CW01160443

Muslim Women Seeking Power, Muslim Youth Seeking Justice

Muslim Women Seeking Power, Muslim Youth Seeking Justice:

Studies from Europe, Middle East and Asia

Edited by

Christopher Adam-Bagley
and Mahmoud Abubaker

Cambridge
Scholars
Publishing

Muslim Women Seeking Power, Muslim Youth Seeking Justice:
Studies from Europe, Middle East and Asia

Edited by Christopher Adam-Bagley and Mahmoud Abubaker

This book first published 2019

Cambridge Scholars Publishing

Lady Stephenson Library, Newcastle upon Tyne, NE6 2PA, UK

British Library Cataloguing in Publication Data
A catalogue record for this book is available from the British Library

Copyright © 2019 by Christopher Adam-Bagley, Mahmoud Abubaker and contributors

All rights for this book reserved. No part of this book may be reproduced, stored in a retrieval system, or transmitted, in any form or by any means, electronic, mechanical, photocopying, recording or otherwise, without the prior permission of the copyright owner.

ISBN (10): 1-5275-3479-0
ISBN (13): 978-1-5275-3479-7

TABLE OF CONTENTS

Editors and Contributors vii

List of Acronyms ix

Foreword and Acknowledgements x

Chapter One 1
Islamic Ethics, Sociology and Social Justice – A Critical Realist
Perspective and a Feminist Viewpoint
Christopher Adam-Bagley and Mahmoud Abubaker

Chapter Two 35
Muslim Women in Management Roles in Western and in Muslim-
Majority Countries: Strong Women Balancing Family and Career
Mahmoud Abubaker, Christopher Adam-Bagley and Afroze Shahnaz

Chapter Three 56
Work–Life Balance Programmes and the Career Aspirations of Women:
A Critical Realist Approach to Issues of Work and Welfare in the Islamic
Culture of Gaza, Palestine
Mahmoud Abubaker and Christopher Adam-Bagley

Chapter Four 74
Muslim Women and the Children of Gaza: Teacher Support for Children
Under Stress - Evidence from Elementary School Case Studies
Wesam Abubaker

Chapter Five 120
Muslim Youth in Britain: Becoming Good Citizens in the Age
of Islamophobia
Christopher-Adam Bagley and Nader Al-Refai

Chapter Six 162
Muslim Women (and Men) and Youth Seeking Justice: English and Dutch
Case studies of Prejudice, Racism, Discrimination and Achievement
Christopher Adam-Bagley and Mahmoud Abubaker

Chapter Seven 182
Discrimination in Action: Three Case Studies of Muslim Women
Seeking Work in England and the Netherlands
Christopher Adam-Bagley and Mahmoud Abubaker

Chapter Eight 212
Exploitation of Girls and Women through Enforced Prostitution
in the Culture of Bangladesh: Denial of Islamic Moral Principles
Christopher Adam-Bagley, Sadia Kadri and Afroze Shahnaz

Chapter Nine 229
Suicidal Behaviours in Bangladeshi Girls and Women, and the Oppression
of Women in an Islamic Culture: Issues for Feminist Conscious-Raising
and Intervention
Christopher Adam-Bagley, Afroze Shahnaz and Sadia Kadri

Chapter Ten 255
Child Marriage as Traumatic Rape: A Cause of PTSD in Women
in Bangladesh and Pakistan?
Christopher Adam-Bagley and Wesam Abubaker

Chapter Eleven 263
Pakistan: The Hard Struggle for the Islamic Equality of Women and Girls
Christopher Adam-Bagley

Chapter Twelve 296
Gender Equality and Peace-Making: Challenges for the Human Rights
Achievement of Muslim Women, Men and Youth in Europe, Gaza,
Bangladesh and Pakistan
Christopher Adam-Bagley

Bibliography 318

Index 399

Editors and Contributors

Mahmoud Abubaker is a Lecturer in International Human Resources Management in the Leeds Business School, at Leeds Beckett University, Leeds, UK. His doctorate is from the University of Bradford, UK, and his masters degrees are from Salford University, UK and Manchester Metropolitan University, UK. His undergraduate degree in business studies is from Birzeit University, Palestine. He was a lecturer in business studies at Al-Aqsa University in Gaza for some years, and has worked in government and business organisations in Palestine.

Christopher Adam-Bagley is Emeritus Professor of Social Science, Faculty of Social Sciences, University of Southampton, UK. He has degrees in education, social policy and psychology from the Universities of Exeter, Essex and London, UK; and doctorates in sociology, and social psychology from the Universities of Essex, and Sussex, UK. He held research chairs of child welfare and social policy at the University of Calgary, Canada, and City University of Hong Kong. He qualified in psychiatric nursing at the Quaker Hospital, The Retreat, York, and has worked as clinical psychologist at the National Neurological Hospital, London; and at the Institute of Psychiatry, Kings College, London.

Wesam Abubaker has a degree in English and education from Al-Quds University, Palestine, and taught in schools in Gaza until 2007. Her master's degree in Educational Studies is from the University of Huddersfield, UK.

Nader Al-Refai has undergraduate and master's degrees in Islamic studies and education from universities in Jordan; and master's and doctorate degrees from the University of Huddersfield, and University of Derby, UK. He has taught Islamic Studies in Muslim Secondary Schools in Manchester, UK and is now Head of Training and Development at Yarmouk University, Irbid, Jordan.

Sadia Kadri has undergraduate and a master's degree in communications and journalism from the University of Bangladesh. She was a public relations consultant in Bangladesh until 1999, before postgraduate studies in the UK. She has a master's degree in community development from the London

School of Economics, and is now an independent researcher in Manchester, UK.

Afroze Shahnaz has degrees from universities in Bangladesh, and a master's degree in public health from the Karolinska Institute of Stockholm. She is now a postgraduate student of nursing at the Karolinska Institute.

LIST OF ACRONYMS

BEM	Black and Ethnic Minority
BRAC	Bangladesh Rural Advancement Committee
CE	Citizenship Education
CR	Critical Realism
CRE	Commission for Racial Equality
CSEWC	Commercially Sexually Exploited Women and Children
CSR	Corporate Social Responsibility
DCR	Dialectical Critical Realism
DES	Department for/of Education and Science, UK government
GCSE	General Certificate of Secondary Education, UK
EHRC	Equality and Human Rights Commission, UK
HRCP	Human Rights Committee of Pakistan
HRM	Human Relations Management
HRW	Human Rights Watch
ICR	Islamic Critical Realism
IDDR-B	International Disease Research Centre of Bangladesh
KSA	Kingdom of Saudi Arabia
LEA	Local Education Authority in UK
LGBI	Lesbian, Gay and Bisexual
LMICs	Low and Middle Income Countries
NVQ	National Vocational Qualification, UK
OFSTED	Office for Standards in Education, UK
PSHE	Personal Social and Health Education, UK
PTSD	Post Traumatic Stress Disorder
PVV	Dutch political party of the 'far right'
QCA	Qualifications and Curriculum Authority of UK government
RE	Religious Education
RSE	Religious Studies Education
SCF	Save the Children Fund
STIs	Sexually Transmitted Infections
UAR	United Arab Republic
UNDP	United Nations Development Programme
UNWRA	United Nations Works and Association
WHO	World Health Organisation
WLB	Work Life Balance

Foreword and Acknowledgements

This is a book of complex and cross-cutting themes, argued and illustrated through different national and local studies in which Muslims and their neighbours of different religious identities or commitments live together: the Islamic-Christian nexus in England and The Netherlands; the Muslim-Jewish nexus in Palestine; and the attempts of the Muslim-majority countries of Bangladesh and Pakistan to construct ethical states based on Islamic principles.

We evaluate the points of tension in these struggles by focussing on the Islamically-expressed aspirations of women and girls, and their hard struggle to achieve rights in education, management and professional roles in developed and developing countries. It is a matter of tragic irony that these rights have least fulfilment in the so-called Islamic Republic of Pakistan.

Women in Palestine are achieving equality in business organisations through Islamically developed Work Life Balance policies, and we argue that Muslim women's experience as "strong family managers" is an asset that is fruitfully transferred to the sphere of business and professional life.

In England and The Netherlands, the research for this book shows that Muslim women still face considerable discrimination in seeking employment, in these seemingly liberal cultures. This discrimination applies to Muslim men and boys, as well as to women. The degrees of alienation this generates is, in absolute terms, unknown. But we argue that recent cases of lone terrorism do illustrate these possibilities, and give an account of Salman Abedi, the 2017 Manchester Arena Bomber, whom we knew but were unsuccessful in counselling.

In Bangladesh and Pakistan the widespread practice of child prostitution and sexual assault, child marriage, and female infanticide are a mark of shame, a fundamental denial of Islamic principles. We review localised solutions for these problems, "saving one child at a time."

We offer the Muslim tradition of peace-making and pacifism as a higher order value for human co-existence, and co-operation with Jewish and

Christian cultures in seeking a Critical Realist programme of "absenting" the many crimes which women and children are subjected to in many world cultures, in their journey towards equality and Islamic fulfilment.

We wish to acknowledge the unnamed research students who, quite literally, risked their lives in Pakistan in data collection on which we have drawn. We also thank our daughter Dr. Abbie Vandivere of Amsterdam University, for her assistance and advice in our work in The Netherlands.

Finally, Mahmoud, Wesam and Christopher wish to dedicate this edited work to the futures of their children: Zain, the Manager; Yousef, the Explorer; Mohamed, the Technologist; Khalid, the Scientist; Michael, the Artisan; Daniel, the Traveller; and Abigail, the Artist.

Oh Allah, we seek refuge in You, lest we misguide others, or we are misguided by others, lest we cause others to err or we are caused to err, lest we abuse others or be abused, and lest we behave foolishly or meet with foolishness in others.
—Hadith of The Blessed Prophet, recorded by Abu Dawud. (Sa'id bin Wahf Al-Qantani, *Fortress of the Muslim*, 2009).

Christopher Adam-Bagley and Mahmoud Abubaker,
Leeds, England, June 2019.

CHAPTER ONE

ISLAMIC ETHICS, SOCIOLOGY
AND SOCIAL JUSTICE –
A CRITICAL REALIST PERSPECTIVE
AND A FEMINIST VIEWPOINT

CHRISTOPHER ADAM-BAGLEY
AND MAHMOUD ABUBAKER

1. Introduction

In Islam, women should be free to become educated and to carry on any work they choose and live as equals to men in society ... with regard to marriage, mutual consent is an essential aspect. Fazeel Khan's essay on *The Final Prophet* (2014).

Here is a statement by a female scholar of Islam, which is both simple and profound, and is based on a clear and rigorous reading of The Qur'an (God's Final Message to humanity); and on The Sunnah, the life, teaching and actions of The Final Prophet, Muhammad (pbuh).[1]

We are two Muslims, both male. One of us, Adam is a convert to Islam and continues an exciting journey, discovering each day a new Scripture and a New Prophet; and a field of scholarship, commentary and ethics which brings great joy and meaning to the journey through life along "the straight path" (Esposito, 1998). Mahmoud is a born Muslim and has a name which honours Our Prophet's first companion *Abu Bakr*, the father of Aisha. Aisha was the Prophet's wife, "the red-haired one" to whom we owe so much in

---

[1] When we mention the name of our Prophet Muhammad, we add the prayer "peace and blessings be upon him", often abbreviated to PBUH, or (pbuh) in brackets. Dear reader, if you are a Muslim, please say this prayer when you say or read The Prophet's name in the text that follows.

the recording of Muhammad's life and teaching, the Hadith and the Sunnah (Eaton, 2008).

How come two men are attempting to offer a feminist approach to Islam? There is no paradox in this, since men and women are equal in Islam, morally, spiritually, emotionally, and intellectually. Both men and women (that is, all humans, whether they acknowledge their Islamic heritage, or not) are descended from the creation of the two original human souls: one is the man Adam; the other is the woman Hawa. You and I, dear sisters and brothers, are all descended from these first two humans, created by a God who is neither male nor female, whose infinite being and dimension are beyond human comprehension. We know God only through the 99 names which God has chosen to reveal to us in the final message to The Prophet (Morgan, 2010).

Furthermore: "There does not need to be any gender injustice within Islamic societies, if you can accept the full humanity of women, the full ontological equality of women with men, right from the point of creation." (Kassam, 2014, p. 143) Taj Hashmi (2000) writing about gender justice in Bangladesh argues that patriarchy and subjugation of women has been built into ancient Greek, Hindu, Jewish and Christian theologies: and patriarchy was part of pre-Islamic culture, in which men claimed that their superior power was divinely ordained.

In this view patriarchy is a pre-Islamic cultural institution. We adduce this from the Qur'an's account of Adam and his wife. Hawa (Eve) was created equally with her male partner and was not responsible for initiating 'original sin'. In this Islamic scripture there is no theological justification for women's inequality: Islamic theology is the first set of ideas in human history which introduced gender equality, in any scriptural revelation or human philosophy.

We join with our American sister Chimanda Ngozi Adichie (2014) in affirming *We Should All be Feminists*. And for the sake of our fragile male egos, we also accept the Australian Robert Jensen's arguments in his *End of Patriarchy: Radical Feminism for Men* (2017).

For us, the most exciting trend in Islamic theology of the past three decades has been the detailed examination by feminist exegesis of The Qur'an; the Hadith (verified observations and recordings of the actions and sayings of The Prophet); and the Sunnah, the verified accounts of how The Prophet lived his life according to The Qur'anic message. Since 1980 a brilliant stream of mostly women scholars from the Islamic world, and from universities and institutes in Europe and America have offered us new or refreshed insights into the meanings of Islam for gender equality[2]. We mention here some of the writings we have studied, and been inspired by: the work of Leila Ahmed (1992), Kecia Ali (2016), Etin Anwar (2006), Asma Barlas (2002), John Esposito (2003), Heba Raouf Ezzat (2007 & 2008); Taj Hashmi (2000); Sherin Khankan (2018); Zayn Kassam (2010 & 2014); Fazeel Khan (2014); Asma Lamrabet (2017); Irshad Manji, 2003 & 2011; Fatima Mernissi (1987 & 1999); and Amina Wadud (1999). Gray (2019) identified 75 women scholars of Islam "teaching from the tent", in various world centres, through electronic media. This growth of scholarship is exponential, extraordinary and exciting.

There is a still, for us, a rich vein of writings in Islamic feminism waiting to be explored – but it is not the purpose of this Chapter to attempt a full review and analysis of this literature. One thing is already very clear however: Islam in no way supports patriarchy, or violence towards women, or the subjugation of women and girls. And like Robert Jensen (2017) we are excited at being able to join a movement which seeks to end the oppressions by patriarchy, not only in Muslim cultures, but in all societies today.

Moreover, the feminist theology that we have consulted is both cautious and conservative in terms of its exegesis of sacred and traditional texts, in order to deal with the voices of protest from Muslim men (including some 'scholars') who perceived their power and privilege to be slipping away (De Sondy, 2015). Feminist theology in Islam does not commit the mistake of selective quotation, but seeks to interpret the Qur'an, Hadith and Sunnah as a unified whole, in which the Message from Allah is always the final authority. Nor does Islamic feminism make the mistake of saying that The Qur'an was a revelation for a desert people, and must be read differently today. Everything in the Qur'anic message was true in the seventh century, and remains true for humanity today.

Commentators on Islamic feminism point to important women in the history of Islam: first was Khadija, the first convert to Islam, a successful business woman who supported her husband Muhammad during the difficult years of receiving The Message. Muhammad was a kind and gentle man, the opposite of powerful masculinity, as the accounts of his life clearly show (Armstrong, 2006; Sardar, 2012; Al-Awadi, 2018). He preached and

---

[2] This feminist movement was originally an expression and by-product of Arab-Muslim nationalism. Qasim Amin (d. 1908) and Salama Musa (d. 1958) considered the liberation of women as an " ... essential foundation for the liberation of Arab-Muslim society from colonial rule." (Mernissi, 1985)

practised forgiveness and compromise, and the accounts of his relationship with Aisha, his fourth wife are quite extraordinary, giving us a very full insight into how this wonderful man lived The Message.

The first modern university was founded by a Muslim woman, Fatima Al-Fihri, in Morocco in 859CE. Now the Fatima Al-Fihri Open University based in Casablanca, it has continuously operated with a library and lectures, as a degree-granting institution up to the present time. It was one of the Muslim institutions which preserved Greek texts in science, medicine and mathematics which would otherwise have been lost, since Christian iconoclasm had no interest in such scholarship (Watt, 1972).

Lamrabet (2016) has observed that: "The Prophet's rejection of all violence against women is recognized by all. Many hadiths denounce the mistreatment of women and condemn acts of violence committed by men. On this topic, the hadiths are too numerous to cite in their entirety but the most well-known are sufficient, to perceive the importance which the Prophet attributed to this problem and his intense action to educate Muslims in order that they behave with decency and respect towards their spouses: *The best amongst you are those who are best to their wives.*" [3] (p. 156)

Consider for example the Hadith for which Aisha is the main source (and which Abu Dawud has recorded). Abu Bakr (Aisha's father) entered Muhammad's house and found Aisha scolding her husband over some domestic matter. Abu Bakr raised his hand to Aisha in order to slap her, saying 'Don't ever let me find you raising your hand to God's Messenger!'. But The Prophet stopped him, and Abu Bakr left the house, angry ... Some days later Abu Bakr returned, and found the couple had made peace, and said to them: 'Bring me into your peace as you brought me into your war!' The Prophet replied 'We have done so, we have done so.' (translated by Mustafa, reprinted by Eaton, 2008). From this action of The Prophet reflecting the divine message, comes the Islamic law that no man may strike a women (and no woman may strike a man).

Although "he" (male gender) is used in Qu'ranic translations, every Qu'ranic injunction and every hadith applies equally to men and women, except where the roles and status of women are specifically described, as for example in giving evidence, or inheriting property. Most importantly,

---

[3] The teaching of The Prophet on nonviolence in marital and adult-child relationships is not, alas, obvious to all of those who call themselves Muslims, as the chapters in this book on Bangladesh and Pakistan, will argue.

women have a right to become educated in a manner and to a level that is equal to that of men, and should have equality in marriage and marital relationships, including divorce. For example, if a man chooses to divorce he must maintain his wife and children at the same level as in the marriage. And a woman has equality with men in initiating divorce, with additional rights concerning property and custody of children.

Verified accounts abound of The Prophet's kindness and gentleness in personal affairs, and in the struggles of Islam to survive.[4] We are particularly delighted by the accounts of Muhammad's relationships with children, for whom he had great tenderness and tolerance. "Abu Qatadah said: I saw The Prophet leading the people in prayer with Umamah [his little daughter] on his shoulder. When he bowed, he put her down, and when he rose up after the prostration he put her on his back." (Bukhari and Muslim). These and many other examples are for us some of the hallmarks of Islam: gentleness, kindness, compromise – not the tyrannical leader of Islamophobic fiction. Many more examples are given in Hesham Al-Awadi's (2018) *Children around The Prophet*.

Muhammad was outraged too at the traditional custom of the polytheists of burying alive unwanted female infants in the desert sand.

Often the Qur'an is a kind of dialogue between Muhammad and Allah, so we are not sure whether the kindness and purity of thought which emerges comes from the joyful spirit which Allah has breathed into Muhammad, or from the wonderful personhood of Muhammad himself, giving breath to Sura and Sunnah. But in the Qur'an's Sura 81 "Shrouded in Darkness" (on the final day of reckoning) among the accusatory voices is when: " …the baby girl buried alive, is asked for what sin she was killed …"[5] Of course, the infant is without sin: the sin belongs to her murderer. (In Chapter 7 we give an account of the widespread, current practice of female infanticide in the Islamic Republic of Pakistan).

Muhammad loved all of his children, but according to Aisha he was most devoted to Fatimah, who was said to be most like Muhammad in character: "Fatimah is part of me. Whatever upsets her upsets me." (Hadith, recorded by Muslim) "One assured route to Paradise is to love and care for one's daughters." (Hadith, recorded by Al Bukhari). In Islam there is, formally

---

[4] Christopher Adam-Bagley, a Quaker before his conversion to Islam and the adoption of the Muslim name of *Adam*, has argued that Islam may embody the pacifist approach for which Quakers are known (Adam-Bagley, 2015a).
[5] We follow our favourite Qur'anic translator, Abdel Haleem (2005).

speaking, a strong tradition of guarding human rights (including those of non-Muslim minorities), and serving the interests and welfare of children (Sidani, 2018). Amongst the rights documented in the Prophet's Hadiths is the right of women to become educated to their full potential, to work, and to enjoy the full support of their husbands whom they, in a spirit of mutual respect, also support.

The American feminist Azizah al-Hibri (2002) in a report to the American Bar Association's Commission on Women in the Law Profession, focuses on the Islamic concept of *Adalah* (Justice), a complex, higher order concept which is the backbone of *Mizaam*, the Islamic concept of harmony and balance which emerges from the Prophet's teaching on modesty, moderation, and the middle path ordained by Islam. *Adalah* rests on a system of basic equality of all human beings (Muslims and non-Muslims – Qur'an 5:8, 17:70 & 49:13). All people were created as equals so that they would know, respect and nurture each other (Qur'an 30:22). There is ontological equality of the two genders. Islam also emphasises the value of education for all people, and the principle that men and women should become equally educated (Qur'an 20:14 & 58:11). Women are denied equality of education and achievements in some Muslim-majority countries through patriarchy, which denies the fundamentals of Islam, argues al-Hibri.

Marriage is not a contract of service; it is a contract of equals, of mutual love and kindness (Qur'an 30:31). Violence between spouses is forbidden by Islam. Although within the family men and women have different roles, each role is of equal status and each partner should support their spouse in their chosen roles (Qur'an 60:12)

We end this section with a quotation of Islam's popular and authoritative spokesperson of "moderate Islam", Ed Husain (who had explored most thoroughly the 'radical' version of Islam, which he firmly rejects):

> *Every erudite Muslim in the world today believes, rightly, that the Prophet was a liberator of women. All recognise their Prophet as being a feminist of his time. Abdullah ibn Abbas, the Prophet's cousin, frequently reminded Muslims that the Prophet commanded his wives and daughters to leave their homes and join the festivals of Eid ... The fault with many Muslims today is to grasp the spirit of the Prophet's actions and the motives behind his divine sanctions relieving the plight of women. Many buried girl daughters [alive] ... Those of today's Arabs and Muslims who have sadly clung on to that mentality have abandoned the progressive ways of their Prophet. He abolished infanticide ... and he changed the rules on dowries – how the money went from the man to the woman directly, so that she owned it, and*

not her parents. Even in the event of a divorce, she would retain her own financial assets. Previously, divorce had been a mainly male prerogative, but the Qur'an granted women the right to divorce their husbands and inherit property. (Husain, 2018, p. 213)

2. The 'Modesty' of Islam, and the Implications for Muslim Conduct and Social Organisation

Allah created in human beings *difference*: in terms of the biological differences between men and women (Qur'an 49:13); between ethnic groups in terms of physical appearance or language; and between human cultures, in terms of national identity, and their different religions and social organisation. Each individual is divinely endowed with a different personality, and a unique pathway to paradise, being presented with choices for action which are tailored for each individual human being, addressing the spirit which has been implanted in the human soul.

The Final Message advises that the three great monotheisms - Islam, Judaism and Christianity – should respect and tolerate one another (Qur'an 5:12-17), This is evidenced, for example, by the long history of tolerant acceptance of Jewish minorities by Islamic countries in the years of the Jewish diaspora (Lewis, 1984).

Prophet Muhammad said: "Every faith has its own identity, and ours is modesty." (An-Nawawi, 1989). Much of Islamic etiquette and social organisation reflects this principle of *modesty*. Neither men nor women may present themselves flamboyantly in dress or manner (except within the privacy of marriage). From puberty onwards the genders in Muslim social organisations congregate and organise themselves separately. In daily prayer for example, men stand in the prayer line shoulder to shoulder and foot to foot with their brothers, and move together (in the prostration of prayer) in a joyful, gendered unity which is both a metaphysical and a physical ecstasy. This physical unity in prayer is for a single gender (a man cannot, for obvious reasons, bond closely to a woman in the prayer line).

Women in their separate prayer lines may be (for modesty's sake) to the rear of men, or elsewhere in The Mosque. But for each group of men or women the prayer line is part of the Ummah, the wonderful institution of brotherhood, and sisterhood, which unites Muslims. We all pray, five times daily in the same manner and reciting the same Qur'anic texts, whether Sunni, Shia, Sufi or of some other Islamic grouping.

Remarkably too (for the Muslim who has made a journey into Islam from another religion) there is no intermediate class of priests. Each Muslim speaks about their fears, faults and aspirations directly to Allah, and Allah in turn offers a daily guide for individual actions to the thoughtful Muslim. Men greet one another with the handshake, exchanging the greeting *As-salamu alaykum* ("may peace be with you"), embodying the prayer that Allah may forgive the sins of the brother whom we greet.

For women parallel rituals exist, and one of us (Adam-Bagley, 2016a) keeps track of his gendered progress, comparing experiences with his biological sister, also a convert to Islam. We follow Mernissi's (1987) argument that the hijab, the women's head covering and her modesty in dress does not separate women from men in spiritual or ontological terms: it is a device of honour, respect and love of religion, and of man for woman, and of woman for man.

Women and men in Islam dress and behave modestly, as The Qur'an requires. This implies for women that legs and arms always be modestly covered, as well as the upper body. Hair may not be styled as an expression of sexuality, and women often cover their hair with the hijab. Neither the veil nor the hijab are compulsory, but are proud symbols of religious identity, and women and girls in the West often wear the hijab as a statement of their Islamic pride, in school, college and workplace. A Muslim woman will not touch or shake hands with a man (Muslim or otherwise), except her spouse, or a close relative such as father or brother.

These are not merely obligations, but rights (and rites) of proud men and women, tolerant of themselves and others, who are now a fundamental part of European and North American cultures. The Islamic ideal of modesty also means that Muslims in whatever culture they find themselves act with caution and restraint, following the Muslim social contract of becoming good citizens in their new cultures - giving to charity, being good neighbours, becoming educated, and seeking tolerance for certain religious customs such as fasting and diet (Khan. 2012). Muslims, like an earlier generation of Jews in Europe and North America, are seeking to integrate (becoming good citizens, while retaining religious values and rituals), following the route of integration rather than assimilation.

Islamophobia (the hatred or fear of a people because of their religion) attracts many nominal Christians in the West today, just as anti-Semitism was the province of the grandparents of these prejudiced people, in Europe and elsewhere (Bunzl, 2007; Cherribi, 2011; ENAR, 2016). There is considerable irony in this: the Islamophobic masses are nominally, but not actually, Christian and they often follow lifestyles of licence and blue-collar ignorance, being the failing generations of Western, capitalist cultures (Standing, 2014; Sawyerr & Adam-Bagley, 2017). For the neoliberalist forces of international capitalism, it is extremely useful if the proletarian class divert their energies from unmasking the alienation that binds them, into having a group whom they hate with profound irrationality, rather than understanding the nature of their exploitation in capitalist cultures (Sawyerr & Adam-Bagley, 2017). In the last century Jews were the convenient scapegoats: today it is those who are visibly Muslim (Cherribi, 2011; Renton & Gidley, 2017).

3. Wider Implications of Islamic Modesty

Syed et al. (2005 & 2010) have written persuasively about *Islamic modesty* and Muslim women making progress in work outside of family settings in Muslim majority cultures (MMCs). They show, from analysis of Islamic textual resources that this principle of modesty clearly applies to both genders. Only the wives of The Prophet were secluded – Aisha (The Prophet's wife) for example preached sermons in her mosque from behind a screen, for many years after Muhammad's death. For women who were not scholars or preachers, Islam made no bar to the "economic agency" of women, many of whom did become business women and traders in the early years of Islam, following the example of Muhammad's first wife Khadija (Koehler, 2011).

Gradually however (and especially in the second millennium), male hegemony re-emerged with vengeance, and the ideology of patriarchal scholars required women to remain confined as 'family managers', with little involvement in the external economy. But, Syed shows, Qur'an and Sunnah teachings and traditions have never required such a constrained role for women, whose opportunities in competing with men on equal terms must follow Islamic principles, not the self-interests of the patriarchy. Islam imposes special duties on men, but gives them no special rights or privileges above women.

In a brilliant essay Miles K. Davis (2013) offers an Islamic perspective on entrepreneurship. With the wealth that Allah has bestowed on us, Davis argues (from Qur'anic instructions) the individual, the culture and the nation must follow the religious principles of *modesty* in the creation, use and spending of wealth. Wealth creation is a form of social service, and through the principle of religious giving (*zakah*, obligatory for all Muslims) must serve the wider community. The 'modest' Muslim entrepreneur, man or woman, does not accumulate wealth for purposes of personal power and self-aggrandisement. Muslims are stewards of wealth, and their exemplar in this is The Prophet himself. Numerous Hadiths support this view: the purpose of economic enterprise is to support the community. In the case of the business woman Khadija, her entrepreneurship supported both The Prophet during the period when he received The Message, and the growing number of Muslims.[6]

Modern businesses and commercial enterprises which are owned and run by Muslims must follow Islamic ethical principles, in whatever culture they are established. The Shari'a guidance for economic enterprise stresses that this endeavour must be integrated with all of the ethical and moral principles of Islam. As Esposito & Delong-Bas (2018) put it:

> *Economic activity, enterprise, and employment are encouraged for all people ... At the same time it is recognized that some people may not be able to work, for a variety of reasons such as age or infirmity, so that welfare benefits are also to be made available ... Shari'a is neither socialist nor capitalist: it takes a middle position between the two, and emphasises the common good (maslahah).* (Esposito & Delong-Bas, 2018, p. 250)

In such Islamic economic enterprise 'moderation and modesty' should ensure that profit is balanced with doing good to the community, using resources wisely, not charging interest on the giving or receiving of loans, not producing products (e.g. alcohol) which are harmful to health, and ensuring that profits made are distributed to the community and to the workers, and not to some remote group of rentiers.

Islamic norms of "respectable, subordinated femininity" which involve stereotyping women's roles as being confined to family duties alone are not compatible with Islam's teaching on the absolute equality of women, and must be renegotiated in countries such as Pakistan, in which very few professional women are able to break "the glass ceiling" of employment. The principles of "modesty" also govern how Muslim men and women present themselves and relate to other cultural groups in Western countries[7] (Roald, 2001). Muslim women in all cultures who enter the world of

---

[6] Imagine, Allah has bestowed an Islamic nation with considerable reserves of, say, oil. How should this nation conduct itself in the world? For a discussion of this dilemma see Sultan et al. (2011).

[7] A "Western country" we define as one in which the majority are of European descent (e.g. England, Australia, USA).

employment outside of the family need, Kamla (2017) argues, to develop "religious-based resistance strategies" in creating for themselves "authentic professional roles." Again, Kadijah is an important role model as Muslim women create for themselves professional identities which are grounded in Islamic texts.

Adam-Bagley et al. (2018) writing about sexual harassment in Western, non-Muslim organisations comment that the everyday, crude sexism which is one way in which men retain power in organisations and block the advancement of female managers (Bates, 2014) is unlikely to occur in organisations in MMCs – when women are employed as managers and specialists, they are usually afforded respect that is in line with principles of Islamic modesty (Abubaker & Adam-Bagley, 2016a). This we discuss in detail in later chapters on Work Life Benefit programmes in Palestine and Jordan, and "the glass ceiling" for women managers and professionals across Muslim and Western cultures. Unfortunately, as Chapter 11 on Pakistan will discuss, "everyday sexism" which includes verbal, sexual and physical harassment and assaults, do occur in a country which is an "Islamic Republic" in name only (Saeed, 2013).

Modesty is a principle which permeates Islamic life and is certainly not confined merely to how the Muslim man or woman presents themselves in terms of dress and physical appearance. Mufti & Salman (2006) offer an overview of Islamic modesty from a scholar's viewpoint: modesty is part of faith, and involves the avoidance of all bad deeds. The exemplar of modesty is The Prophet: "A strong person is not one who throws his opponent to the ground. A strong person is the one who contains himself when he is angry." Al-Bukhari (quoted by Mufti & Salman, 2006)

Modesty is the means by which, for the Muslim in whatever culture he or she finds themselves, the overwhelming importance of morals and ethics in society is pursued and maintained. Modesty involves love and respect for all human beings, and all of nature. Modesty is the "underlabouring" principle we offer in our critical realist analysis of both Muslim social institutions, and of society as a whole.[8]

---

[8] In previous writing on abused, oppressed and neglected children we used the concepts of "child-centred humanism" as the Hobbesian underlabouring principle in critical realist analyses (Sawyerr & Adam-Bagley, 2017). In our current writing, we use "modesty", "child-centred humanism" and "non-violent peace-making" as underlabouring principles.

4. Islamic Justice and Shari'a Principles: Prelude to Case Studies of Bangladesh and Pakistan

In a later Chapters of this book we consider how two Islamic nations, Bangladesh and Pakistan provide through Islamic observance: the translation of Qur'anic principle and The Prophet's example (in Hadith and Sunnah) for the care and treatment of children, girls and women. We will discuss profoundly non-Islamic practices firstly in (sexual prostitution of children, girls and women; child marriage; and high rates of suicide in girls and young women); and then in Pakistan (high rates of female infanticide; culturally ordained murder of young women for reasons of 'honour'; and the stoning and burning to death of abused girls and women). In Bangladesh and Pakistan today, many thousands of girls and women are abused, tortured and murdered each year, and are denied the basic protection which Muslim cultures should offer.

Surely these practices conflict with the care which Islam offers to children, and the respect and equality which The Qur'an gives to women? Yes, is the definite answer. In this regard we refer to the declaration of 200 women religious scholars from all regions of Pakistan after their meeting in Lahore in June, 2016 (Mahmood, 2015). The scholars, under the leadership of Jamia Sarajia Naeema of Lahore, declared:

> *Islam does not allow the killing of a mother, sister, daughter or any woman in the name of a family's honour, by any family member or by their agency.*
>
> *We condemn the most heinous acts of burning of women, of acid attacks or beating of a woman for any purpose.*
>
> *Any Muslim man or woman who has reached the age of majority [18] may if both parties freely consent, enter into marriage with a believing Muslim. All Muslim women (and men) have the right to refuse to accept any man as a marital partner, whatever their family's wishes.*
>
> *Vani[9] belongs to pre-Islamic times. No woman may be forced to marry, or be required to marry to compensate for the sins of her male relatives.*

---

[9] *Vani* (from the Pashtu word for "blood") involves the surrender of a child as compensation for inter-family conflicts which involved the spilling of blood. In 2012 'only' 13 girls aged 4 to 16 were sacrificed for this purpose according to official data. As always in Pakistan, the real figure is likely much higher.

> *Islam requires that all, male and female alike, shall become educated to the fullest of their potential.*
>
> *Shari'a divorce law should make men and women equal in seeking divorce, with a woman's special right for maintenance for herself and her children at the same material level as before the divorce. Qur'anic prescriptions on dowry payments (which the Qur'an requires shall be paid by the husband to the wife) must be followed.*
>
> *Family members **may not** impose stoning, beheading, other forms of execution, cutting off limbs, or whipping, on members of their family. If punishment is necessary, it can only be imposed by Judges of an Islamically-guided court.*

There is some evidence that women in migrant Pakistani families in Europe, having options in marriage and divorce beyond those of Shari'a law, are able to negotiate a more just and Qur'anically accurate form of divorce settlement than would be available to them in Pakistan (Mehdi, 2003). There are broader issues here too, of Pakistani and Bangladeshi women seeking avenues of personal equity, higher education, and occupational advancement following migration to Western countries (e.g. Hussain & Bagguley, 2007; Archer, 2009; Hussain, 2017). We would expect (or hope) that these Qur'anically-focussed activities of the Ummah (the international sisterhood and brotherhood of Islam) involving both modesty, and the desire for occupational and educational progress, will spread amongst Muslims across the world.

On this theme, further important points emerge in Ayesha Shahid's (2013) comparative study of divorce laws in Pakistan and Bangladesh. On the "plurality" of systems, in which Qur'anically derived principles are mixed with secular ideas in framing divorce customs and legislation which disadvantage women, she comments:

> *In both Pakistan and Bangladesh the patriarchal ordering at the state, judicial and societal levels exacerbates this situation ... patriarchy has silenced the more egalitarian aspects of Islam ... It is therefore pertinent to maintain a clear distinction between the normative teachings of Islam and the male-dominated patriarchal norms prevalent in Muslim societies.* (Shahid, 2013, pp 211-212.

5. The Crucial Importance of Ethnography in Understanding Muslim Women's Search for Justice and Social Power

Problems in elevating issues of "Muslim women's rights" to the level of political and international action, or the level of debates between the religious scholars of Islam must be acknowledged. Several important scholars have urged that we cannot understand how and why Muslim women are making some progress in MMCs without an ethnographic, or sociological understanding of how people at the grassroots level experience and assert their rights and duties (which they believe to be derived from their traditional understanding of Qur'an and Sunnah – or in the case of Pakistan, from pre-Qur'anic tribal cultures). Thus for example Mounira Charrad (2011) in her sociological review of the status of women in Middle Eastern countries argues that assertions about gender equity expressed through international agencies ignore (or miss) how women's agency is expressed as part of kin-based solidarities.

The crucial importance of the ethnographic analysis of the "women's rights" movement in Islam is expressed by Lila Abu-Lughod (2010 & 2013) in what for us, is a powerful analysis of the social movements in Egypt and Palestine which have been emerging and developing at the local levels, and form the basis of real social change in the movement of Muslim women achieving the equality rights afforded them by Qur'an and Sunnah. Abu-Lughod, a Palestinian-born, American-based anthropologist offers a *realist* understanding of the movement for the realisation of women's rights in Muslim cultures. She makes a detailed analysis of how ordinary women liaise with ordinary men, in the sphere of Muslim worship, ritual and social relationships in asserting and achieving the gender equality that reflects Qur'anic principles.

Abu-Lughod criticises international bodies advocating 'women's rights', based on Judao-Christian ethics (e.g. the UN Convention "on the elimination of all forms of discrimination against women") offered as an often hidden but barely-negotiable part of World Bank, Ford Foundation, UN and other aid packages channelled through Non-Governmental Agencies (NGOs) to Egypt and Palestine.[10] The pressure from these NGOs to adopt a certain brand of 'women's rights' can be counter-productive, just as the attempt to impose Western models of democracy are reluctantly received by Middle Eastern countries which have fallen, through warfare, colonialism or chronic

---

[10] This problem also pertains in Pakistan – see Chapter 11, below.

poverty, under the European-American sphere of political guardianship and influence. NGOs were, according to Abu-Lughod becoming imbricated (like the layers of fish scales) with government policies which still deferred to Western influence. The grassroots Egyptian agency analysed by Abu-Lughod, works in parallel to the Egyptian Center for Woman's Rights, a UN-sponsored agency which campaigns against spousal violence.

Ordinary women in the grassroots agency studied by Abu-Lughod express and perceive their Islamic rights quite differently from those advocated by international aid agencies, ignoring the "growth industry" of internationally financed NGOs whose actions were interlaced with government policies. Instead there has, since 2000 been a growth of low-budget, indigenous organisations such as the Centre for Egyptian's Women's Legal Assistance (CEWLA) whose activities Lughod describes in detail. Shari'a compliance is emphasised, and Qur'anic texts are emphasised which guarantee educational, social and occupational equity between genders. Evidence shows, for example, that the pressures of ordinary men and women within an overtly authoritarian state have in fact achieved remarkable achievements for women's rights in the female-friendly (and Shari'a compliant) Egyptian law on divorce described by Sonneveld (2019), discussed later.

Abu-Lughod (2010) is deeply critical of mainstream American writing on Palestine, which largely ignores the condition of the lives of ordinary people. Writing of the situation in 2009, she introduces the section of her writing on Palestine thus:

> ... *the Israeli attack on Gaza that was launched in December 2008. In 23 days, over 1300 Palestinians were killed, buried alive in houses bombed by F-16s, shot at close range in their beds, machine-gunned from the sea, shelled by tanks using flechettes, and burned by white phosphorus, which acts like napalm. How many were women? We know that over 300 of the dead were children. Human rights groups say 900 of the men killed were civilians. No one gives a separate count for women but cases of women killed or wounded are described in all the reports.* (Abu-Lughod, 2010, p. 17)

This is the reality of life in Gaza, repeated in 2012 and intermittently every year since that time. Within this matrix of violence, ordinary people struggle to achieve their Islamic rights and to cope in non-violent ways with external aggression, since it seems clear that this is the bravest (and only effective) way to face a violent and unprincipled enemy, as Wesam Abubaker argues in Chapter 4.

Some rather similar points are made by Nadera Shalhaub-Kevorkian (2004 to 2015). Shalhaub-Kevorkian, a Palestinian social scientist and Professor of Public International Law at the Hebrew University of Jerusalem, writes powerfully about women's experience of loss as their homes are destroyed, and their loved one's murdered by Israeli terrorists: " ... watching your son's brain spill on the ground as Israeli soldiers trample his body ... the quiet, stunned children trapped ... overwhelmed by the smell of blood and urine." Like Abu-Lughod, she laments the political silence amongst Western feminists about the "slavery" imposed on women and children in Gaza and the Palestinian West Bank.

Abu-Lughod (2010) cites a variety of international organisations campaigning against violence expressed towards Muslim women, by Muslim men: "But where is the global feminist campaign against killing such significant numbers of (mostly Muslim) women, by the Israeli army?" Abu-Lughod describes the "organic feminism" of ordinary women who incorporate stories of loss, of tradition, of suffering, of Islamic principle and assistance as it affects the everyday lives of folk. Institutional arrangements like *qayma* (the value of house and household goods at marriage) which will form part of a woman's property if she is divorced had been ignored by what she terms "the femocracy" of Egypt and Palestine, the foreign-born or foreign-trained women who run the international NGOs. The alternative model of women's rights, in this argument, is built from below through centuries of tradition, with powerful religious roots. Everyone in every Arabic culture has a manual of guidance for such radicalism: this book is called The Qur'an.

One important implication for Abu-Lughod's ethnographic approach for our understanding of the struggles of the women of Gaza and Palestine for Islamic justice and equality is that these concepts and ideas are embedded, and have their genesis from interactions *within the extended family*. In an extended family dwelling, several daughters or sons of the senior couple will live with their children, incorporating several families. Often a married couple will have their own flat in a multi-story building, with other couples of the extended family living in flats in this shared building, but often eating together and caring for each other's children. In this family intimacy, values are generated and shared (sometimes mediated through the never-ending TV soap operas from Egypt, so beloved of Palestinian families).

Often a woman will choose to follow higher and professional education, with the support and encouragement of her brothers and sisters, and of her husband. She will be a valuable person of prestige as well as an income resource, and her sisters will often offer childcare for her. From our ethnographic work in Gaza we can observe that violent or dissenting husbands can be expelled from this tightly-knit household system, which observes the five daily prayers of Islam, and instructs children in reading of the Qur'an, giving them accounts of the life and teaching of The Prophet. As Sania Ahmed and Sally Bould (2004) put it, based on their ethnographic work with women in the external labour force in Bangladesh: "One able daughter is worth 10 illiterate sons."

That such quiet but strong value change can flow from wishes and expressions of ordinary people is exemplified by recent changes in Egyptian law on divorce (Sonneveld, 2019). The most conservative interpretation of Shari'a canon law had in the past clearly disadvantaged women. But the new law which is Shari'a compliant (in Egypt at least) permits women to declare a non-consensual, permanent end to the marriage (i.e. the husband cannot nullify his wife's wishes). Such a divorce is also non-fault, in that a woman does not have to prove any grounds for wanting the divorce. The woman acquires the material assets of *qayma* – the material assets provided by various family members at the beginning of the marriage (including ownership of house or flat, if she has children). The *dower* given by the husband at marriage will be returned to him upon divorce: this is the equivalent of the cost of gold approved in traditional canon law, and cannot exceed about US$30.

In the Egyptian case, the husband must move out of the marital home under the order of the Shari'a divorce court, and the woman retains custody of both male and female children until they are 15. At that age the children may choose which parent to live with. If the husband has continuing wealth he is required to make maintenance payments for children, with some guardianship rights such as approving choice of a school. Sonneveld (2019) offers interesting case studies of weak, occupationally failing and sometimes violent husbands whose career-successful wives have found them unbearable to live with.

This new law, while entirely compatible with Qur'anic guidance, is quite different from how Shari'a canon law viewed divorce in Egypt and Palestine in previous decades and centuries (Hallaq, 2009). The critic can appreciate international changes in Shari'a family law by comparing the accounts of such law by Esposito & DeLong-Bas published in 2001, and then in revised form in 2018. The Qur'an remains across the ages, unchanging. *Exegesis*, interpretations of the Holy Qur'an, is in a constant flux of debate, criticism and change.

For a further understanding of how "honest Muslims", the ordinary people and women in particular, engage in local democracy we must turn to "realist studies of oppression, emancipation and resistance" (O'Mahoney et al., 2018); and to accounts of *morphogenesis*, how ordinary and often oppressed people (including "Muslim women seeking power") engage in conversations and movements which bring about social change, through *critical realism*.

6. Critical Realism and a Value-Based, Islamic Understanding of Society

The concept of Critical Realism (and its later development using ideas from Hegel and Marx) known as dialectical critical realism (DCR), comes from philosophy, and not from social science. It uses philosophical language and reasoning, which is often challenging for the social scientist who has had no grounding in formal logic, or in the discipline of philosophical analysis. DCR is not an account of social science, but rather a philosophy of how knowledge about people and their social structures may be construed, interpreted, described and fitted together. DCR assumes that although the ground of knowledge is real, it also has a value base: there is no such thing as value-free social science. Moreover, what are often regarded as "facts" by positivist social science (and indeed by its post-positivist manifestations) is merely a superficial description of the real ontology of a phenomenon:

> Critical Realism (CR) clearly prefers social science research which employs qualitative, case-study methods, but acknowledges that multiple methods (including surveys and statistical analyses) can be used in order to gain the fullest information about "a case". (Alderson, 2013)

Critical Realism emerged from the writings of the philosopher Roy Bhaskar who was seeking an alternative to what he saw as ambiguous and often confusing models of scientific methodology, particularly the Popperian doctrine of "falsifying hypotheses" (Popper, 1992). He extended his critique to the methodologies of social science (Bhaskar, 1978), attempting to find a way forward from what he saw as the stultification and confusion of "positivism", "phenomenology", "post-modernism", and "social constructionism" as forms of analysis and explanation of the world of social relations, and social reality.

Critical realism has been attractive to social researchers and theorists who are committed to a firm ideological basis for viewing human action (e.g. Marxists, Muslims, Catholics) in asserting that *structures* within society are real and although their influence may be debated, their *being* or ontology (e.g. class exploitation, alienation, the nature of spiritual being) can be accepted as givens.

It is of course possible that Marxists and Catholics will disagree profoundly on what is or should be salient (Creaven, 2007) but CR nevertheless also lays the way open for dialogue and compromise between seemingly incompatible systems through the process of dialectical critical realism (Bhaskar, 1993/2008). Bhaskar adapts the Hegelian model of dialectical debate (traditionally: thesis, antithesis, synthesis) and goes beyond this model in positing a fourth level in the dialectical process which leads to action for, or advocacy of change. Moreover, this process of dialectical critical realism (DCR) is a continuous process in the lives of social systems, dyads and individuals, and there is continuous feedback between the 'agents' (the actors or individuals in DCR), or between various individuals: through these reflexive ideas and exchanges, organisations are in a process of continuous change and adjustment to new feedbacks, and the changing of social structures.

At this stage, a challenge in reading CR theoretical texts and research emerging from that theory should be mentioned: Critical Realism has developed its own vocabulary, and has coined new words ('neologisms') which the student may have difficulty in learning, or retaining. Furthermore, common English words are used in a way which attributes a rather different meaning to that of everyday language. The use of the word *absence* is a case in point. The difficulty of grasping CR concepts may be illustrated by this quotation from Alderson (2015):

> *Absence as a noun or verb is central to the DCR process of absenting absences, constraints, ills, contradictions, oppressive power, relations or inequities. Absence is the crucial empty physical, social and mental space that enables movement, imagined alternatives, processes and change.* (p.166).

Thus "absence" actually implies (in some, but not in all situations) the presence or existence of some positive force for social change.[11] Despite the

---

[11] "At its philosophical core lies a theory of *absence*, which Bhaskar combines with his pre-existing arguments from critical realism for the significance of ontology. This is a basis for the realist understanding of human *being* in society and in nature which, through the account of absence, is aligned to a theory of *becoming* and change in a spatio-temporal world. The alignment of being and becoming is achieved in a manner that displays both a uniqueness of individual philosophical voice and

complexities of her CR model, Anderson in her two volumes on *The Politics of Childhood Real and Imagined* (2013 & 2015) has many valuable things to say, and we have tried to utilise her insights in this Chapter.

What one finds in CR writing is an absence of dogma, and a willingness to engage in debate (the essence of DCR) to reach compromise. Thus Collier (1994) offers a useful synthesis of Weber's "individualism" and Durkheim's "collectivism" showing (pp 144-145) that these are not alternative models of individuals within social systems, but in the DCR mode, interactive ones, which coexist and offer simultaneously ways of promoting social action for change: individuals co-operate collectively, but remain individuals, is the message. Thus, in Collier's (1994 to 2002) analysis of Marx's writing on *Capital*, most wage earners are 'mystified' by the nature of capitalism that exploits them: their alienation remains unmasked. But in the Dialectical Critical Realist model they are capable of understanding and changing both their modes of thought and their social actions, their necessary "underlabouring" (using a technique borrowed from Locke) in addressing capitalist exploitation. The worker who fails to grasp the nature of his or her exploitation remains in a state of "non-realism" (Collier 1994, p. 12).

In response to critics of this Marxian approach, Collier (1994) says:

> ... *modern non-realists often accuse realists of dogmatism because of our defence of objectivity. They accuse us of arrogance in claiming truth for our theories ... [but] ... to claim objective truth for one's statements is to lay one's cards on the table, to expose oneself to the possibility of refutation.* (p. 13)

This bold claim to recognise "reality" (which is, of course, initially an intuitional process) rejects postmodern ideas of the relativity of knowledge and the impossibility of constructing linear models of basic cause; and the rejection of social constructivist ideas that knowledge and values are relative, and are generated through unique sets of social interactions. "Reality is a potentially infinite totality, of which we know something but not how much." (Bhaskar, 2008, p. 15)

One understands why CR has proved attractive to the Muslim scholar Matthew Wilkinson (2013 & 2015a):

---

boldness of intellectual vision, and these gave Bhaskar a fair claim to stand ... in the first rank of western philosophy today." (Norrie, 2010, p. 3).

> ... *both Islam, authentically understood from its primary sources, and critical realism share a foundational commitment to philosophy and existential "seriousness". Seriousness in its critical realist sense means that your behaviour is consistent with your beliefs, and that your practice is consistent with your theory and knowledge.* (Wilkinson, 2013, p. 429-30)

In "making sense" of his experience of teaching in a Muslim school he says:

> ... *this book draws upon the tradition of dialectical European philosophy, epitomised by Hegel ... Most recently, this tradition has been brought with great energy and conceptual sophistication into the contemporary academy by the founding figure of the philosophy of critical realism, Roy Bhaskar, as well as others following his lead, such as Alan Norrie, Andrew Wright and Margaret Archer. Critical realism is exceptional in its coherent articulation of a contemporary philosophy of being, of knowing and real personal, ethical and social change, and its <u>refusal</u> to reduce being of all types, including spiritual being, to socially constructed epistemology or merely psychological or semantic meaning. This makes the philosophy of critical realism at its original, dialectical and spiritual moments an ideal vehicle for the development of a systematic rationale to interpret Islam and Islam-in-education in a multi-faith world.* (Wilkinson, 2015a, p. 10)

Wilkinson draws on both Islamic and critical realist thinking in arguing that Muslim education should be "a philosophy for success", an empowerment (or, as Marxists would put it, the unmasking of alienation). *Success* is seen by Wilkinson as embedded in the multidimensional development and self-realisation of human social interaction within and between the four planes of social being defined by CR theorists. These planes are:

> The Real: *material transactions with nature (e.g. "the ground of being", "the essence of humans", "the uniqueness of each human being" counterpoised with forces of nature, polity and economy which impose themselves on humans; and the divine revelations of various world religions);*

> The Actual: *Inter-subjective (interpersonal) transactions between individuals or 'human agents' in different settings, including socialization and social control, the imposition of racialized identities; economic deprivation; forced migration et alia: and the understandings which humans have of these controlling forces, in dialogue, in writing, in protest, in political movements;*

> The Empirical: *Social relations at the non-reducible level of structures, institutions and forms;*

> The Transcendent: *The embodied personality's liberation through mutual tolerance, the shedding of false consciousness, spiritual fulfilment; awareness of self-potential, self-actualization. (Adapted from Bhaskar*

1993/2008 – *this is also the basis of Alderson's MELD model, explained below).*

Wilkinson (2015a) focuses his analysis on "the embodied personality" and his or her spiritual, intellectual, affective-cultural, civic, and instrumental dimensions. Each of these dimensions has distinct and interrelated or "articulated" ontologies. "Ontological realism" concerns the philosophical study of *being* (the first level of being in CR theory), and is a central concept within DCR:

> A basic understanding of critical realist ontology, the philosophical study of being is ... that being exists independently of our knowledge of it and in particular, our ability to describe it, so that it cannot be reduced to discourse, nor is it merely contained or constructed in the semiotics of our speech." (p. 50)

Priscilla Alderson (2015) in construing "the politics of childhood" offers the following explanations of DCR's 4-levels of analysis, which, following Bhaskar, she terms **MELD**. The first level is **1M** - DCR concepts of basic reality e.g. moral realism, which consists (in social science) of ethical naturalism. The 'moral realism' inherent at this basic level of DCR:

> ... accepts that harm and benefit are universal, causal, moral realities, which are defined and experienced in varied local and personal ways. To deny moral realism would set up theory/practice inconsistency ... Because humans are vulnerable, sensitive, social beings, able to flourish and to suffer, moral realism is part of human nature and daily life, and is not artificially introduced (Archer, 2003; Bhaskar, 1986; Collier, 1999) ... *1M* seeks to avoid the anthropic fallacy that places humans at the centre of the purpose and meaning of the universe (Bhaskar, 2000, 26). Instead, *1M* sees that we are <u>part of</u> nature ... A related problem is the adultist fallacy. This sets rational adults at the apex of morality, and regards childhood as a slow climb up from lower, natural, pre-social, pre-moral babyhood to higher, socialised, moral adulthood. Alderson, 2015 pp 28-29)

Priscilla Alderson in her two volumes on 'the politics of childhood' offers a vigorous and often moving account of the children she has been involved with in her research over a 30-year-period, but admits that she is a recent 'convert' to DCR:

> The challenge of rethinking my past research in relation to DCR, and of writing this book, has helped me, and I hope it will help readers, to see how DCR enlarges research theory and analysis. Since learning about DCR, I have revised some of my former ideas and discarded others, on the continuing journey of learning and changing. (Alderson, 2013, p. 8).

Alderson terms the second level in her DCR analysis **2E** (second edge) "… which concerns the transition into intervention and *process in product*. **2E** concerns actively negating problems that were identified at 1M (Bhaskar, 2008, 97-8). This involves absenting *aporia* (contradictions and constraints, ills and untruths) (Alderson, 2016. p. 34). Exactly how this is done is problematic however, and often one is challenged to know where to "fit" one's research findings within the four levels of analysis, and how to interpret findings (and undertake further research) in terms of absence, dialogue, dialectic or change – for example, the research studies on children which Alderson presents us with. She continues (p. 36): "A seven-scale DCR framework for interdisciplinary analysis (Bhaskar & Danemark, 2006) helps to connect many themes …"

We move to Alderson's third level called **3L**. She terms this level the *totality of change*, and comments:

> … **3L** recognizes that we all share the core universal human nature, our common humanity, and we are all unique and ethically different … We are interconnected and interdependent, dialectic replaces dichotomy, 'is' connects to 'ought', and 'ought' connects to 'can' (Bhaskar, 2010, 146-8) Alderson, 2016, p. 41).

It is at this level of understanding social structure that Margaret Archer's ideas (1995, 2000, 2003) of *morphogenesis* (personal change through dialectic interchange, and self-reflection) become increasingly important. And then at the level of the fourth dimension **4D**, there occurs the fullest realisation of *reflexive analysis*.

The transformative agency of **4D** aims for:

> …*emancipation … in the free society where each individual's flourishing depends on everyone flourishing.* **4D** *works to overcome the false sense of self as separate and isolated. We relate to the world and to other people through recognising what we share in common (Bhaskar, 2002, 305). The key questions concern identity (who am I?) and agency (what am I to do?).* (Alderson, 2015, p. 46).

At this stage then, false consciousness is shed, and alienation is unmasked.

The combined model is thus called **MELD** – in summary:

> *1M: Basic values, which are often unseen or unrecognized, but which inform or control action (e.g. covert power systems and alienation)*

2E: *Seeds of hope, and the dawning of understanding and dialectics. The realisation of absence, of lack of fulfilment, and yearning for change.*

3L: *Understanding of how social structures constrain us.*

4D: *Critical reflection and social change.*

Clearly, this is an ideal (and idealistic) model, and Bhaskar (2000, pp 8-9) warns us of the possibility of "malign MELD", in which negative, coercive powers subvert consciousness, control debates (e.g. through newspaper campaigns), and ensure that the powers of capital are unassailed, however much information we have (e.g. on health inequalities, on educational underachievement, or on poor quality schools). The 'seeds of hope' of 2E are often dashed.

Alderson devotes her two volumes to accounts of how, effectively, to liberate children so that their rights are fully realised. She uses the 1E assumptions about the "real" world and its state in nature (what Wilkinson in his Islamic formulation would call the original garden of paradise in which, following the acquisition of knowledge, Adam and Hawwa (Eve) are charged with "naming all things"):

> *Childhood and nature overlap in symbol and in practice ... ways in which children are treated reflect activities towards nature. These range from neglect and abuse to violence that wastes potential and ends the lives of millions of children.* (Alderson, 2015, p. 46)

Considering alienation's ending, Alderson (a Quaker) speculates about the 'natural communism' that would follow – what Quakers would call the Kingdom of Heaven existing on earth now, through the process of constructive relationships and harmony with the environment.[12]

In Alderson's formulation this communism goes beyond Marx (who merely wanted 'from each according to his ability, to each according to his need'): "Marx's ... generous giving and taking is not possible if everything is already shared."[13] (p. 159). In this model, the needs, rights and interests of children are not separate, but shared, in the utopia which Alderson anticipates. Alderson's (2013) chapter on "Inner Being: Alienation and

---

[12] See Alderson's account of "respecting children" from a Quaker viewpoint (Alderson, 2017).

[13] There is an intriguing parallel with Flaschel's (2009) idea that Marx's "reserve army of labour" will disappear if the social democratic state gives <u>all</u> citizens, whether working or not a generous living allowance, in his model of 'flexisecurity'.

Flourishing" sums up, for us what is most inspirational in critical realist theory of social science. She comprehensively demolishes the myth of "value free social science". Research with children, she argues, is not only value-informed: its entire goal in showing how children can "flourish" at the highest level of the MELD model is, as Bhaskar put it "value saturated" at each step in the MELD framework:

Although DCR is a complex philosophy for social science research, Alderson's reconstruction of her previous research with children using the DCR framework, which she elucidates in the passage quoted above, is both enlightening and enervating. The reader's journey in following this difficult intellectual model seems justified. According to Bhaskar (1993/2008):

Practical, concrete utopianism stands in contrast to abstract, intellectual utopianism ... being practical involves absenting constraining absences, as each in their own way, human beings try to overcome power2 and 'master-slave' relations' in society and nature ... the dialectic is an inner urge that flows universally from the logic of elemental absence (lack, need, want, desire) ... against power relations towards freedom as flourishing." (p. 14)

Consideration of the soul, the inner or spiritual self, may be outside of the bounds of conventional sociology, but for Alderson:

DCR explores unseen deeper realities, and shows the problems in social research that ignores them ... Without some explicit theories of human nature and the young self ... [research] ignores concepts of harm and benefit to children ... ideas from religion and philosophy seep into common imaginings of the self ... they [Jesus, Muhammad, Buddha] exemplified 'childlike' humility, poverty, humility, vulnerability, willingness to admit ignorance and to learn, with obedience to a transcendent goodness and an innocent detachment from worldly power." (Alderson, 2015, pp 141-142)

7. Matthew Wilkinson: Dialectical Critical Realism from an Islamic Perspective

The generosity of the shared dialectical process also flows from Wilkinson's (2012, 2015 a & b) analyses of CR's links with Islamic theology, law, education and moral practice. He too uses the MELD hierarchy, and concludes his **1E** analysis:

The Islamic Critical Realism (ICR) fulcrum offers the philosophical possibility that God may have granted genuine spiritual insight to those who fall outside one's own religious tradition and this can enrich rather than threaten one's own commitment to faith and facilitate a genuinely respectful engagement with the 'other'. (p. 64)

Moving to **2E**, Wilkinson observes how Bhaskar (1993/2008) adapted Hegel:

He radically alters the phases of dialectic into non-identity, to absence, to totality to transformative praxis in an extension of the 'revindication' of ontology and the positing of a new ontology of original critical realism. (p. 66)

Further, on *absence*, Wilkinson observes:

According to critical realist thinkers, absence, negativity and change are essential parts of the duality of presence and absence in being (Norris, 2010). For example silence is the precondition of speech, rests are indispensable to musical sound, and as we know from natural science, empty space is a necessary condition of solid objects. In the experience of selfhood, a sense/knowledge/belief that 'I am this' necessarily entails a sense/knowledge/belief that 'I am not that.' (p. 66)

In DCR absence is, crucially, transformative. "Indeed, dialectical change is understood by critical realists as the process ... of remedying or removing absence." (Bhaskar, 1993/2008) For Bhaskar, positive change is often the removal of, or progression from, something negative. The archetype of this movement is the process of abolishing (i.e. absenting) the conditions of slavery – and on the meaning of the "master-slave" relationship Bhaskar has much to say.

In Wilkinson's (2015a) account of the journey towards combining British and Islamic citizenship in Muslim adolescents, he first paints the **2E** picture of absence, and the 'absence' of seriousness' in National Curriculum goals concerning citizenship education. But as his research progressed, Wilkinson moved to 3L, the level of 'seriousness'. As an example, he cites Lovelock's (1979) idea of *Gaia*, the self-regulating, self-healing universe, which he relates to the Qur'anic idea of *kalifa* or stewardship of the earth. At this level, DCR concepts allowed Wilkinson to focus on transformative ideas, on the notion of the primacy of structure over individual agency. At the **4D** level, the meaning (and pedagogy) of citizenship education was taken outside of the classroom into 'the world', so that:

*... unity-in-diversity is the bedrock of society, in which institutional structure both predominates over individual agency and can be transformed by it. This task of linking agency with structure means that more than any other subject at the level of **4D** (Fourth Dimension – transformative praxis),*

citizenship education needs to be carried outside of the classroom into the community. (Wilkinson, 2015a, p. 246).

8. Margaret Scotford Archer[14]

Archer is, in our reading, the most impressive of the sociologists who have been inspired by Bhaskar's critical realism, and its unfolding from and through Marxism and Hegel, into dialectical critical realism – and then into realms of theology, and how in critical realist theory, we may understand and apprehend notions of the divine (Archer et al., 2004).

Bhaskar's (1993/2008) earlier consideration of (and modification of) Marxian theory had led some American commentators to label him as a Marxist (and hence the neglect of DCR by American sociologists – Gorski, 2013). However, transcending the purely material concerns of Marxian ideology, Bhaskar embarks on a spiritual journey, exploring Hindu and Buddhist concepts of self and soul (Bhaskar, 2002). Certainly, as Wilkinson (2013 & 2015a & b) saw in adapting DCR in Islamic terms, there are profound possibilities of DCR transcendence in reconceptualising Islamic (and other theologies') approaches to citizenship education.

Archer's fullest and most eloquent account of "the internal conversation" for us is her 2003 volume *Structure, Agency and the Internal Conversation*. Her arguments concern "structure" (which has variable meaning in philosophy and sociology, but is seen as an enduring form), and "agency" (with similar debates about its meaning, but intuitively, concerns how individuals relate, subjectively, to structure). Both structure and agency exist independently (i.e. have ontological reality), and causal relations between them remain to be investigated. Structure and agency "are two distinctive and irreducible properties and powers, and ... human reflexive deliberations play a crucial role in mediating between them." (p. 14) Thus *reflexivity* is central in Margaret Archer's sociology:

> *Were we humans not reflexive beings there could be no such thing as society. This is because any form of social interaction, from the dyad to the global system, requires that subjects know themselves to be themselves. Otherwise they could not acknowledge that their words were their own nor their intentions, undertakings and reactions belonged to them ... not one social*

---

[14] Margaret Archer has been for some time, principal adviser to Pope Francis on women's issues, and President of the Pontifical Academy of Social Sciences.

> *obligation, expectation or norm could be owned by a single 'member' of society.* (p. 19)

Moreover, the reflexive, internal conversations and self-appraisals of individuals in their interactions with others have, in Archer's model, causal power in modifying structures: these "extrinsic effects ... mediating cultural and social properties of their societies ... and the private lives of social subjects are indispensable to the very existence and working of society." (p. 52)

Archer draws ideas and insights on the social psychology of the self, described in the writings of William James (1890) and George H. Mead (1964; Joas, 1997), whose ideas of self-other, and I-myself she analyses in detail, and is critical of their ideas of "personal reflexivity": their idea of the "inner world" lacks autonomy in relation to the individual's "outer world". This is a crucial shortcoming, in Archer's goal to "reclaim the internal conversation" as talking "to" society, not merely "about" society. Only then, Archer proposes "... we are in a position from which properly to consider the potentialities of our reflexive deliberations as the process which mediates between 'structure and agency'." (p. 129) Archer illustrates her thesis by analysing the "internal conversations" of twenty adults, making each a unique case study, in showing *inter alia*, "How the different *individual* modes of reflexivity, which mediate constraints and enablements in quite distinctive ways, are also related to *collective* action." (p. 166)

Reflexivity does not usually lead to structural change, of course, and Archer illustrates why this is so in her analysis of types of reflexivity. But, reflections upon reflections, refined, shared and polished reflexives:

> ... *'meta-reflexives'... are such because they pursue cultural ideals that cannot be accommodated by the current social structure and the array of contexts it defines ... By personifying their ideals of truth and goodness, the meta-reflexives awaken them and re-present them to society. In so doing they re-stock the pool of societal values, by displaying alternatives to the aridity of third-way thinking – and its repressive consensus ... (Archer, 2003, p. 361).*

A useful critique of Archer's "reflexivity and conduct of the self" has been offered by Akram & Hogan (2015), who examine among things, how Archer's idea of self-reflexion may challenge ideas of the "taken-for-granted" everyday events in the lives of individuals which form part of Bourdieu's (1989) account of *habitus*. Bourdieu downplays ideas of freely willed choice in making decisions, focussing instead on how social and economic classes create reserves of social capital, through socialising those below them into "unconscious acceptance" of everyday lifestyles. It's almost as if some wealthy elite in Britain had devised a newspaper called *The Sun*, which the workers may enjoy as their daily intellectual succour: this same cabal would have been responsible for creating 'sink estates' and poor quality comprehensives (Sawyerr & Bagley, 2017a). This habitus of the labouring classes, and of the reserve army of labour is deeply entrenched (Stahl, 2015). The proletariat's only mode of upward mobility, like that of the proles in Orwell's *1984*, is to win the lottery.

Yet despite this gloomy continuity of class, Bourdieu allows that 'misrecognition' (akin to Marx's 'false consciousness') can change over quite lengthy periods of time, or change in response to sudden upheavals, such as war. Bourdieu has appeal for some radical sociologists in that he seems to have identified how socio-economic classes perpetuate themselves through symbolic rituals which can be enduring across generations: but these rituals may also be identified, and changed (e.g. Carlile, 2013; Savage, 2015).

Archer's idea of morphogenesis, as part of a self-reflexive change in self-concept, being a path to "social mobility" seems a light year away (or perhaps a "second edge" away in CR terms) from the rather depressing portraits of everyday social life which come from detailed ethnographic portraits of working class life which students of Bourdieu paint. For Akram & Hogan (2015) Archer proposes:

> ... *a seismic shift [from Bourdieu's account] in how people form and conduct themselves in everyday life, a process that would result in the realization of extremely high levels of ethical autonomy ... she goes beyond Giddens' and Bourdieu's notions of everyday, routinized taken-for-granted actions ... offering an entirely new view of how people form, manage and understand themselves in everyday life. (p. 610).*

Archer (like Alderson, 2013, p. 80) does not reject Bourdieu's account of "everyday habitus", but offers instead a novel form of the social psychology of everyday life. What is novel (among other things) is Archer's idea of *agency*, which is developed within the framework of Bhaskar's dialectical critical realism. Personal reflexivity (renewing one's own thoughts, feelings and actions in relation to those of others) is shared, according to Archer, by all people who find themselves in a common social situation. Akram & Hogan (2015) sum up their understanding of Archer's position:

> *Reflexivity is the regular ability, shared by all normal people, to consider themselves in relation to their social contexts and vice versa ... Reflexivity in modern society means a transition from a morphostatic to a morphogenetic society of constant change. Reflexivity is also linked to our emotional commitments and our moral concerns ... all of which help to maintain 'the internal conversation' which reflects ongoing conversations in agents about who they are, and how they see their lives progressing ... Archer's work raises the idea that individuals think about who they are (in the sense of personal and social identity) and modify their identity in the course of everyday being ... Central to such a practice of the self is a deep sense of awareness of who one is, how one became who they are, and the benefits of pursuing such new performative aspects of identity.* (Akram & Hogan, p. 620)

In this new world (for it seems to be too exciting to be like the old world which we all remember):

> *Reflexivity emerges from a new social and cultural order, which creates novel situational contexts, and which they must negotiate ... In such a scenario, agents draw upon their socially dependent, but nevertheless personal powers of reflexivity to define their courses of action ... Reflexivity is not necessarily positive, because it can also have negative outcomes ... some will be taking the best course, but may make mistakes ... not all reflexion is successful, but all are crucially trying to be reflexive.* (Archer, 1995, p 110).

This is a fascinating area for qualitative research, for eliciting extended accounts of how people in specific communities, or with shared pasts (e.g. those based on religions, ethnicities, childhood experiences) construe themselves through their intellectual, moral and emotional histories, their reactions to others, and how they share thoughts, feelings and opinions. The agents in such a study might be people undergoing change in their lives and who are making choices for the future, reflecting on their past: a population of senior high school students might be ideal for such a study. This research could also be carried out with an ethnographic methodology, with women (e.g. Muslims) seeking empowerment and change.

9. Critical Realism's Marxist Dimension

Throughout Critical Realist writing there is mention of Marx, much of it critical, although Roy Bhaskar (1992/2008) clearly draws inspiration from Marx and Hegel, even when he is moulding their ideas creatively into an entirely new way of understanding "society and nature."

Creaven (2007) argues that critical realism should, like Marxism, be concerned with alienation, the separation of the individual from the 'natural' status implied by their relationship to the social equity required by 'labour' (employed, for example, in schools in the world of subordinated learning, or employment). This alienation, a form of habitus, is an "enslaving ideology" transmitted between generations: CR's (and DCR's task) is to 'unmask' this alienation, and replace 'false consciousness' with reflexive knowledge which enables social structures, and individuals interacting with structures, to reach a state of self-hood that melds them in the utopian awareness that may be the natural state of humankind.

There is lyrical parallel to morphogenetic insights, in the model of "wonder" which Ahmed (2004) derives from the writing of Descartes (on the body's first passions of cognitive surprise) and the "sensuous certainty" which Marx describes in the first dawning of consciousness in the unmasking of alienation:

> *The body opens as the world opens up before it; the body unfolds into the unfolding of a world that becomes approached as another body. This opening is not without its risks: wonder can be closed down if what we approach is unwelcome ... But wonder is a passion that motivates the desire to keep looking; it keeps alive the possibility of freshness, and vitality of living that can live as if for the first time ... wonder involves the radicalisation of our relation to the past, which is transformed into that which lives and breathes in the present. (Ahmed, 2004, p. 180).*

Critical Realism, in Daniel Little's (2012) analysis sees critical thinking as "emancipatory". In both Marxist and CR traditions the term "critical" has specific meaning. Bhaskar cites Marx's Feurbach thesis: "The philosophers have sought to understand the world: the point however is to change it." In this model, critical science is an engaged or committed scientific endeavour, aiming to construct knowledge that may be, according to CR's emancipatory paradigm, for humanity's long-term benefit. Like Marx's *Capital*, which was subtitled "a critique of political economy", CR also attempts to expose the underlying ideologies of powerful interest groups, and to expose "false consciousness".

On the difficulties of research findings actually leading to change, Alderson (2013) observes:

> *Many childhood researchers are disappointed that their 'participative research' [that] ends with the neat reported findings (words) seldom leading to real, messy, transformative change (deeds). DCR helps to identify and remedy this problem, in following Marx by identifying five types of practical*

contradictions to be resolved if real change is to occur." (Alderson, 2013 p. 91).

Alderson continues her analysis of DCR in Marxist mode in discussing Bhaskar's (1993/2008) borrowing from Marx of the idea of "the master-slave relationship", which goes beyond the power of "masters" in older societies to all kinds of power relationships:

> *'Master-slave' relationships involve Marx's understanding of concepts that are central to DCR [identifying] ... forms that have immanent contradictions that can suggest an ideal and misleading representation of the world; and also a real world that can be described, classified and explained in various, changing and developing ways. Marx, as a scientific realist, believed that explanatory structures are essentially not only distinct from, but are often ... in opposition to the phenomena they generate. Examples include the way many schools fail many of their students ... (p. 111)*

We observe with satisfaction the views of Creaven (2007, 2012 & 2015), who is the most enthusiastic of the "Marxist critical realists". He examines how Marx and Engels worked together, and observes (following Bhaskar) that Engel's was the "underlabourer", clearing away the underbrush of false ideas and philosophical nonsense that impeded the clarity of Marxian ontological analysis. Wilkinson, (2015) too uses the Hobbesian idea of underlabouring, which clarifies the road to Islamic emancipation in the critical realist model, focussing on the Sunnah (life and teaching of Prophet Muhammad) and Shari'a legal principles, providing a truthful or real interpretation of the Qur'an, in contrast to the distorted and false interpretations of groups such as Al Qaeda and other islamist groups (Wilkinson, 2015b, 2017 & 2018).

10. Conclusions and Reflections on Critical Realism

In reading Bhaskar, Alderson, Wilkinson and Archer and other critical realists, we have been struck by a new facet of communication and information which influences all of our lives: the electronic information system of the web from which we are constantly gleaning information; and as well as sending frequent e-mails and texts, the sharing of ideas and images with friends (and others) on numerous media and messaging sites. The youngsters among us are no longer truly part of themselves: we share ourselves, reflexively, with a much wider world than when Roy Bhaskar published his first book in 1978. What is the meaning of this electronic world? Alderson (2013, p. 102) is worried about the covert collection of children's electronic data as a means of controlling them, an electronic version of Bhaskar's (1993/2008) 'master-slave' relationship. But there is also a powerful anarchy in the data which is collected on all of us, and liberation when it is released through the integrity of 'whistle-blowing'.

And, returning to Alderson's (2013 & 2015) reconstruction of her earlier work with children, how might the researcher help these adolescent women achieve a self-actualization of identity?

Alderson observes that:

> *Children and adults learn about their needs through their bodily experiences within relationships; they express their needs and views through their bodies; and they are respected or disrespected in the casual or harsh ways in which their bodies are treated in practice.* (Alderson, 2013, p. 94)

She is writing about her research with physically challenged children: but these words could have been written of physically and sexually abused children, including the abused and exploited children and women of Bangladesh and Pakistan, who we discuss in Chapters 8 to 11.

Finally, we want to emphasise how exciting critical realist theory can be. Once you have absorbed it (or your personal version of it, since individual researchers and scholars will perceive DCR writings differently, and take away different aspects of the model in their quest for truth-telling and social change) your thinking and feeling about the world will never again be the same. Reflecting, thinking, feeling, relating to one's own thoughts and those of others is exciting, a daily excitement which is never lost[15]. And when one is absorbed within the intellectual milieu of Islam, it is transcendent.

We are empowered in being confident that *our* value judgements and the actions that derive from them can be important: in research we now move easily from 'is' to 'ought', to 'can', and reflexively through dialogue and debate with our academic and professional partners, set new goals and horizons for achieving liberation, seeing ways of escape from alienation and 'false consciousness' imposed on ourselves and others.

Critical realism gives to the student what Sara Ahmed (2004) calls a sense of "wonder" in rediscovering and redesigning the social matrix of her world:

---

[15] For the convert to Islam, this is like the daily excitement of the conversations with Allah, through prayers, both the prescribed daily prayers, and the silent prayers we murmur at the end of each formal prayer session.

This critical wonder is about recognising that nothing in the world can be taken for granted, which includes the very political movements to which we are attached. It is this critical wonder about the forms of political struggle that makes Black feminism such an important intervention, by showing that categories of knowledge (such as patriarchy or 'women') have political effects, which can exclude others from the collective. (Ahmed, 2004, p. 182).

For Muslim scholars and reformers, advocating the realisation of human rights and equality for women, men and young people which are offered to us by Qur'an and Sunnah, Mathew Wilkinson is the lead scholar, not only in the West but in the world also. His massive book *The Genealogy of Terror: How to Distinguish Between Islam, Islamism and Islamist Extremism* (2018) deserves to be widely read, since it offers a clear, comprehensive and brilliant exposition of the true foundation and meaning of Islam, and how islamist terror groups have distorted and corrupted Islam. Wilkinson artfully interweaves the Shari'a underlabouring principles in his critical realist account in a text meant to be read by policy makers as well as scholars. He shows that the different worldviews of Islam " … explain, for example, why Malala Yousafzai campaigns for the Islamic right to female education and why the Taliban shot her for it."

Chapter Two

Muslim Women in Management Roles in Western and in Muslim-Majority Countries: Strong Women Balancing Family and Career

Mahmoud Abubaker, Christopher Adam-Bagley and Afroze Shahnaz

1. Introduction: All Women Experience Discrimination in Employment

The authors of this chapter have two major concerns. The first is the problem discrimination against Muslim women by employers in Western nations (those countries in whom the majority of the population are of European heritage). Our second particular concern, as Muslims, is the discrimination against women as managers and as professionals, in Muslim Majority Cultures (MMCs)—the Muslim cultures of Africa, the Middle East, and Asia. We cannot address these two concerns without first considering the range of factors which can impede women (of whatever ethnicity or religion) from reaching management roles at a variety of levels, in the companies and professional centres in Western nations which choose to employ them. We shall argue that the identified strengths of women managers in Western countries may also apply, in a culturally modified way, to Muslim women seeking occupational advancement in MMCs.

The first tier of literature which we consider concerns the barriers to the employment of women (*regardless* of ethnicity and religion) in management in American and European cultures. The second tier of literature concerns the issues of *intersectionality*, in which Muslim women seek professional, management and executive roles in the external workforce in Europe and America, following "the Muslim diaspora" (Syed & Pio, 2016).

The third set of literature is concerned with the progress of women in management and professional roles in Muslim-majority countries. We want to see if there can be a coherent model of research and understanding which covers these three tiers or domains of literature, as a prelude to proposing both quantitative and qualitative studies on problems encountered by Muslim women in particular types of business organisation in Muslim Majority Cultures.

2. Women in Management: 'Western' and International Studies

The barriers to women's progress in taking management roles in Muslim countries such as Palestine, Jordan, Pakistan and Bangladesh may first of all, be similar in a number of ways to the issues facing women in Western countries, including minority women who seek to attain status in managerial roles (Rizzo, Abdel-Latif & Maeyer, 2007). The study of women in management roles, and the barriers to such attainment in Western countries has recent genesis (Alvesson & Billing, 1999). It remains clear that in all countries of the world there remains a "glass ceiling" (of variable height and thickness) which prevents women attaining the highest ranks in professional and business organisations—when they do succeed, it is often in specialised roles such as human resources management, or in specialised technical areas which do not require male-type aggression (Paludi, 2013).

An ILO (2015) study, updating World Bank (2012) profiles of women in management, surveyed 108 countries and reported significant advances in the proportions of women in middle and senior management roles. While women outnumbered men in the areas of human relations, publicity and communications, they were underrepresented in fields such as sales, marketing and higher management. The ILO study identified many different ways in which women said that they could advance their careers, including peer support and mentoring, and the pressure for adequate Work Life Balance (WLB) benefits. Certain nations had not made progress in women's professional role advancement however, and the eleven nations ranked lowest by ILO were all Muslim-majority cultures, many of them bracketed as "low to middle income" countries. Only Turkey and Palestine ranked with "developed" nations in the proportions of women in more senior managerial roles.

In 2016 women occupied 24 percent of senior roles in the North American Fortune 500 companies, an increase of 3 percent since 2011. But in 2016, in 33 percent of global companies there were no women in senior management. The authors of the report reaching these conclusions commented: "The percentage of women in senior roles is slowly growing worldwide, but at this pace we won't reach parity for decades." (Catalyst, 2017).

In a British analysis Francke (2014) pointed to "the power of role models"—the prominence and activism of powerful women in British institutions and companies who are exemplars of how success may be achieved. In fact, this report shows that knowledge of discrimination, potential or actual, can make women grudgingly accept rather low levels of reward and responsibility in organisations.

Carter & Silva (2010) observing that only three percent of Fortune 500 companies were headed by a female CEO, report on a follow-up study of cohorts of male and female MBA graduates in America. They showed that after graduating women were significantly more likely to be appointed to positions of lower rank and salary than their male counterparts. But an early appointment to a lower ranked or rewarded managerial post tended to determine a woman's whole career pattern—a similar finding to that of Metcalfe (2011) in her research on a number of Muslim-majority cultures.

Women in Carter & Silva's study who did not take "child-care breaks" also remained disadvantaged in American organisations. In this analysis, all too often women managers were seen as "taking care", while male managers were viewed (by the senior males who hired them) as "taking charge" and were the likely candidates for further promotion. However, we argue below for a Muslim-model in which the "caring" role of being a strong family manager can translate into a senior management role in an enterprise, successfully fulfilling both ethical and financial goals.

The positive aspect of women's role as senior managers comes from the influential work of Americans Sally Helgeson and Julia Johnson. The first edition of their insightful and ground-breaking book *The Female Vision: Women's Real Power at Work* appeared in 1990, and a largely rewritten version of this book, taking account of the financial decline of 2008, was published in 2010. Their accounts of the successful female manager which have emerged from this research have been broadly acclaimed, and their model is persuasive. In their original research they conducted extensive interviews with 80 successful women managers, and "tracked" the daily routines of a number of the managers. Women perceive differently, relate differently, and control differently when compared with their male counterparts (Helgeson, 2017).[1]

In the model which emerged from this research, women managers "take in" more detail in arriving at decisions—they are more analytical, rational and thoughtful. They act and organise differently from men, in ways which reflect a superior "emotional intelligence" compared with males. They are more attentive to the emotional needs of those below them, and above them. These are skills which the alpha-male manager often lacks. When the organisation is under threat, the male leader may enter a "fight or flight" mode, while the woman leader may "circle the wagons", using her male counterparts with strategic intelligence. Women managers support depressed and troubled employees, rather than firing them. In Helgeson's (2017) account, they get the best out of people. Their approach to management is qualitative, rather than quantitative. Any male bean-counter can calculate the bottom line: it takes a person who combines emotional and strategic intelligence to know how the organisation should change in order to improve the bottom line. This is one of the (several) ways in which women may excel in management. Woman (reflecting a different kind of family experience) are more empathic, less interested in profit for its own sake, more interested in the firm as a socially responsible organisation—although, as Belinda Parmar (2014) argues, empathy in business enterprise, including marketing, may be the royal road towards profitability.

In this feminist model, women may diminish (or ignore) any innate drive to "control and subjugate": their major driver, rather, is for most managers to meet the personal needs of employees and customers alike, through co-operation and understanding in seeking to maximise a company's potential and profitability. Empathy with potential customers and clients is another important way in which women often outmatch men. Intelligent women executives do not engage in needless battles, and they may exercise the

---

[1] There is no evidence from neurobiology or neurochemistry that there are any significant differences in basic abilities and dispositions between the genders. Thus, for example, women's "failure" to achieve on a par with men in science, mathematics, engineering and management is entirely due to socially prescribed roles, and socially constructed biases and disadvantages (Rippon, 2019).

option to walk away from situations in which an unintelligent alpha male manager spoils for a fight (Parmar, 2014; Gordon, 2016).

An important question is this: if women, as a group, possess such excellent management skills, why are they underrepresented, and discriminated against, in so many Western enterprises (Bullough, Moore & Kalafotoglu, 2017)? One answer seems to be that not only are many men aggressively hanging on to positions of power in ways which are dysfunctional for their organisations: they often operate, cognitively, within a realm of cognitive dissonance, their innate prejudices unshaken by contrary evidence (Burnes & James, 1995).

In reading these accounts of successful women managers, we are struck by the similarity of this model with the accounts of the successful woman in Muslim cultures, past and present, who is not only supremely successful as a "strong family manager", but also in modern times when she graduates from university and enters professional employment, where she is successful *because* she is also a successful wife and mother, effectively running two organisations according to the same principles based on "emotional intelligence" (Murphy & Smolarski, 2018).

We should add that this account of women managers' potential for success is based on an idealised model, and there are a number of ways in which men can undermine the "emotional friendliness" of women in organising work settings and commercial enterprises. Men can disrupt women's organisational power through "the masculine managerialism of conquest, competition and control" (Kerfoot & Knights, 1994; Knights, 2017). Male sexism moves non-formally into many situations in the workplace, into sexually demeaning and even sexually assaultive comments, strategies and behaviours imposed on those women below them, or who are perceived as threats to their hegemony (Bates, 2014).

In profound contrast, the Islamic solution to the mixing of genders within social institutions is to emphasise the ethical ground of respect and modesty, in a system of gender plurality. Contrary to Knights' (2015) thesis that "if bodies are to matter, binaries need to shatter", Islam asserts the divinely inspired plurality of male and female sexuality, linked together by the ethics of modesty and mutual service. Women in organisations in which a majority of employees are Muslim will not, we hope encounter sexual harassment[2]. Such behaviour should be anathema within a culture which is extremely

---

[2] But there are contrary examples from modern Pakistan, cited in Chapter 11.

cautious about sexual expression outside of the family unit. This may not be the case in Pakistan, however in which sexual bullying and workplace assaults on women are said to be common (Saeed, 2013)

In organisations in Muslim Majority Cultures (MMCs), women are not treated in the same way that men are treated: rather they are perceived as significantly different, having special needs (for respect and modesty), with personal rights in their child-care roles not afforded to men. Muslim organisations are most likely to discriminate in failing to hire women for managerial or professional positions on grounds of patriarchy; but once women have been hired, although their promotion may be slow, their treatment should not involve sexual harassment of the kind recorded by Laura Bates (2014) in Western cultures. And, perhaps paradoxically, in Saudia Arabia, a culture in which norms of Islamic modesty have such a strong expression to the extent that educational and health systems (including universities) are gender-segregated, women have achieved the highest ranks in any Muslim Majority Culture, as Deans of Faculties (in women-only universities), and as Medical Directors: Saudi Arabia is experiencing the rapid advancement of women professionals through this gendered segregation, in a time of rapid social change in which women in KSA are making major advances within the Islamic tradition of strong, professional women. The Kingdom of Saudi Arabia (KSA) is described as "a most masculine state" (Al-Rasheed, 2013), with extreme distancing of men and women in schools, colleges and universities; and many health care facilities are also gender-segregated (Al-Sudairy, 2017). The paradox is that within these segregated institutions women rise to the highest levels of leadership and administration, so that in KSA there are more women in high levels of leadership in educational and health sectors, than in many other Muslim majority cultures (Almansour et al., 2016; Alsubaie & Jones, 2017).

Economic analysis of potentials for growth in all world cultures suggests that if all women were educated to the same level as men, and were recruited to employment without discrimination, there would be a net growth in national wealth across the world of about US$12 trillion, within a decade (Woetzel, 2015). Schwab et al. (2017) in their survey of 142 countries suggest that these gains could be made within eight years, in any country which manages to achieve gender equity in employment, education, health care and education – the figure for the United Kingdom is a net gain in GDP of US$250 billion by 2025 if gender equity were to be achieved.

The periodic surveys on "the gender gap" issued by the World Economic Forum (Schwab et al., 2017; WEF 2017-2019) are instructive and important, since they show progress made in achievement of women's equity in four areas: economic participation and opportunity; educational opportunity and attainment; health and survival; and political emancipation (access to democracy and being candidates for, and members of ruling assemblies). All figures from these indicators are expressed as the proportion of women in any culture who have achieved equal status with that of men. For all of the 142 countries studied, the overall equity figure was 68 percent, meaning that women were disadvantaged compared with men, by 32 percent, on average. This proportion (in 2018) had barely moved since the publication of the previous report, and it was estimated that at this rate of progress it would take 99 years for world gender equity to be achieved. The report for 2019 (Zahidi et al., 2019) showed net progress of only 0.03% on the previous year, with 89 countries improving, but 55 showing an actual decline. Those countries with the least gender equity, and with low or negative growth in women's opportunities were Syria, Iraq, Pakistan and Yemen.

Most gender inequity was found in the official data for Middle Eastern and North African (mostly Muslim) countries, with an estimate of 157 years before equity would (if ever) be achieved. Only four mainly Muslim countries, Bangladesh, Bosnia, Indonesia and Malaysia, scored above the median on the indices of gender equity. Two Muslim nations, Pakistan and Yemen placed last in the rankings.

3. Minority and Muslim Women Seeking Managerial and Professional Employment in 'Western' Organisations

Women (and especially minority women) who seek to rise in business organisations face the problems of "intersectionality", in which several disadvantaged statuses (e.g. gender, ethnicity, migration status) coincide or intersect, perhaps with synergistic or additionally negative effects (Phoenix, 2006; Shen et al., 2009; Sternadori & Prentice, 2016). In the complex identities with which the intersection of roles and statuses challenges women, polite compliance - acknowledging and supporting the ambitions of male managers if they are themselves to seek advancement, is one possible pathway which women may choose (Purdie-Vaughns & Eibach, 2008; Ng & Sears, 2010).

Women in such settings may have to adopt "fluid identities" in order to be successful, knowing how to "present themselves in everyday life" (Goffman, 1978) in roles in which they seek to avoid imposed stereotypes

(Afshar, 2012; Veenstra, 2012). In these accounts the very flexibility of a woman's identity in a male-dominated world of industry and commerce allows them to find niches and avenues of power (Afshar, 2012). In Muslim Majority Cultures (MMCs) the 'career woman' has to manage expertly a complex identity in which she is simultaneously wife, mother, family manager, professional and entrepreneur (Rossenkhan et al., 2016).

It may be, as Parmar (2014) argues, that a woman's successful development of multiple-role management is equalled by her capacity for warmth and empathy, enabling her to understand the nuances of managerial roles in organisations which men control, in ways which allow such women to both successfully serve and to manage important organisational roles. Men have lesser role complexity: 'merely' being expected to offer social and psychological support and to serve their wife, 'the strong family manager'; and to earn enough in the marketplace to enable them to fulfil this supporting role in economic terms.

On the issue of self-identity in Muslim career women in MMCs, Arar et al. (2013) studied Palestinian and Jordanian women who travelled from home to residence in tertiary colleges for professional education. They found that developing a group experience with fellow students led to a change of identity and self-concept which made them not only successful professionals in the making, but also women who were, effectively, pioneers of Islamic feminism. Such upwardly mobile Muslim career women were creating for themselves new "spatial identities" (Abu Oksa Daoud, 2017). These new movements in Islamic feminism in the Middle East call for better Work-Life Benefits (WLBs) to support dual-career roles, and fresh thinking by Human Resources professionals in both the West and in MMCs.

Professional developments in HRM (Human Resources Management) practice have too often reflected public stereotypes of ethnic minority women (Shen et al., 2009). In response to such prejudice and misunderstanding, self-help groups have been developed for mentoring Muslim women seeking advancement in management roles (Grine, 2014); in addition, explicitly multicultural policies in countries such as Canada (Mahadevan & Mayer, 2017) may be helping the rise of Muslim women in management roles. But even "progressive" HR managers in North America have tended to tend to focus on gender rather than on ethnicity or religion, when promoting policies for employment equity (Kameneau & Fearful, 2006).

Indeed, Muslim women seeking occupational advancement in non-Muslim societies in Europe and North America face the additional challenge of ethnic and religious prejudice, which when combined with sexist values, can be major obstacles to obtaining professional employment, or executive roles in commercial organisations (Kumra & Manfredi, 2012).

Ali et al. (2017) place such discrimination within a three-tier framework, in which workplace discrimination (including the failure to provide adequate Work-Life Benefit support) combines within macro, meso and micro-level factors with complex "relational intersections" which act to exclude Muslim women in Western countries from having access to the external labour market at a level which matches their education and aspirations. We have adopted this heuristically useful three-tier model of Ali et al. (2016) in framing the present review of literature.

In all Western countries, women of "the Muslim diaspora" face particular challenges, since the wearing of the hijab (head covering) and modesty of dress marks a woman for discrimination and abuse in public places, schools and higher education, and in employment situations (Syed et al., 2005; Ali et al., 2017; Busby, 2018). Muslim women face greater amounts of employment discrimination than do Muslim men. This is a major challenge for research on human relations practice (Ali et al., 2017), and has led the researchers working under Syed's leadership on the study of prejudice, discrimination and their impact on women in the labour force in 18 different countries, to seek, largely in vain for common threads in gender and diversity polities in a variety of cultures in which Muslims form varying proportions of the population.

Syed and Colleagues (2008 to 2016) argue that HRM policy in societies marked by ethnic and religious diversity must adopt complex, individualised models of practice reflecting a country's particular history and social structure with regard to the treatment and power relations of majority and minority groups. This approach, though manifestly sensible is difficult to adopt systematically in practice, and we have yet to see an example of how it has been successfully applied as a comprehensive, explanatory framework, either for explaining or for diminishing discrimination against Muslim women's employment. The question, as Rodriguez et al. (2016) posed with regard to gender, ethnicity and "intersectionality" is: "Where do we go from here?"

Eden & Gupta (2017) do offer valuable data analysis in exploring why women are underrepresented in management roles in countries at various stages of development. In this analysis, economic growth is by no means a guarantee of increased gender equality in management. According to the international data from this study, not only are gender inequalities in management unchanged by economic development in "rich" countries: in some developing countries gender inequalities are actually decreasing, with very slow overall growth in women's advancement into senior roles.

That questions about increasing the role of "minority women" in organisations must be asked, is clear from the work of Mahadevan and her colleagues (Mahadevan et al. 2017). They attempt to develop relevant models through European and international descriptions of HRM practice (focusing in particular on Muslims of both genders who are part of the "Muslim diaspora" in Germany and elsewhere in mainland Europe). Their emerging model is one of "reflexive HRM practice" (Mahadevan, et al. 2017). This is a bold model, since it requires HRM managers to engage in reflexive dialogue in how they perceive and understand the aspirations of upwardly-mobile Muslims.

Translated into the critical realist model outlined in Chapter 1, this implies that the phenomenon of *absence*, of ignoring Muslim aspirations, is being replaced in a reflexive dialogue as a prelude to morphogenesis, the foundation of structural and value change. Britain has certainly not yet gone much beyond the stage of denial (the state of absence), that of ignoring the reality of Muslim women's occupational presence and their aspirations, in anything other than stereotyped terms. Muslim women in management roles in countries such as Britain are a small fraction of all women in management (Tariq & Syed, 2017). In order to succeed, these women have to draw on intersecting support networks, and to engage in pioneering education on behalf of Muslim women in leadership roles.

However, the commonly used idea of "intersection" (when different statuses which imply disadvantage and discrimination, coincide) is problematic. Do the aspects of disadvantage combine in a simple additive model? Or are some statuses more important than others? And is there interaction between the statuses so that particular statuses in combination (e.g. being a woman, a woman of colour, and a woman identifiable as a Muslim) create a profound disadvantage which is greater than in the sum of the individual effects? Critical realists approach the problem of intersectionality in a particular way, arguing that awareness of intersectionality is part of the dialectic process of women talking to women (and to men) about the meaning and reality of such discrimination as part of their "lived experience" (Chis, 2016). Certainly, as Abu-Lughod (2010) argues in her account of the Muslim feminist movement in Egypt and Palestine, the understanding for action must be grounded in ethnography rather than in politics. And such research understanding must reflect the fundamental principles of Islam, as we argue next.

4. Women's Role in Traditional Islamic, Muslim-Majority Cultures

Traditionally, women have held both powerful and protected roles in Muslim societies. Their duality of role—supporting and leading their family, and exercising wider social power—is not usually understood by non-Muslims. Muslim women's equality has been proportional rather than absolute, and specific portions of The Qur'an specify that women require special treatment and respect in roles concerning family relationships, child care, marriage and inheritance (Mernissi, 1991). Nevertheless, the Qur'an clearly prescribes the absolute moral, structural and spiritual equality of men and women in many roles and social institutions (Wadud, 1999; Esposito, 2003).

Women in Islam have played important roles as leaders of commerce (following the example of Kadijah, the first Muslim woman); as religious scholars (Aish'ah, Umm Salama, and many others); as governors and administrators; and as military leaders (Ghandanfar, 2001). The "golden age" of the Caliphates until 1258 (Esposito, 1998), and the many prominent women in Islam are often forgotten, and today a sub-Islamic patriarchy in nominally Muslim countries often prevails, in ways which oppress women (Hashmi, 2000; Khan & Ahmed, 2010). This is despite the abundant evidence from Qur'an and Sunnah (the teaching, and the lived example of Prophet Muhammad) that women have in virtually every domain, equal rights with men (Mernissi, 2001; Roald, 2001).

Anwar (2006) too draws on Qur'anic and Sunnah sources in developing a philosophical argument about "the ontology of selfhood" for Muslim women. She develops a pluralistic model—women, from the time of Adam's wife Hawa, have profound differences from men, but they also have the rights of equality of selfhood in terms of sexual identity and aspirations. In this model, women should not be subordinated to men in Islamic cultures. Modern Islamic feminists draw on the traditional writings of Islam in showing that this theology asserts the net equality of all women, including all Muslim women (Lovat, 2012).

In the Arab world, according to the Moroccan sociologist Fatima Mernissi (2001), male hegemony leads to distorted and biased interpretations of Qur'an and Sunnah. For Mernissi the essential first step is for all women to achieve at least full secondary education, and then to equal men in the number of university graduates. These arguments parallel the equally strong account of women's equality in Islam advanced by Anne-Sophie Roald, from her analysis of Qur'anic and Hadith sources (Roald, 2001).

In many Muslim-majority societies today women are making considerable strides in educational equality, the first step in attaining the full gender equality which Islam ordains (Ahmed, 1992). And as Ramadan (2010) urges, women achieving structural and value equality with men in Islam, have the right to choose their own route along "the straight path of Islam", not that which men (including some "liberal" scholars) think that they should follow. For example, the wearing of the hijab is a proud (and also voluntary) statement of the identity of a Muslim woman, and not a subordinated form of obligated religious attire.

There are now eloquent voices in modern-day Islamic feminism which argue the case for women's role in the worlds of education, the professions, commerce and industry. Foremost amongst these is the Egyptian scholar Heba Raouf Ezzat (2007, 2008). She argues that Muslim women who seek equality are seeking a dignity which links with a worldwide movement for women's equality, regardless of their religious identity: "Through networks of mobilization, fair trade campaigns, alternative media and grassroots projects woman can create spaces where sustainable development comes close to realisation." (2007, p. 190). For Arab countries she advocates the feminist reform of authoritarian regimes. Furthermore: "Unless women's struggle for dignity is rooted in Islam, we risk losing our compass." (Ezzat, 2008, p. 109). On Muslim women in business organisations Ezzat develops the model of zakah, the Islamic principle of gift-giving and engaging in economic activity in order to contribute to fellow citizens for welfare purposes, within a commercial framework which avoids exploitation through usury and the charging of interest. Thus Islamic capitalism is (or should be) fundamentally welfare- rather than profit-oriented. In this model women may be managers of an industrial, welfare enterprise which is like a family, large or small: and men may be the worker bees whose industry makes the system work. These ideas are elaborated by Murphy & Smolarski (2018).

Ahmad (2004) also observes that:

> *Islamic economics represents an effort to search for a new participation ... The idea is to address basic economic problems from a moral and socially responsible perspective. We seek to reintegrate economics with ethics ... our approach is more holistic, and all embracing ... While abolition of interest*

and introduction of zakat are two pillars of the Islamic economic system, Islamic economics represents much more than that... Productive efficiency and distributive justice are twin objectives, inalienable elements of an integrated whole. (p. 39)

There is an interesting parallel between this model of women managers in Arab countries who transfer their skills as "strong family managers" into the management of public and commercial enterprises—bringing with them, intuitively, the model of the empathic, perceptive and psychologically strong women professionals—and the model of women managers and executives identified in Western cultures by Parmar (2014), and Helgeson (2018). Islam in this ideal model simply draws out the best of women's "natural" managerial skills (Anwar, 2006). However, it is clear from the accounts of Middle Eastern human relations policy that a just and rational model of women's equality in employment is still struggling to emerge (Jamili, Sidani & Safieddine, 2005; Sidani, 2005; Kalafatoglu & Mendoza, 2017; Spierings, 2015).

Ezzat's (2007) account of enterprises in Muslim countries being service rather than profit oriented is, we believe, crucially important, since Western entrepreneurs investing in Arab and other Muslim-majority countries risk making the mistake of failing to understand the reluctance of Muslim businesses to employ the sharp-edged, competitive techniques imported from Western capitalism (Branine & Pollard, 2010). However, business enterprises in Muslim-majority cultures only atypically operate according to Islamic norms (Sidani, 2005; Sultan et al., 2011; Branine & Pollard, 2010). An important factor in Muslim majority cultures influencing how businesses organise human relations management may be that non-Muslim, international investors import models of management without much understanding of how Islam requires ethical conduct and relationships between individuals (Hutchings et al., 2010).

Another interesting possibility is that women managers serving in patriarchal business systems in Muslim cultures in North Africa and the Middle East, operate with smart intuition in drawing on social capital resources, obtaining for the firm the best kinds of finance, trade deals, and entry in international marketing—successes for which the senior manager, the "elderly patriarch" will take credit (Kalafatoglu & Mendosa, 2017). For Muslim women seeking progress in employment and other realms, established patriarchy employs many strategies to maintain positions of privilege and power (Derichs & Fennert, 2014).

Perceptive analyses of the roles of Muslim women in managerial positions in some Middle Eastern countries comes from the group of scholars led by Beverly Metcalfe (Metcalfe et al. 2006 to 2011; Hutchings et al., 2010; Mellahi et al., 2011). Metcalfe observes that:

> *If one examines Muslim-majority countries governed by Shari`a, one will find that Islamic interpretation is highly variable and has differential impacts on the role of women ... due to historical events and male domination in Gulf society, there is much confusion between what Islam is, and what is merely culturally associated with Islam. While there is ongoing debate on interpretations of Islamic jurisprudence and women's role... at the root of the barriers to women's progress in the Gulf are traditional masculinist attitudes, which I will call an Islamic Gender Regime... premised on the biological differences between men and women, and it is these biological differences that determine social function. As such, men and women have complementary but different family responsibilities. Cultural processes assume that a woman will marry early; that her contribution to the family will be as homemaker; that the household will be headed by a man and that the man will provide financially and 'protect' the family. Male protection is seen as justification for the exercise of authority over women in all areas of decision making that relates to the public sphere.* (Metcalfe, 2011, p. 13) - views supported by the observations of Mernissi (2001), Roald (2001) and Metcalfe & Rees (2010).

The interpretation of the Muslim authors of the present Chapter concerning the Islamic perspectives on women as "leaders", is that a man's role as "protector and supporter" of the family means that he is an external person who earns money or who farms for food which he offers to the family manager (who is always a woman). The woman, like Kadijah the first wife of The Prophet, is the manager not only of the household but also of the family business. The subversive patriarchy which tries to assert that men are rulers of women, is un-Islamic (Hashmi, 2000). A husband acts as the external guard of the household, but his role should be complementary to that of his female partner, rather than one of being that of a dominant or controlling male.

Thus women in traditional Islamic societies, are powerful managers of a particular domain, the family. Men are expected to work outside of this domain to provide financial support, but nevertheless their roles are subordinated (or at least, complementary) to those of women on many issues. Muslim women in some Arabic countries are now exercising power outside of the family, in professional roles, which require the management of companies to provide Work Life Balance benefits which are appropriate for a Muslim culture, benefits which are often different in kind and quality from those offered by Western organisation. The "civility" of life in an Islamic organisation is matched by the dignity which a fully developed Muslim culture affords to society at large, including people of all ethnic groups and religions.

But in many Muslim-majority countries today male hegemony rather than religious principles derived from Qur'an and Sunnah, governs the conduct of everyday life, including the emancipation, education, employment and promotion of women (Hashmi, 2000; Rizzo, Abdel-Latif & Meyer, 2007). How the needs and interests of women in Muslim-majority societies are addressed by human resources management (HRM) policy and practice when they enter the workforce remains unclear in any holistic sense. Indeed, the nature and variations of HRM policies in Muslim-majority cultures have not yet been definitively described, but studies so far undertaken imply that a complex, multi-level model of understanding, integrating cultural, social system and localised variables must be applied (Ali et al., 2016).

Budhwar & Mellahi (2006) draw together accounts of HRM practices in Iran, Oman, United Arab Emirates, Qatar, Turkey, Egypt, Sudan, Tunisia, Algeria and Morocco, examining the degree to which Islam as a national religion has influenced the values and practices of Human Resources Management in particular countries. They conclude that there is no common pattern, and other factors must be implicated, including recent political and colonial history, localised values, the actual extent to which Islamic values influence social values and social norms, and contrasting cultural aspects - all influence to a certain degree how human potential is managed in different enterprises, in contrasted countries. They offer their overview as a "catalyst" for further research, but could offer no unifying model of how different Muslim cultures address women's needs and aspirations in the workplace.

Omair (2008 & 2010) offers a useful review of literature on women in management in Muslim majority cultures (MMCs), as well as a qualitative analysis of women managers' career patterns in the United Arabic Emirates. She argues that most studies of women managers in MMCs have not regarded women as the equivalent of men in pursuing managerial careers: rather, what has been examined has been their motivations in seeking atypical roles. Omair classifies the women in her study into four types: progressive career women, who seek to compete on equal terms with men, in seeking higher managerial roles; moderate career women who seek management positions, but not at the highest level, often taking long periods away from paid work for family roles; facilitated career women, who occupy senior managerial and professional roles within family-owned businesses; and idealist career women, occupying senior roles in medical, educational and social service management. This typology has yet to be examined with larger, cross-cultural samples, but may offer a useful model for subsequent research (Panjalingan, 2012). Saeed, Yousaf & Alharbi (2017) also offer useful findings on women managers in family-led firms: when such firms expand internationally or are awarded state contracts, women managers and male directors both gain status and power.

Kemp et al. (2015) offer a statistical analysis of characteristics of 2,805 companies in six Gulf states (KSA, Oman, Qatar, UAR, Bahrain, Kuwait) and partially replicate factors identified in previous research shown to influence proportion of women employed as managers (average, 5.2% in organisations in these six countries). These influences include the survival of patriarchal values; local or biased interpretations of Islam; public sector employment favouring women; women perceived as costly in terms of benefits required; women seen as more likely to be short-term employees; and local political and/or ethnic particularism. Their conclusion that the rapid increase in the numbers of women graduates will lead to more women entering management in these countries, with new pressures and models emerging, is important and should lead to further research.

Muslim women who break 'the glass ceiling' are rare enough for their success to be feted in the media (e.g. Kholoud, 2015; *Forbes Magazine*, 2017; Bakar, 2018; Qazi, 2018). There is positive social change, certainly, but its progress is uncertain. The *Global Gender Gap Reports* for 2013 and 2018 showed that all Muslim Majority Cultures were below the global average in proportion of women managers in larger organisations (Bekhouche et al., 2013; Schwab, 2017; Zahidie et al., 2018; WEF 2013 to 2019), because of *inter alia* women's lack of "masculine qualities"! (Jalalzai, 2013). Where there has been progress, it has been in Muslim women's advancement in the health, welfare and education sectors – but in all cultures, not only in MMCs, women are underrepresented in managerial and executive roles in engineering, manufacturing, construction and technology (Schwab, 2017). Sidani (2005) called for a more radical or accurate interpretation of Islamic texts and principles which would allow women's progress in management roles in Muslim countries: 15 years later, her call remains valid.

There is evidence that women in MMCs are making most progress into senior roles in public service organisations involving education, health and social welfare (Schwab et al., 2017), or (as in Turkey) where proportion of women to be employed is specified, by governments and business (Culpan et al., 2007). Thus in Saudi Arabia where negative attitudes to women executives are as strong as in any other Muslim country (Al-Sudairy, 2017) Muslim women as a proportion of those qualified seem more likely to occupy senior positions in health, education and welfare *because of* strict norms of gender segregation leading to female-only, but also to female-led institutions (Abalkhail, 2017; Abalkhail & Allen, 2015 and 2016). We are not advocating an emulation of this policy, merely pointing to the irony of this proof that Muslim women are effective leaders in modern institutions.

There is still no clear or unified model of how women are recruited to, and successfully survive in managerial roles in Muslim majority countries (MMCs). We appreciate this lack of clarity about MMCs from our work in Bangladesh, in which (as Muslims) we have, like others, observed the failure of a supposedly Islamic country to address the needs and aspirations of women and children which would fulfil the ideals of Qur'an and Sunnah (Abuznaid, 2006; Shanaz et al., 2017).

In Pakistan too, despite ideals concerning the inclusive ethics of a Muslim economic enterprise which give equal participation to women, in practice the education of women (and their high rates of illiteracy) compares unfavourably with that of men, and very few Pakistani women achieve professional or managerial status – this is the situation described by Nigar Ahmad, founder in 2004 of the *Aurat* Foundation of Pakistan, a strong advocate for women's equality. The scarcity of women in managerial roles means that no women managers had been studied systematically in Pakistan (Coleman, 2004), nor at the time of this review, in May, 2019. In the ILO (2015) survey of women managers in 108 countries, Pakistan ranked last, with only three percent of managers being women, often in junior positions with little possibility of advancement. Male authoritarianism in Pakistan contrary to Islamic principles, generally denies the access of qualified women to managerial positions (Morin, Fatima & Qadir, 2018).

Women have only begun to enter executive and managerial roles in business in some Muslim-majority countries in the latter part of the twentieth century, but in increasing numbers—reflecting several factors: the increasing educational attainments of women; the influence of international organisations who have an increasingly prominent role as investors; and through employment policies of NGOs and aid agencies in some Middle Eastern countries (Abbas, 2005; Sultan, Weir & Karake-Shalhoub, 2011).

In one Muslim Majority Culture, at least – Malaysia - women are making advances in professions and in industry which reflects the positive views of men towards women's equality in Islam (Grine, 2014; Hilal, 2015; Schwab et al., 2017). Ibrahim & Islam's overview of *Management of Resources in Muslim Countries and Communities* (2012) based on their Malaysian experience (including Panjalingam's analysis of Muslim women achieving equality in management roles) strikes us as a most forward looking understanding of ethical and effective business models founded in Islamic principles.[3] This is not to say that Muslim women have achieved employment equity in Malaysia, and there are still many hurdles to be overcome (Schäfer & Holst, 2014).

An emerging pattern is for women of wealthier parents in Muslim-majority societies to attend college, and work successfully after graduating, but then to retire from the world of external work to become the traditionally strong family member, a matriarchal role familiar in Arab culture (Ezzat, 2007). Increasingly however, Muslim women in all MMCs are choosing to remain in professional and managerial roles, effectively managing two domains, work and family.

Examples of how organisations in two Arab countries accommodate the needs of dual-career women come from studies of how employers in the expanding telecommunications industry (in which women graduates make up about a third of the workforce) regard Work Life Balance benefits in Gaza, Palestine and in Jordan. This qualitative work elaborated in the next Chapter, shows a range of benefits which do not exist in Western companies. In describing and evaluating women's entry and progress in the world of external work, it is clear that the family context has to be studied. Since a common pattern is for siblings and their partners to live together in a shared (usually patrifocal) household, sisters and sisters-in-law will be at different stages of child-bearing and career development. The successful 'career woman' from a Muslim extended family needs the support of *all* of the influential adults in the family, for whom she will be important as a source of economic support. Some of her sisters may choose to be full-time carers of children, as well as (for shorter or longer periods of time) those of her sisters who work outside of the family. Men who object to the enfranchisement of their wives, even to the point of violence, may be ejected (even divorced) by the woman who asserts her Islamic identity. There is important further work of an ethnographic kind to be undertaken here, and

---

[3] Malaysian attitudes to, and services for, young women who become pregnant (including rape victims) without support, stand in profound contrast to attitudes and behaviour in Pakistan (another Muslim majority culture): see Jamaluddin et al. (2018).

we are impressed by the accounts of the grassroots Islamic feminist movement in Egypt and Palestine offered by Lila Abu-Lughod (2010).

Table 2.1. Differential Levels of Challenge, and Outcomes, for Women, and for Muslim Women in Management

	All Women	Muslim Women of the Diaspora	Women: Muslim Majority Cultures
Macro-level	*Positive trends* Government & firms recognise women's strengths *Negative trends* Glass ceiling remains & discrimination vs women	*Positive trends* Western countries' (e.g. UK) have equal opportunity laws *Negative trends* Discrimination vs ethnic minorities & Muslims marked, laws not enforced	*Positive trends* Islam empowers women, extends 'family strength' to 'occupational strength' *Negative trends* Patriarchy prevails in many MMCs, blocking women's professional entry
Meso-level	*Positive trends* Positive hiring of women by government & some firms *Negative trends* 'Glass ceiling' remains in many commercial sectors	*Positive trends* Muslim women some prominence in media & politics *Negative trends* At local levels many Muslim women face marked prejudice & choose not to seek external work	*Positive trends* Some firms have good record in hiring women & WLB benefits *Negative trends* Most have 'poor' record of recruitment & promotion of women managers/ professionals

Note: Format of model based on conclusions and proposals of Mahadevan et al. (2017), and Ali et al. (2016). "Western" indicates nations in which a majority of the population are of European ancestry.

5. Conclusions: Muslim Women as Ideal Leaders, Professionals and Administrators

In writing this chapter on Muslim women's progress towards executive managerial and professional roles in both Western and Muslim majority countries, we realised that we had to consider first the literature on women in management in Western society, regardless of their ethnicity or religion. This exercise has given us insights, from the work of Helgeson and Johnson (1990 & 2010; 2017) into how women managers have (or deploy) special strengths in managing complex situations, by means of empathy, astuteness of perception, emotional bonding, caring for employees, holistic perception and other traits not greatly used, or used to similar effect, by their male counterparts.

We are impressed too by the similarities between the feminist managerial models of Helgeson & Johnson (2010) and the accounts of women in Islam, as enjoying a duality of roles as family managers and community leaders in ways which are quite different from the roles normatively (and spiritually) prescribed for men. Women in Islam have special strengths based on their family roles which should enable them to be strong, caring, intuitive, empathic, perceptive managers. Moreover, in the commercial world of Islam in which service rather than profit is an over-riding goal, woman as super-managers of family and firm may have a strong role.

This is of course an ideal model, and is emerging only in some modernising Arabic cultures in which values of patriarchy are giving way to those of Islam. The renaissance of Islam in the West is described eloquently by Tariq Ramadan: Muslims in the West are not merely first or second-generation immigrants. Islam is a major force in multicultural Europe, with an equality of intellectual and moral energy that matches other groups in multicultural, plural societies (Ourghi, 2010; Ramadan, 2012; Adam-Bagley & Al-Refai, 2017). This firm Islamic identity has an interesting interplay with modernising Arabic and Muslim societies across the world (Sultan, Weir & Karake-Shalhoub, 2011). Women in Muslim majority cultures are gaining power through their educational advancement, which inevitably leads to pressures to achieve occupational success.

What we advocate, in conclusion, is a series of qualitative studies of companies in MMCs in which, as did Helgeson & Johnson (1990/2010 & 2017), researchers can identify successful women in management, and through their biographies and accounts of daily decisions, show how Muslim women may absorb and balance Islamic and Western norms and values in making a success of being "super managers". In our critical realist model the Muslim model of gender relations, equality, modesty and mutual respect between men and women, are structural "givens" which forms the value base of such a research programme. In this dialectical research model, our intuitive, initial hypothesis is that Muslim women become strong managers *because of* their family status, and in commercial and industrial settings women will carry forward their strengths as "strong family managers".

This model, we believe, is compatible with the theologically derived management and business models which Islam implies, as outlined by Murphy & Smolarski (2018) who argue that:

> ... *large firms within Muslim majority countries have the moral obligation to assist governments in addressing challenges related to sustainable socioeconomic development and in advancing human rights ... we draw upon the Islamic business ethics, stakeholder theory, and corporate governance literatures, as well as the concepts of Maqasid al Shariah (the objectives of Islamic law) and fard al 'ayn (obligation upon all individuals within society) ... to introduce a normative model elucidating critical Islamic precepts.* (p. 1)

Chapter Three

Work–Life Balance Programmes and the Career Aspirations of Women: A Critical Realist Approach to Issues of Work and Welfare in the Islamic Culture of Gaza, Palestine

Mahmoud Abubaker and Christopher Adam-Bagley

1. Introduction and Overview

Finding a balance between the demands of the role requirements of work, family, and social life is a challenging problem for modern society and is particularly relevant for the growth of women's participation in the workforce. These role conflicts may result in significant psychological stress for individuals. For corporations, stressed employees are also a problem. Work–Life Balance (WLB) programmes to address these issues have emerged in Western countries in the past three decades and have been evaluated in various ways in multidisciplinary studies which have used sociological and psychological methodologies. WLB programmes in developed countries often reflect the ethos of particular cultures, and Western models may not be wholly (or at all) relevant for trans-cultural application.

The present study explores these issues using the methodology of critical realism in companies in the telecommunications sector of Palestine. This qualitative study develops a model of a newly identified set of factors, which may be relevant for other Arabic cultural settings.

The study of the social psychology of complex organization in business, health care, and government requires an interdisciplinary approach. For this purpose, techniques developed in industrial and organizational psychology (Anderson, 2012; Jones et al., 2013) must be complemented by sociological and ethnographic methodologies (Poelman et al., 2013), and both quantitative and qualitative research approaches are necessary to achieve the fullest picture of the nature and delivery of developing policies such as work–life balance (WLB)—policies which aim to reduce strain on workers and improve their well-being and efficiency, in balancing the often stressful, competing demands of work roles, leisure time, and family commitment.

In the language of business, WLB is defined as: "A comfortable state of equilibrium achieved between an employee's primary priorities of their employment position and their private lifestyle" (Business Dictionary, 2015). In the past three decades, employers, employees, and government have recognized the need to address these issues, especially as higher proportions of women enter the workforce (Gambles et al. 2007).

Methodological Issues: Using the Critical Realist Approach

Social science methodologies for studying industrial organizations face the dilemma of using quantitative methodologies (often with positivist assumptions) that tend to ignore social context; or qualitative methodologies (often construing the research universe as a singular phenomenon) that provide detailed information of an apparently unique situation from which generalizations may be difficult. One solution to this problem of the paradox of competing methodologies is to engage in follow-up research, constructing psychological instruments that build on the insights generated by qualitative work (Rogelberg, 2002). It is surprising how rarely this is done, as researchers are only atypically trained in more than one type of research methodology (Poelman et al., 2013).

Another potential solution to these dilemmas of methodology has emerged in recent years, that of critical realism, which is based on a philosophical critique of how knowledge is produced, perceived, analyzed, and interpreted (Archer, 1995, 2003) and offers a new way of addressing methodological dilemmas in the study of organisations (Fleetwood & Ackroyd, 2004; Easton, 2010; Zacharlias et al., 2010; Edwards et al., 2014). Critical realism reflects both sides of the quantitative versus qualitative debate: it accepts that reality is in part subjective and in part objective (Bhaskar, 2010). The critical realist paradigm utilizes a stratified or deep, ontology (Sayer, 2002). This deep ontology comprises three distinct layers: the empirical, which is what is observable by human beings; the actuality of what exists, such as social institutions and collective organizations, including the state; and a conception of the real that goes beyond facts, perceptions, and experiences, which seeks to explicate underlying social mechanisms that are independent of the observer but which serve to condition the social life, and therefore the subjective perceptions of social actors (Bhaskar, 2010; Sayer, 2002). According to this approach, a researcher should be able to grasp the subjective as well as the objective realism of the WLB practices within the cultural and organizational context under study.

In other words, the researcher will consider the social mechanisms of the culture, the norms of the society, prevailing economic ideas, and other existing aspects of reality behind the events observed (Bhaskar, 2010). These should then be combined with accounts of the experience of the social actors, in order to generate a comprehensive set of recommendations for WLB practices in the organisations studied.

In its most basic form this means that knowledge of the social world is to be produced by a study of factors such as governmental rules and regulations, as well as prevailing social and cultural norms, the labour unions, the organizational structure and by an assessment of the effect which these objective factors may have on individuals' subjective perceptions, decisions, actions, and social roles, as they themselves interpret them (Reed, 2001 & 2005).

Social mechanisms are never entirely fixed and determined but are constantly open to stress, flux and dialogue and therefore to change over time (Bhaskar, 2010). This is a process of change dependent on the human social actors themselves and also in part on factors outside of the control either of individuals or of collective organizations (Archer, 2003). In effect, we are seeking to identify in our research a "a still point in a world of change", which over time, will be subject to modification as the social reality it reflects undergoes morphological or dialectic changes (Archer, 1995).

For example, in order to understand the barrier of taking up the WLB practices by employees, critical realism will likely oblige the researcher to move progressively from surface appearances—from a flat ontic reality— to a deeper, stratified ontic level in order to determine the social mechanisms involved in any social practices and the objective mechanisms which in turn are embedded in either social or cultural conditions, or most likely, in both. Under each layer, there are usually to be found one or more sublevels, so that under the general category of society, we need to consider how the individual participates in family life, ethnic group friendships and exchanges, religious organizations, and so on. All of these interconnections, taken together, reflect the whole reality of (for example) the barriers to take-up of WLB practices by employees (Archer, 2003; Fleetwood, 2005).

The critical realist does not take their findings to be necessarily fixed and objective over time. Change is accommodated within the methodology by means of a feedback loop between ideas and real social practice and outcomes (Fleetwood, 2005; Fleetwood & Hesketh, 2008). Critical realism holds that the reality of the social world is always relative and that any scientific theorizing, while presenting the best means of deriving knowledge of both subjective and objective factors, is fallible and open to change. While most methodologies seek to determine the outcomes of the policies they advocate, critical realism goes further by recognizing that any change to the social practices dominant within a culture will inevitably feed through into other aspects of the life of a society, aspects of which are not usually considered to be direct consequences stemming from those practices (Boyd, 2010; Fleetwood & Ackroyd, 2004).

Critical realism argues that, despite any epistemological relativism it is always possible to combine its findings with a judgmental rationality which asserts that a science is not an arbitrary practice but rather the product of rationally determinable criteria by means of which it is possible to judge whether certain theories are better than others (Boyd, 2010). This feedback loop, and its potential to facilitate an internal modification of the study, will be represented in a triangulation of the findings from the perspectives of different groups, as well as by reference to existing theory and the observable factors supporting any particular viewpoint.

In effect, critical realism is a self-booting approach to the study of social and economic conditions, providing the researcher with tools that permit first the formulation of a theory and then the opportunity to test this theory against objectively determinable practical outcomes. In other words, it attempts the unity of both theory and practice (Boyd, 2010). The critical realist research model therefore stresses the importance of developing new theoretical models for further research (Ollier-Malaterre et al. 2013).

2. Research Setting and Design

This research examines first of all, whether certain Work-Life Balance policies and practices identified in European and North American research (e.g. Heinen & Mulvaney, 2008) are available or relevant to employees in key organizations in a developing country (Palestine). Little previous research in this field in any Arabic country can be identified (Al-Hamadi, Budhwar, & Shipton,2007; Aycan & Eskin, 2005; Abu Bakir, 2018) and there is no previous research on WLB policies in Palestine. This exploratory research examines within a critical realist research model, how the benefits identified may differ from those found in Western and other international research; how particular cultural, religious, social, and political factors in Palestine may influence the application of a particular set of WLB policies; how these policies are applied in practice; and how line managers and employees perceive the application and uptake of these policies.

The research setting and subjects are a sample of the headquarters staff in the two largest, privately owned telecommunication organizations in Gaza, Palestine, which offer mobile and landline services. The companies have received significant international investment and technological innovation in the past two decades, particularly from European corporations. Although investment and technology come from international organizations, the two companies operate independently with local board members and CEOs. The implicit message from the international corporations seems to be that profits are maximized when local customs regarding employee benefits are supported.

Palestine, previously a single state, was split into two halves following the founding of Israel in 1948, and since that time there has been an uneasy relationship between Israel and Palestine, sometimes resulting in violent conflict between the two countries, most recently in 2014. Movement of Palestinians between the two halves of the Palestinian state is often difficult or impossible, which has split some extended families (Taraki, 2006). This has meant that a higher proportion of women than would be expected in an Arab country do not have the support of an extended family for child care when they take up paid employment outside of their home (Kultab, 2006). Although the unemployment rate in Palestine is around one third in males, 20% of the workforce is female (Palestinian Central Bureau of Statistics, 1997–2014). The women employed in the telecommunication industries in the present research (22% of the total number of employees) were frequently graduates, bilingual in Arabic and English, with highly marketable skills and experience.

Palestine, like other Arab countries, is marked by the collectivist mode of culture (Heinen & Mulvaney, 2008) in which individuals share allegiance and mutual obligations across extended kindred and social groups, of whom the majority follow Islamic principles concerning family obligations and care, and norms concerning the primacy of family institutions embedded in a collective identity of shared norms and values, of the large majority of the population. It was expected at the outset that explanatory models for WLB policies derived from Western research (Hegewisch & Gornick, 2011) might well be inadequate in explaining the development of, and the need for WLB policies in the largely Arabic culture of Palestine.

Palestine has many features of social organization which are similar to those described in other Arab societies (Nydell, 2012), and in many sectors of society has well-developed economic and educational institutions, although the effects of continuing conflict between Palestine and Israel have increased unemployment levels in Palestine since 2014. This internecine conflict has involved a blockade which makes the import of many types of raw materials difficult, and actual warfare in which the well-armed Israeli neighbour is capable of imposing massive damage to infrastructure, with significant loss of human life and injury to many individuals (Pappe, 2017).

As no clear research hypotheses could be adduced to account for the emergence and application for WLB policies in Palestine (which only began to host transnational companies in the late 1990s), the present study is exploratory and qualitative in nature, within the critical realist research paradigm. A qualitative research programme collecting contextual and observational data for the two telecommunications organizations was undertaken, with purposive samples: the two most senior managers, and all of the 15 middle-ranking managers (two of them female) in the two telecommunication companies; and 32 employees (half of them female) with varying degrees of experience and technical skill. Employees sampled were equally divided between the two companies. Female employees were oversampled as we were particularly interested in how women perceived and had access to WLB policies, in the light of traditional role expectations for women in Islamic cultures, and our interest in and support for the economic advancement of women. Extensive, open-ended and semi structured interviews were conducted with each individual. Sampling of employees (similar proportions in each of the two organizations) ended at the satiation point, when additional interviews appeared to yield little or no new findings or insights (Gomes, 2013).

3. Data Analysis in the Critical Realist Mode

The Arabic language interviews were recorded, the tapes being transcribed into a format suitable for N-Vivo processing (Silverman, 2011, 2013). The interview transcripts, which are in Word format, have been subjected to an exhaustive process of qualitative analysis, which is not limited to a single systematic method as would likely be the case with the quantitative approach (Sandiford & Seymour, 2007). There are different approaches that can be utilized, such as grounded theory, thematic analysis, and other methods which rely on an abductive principle of critical realism for applying the coding process (Bryman & Bell, 2007; Dey, 2003; King, 2004).

According to the paradigm of critical realism, the codes for data analysis derive mainly from a top-down coding taken from the personal knowledge and intuitions of the researchers, rather than from a bottom-up system of coding from data itself; in this respect, the researcher considered the existing theoretical framework of the study in terms of, for example, the role of government and labour unions, and examined them in subsequent interviews (Urquhart, 2001). The researcher (MAB) did however, derive certain significant themes from the interviews themselves and has added these to the theoretical framework of the study (the abductive approach). These derived concepts related to socially influenced WLB practices, and their links to the political and Islamic belief of individuals, and the culturally embedded identity of the individuals studied.

The themes concerned with reasons for adopting WLB practices were identified by the following N-VIVO 'codes': government rules and regulations, labour unions, women in the workforce, workers with dependants, religion and cultural values, the position of women in society, and the existence of competitors in the market. The data transcripts were translated from Arabic to English, a language suitable for the software employed.

4. Case Study Findings in Light of the Cultural and Religious Setting, Compared with Previous Findings in Contrasted Cultures

The qualitative data analysis has identified four salient types of WLB policies in the case studies of the two telecommunications organizations. These are: (a) flexible WLB policies, (b) leave arrangement WLB policies, (c) childcare and financial policies, and (d) social and religious policies. The policies available to workers were largely similar across the two organizations.

The first type, flexible and leave policies generally resembled those available to employees in Western organizations: these reflected the desire (because of market forces) to retain the loyalty and work commitment of valuable employees, pressure from unions, and the requirements of governmental regulations (described in other contexts: Den Dulk, Peters, & Poutsma, 2012; Pasamar & Alegre, 2014). These include part-time work, flexitime, school term-time work, compressed working, and some other benefits which are offered to enhance the balance between working time and private life. But the Palestinian organizations applied only a few flexible policies involving part-time working and flexitime systems. For example, flexitime working was offered only with one-hour variability of working hours for male and female employees; and teleworking was available only on a very limited scale. This finding is in line with studies in Spain, India, and China which pointed to the limited adoption of flexible polices, because of plentiful labour supply; and with studies identifying a variety of cultural, political, economic, and social factors (Baral & Bhargava, 2011; OllierMalaterre, 2009; The´venon, 2011; Wang et al, 2008).

Findings from the present study of the two Palestinian corporations indicate that the right for men to have parental leave hardly exists: men have only a very short paternity leave of 3 days, available only in one organization. The present study indicated overall, rather low interest among male employees concerning the balance between working and family lives in the two telecommunication organizations: men in general believed that external work did not conflict with family life. Rather, and in line with studies from India and China, Palestinian men seem to be satisfied with longer working hours (provided there was adequate remuneration), because working and personal lives, in cultural terms, complemented each other.

Higher remuneration of the male bread winner usually supported family welfare in the absence of well-developed state support. If any conflict occurs between the two, work is given priority over family life, reflecting cultural values concerning how roles are prioritized, with women's roles being more home-focused (Spector et al., 2004; Wang et al., 2008). Researchers in developing countries have found a limited relationship between flexible policies and reducing the conflict between work and personal life in comparison with many Western countries: but in the latter, WLB benefits are more likely to benefit both genders (Idiagbon-Oke & Oke, 2011; Spector et al., 2004).

Reflecting this, the adoption of flexible policies by organizations (including the two in the present study) is limited to part-time and flexitime policies which generally fulfil the needs of the women workforce, in contrast to studies in Western settings (Chandra, 2012; Spector et al., 2004). These different cultural styles are derived from what has been termed 'squeeze time pressure' (Lewis, Gambles, & Rapoport, 2007; Stalker, 2014; Zuzanek

& Manhell, 1998). This literature suggests that, in comparison with developing countries, many individuals in Western or developed countries frequently experience the strains of separating work activity from personal life within a crowded day. But in Palestine and also in many Arab and developing countries, business and individual life is not so often squeezed into separate compartments: for men at least, work, family, and leisure roles are integrated, rather than being separated and potentially conflicting.

The second type of WLB policy which emerged was special leave arrangements, and these were more strongly developed in the Palestine case studies than those recorded in Western organizations. These were mainly aimed at helping women to balance the demands of family and childcare with the time demanded by work. These included paid maternity leave for three months, and after return to work an hour's leave each day for breastfeeding a new-born for up to 24 months; and emergency paid leave of up to 10 hours a month for a child's illness.

In several developed countries flexible policies for WLB to some extent accommodate women's interests, although feminist critics argue that there are still, in Europe, many reforms yet to be enacted or applied (Crompton, Lewis, & Lyonette, 2007; Hantrais, 2000; Pasamar & Alegre, 2014). In Palestine, the movement toward meeting women's interests can be observed in the emergence of part-time working, including a one hour reduction every day for women's working hours in the winter season. This policy derives from the Arabic belief that women need to be protected, in both family and work roles: for example, they are not expected to go outside alone during darkness, except when protected by a related male chaperone (e.g. father, or brother).

Palestinian society, like other Arabic cultures, has strong values concerning the "protection" of women, principles supposedly derived from Islam, but also owing much to long-standing patriarchy in which women are not so much "protected" as "owned". The anthropologist Lila Abu-Lughod (2013) offers a scathing analysis of this ownership of women in the name of Islam. The "critical self-reflection" for women in Palestine (and in other Muslim countries, such as Egypt – Abu-Lughod, 2010) which she advocates is a further step in the critical realist understanding of change in women's roles, elaborated by Margaret Archer (2014) in a variety of cultural contexts.

There remains in Palestine a strong masculine gender culture in which men are seen as the main 'breadwinner', while women's roles are more focused on the home (Kabasakal & Bodur, 2002; Tlaiss & Kauser, 2010). The unresolved tension concerns the questions: should Muslim women be educated to the same level as men; should they follow career tracks external to the family; how can an Islamic society which sees men and women as equals support women's roles both within and external to the family; and how can men abandon the idea of 'ruling' women, to one of supporting them as equal partners?

These issues are unresolved not only in Islamic countries such as Palestine, but also in Europe in cases where female employees have rights to statutory maternity leave, the right to maternity paid benefits, and protection against unfair treatment or dismissal because of pregnancy, and also the right for leave for child illness.

These policies have been developed over time in various ways within Western countries and with varying outcomes: for example, maternity leave is quite long in Germany and Scandinavian countries compared with the United Kingdom and Spain (Ollier-Malaterre, 2009; Poelman et al., 2013; The´venon, 2011). Differences in the period of maternity leave are related mainly to birth rates and publicly funded welfare systems which reflect varying political value systems (Den Dulk et al., 2012). Women in the two Palestinian organizations studied had only 70 days of paid maternity leave, and in addition unpaid parental leave of one year, with guaranteed job return.

This finding is consistent with studies in developing countries which have found that maternity leave and other benefits are rather meagre, in contrast to those documented in the United States and European WLB literature (Gregory & Milner, 2009). However, some WLB leave policies in the two Palestinian organizations were more developed than those in Western countries, with regard to four areas: emergency leave (e.g., urgent illness or injury involving a family member), bereavement leave, breast-feeding, and honeymoon leave. These policies are found in some Western countries, but the periods of leave are quite short, and usually allowed only to fulfil atypical personal needs (Ollier-Malaterre, 2009; The´venon, 2011). In the Palestinian case studies there is evidence that emergency, bereavement, and honeymoon leaves are applied on a larger scale than in Western settings: for example, 10 days for honeymoon, and 10 hours of emergency leave every month, which could be extended. Such emergency and bereavement leaves are also part of the Labour Law of Palestine; this code also provides for women to have breast-feeding leave for one hour every day, for two years.

Legal protection for workers is a recent development in Palestine, as in other Arabic countries, and dates from around 1990. Based upon the findings of the current research, individuals in Palestine need a long bereavement, honeymoon, and emergency leave to satisfy the needs of not only of their close family but also of relatives and friends, in ways which are strongly influenced by the traditions of culture and religion. This reflects both Palestinian values, and Islamic ethics (Metcalfe, 2007; Nydell, 2012) which require assistance be given 'to the seventh degree of relationship'.

When governments and organizations in Palestine develop policies, they are often implemented according to how the principles of Islam are traditionally understood. Concerning childcare and financial policies, in both organizations described in the present research there is an on-site childcare centre for children of employees, with 50% discount of normal fees, for all individuals. The childcare centre concept is also found in Western contexts, mostly provided by the private sector (Dex & Smith, 2002; Glass & Finley, 2002). The existence of such centres was not expected, given the extended family culture of Palestine. Setting up a childcare centre requires staff trained in child development, as well as management costs and skills. Such organization would not be undertaken unless it appeared to be vital for the workforce, or for the image of the employer, or for conformity with religious norms.

Some married couples in Palestine are now beginning their lives independently of extended family, for a variety of reasons including the splitting or decimation of extended families between the two halves of Palestine, and migration to other countries when this is possible (Taraki, 2006). This situation does not seem to have decreased individual obligations on the part of young adults towards their father, mother, and close family members, and individuals accessing WLB benefits still needed many leave policies to fulfil obligations of care toward their parents and extended family. For religious and other cultural reasons, ties of kinship and the extended family remain powerful (Kamali, 2003; Sidani, 2005).

In the Palestinian context there are many emerging WLB policies that enhance the welfare of individuals. Financial grants were also offered by the organizations studied to assist individuals with respect to education, healthcare, hardship and crises, and family vacation expenses. These financial policies are a crucial part of WLB policies of both the organizations and had the overt intention of fulfilling and harmonizing individual lives within workplace, family, and society. In effect, the company was becoming like a surrogate family for many of its employees.

This finding emerged from both of the organizations studied, notwithstanding the fact that they are working within the stressful economic and political situation of Palestine. As in many developing countries (Baral & Bhargava, 2011; Idiagbon-Oke & Oke, 2011; Wang et al., 2008), in Palestine there is a lack of developed comprehensive, free health systems, or any kind of welfare state. Parents are expected to cover costs of education, buying or building a house for sons, and much more. Most Palestinian parents work to save money for the future educational and medical care of their children (Devi, 2004; Lundblad, 2008).

In Palestine, there is also the constant threat of conflict with Israel: four major conflicts have occurred in previous decades. The consequences have been extensive damage to housing, and the risk of death or serious injury to employees and their extended families. Numbers of employees have died or were injured not only in conflict with Israel but also from local political infighting. The two telecommunication organizations studied have, remarkably, paid the cost of house refurbishment and have also secured financial support for individual families after a breadwinner had been killed, in the random bombing and rocket attacks which have killed, maimed and traumatised many innocent men, women and children, as the following Chapter by Wesam Abubaker details.

Such financial policies greatly enhance the welfare of employees in the current context of Palestine. WLB policies of the Western type rarely encompass financial WLB policies of this type, perhaps because they are rarely needed. Only a few studies have identified specific financial benefits in other developing countries, such as healthcare premiums and subsidies for study (Bach & Sisson, 2000: Idiagbon-Oke & Oke, 2011). These have usually been categorized as fringe benefits, or financial incentives rather than being true WLB practices available to all members of a workforce.

Concerning social and religious policies, the present research has identified WLB policies which do not exist in the policy models of most Western corporations or labour laws: benefits in both of the organizations studied included 30 minutes for daily prayer, one month's paid leave for the Hajj pilgrimage (an obligation at least once in a Muslim's lifetime), reduction of working hours during Ramadan (the fasting month), as well as other concessions and benefits related to family obligations and the perceived roles of men and women.

These are offered to allow individuals to comply with the five pillars of believing in and practising Islam (Kamali, 2003; Kamal-ud-Din, 2010).

Suspension of conferences or meetings during the prayer time is customary in Palestine as in many Arab countries, since individuals pray together (Abuznaid, 2006; Budhwar & Mellahi, 2006). Reducing working hours in Ramadan (when individuals take no food or liquid during daylight hours, for one month) is due to the fact that the individual has less energy during the long fasting hours. Individual work efficiency may fall and absences from work increase.

Such policies reflecting religious practice are also incorporated in regulations of the government of many Arab countries. In many Western countries, religious benefits are usually confined to the granting of particular religious holidays for Christians, Jews, and Muslims. But aspects of how religious culture frame individual work values and identity, and in turn influence WLB policies, has not been discussed in the research literature in industrial and organizational social psychology. In the Palestinian culture, boundaries between work, society, and family are porous rather than fixed, and this has clearly had an influence on WLB policies. In the two case studies, individuals had informal rights to have personal visitors during office time, regardless of work-related task demands, as well as the right to make and receive personal phone calls from friends and family members during office hours, not merely when some family crisis was involved. A parent of any employee could stay for 20 to 30 minutes with their son or daughter in their workplace, to have a cup of coffee. Even if one is busy, it is unacceptable not to meet with the visitor. Arabic society is still less concerned about time and the meeting of mundane productivity goals than is customary in the West, whether in business or family life; in both of these aspects, the individual in Palestinian culture brings little pressure to be on time. The social WLB policies for these aspects of cultural behaviour and obligations are largely absent in the Western context (Chandra, 2012; Heinen & Mulvaney, 2008).

Compared with limited availability of flexible and leave policies which are conventional in Western organizations, those in the present study have concentrated more upon policies that meet the requirements of an employee welfare system within a specific cultural, political, and religious context. This finding supports the ideas of earlier researchers, who suggest that human relations management (HRM) policies cannot be predicted or understood without reference to the values and social structure of the countries in which they are developed.

Flexibility in WLB policies was offered by the organizations in the present study, due to particular social, culture, and market characteristics. Some leave policies in the Palestinian context are essential but are quite unlike those typically encountered in Western WLB policies. The non-leave, financial policies were of importance to make up for deficiencies in the welfare system of the Palestinian government. These financial incentives have also been found by researchers to be motivating factors for WLB policies in Arabic countries such as Egypt, Saudi Arabia, Jordan, Oman, and Libya (Mellahi, Demirbag, & Riddle, 2011; Mellahi & Wood, 2004; Metcalfe, 2007).

Two other salient findings emerged from the critical realist analysis of the case study material: first, the role of *wasta*, a cultural practice of favouring those whose status or values apparently deserve deference; and second, the role of line managers in administering (and sometimes blocking) access to WLB benefits. Wasta is common in Arab cultural life and can be an advantage or disadvantage (Jamal, 2009). It involves treating favourably those to whom the individual feels a social or ethical obligation. This can be toward members of a religious group, a political affiliation, a gender group, or those ranked by age. Thus women in the case studies had better access to WLB benefits, and indeed many such benefits were designed with women's dual-career status in mind. The value of deferring to the elderly also meant that older males were more likely to be given access to WLB benefits.

Both of these two types of favouritism reflected cultural and religious values. However, despite formally written HR policies, middle-rank line managers were often ignorant of the full range of WLB practice in their organization and refused requests either through ignorance or through the practice of favouritism. Employees interviewed also reported uneven practice by some line managers. There are lessons here for more efficient administration of WLB benefits in this cultural context, which can be crucial in accommodating the needs of all employees.

A Theoretical Model

Derived from the case study interview and observational data using a critical realist methodology to gain insights, there are several main reasons for applying WLB policies. These emerging themes form the basis of a theoretical model whose viability can be tested both in Palestine in further quantitative and qualitative studies, and in other developing countries both within the Arab world and beyond. The potentially synergistic and interacting elements of the model which appear to inform and underpin WLB policies and their application are:

Social and religious factors of the culture which inform and influence values and actions in many institutions;

International investment and technology adoption, in which norms of international organizations are to some extent absorbed— both of the organizations in the present study have strong links with European communications technology, and investment;

Rules and regulations of government enacted in Palestinian labour laws;

The presence of a significant number of women workers whose expertise is essential for the organization, and whose presence may have resulted in a unique set of WLB policies which assist women in balancing the culturally prescribed role obligations of family and child care, and the demands of the workplace.

The relative influence of labour unions, enabled by competition for skilled labour, both male and female.

These theoretical influences on WLB (Abubaker, 2015) are novel in character and quite different from those offered by studies based on research in Western organizations. The WLB policies in the two Palestinian organizations studied were focused upon financial, social, and religious WLB benefits, rather than upon the flexible policies typically found in Western settings. In Palestine, there exists the potentially unique combination of WLB polices: crisis financial support, healthcare insurance, war hardship support, time for prayer, time for Hajj (pilgrimage to Makkah), and receiving personal visitors.

This study also offers insight into the nature of a number of leave policies which are relevant for Muslim and Arabic countries, such as emergency (e.g., accident or illness) and bereavement leave, which are more developed than in the West. The organizations in the present study have concentrated upon policies that meet the requirements of an employee welfare system within the relatively homogenous Islamic context of Palestine. This finding supports the idea that HRM policies cannot be predicted or understood without reference to the values and social structure of the countries in which they are developed (De Henau et al., 2007; Den Dulk et al., 2012) and explains the uniqueness of the Palestinian WLB profile identified.

This evolving structure of WLB policy includes new elements likely applicable as theoretical bases or elements for further studies in Palestine and other Arabic nations. The homogeneous Islamic culture is common across many Arabic nations, governed by religious rules, values and obligations (such as Ramadan fasting, and Hajj pilgrimage). All of these obligations can be accommodated within WLB policies. Flexibility is generally practised in Western countries, given their much more heterogeneous cultural and religious social systems, and these could also accommodate Muslim workers' needs.

For example, according to an Australian study (Sev et al., 2012), which examined how a sample of Muslim men adapted their work roles in relation to religious obligations and practices, it was found that Muslim men may preferred to reduce their working hours through the use of flexible policies in Ramadan, and also sought to have a holiday each Friday since (as in Muslim countries) this is the day of attendance at the Mosque for *jummah*, the obligatory prayers at the mosque — rather than the conventional weekly holiday of Saturday or Sunday.

Likewise, the effects of Muslim business ownership are notable; in Bradford, United Kingdom, many Muslim-owned shops are closed and work is suspended on Friday afternoon, which will affect employees' work hours. Previous theoretical models derived from Western research have not encompassed such socio-religious factors as salient reasons underlying the adoption of WLB policies (Chandra, 2012). The critical realist findings of the present Palestinian study are a novel contribution to the theoretical framework of the literature on why organizations adopt WLB policy and practice in various cultures. Social and religious influences of Islam are essential elements in formulating research for understanding organizational business environments in developing, Islamic-majority countries and should be part of any initial theoretical framework for understanding these contexts.

Conclusions

A critical realist methodology has combined attempts by external observers to construct what they perceive to be the realities of a research setting, leading to a qualitative case study and interview study of managers and employees in two telecommunication companies in a developing country. Based on the data generated, a complex model of potentially interactive elements has been constructed, which influence the policy and practice of delivering WLB programs. As the initial observation was that WLB policies were meeting the needs of women rather than of men, reflecting the fact that a particular focus of research was on female employees, who were purposely oversampled (two women compared to each man studied) as the research proceeded.

Standard techniques for analysing qualitative data found a number of contrasted themes within the data generated. While some WLB policies identified in Western literature also emerged in the Arabic culture of Palestine, new forms of benefits to help workers balance the demands of work, and cultural, social, religious, and family life have been identified. While various factors have influenced the development of such WLB policies in Palestine, cultural and religious factors have meant that women have been a major focus of such policies. We offer these as important findings since they imply that further research and policy development should be initiated using more quantitative research methodologies that build upon the information and insights of the qualitative study.

A psychometrically validated scale relevant for cross-cultural use would be ideal - for example, the scales developed by Hayman (2005) and Hayman and Rasmussen (2013) which combine psychometric and qualitative methodologies to understand the nature and impact of WLB policies. Future research should also measure stress experienced by individuals in relation to the success or otherwise of WLB programmes in particular cultural settings. This we have attempted to do in a psychometric study of WLB stressors in an English sample of nurses (Adam-Bagley, Abubaker & Sawyerr, 2018).

Both qualitative and quantitative techniques should be combined to give the fullest picture of the problem we are focussing on. We take to heart Abu-Lughod's (2010) ethnographic approach to Muslim women's movements in Palestine and Egypt. Research on women entering the external work force must focus not only on structural factors which enable women's advancement, such as public and private investments and recruitment to consumer and manufacturing sectors. It must focus first and foremost on *the family*, understanding why particular girls and women in a household seek firstly to become educated at degree and professional levels, and then why they choose to be dual career (or single career) women.

The typical household in an Arabic culture will consist of several families living in the same or adjacent dwellings, usually with a paternal grandfather as the nominal spiritual adviser. The *whole family* will reach a consensus on how boys and girls should be educated, whom they might marry, and what careers they should pursue. Often women will decide at what stages of their career they will have children (and care for their sister's children, if need be). A working woman is a source of income and welfare for a family in a struggling economy such as Palestine, and families organise themselves in the best way to maximise employment, income, welfare, and good child care. At this level of ethnographic understanding, women's achievement emerges from family interactions, and her consciousness in this regard will influence how she will negotiate her way in the previously male-dominated setting of the commercial firm or agency.

The office setting in a Muslim organisation also operates in some ways like a family, in which the norms of Islam have strong influence on how the firm behaves as a commercial organisation, and how women and elders are treated with care and deference. The Islamic importance of the family is deferred to and regarded in a way which is quite different from how commercial organisations in the West regard women who have dual careers.

Chapter Four

Muslim Women and the Children of Gaza: Teacher Support for Children Under Stress - Evidence from Elementary School Case Studies

Wesam Abubaker

Souls cannot be imprisoned, dreams cannot be shot down with tanks. The City will not have one colour as they wish. The City is coloured with colours like the butterflies. (Quoted by Sherin Khankan *Women are the Future of Islam*: *A Memoir of Hope*, 2018)

1. A Summary of the Evidence and the Arguments

The object of this chapter is to try and establish some ways by which teachers and educational systems in Gaza may help children traumatised by intermittent warfare to overcome post-traumatic stress disorders, achieve normal lives, and reach normal levels of achievement. This is explored through a systematic and comprehensive review of academic studies of the psychosocial impact of blockade and bombardment on Gazan children, and studies of attempts to heal these psychological wounds; and through my own research, a case study of two elementary schools in Gaza, based on telephone interviews with five teachers in each school. The literature analysis has identified the many ways in which experience of warfare (and continuous blockade which causes poverty, and lack of health and nutritional resources) imposes profound psychological harm on up to a half of children who have suffered the trauma of warfare. The analysis of published studies identifies several models of therapy which have been evaluated, as having positive outcomes (yet after 2 years, at least a quarter of children 'in therapy' still manifest symptoms of post-traumatic stress disorder).

Gaza is resource poor in terms of qualified professionals who can offer such programmes, and my interviews with teachers, and the case study of two elementary schools indicate that it is left to teachers to be the main therapists for the many traumatised children who need help not only with learning tasks, but also with problems of adjustment. The interviews with 10 teachers in two schools offer numerous case examples of traumatised children who have been effectively 'reparented' by staff and older students within the school, drawing to some extent on validated models of treatment and care, such as cognitive behaviour therapy, and group counselling.

I argue that these teachers are "strong women" within the tradition of Islamic feminism. Given the intractable nature of the conflicts which afflict Gaza, the strength of these women and other professionals like them, must form the main type of protection and therapy offered to children. The findings of this study, of the ways in which teachers are adapting professional programmes of therapy for front-line use with very traumatised children offer an important starting point for a larger programme of how teachers can assist both the learning and adjustment of severely traumatised children, in situations of chronic stress, drawing on elements of professionalism and of Islamic feminism.

2. Introduction: An Autoethnographic Approach

Vignette:

Manchester, England - January 2009. Finally, after a hazardous journey through Egypt my husband and I and our two children have arrived in Manchester, England from Gaza, and step out into the street on the first day in our new mother country. A helicopter flies overhead. My two-year old son Khaled screams in Arabic: "Mummy, mummy, run, hide", tugging my hand. He thinks the helicopter is going to fire rockets at us. A few weeks earlier in Gaza we were experiencing rockets, tank fire and bombs, huddled for 10 days under a kitchen table, with limited food and water. I had just given birth to my second son, Mohammed, and still needed medical care, which we could not reach. There were no "pampers" for my new-born. When we try and escape, we are in constant fear of rockets, bombs and machine gun fire. These memories are not easily forgotten.

It is clear from my personal experience of Gaza that continuous blockade and intermittent warfare since 2008 has imposed a heavy toll on the adjustments and scholastic progress of many children. I have set out to explore how therapists have offered various kinds of programme for offering therapy to the many children suffering post-traumatic stress disorder, and how teachers have used or adapted these approaches in developing school-based systems of support and therapy for traumatised children.

The purpose of this Chapter is firstly, to systematically review the literature on the psychological effects which continuous blockade and frequent bombardment have had, and continue to have on the mental health adjustment of Gazan children and adolescents. The second purpose is to examine description of programmes described in the professional literature for Gazan children facing potential and actual trauma, and how these programmes might help the young people in overcoming these traumas.

A third task is to examine how such programmes could be administered in two schools (one UN-funded elementary school, and one Government elementary school) included in an "ethnographic case study" (Gone & Alcántara, 2010). Since entry to Gaza for research is extremely difficult, I have relied on extended telephone interviews with the two headteachers known to me from my experience as a teacher in Gaza, and with an additional four teachers in each school - supplementing and filtering this information through the lens of her experience as an "auto ethnographer", someone with a profound and intimate experience of their subject matter (Short et al., 2013). According to Baxter & Jack (2008) the qualitative case study report is available as an "easily applied" methodological approach but which nevertheless can " … help develop theory." (p. 545)

An Autoethnographic Theme

This chapter is partly auto-ethnographic (Short et al., 2013), in that my experience informs the direction of the research, and the discussion of evidence. I try and stay as "objective" as possible (despite retaining a strongly held value perspective), reviewing and integrating relevant literature systematically, in drawing on qualitative accounts of two Gazan head-teachers whom I knew personally, and on the accounts of experienced teachers in each school - contacted for the present research though telephone interviews. Each of the headteachers nominated members of her staff who were particularly experienced and dedicated to helping traumatised children.

The teachers I interviewed related to me as a colleague, rather than as a researcher. In this role my "reflexive, ethnographic self" had both to enter the world of the elementary school, at the same time maintaining an "analytical distance". Gray (2018 pp 448-9) comments on the difficulties and tensions within such a role, since "the ethnographer" herself is entering (once again) this world of trauma. This reflexive research task is a challenging one.

Literature Review and Research Themes

The review of literature and research is divided into the following sections:

(a) The recent history of Gaza, and prospects for change.

(b) How young children, teenagers and adults are surviving physical and emotional health hazards, and the chronic fear, anxiety and stress which is imposed by blockade and bombardment of Gaza.

(c) A survey of programmes of help and support for various groups, and how in particular programmes for children and adolescents can be school-based and teacher administered.

(d) A review of what success there has been for such programmes, in systematic evaluations.

(e) From my own experience, and research, based on telephone interviews with two elementary school principals and eight of their staff, a perspective on how teachers may deploy previously evaluated programmes for war-traumatised children, and what new programmes might be developed which teachers can apply. I am interested too in the views of the interviewed teachers on the general utility of these programmes, and what programmes of their own they have developed, as well as their personal strengths and modes of coping when faced with extreme stress.

Context: Gaza - Brief History of Recent Developments

My focus will not be on the causes of conflict between Gaza and Israel, nor on how such conflict might be ended. But briefly, in 1948 the State of Israel was imposed by UN Resolution on the land of Palestine, and after various struggles Palestine was split into two halves, the West Bank and Gaza (Ellis, 2002; Macintyre, 2017). The population of Gaza is approximately 1.8 million, of whom 1.3 million still live in refugee camps. More than a half of

Gazans are aged less than 18 (UNRWA, 2018). Large numbers of Palestinians also fled from their homeland in what became Israel, into refugee camps in Lebanon, Syria and Jordan (Berry & Philo, 2006; Abu-Rmeileh at al. 2011; Pappe 2016 & 2017; Macintyre, 2017).

Because of Gazan resistance to segregation, this small territory has been subject to intermittent bombardment, and continuous economic blockade by Israel. Leaving and entering is extremely difficult, and the airport and seaport have been destroyed. Following Israeli rocket bombardment and canon fire from helicopters, ships and fighter-bomber aircraft, and troop and tank invasions in 2008, 2011 and 2014, several thousands have been killed, and many more permanently injured (at least 90 percent being the elderly, the unarmed male civilians, and women and children). The Israeli Defence Minister declared in October, 2016 that: "The next war with Gaza will be the last, because we will completely destroy them", implying the complete destruction of the entire population of Gaza (McKerman, 2016). Certainly, the massively armed state of Israel has the capacity to do so, receiving several billions each year in armaments aid from the US government, according to *The New York Times* (Alexander, 2019). May, 2019 has seen a further campaign of bombing civilian targets in Gaza, by Israel, with vain attempts by Hamas to fight back using hand-made rockets (Halbfinger, 2019; Prashad, 2019).

Materials for reconstructing destroyed infrastructure cannot be imported into Gaza because of Israel's blockade, which also restricts imports of fuel for generators: power supplies are often limited to one or two hours a day. Sanitation systems have been destroyed, and clean drinking water is scarce. Construction of water purification and desalinisation plants is blocked by Israel (OXFAM, 2018). According to Trew (2019) the lack of a viable sewage system means that all sources of drinking water are polluted, causing frequent illnesses. Children suffer from high rates of gastroenteritis, water-borne infections, malnutrition, stunted growth, vitamin deficiency, and high rates of morbidity and mortality (see references below). Medical facilities are limited, and many food and welfare services are delivered by international aid agencies, which are themselves the subject of severe cutbacks (Emmott, 2018). By January 2019 all aid channelled through UN auspices funded by America had ceased, with programmes offered by UNRWA and various NGOS severely reduced (Trew, 2019).

Employment opportunities for graduates are diminishing, since the employment infrastructure has been disrupted or destroyed by continuous blockade, and bombardments (World Bank, 2017 & 2018). Despite this,

Gazans place a high value on education, and the proportion of graduates is high: pursuing educational goals is for many, a goal that can be fulfilling in a setting where occupational opportunities are few, and education becomes an end in itself. Thus, literacy levels, and the acquisition of degrees and vocational diplomas are high, despite bleak employment prospects. Gazan universities are noted internationally for their high quality, providing an intellectual link with the wider community of scholars and reformers in many countries (Kolda & Cirakli, 2019).

In 2013 (prior to massive bombardment, which destroyed many schools, killed 1200 students, and wounded many more – UNESCO, 2014), the UN Relief Agency operated 252 schools in Gaza, serving 240,400 students. "These children grow up in bleak conditions, frequently surrounded by poverty and violence. School provides them with one place where they are able to learn the skills for a better future." (UNRWA, 2013, p. 4) Since then many schools have been destroyed by warfare, and it is common for schools to operate morning and afternoon shifts, a completely new group being taught in the afternoon. Classes are very large, and it's sometimes difficult for teachers to recognise or remember individual children. The same is true for the government-funded schools, which serve about 50 percent of children in Gaza.

The quality of schooling is under threat however, and 2018 saw another 5 percent year-on-year decline in national wealth, according to a World Bank report (Trew, 2018). By late 2018, 70 percent of Gaza school leavers and graduate were unemployed, with no prospect of any unemployment.

So far as I can establish from the published literature, this is a unique study, since no previous practitioner or researcher has tried to pull together and compare various programmes devised to address the trauma and difficulty which Gazan children experience, nor how they can be applied within the everyday working of a typical elementary school. I also want to develop an approach which draws, fundamentally, on Islamic feminism, in offering non-violent futures for the youth of Gaza. I generally avoid political issues, except to advocate that violence is not the way forward, and to hold the belief that Palestine should be a free and independent nation.

3. Review of Studies on Women professionals, and Health and Psychological Adjustment of Gazan Children

This review covers several themes: (a) Women in Islam, as strong leaders; (b) Women and girls in Gaza, "strong and smart"; (c) The multiple psychological and physical assaults which blockade and bombardment imposes on children and youth of Gaza; (d) The effects of these assaults on children and youth growing up in Gaza; (e) The potential of women, especially trained teachers, to be supporters and counsellors for children and youth, and change agents supporting the psychological welfare of children and youth in a system of complex and sustained stress and conflict.

Women have a strong and prominent role in Islam as business leaders, administrators, philosophers and scholars (Ahmed, 1992; Al-Khayyat, 2003; Anwar, 2006; Esposito, 1998 & 2003; Ghandanfar, 2001; Hutchings, Metcalfe & Cooper, 2010; Kalafatuglu & Mendosa, 2017; Roald, 2001). In the past three decades these themes of "strong women" have been increasingly developed in women's professional roles in Muslim organisations and businesses (Merniss, 2001; Omar, 2008; Panjalingham, 2010; Sidani, 2005; Spiering, 2015; Syed, Ali & Winstanley, 2005; Wadud, 1999).

Women in Gaza

Drawing on these strengths, women have potentially powerful roles in Gaza as "strong and smart" leaders in education, group work and counselling of children and youth, and of women as mothers and supporters of their extended family (Bates et al., 2017; Diab et al., 2018a & b; Mohammad et al., 2016; Heszlein-Lossius et al., 2018a; Jaques, 2018; Kalatoglu & Mendosa, 2017; Khawaja, 2002; Sabbagh, 1998; Pepe et al., 2018). This literature shows that women in Palestine have been able using traditional Islamic family models, to support not only girls, but also boys and men who are harassed and disturbed by the continued blockade and barrage of Gaza. Gazan (and Palestinian) women have to negotiate and construct what Abu Oksan Daoud (2017) calls "gendered spaces", areas for competence, authority and initiative which simultaneously cope both with the masculine hegemony of Gazan men (Thabet et al., 2015), the brutal realities of life under Israeli occupation, and continuous threat of further bouts of brutal violence. Jong (2018) writes about Palestinian's women's resistance to externally imposed violence and offers a feminist awareness, a women's movement against oppression to counter the "femicide ... of being dead without dying."

I argue here that Arabic (and Gazan) women's strength as "strong family managers" in the Islamic tradition, offers skills and strengths which can be extended successfully into the workplace, and into society at large, comforting and healing victims of blockade and bombardment. Gazan women carry forward the ethic of powerful but peaceful resistance in the face of multiple assaults and injuries, drawing in particular on the teaching and actions of The Prophet and his companions during the early years of Islam in Makkah (Pal, 2011).

The Multiple Psychological and Physical Assaults on Children and Youth: Deaths and Severe Injuries of Adults and Children

The blockade and often prolonged bombardment of Gaza takes a heavy toll, and a half of the more than 3000 people killed since 2008 have been women and children; only a small proportion of those killed, perhaps less than five percent, were actively involved in armed resistance to the Israeli attacks. More than ten times the total number of dead have suffered severe injuries from being crushed, burned, shot or struck by shrapnel (Abuelaish, 2011; Abu-Shaban, 2018; Blanchfield, 2018; Heszlein-Lossius et al., 2018b; Hodson, 2014; Holmes & Balousha, 2018; Rubin et al., 2018; SCF, 2018; Summerfield et al., 2018; UNESCO, 2014; Vaktskjold et al., 2016). Deaths and severe injuries have continued, in the conflicts of 2018 (Elessi, 2018).

Maternal and Child Health, Physical Morbidity and Mortality

The blockade since 2007 has enforced a declining standard of living, and this is measured by declining maternal and child health, vitamin deficiencies, stunted growth in children, chronic anaemia and diarrhoea, and high rates of illness and death in vulnerable children (and their mothers) from causes other than those directly inflicted by violence (Abdel Rahim et al., 2009; Ghattas et al., 2017; Al-Laham et al., 2018; Altamimi, 2018; Alyacoubi et al., 2018; Bottchner et al., 2018; Chaudhry et al, 2018a & b; El Habil, 2018; El-Kishawi, et al., 2018; Kitabayashi et al., 2016; Legge et al., 2018; Manduca et al., 2017; Mosleh et al., 2018; Punamäk et al., 2017; Rahim et al., 2009; SCF, 2018).

These rates of illness and early death in children and adults greatly exceed those expected in a country with Gaza's level of economic development (Jonassen et al., 2018). The rate of these non-trauma illnesses and death are increasing, as medical supplies and personal are blocked from entering Gaza because of the US-sponsored Israeli blockade, and the blocking of international aid funding (Trew, 2018; World Bank, 2018).

4. The Chronic Psychological Terror Endured by Many Children Takes a Heavy Toll on their Mental Health

Post-Traumatic Stress Disorder

While socio-economic and nutritional deprivation increase vulnerability to physical health problems, it is the extraordinary nature of the external trauma in Gaza that inflicts a particularly devastating toll. In three periods, 2008-9, 2011 and 2014 attacks by the Israeli Defence Force involved bombing from jet fighters, fire from helicopter gunships and tank cannons, drone-directed explosives, fire from ground troops, and from naval vessels. The attempted defence of Gaza by the Hamas government to counter these attacks has proved to be completely ineffective.[1] The several hundred deaths of adolescents and young people in 2018 were due to the fact that unarmed young people stood in bleak protest, at the wall barring their entry to the rest of Palestine, waiting to be shot by the Israeli Defence Force. The number of these innocent deaths became so great (and international condemnation so loud) that the IDS then used a different strategy, that of firing at the legs of the adolescents, so that they are permanently crippled (Abu-Shaban, 2018). What factors can account for the despair of Gazan youth?

Every single person aged over five years in the crowded and tiny enclave of Gaza will have heard and seen these Israeli bombardments in progress; will have seen public buildings, schools and hospitals destroyed; and will have known someone, including family members or school class mates, who have been seriously injured or killed: huddled in homes or shelters, waiting for the next bomb or rocket.

The main psychological impact of experiencing such bombardment is *Post-Traumatic Stress Disorder* (The PTSD syndrome). Panos Vostanis a psychiatrist based at Leicester University, UK has worked with children who have been victims of, or refugees from warfare in various settings, and he has teamed with Professor Abdel Azis Thabet of Al Quds University,

---

[1] The popular stereotype of the Western press is that the Hamas defence force attacks Israel, and thus justifies the Israeli countermeasures. We suggest that the opposite is the case: the Hamas police-cum-defence force is tiny, and poorly armed, and cannot possibly hold any threat for Israel's highly armed nation. It acts as a defensive, not an offensive agency. Hamas was elected by popular vote in 2005, and since then has administered, through a democratic mandate, a variety of educational, social and welfare programmes (Roy, 2013). There is no evidence that Hamas uses "innocent civilians" as human shields, an idea generated in some false media commentaries (Macintyre, 2017; Charrett, 2019).

Gaza, and Dr. Sanah Sabah Thabet, Director of the Family Training and Counselling Center, Gaza in developing intervention programmes for traumatised children. Vostanis writes in his 2014 book (*Helping Children and Young People Who Experience Trauma: Children of Despair, Children of Hope*):

> *[PTSD leads to] ... separation anxiety, depressive symptoms and sleep disturbance ... Complaints can be subject to cultural variation, and be communicated through somatisation such as headaches, other kinds of physical pain, dizziness, sickness and unusual body experiences not explained by physical health causes. Some presentations are specific to the impact of trauma, with the vast majority of research unsurprisingly focusing on the construct of post-traumatic stress disorder.* (p. 181)

According to Vostanis (2014 & 2016) and Thabet, Thabet & Vostanis (2016) PTSD in children and adolescents includes problems of behaviour, cognitive issues, psychosocial behaviours, and various kinds of chronic emotional responses.

The ***behavioural changes*** following trauma include:

> *Reckless behaviour.*
> *Regression to an earlier stage of behavioural development.*
> *Re-enacting the trauma events through play.*
> *Autistic withdrawal, including 'frozen stillness', and loss of interest in previously enjoyed activities.*
> *Irritability and unprovoked anger outbursts.*

The ***physical manifestations*** include:

> *Sleep disturbance.*
> *Headaches and stomach aches.*
> *Smaller hippocampal volume, and/or changes in brain metabolism which impair capacity to cope with potential, new threats.*
> *Changes in metabolism (including changes in cortisol level) involved in "reliving" the traumatic event(s).*

Cognitive changes of PTSD may be manifested as:

> *Decreased ability to concentrate on school work, and other cognitive tasks.*
> *Chronically increased arousal, and hypervigilance.*
> *Feeling that the trauma is about to reoccur.*
> *Jumbled, out of sequence memories of the trauma and of prior and subsequent events,*

Psychosocial Symptoms of PTSD can include:

Being emotionally numb.
Avoiding places or situations that could trigger memories of the trauma.
Experiencing 'flashbacks' of all or part of the event.
Having intrusive memories of the trauma.
Frequent nightmares, and night terrors
Worrying about death, in self and others.
Obsessional behaviours including 'safe' routines.
Sadness, guilt and depression.
Poor self-esteem.

Some children and adolescents can survive severe psychosocial trauma without long-term sequels, but the clinical consensus seems to be that well over a half of victims of the kind of war-trauma which Gazan children and adolescents have experienced will have chronic PTSD-like symptoms (Hodson, 2014; Vostanis, 2014; Thabet, Thabet & Vostanis, 2016). PTSD also effects older adolescents and adults (Qeshta et al., 2019; Diab et al., 2018 a, b & c), although this is not an area on which I will focus, confining my study to effects of warfare on children and young adolescents. PTSD following war trauma in Gaza extends into late adolescence (Qeshta et al., 2019), and likely has a negative effect on mental health and social adjustment throughout life – manifested in women as extreme anxiety and depression, and in men as externalised, aggressive disorders (including aggression against the self, in despairing, suicidal actions) (Qeshta et al., 2019).

The complex array of symptoms resulting from PTSD presents teachers and therapists in Gaza with a series of challenges (Pepe et al., 2018): Where and when should therapy and cognitive behaviour training begin? What particular techniques work best? Should we focus on the results of the trauma, or focus on the origins of the trauma itself? How should approaches be modified when most children (as in Gaza) have experienced trauma-provoking events

I list the more than 40 studies in tabular form (in Tables - Appendices 1 & 2), giving a fuller exposition of approaches in which both have had some success, and which could be utilised by teachers in elementary schools in Gaza. There is a slight overlap with the studies identified in Table 4:A1 (on psychological effects of trauma) and the studies summarised in Table 4:A2, since some of this work has been extended into the realm of therapy and symptom reduction.

These studies show that children and youth (and adults whom these youth are becoming) have much higher rates of psychological problems that would be expected in a middle-income, developing country. Indeed, the continuing economic blockade (since 2007) of Gaza has resulted in a steadily declining standard of living, and increased morbidity and mortality (with reduced access to health care - access to specialist paediatric care is often blocked by Israel), and there are inadequate levels of sanitation and nutrition. Poverty and deprivation create pressures which increase the risk of poor mental health and vulnerability to trauma, as several of these studies show (Abu-Zaineh et al., 2018; Altamimi et al., 2008; Punamäk et al., 2017; Thabet et al., 2011).

Overview of Various Interventions Aiming to Overcome PTSD Symptoms, and Create Psychological Resilience in Children, Adolescents and Women in Gaza and Palestine

I have identified 23 studies with findings which might be applied in elementary schools in Gaza. These studies are briefly summarised in Table 4: Appendix 1, below. This Table includes the description of a number of studies which could be relevant for elementary schools in Gaza, ideas which are explored in the interviews with the teachers in the Case Study of Elementary Schools in Gaza.

These evaluations rarely address the roles, status and psychological distress experienced by men (e.g. Helm, 2018), largely for political and cultural reasons. Indeed, my own study will address, explore and attempt to extend the work of women in building psychologically resilient strengths in themselves, their peers and pupils, and in their own families, building on the studies reported by Fassetta et al., 2017; Samuels et al., 2017; and Pepe et al, 2018. I am particularly impressed by the work of Thabet & Thabet (2015) who use a modification of cognitive behaviour therapy pioneered by their mentor, Professor of Children's Mental Health at Leicester University, Panos Vostanis (Vostanis, 2014 & 2016; Thabet et al., 2011). Further, I wanted to explore in the case studies the potential validity of Veronese & Barola's (2018) "healing stories" recounted by children, as the basis for cognitive behavioural methods administered in a group setting (Veronese & Pepe, 2017a & b; Veronese at al., 2018; Vostanis 2014 & 2016).

The following is a brief summary from Table 4: Appendix 2, with the various approaches to therapy with traumatised children and adolescents, grouped into conceptually similar areas:

One: Enhance the psychological and social strengths of traumatised individuals in different areas, co-opting teachers, peers, family and community (Abu-Zaineh et al. 2018; Mohammad et al., 2016).

Two: Group treatment to share traumatic memories, offer mutual comfort and support, consider future goals – linked to art work, relaxation and mind body exercises (Diab et al., 2018a, b, c; Gordon, 2014; Lange-Nielsen et al., 2017; Qouta et al., 2012; Samuels et al., 2017; Veronese & Barola, 2018).

Three: Rapid screening and referral for traumatised children following warfare (Hashemi et al., 2017).

Four: Enabling women through "spiritual support and counselling" to help traumatised children (including their own children) (Diab et al., 2018b; Qouta et al., 2007; Thabet & Thabet, 2015; Thabet et al., 2015).

Five: Treating parent-child dyads, so that healing a mother's trauma helps her to heal and protect her traumatised child(ren) (Thabet et al., 2009; Veronese at al., 2018)

Six: Designing school programmes in advance of any external trauma from warfare, in ways that can enable adolescents to cope with trauma (Thabet at al. 2017; Veronese & Pepe, 2017a & b; Veronese at al., 2017)

Seven: Various models of 'brief intervention therapy' can be employed in Gaza, provided that they are theoretically sound, are administered by trained professionals, and can be evaluated (Vostanis 2014 & 2016).

Abdel Azis Thabet (2019) in an important review of 24 studies on children's reactions to violence in Gaza concluded:

It is apparent ... from the reviewed studies that severity of violence in changing from time to time but types of traumatic experiences are similar including the mutilated bodies ... hearing and seeing the shelling, exposure to sonic bombs, and witnessing home bombardment and demolition. These traumatic experiences and violence affect the young Palestinian's well-being and increase rates of psychological problems in the targeted group. For primary intervention most of the organizations working in West Bank and Gaza Strip are delivering such services through public meetings, workshops, home visits, group intervention in the community and schools. This includes UNRWA, Ministry of Education, counselling centers and early childhood centers. Studies of impact of different types of prevention are increasing in the last few years with different protocols of intervention including group crisis intervention, psychodrama, school mediation, non-curriculum activities in schools and summer camps, and expressive writing therapy. New studies must be carried out to target with new research people with special needs and marginal populations such as older aged and very

> *young children ... We need a study aimed to investigate other biological and organic factors as risk factors for mental health problems in the area ... We need more qualitative and applied research in the field of mental health of adults and children and we need to conduct new controlled trial studies to evaluate the effectiveness of new protocols for psychosocial intervention such as cognitive behaviour therapy, and group intervention with bereaved children.* (Thabet, 2019 p. 204)

Evaluation of interventions poses a challenge. Either an 'untreated control group' is identified (but for obvious ethical reasons, this is rarely possible in Gaza); or the group to be treated is randomly divided into two halves, the second group forming the 'wait-list control group' to be treated later. The evaluations reported in the professional journals all report some degree of success: but that success is always partial, and at least a quarter of treated children and adolescents do *not* improve at all following therapy – bearing in mind that it is the most severely traumatised children who are referred for treatment.. About a half of all traumatised children will, over a period of years, have symptoms which "remit spontaneously", without direct clinical treatment. By the same token of measurement, a half will have chronic symptoms of mental health disturbance, dominated by PTSD.

None of the interventions described in the published literature have addressed the problem of *multiple trauma*. All young children aged three or more experiencing the bombardment of 2008-9 would experience general trauma in 2011, and again from the warfare of 2014. The imported programmes were designed to treat children who have experienced a single trauma, with little likelihood of reoccurrence. But we cannot say that the imported programmes (from England, Italy, USA and Scandinavia) are of no use for such multiple trauma: they do offer training and graduate scholarships for Gaza professionals, and the publications that flow out of these contacts are valuable in bringing the suffering of Gaza's children to the notice of the world.

Women as 'Change Agent' Pioneers

I have selected in advocating for the role of teachers as counsellors from the overview detailed in the appended Tables 4:A1 and 4:A2, interventions which can be adopted (or adapted) by the women who deliver elementary education programmes in Gaza. Several writers have advocated, as having primary importance, the model of Cognitive Behaviour Therapy (Curwen et al., 2001; Stallard, 2009; Vostanis, 2014 & 2016), in which women teachers may enable children and youth to think creatively and positively about themselves, addressing their stressful environment through various coping mechanisms (Veronese at al., 2018 a & b). This model is adaptable in drawing on Islamic feminism, outlined above, which sees women as natural leaders in conflicts which endanger families and children. This model from my experience as a teacher in Gaza, also seems to be particularly appropriate. In the exploratory case studies, based on telephone interviews with the ten teachers in two Gazan elementary schools, I planned to explore these ideas further.

Conclusions from the Literature Review

The tiny enclave of Gaza (population some 1.8 million) in Palestine, has been the subject of continued blockade which prevents the easy transit of people and goods; and has experienced periods of heavy onslaught by bombs, rockets, tanks and artillery in 2008-9, 2011-12 and 2014. More than 6000 individuals have been killed or permanently maimed, most of them infants, children, adolescents, women and other innocent civilians. There seems little prospect of an end to this blockade, and the periods of intermittent warfare. By Winter of 2018, in one year more than 200 Palestinians were shot and killed as they protested at the hideous fence – in this period around 100 children and adolescents were killed, and many more (in excess of 2000) had been severely injured in 2018 (Holmes, & Balousha, 2019). The youth of Gaza raise their fists, and throw stones. For this crime they are likely to be shot.

Warfare and its continued threat has imposed severe psychological stress on children who have experienced the death and severe injury of parents, siblings and other family members (as well as painful and crippling physical injuries to themselves). This traumatic threat is not based on a single incident in the past: it is chronic and imminent. There have been three major wars since 2008, and intermittent attacks occurring in 2018 and into 2019, which over a 16-month period killed more than 200, mostly innocent civilians, including children and adolescents.

Many services to Palestinians still living in refugee camps are provided by the UNRWA (United Nations Relief and Works Agency). In 2018 at least a third of UNRWA's budget was cut, since the American President no longer wished to support this aspect of the UN's activity.

Continued blockade and the frequent threat of bombardment has taken its toll on the physical and mental health of children and their families, as evidenced by the well-conducted studies reviewed in this Chapter. The most frequent outcome for children is Post Traumatic Stress Disorder, which creates many long-lasting and difficult to treat psychiatric symptoms. I have reviewed therapeutic programmes in this field, with emphasis on the role of teachers in supporting their highly stressed pupils. A number of therapeutic approaches have been described and evaluated, and all work to some degree, and can certainly be administered by teachers after appropriate training. It is problematic however in finding the resources and the time to train teachers to engage in these therapeutic programmes.

At last a quarter of children with severe PTSD will not recover, even after the application of validated, prolonged programmes of therapy. About a half of all Gazan children have some symptoms of PTSD, and they are especially vulnerable if (or when) the next war begins.

The warfare and its continued threat has imposed severe psychological stress on children who have experienced the death or severe injury of parents, siblings and other family members. This traumatic threat is not based on a single incident in the past: it is chronic, and further warfare seems possible in 2018. A quotation from an article in the *British Medical Journal* by Abu-Shaban (2018) in response to a report by Summerfield et al. (2018) on *The Maiming Fields of Gaza* illustrates the situation in mid-2018, when the research which I report below, was undertaken:

> *Further to Summerfield and colleagues' correspondence on the situation in Gaza, I respond as head of plastic and reconstructive surgery in the country. The death and injury toll is still rising—as at 18 May, 2018 117 were dead, including 13 children, and 12,271 injured. 6,760 have been hospitalised, including 3,598 with bullet wounds. Nineteen clearly identified medics have been shot ... In June, 2018 we had 300-350 high energy compound tibial fractures in Gaza. Complex lower limb injuries of this severity can require 5-7 surgical procedures, each operation taking 3-6 hours. Even with state-of-the-art reconstruction, healing takes 1-2 years. Most of these patients will develop osteomyelitis. A steadily increasing toll of secondary amputations is inevitable. The only rehabilitation hospital in Gaza was destroyed by Israeli bombing in 2014. Mass lifelong disability is now the prospect facing Gazan citizens, largely young, who were merely gathering in unarmed protest ..."*

5. Methodological Approaches, and Choice of Case Study Methodology

Contrasting approaches to methods of research involving human values and actions have been described by Pathirage et al. (2005). The options available include *positivism* (attempting to measure variables objectively, with statistical management of 'valid and reliable' measures); *social constructivism* (assuming that what is to be measured has been socially constructed through the interaction of individuals and social systems, requiring a social and 'qualitative' understanding by the researcher); and *critical realism* (in which the researcher declares a value position, and 'ontologically' defines a social system including a set of intuitively defined strata, which are investigated by both quantitative and qualitative and methods). Ideally, I prefer this last approach since it has been used to some effect in the situation of Palestine (see previous Chapter).

My chosen model of case study research fits with the 'mixed methods' model of critical realist research. The strongest case for using a critical realist model of research comes from the studies of childhood disadvantage by Priscilla Alderson (2013 & 2016), based on her exposition of the philosophical account of post-modern methodology offered by Roy Bhaskar (Bhaskar 1986 & 2008; Hawke & Alderson, 2017). This model of research is attractive to those with a strong spiritual base (e.g. Muslims, Catholics, and Quakers such as Alderson) who approach the subject matter of research with a strongly held value position, establishing first of all the often hidden part of social structure (e.g. alienation of workers, the silent oppression of children, the 'hidden pulse' towards the dialectic of freedom) which has to be identified and exposed for a proper critique of a social structure to be made, with the strongly held purpose of revealing, and ending, oppression.

Philosophically, the model owes much to Locke's idea of *underlabouring*, establishing the real language of dialogue by which oppression (in Marxist terms) is unmasked (Wilkinson, 2013). Wilkinson (2015a) applying the Critical Realist model to Muslim education in Britain identifies Islam as providing an "emancipatory dialogue" for realising the moral energies of youth. Sawyerr & Adam-Bagley (2017) use critical realism to analyse the oppression and alienation of children and youth in a variety of settings, focussing on "the real but absent" (in the dominant culture's epistemology) forces which perpetuate oppression. This is the model which I wish to apply to the oppression of the children of Gaza.

Writing about Gaza, I identify the mass traumatisation of children and youth through blockade and barrage as the "hidden strata of knowledge" (Alderson 2013 & 2016) which must be identified and exposed for emancipatory change to be made, beginning in what Archer (2014) describes as the "transcendent dialectic" of value-based social change.

Critical realism is essentially a qualitative exploration of social structures, although "mixed methods" exploration of evidence is often used, as in Sarra's (2011) case study of Aboriginal youth seeking power in an Australian school. I have therefore chosen the Case Study method for the research reported below, as well as a comprehensive literature review to establish the multiple trauma affecting children and youth in Gaza.

Research using qualitative case studies is widely used, and the various methodological approaches used in most disciplines are quite well established (Yin 1995 to 2018). There is good evidence too of ways in which qualitative case studies can be enlightening in educational research (Thomas, 2014 & 2015). Such research can be either exploratory or hypothesis testing and can serve different theoretical positions and epistemological assumptions (Yin, 2018). In the present study my case study research is exploratory, with a sub-text of 'hypothesis testing', in addressing the questions:

How are teachers experiencing and focussing on traumatic outcomes of warfare for pupils in two contrasted types of school: an UNRWA elementary school; and a government funded elementary school?

What is the relevance of previously described and evaluated programmes of intervention for use by a specially selected group of experienced teachers, in each school?

How might the selected group of teachers apply different programmes for helping traumatised children, based on their experience of pupils within their schools?

Research Objectives: Undertaking Qualitative Case Study Research (CSR)

Yin (2018) offers clear guidelines for a variety of kinds of CSR. The researcher should be knowledgeable and sensitive, have clear value commitments, but should also be a good listener, and flexible in accessing a variety of kinds of information, including personal accounts and opinions, observation of interactions, and documentation. The research may be theory-driven but may also be descriptive rather than hypothesis testing. In the case studies that I planned I aimed to develop initial qualitative information which could be developed into a more extensive case study. There have been no previous school-based evaluative case studies in Gaza that I can discover, and this could be an important area for future research.

Following the lead of Gone & Alcantara (2010) and Levitt et al. (2017), my focus on Gazan elementary schools is "ethnographically textualized", based on my intimate knowledge of what being a teacher in a war-torn region entails. The research I planned was limited by the fact that I could not be physically present in Gaza now (since the occupying power will not permit my entry for this purpose). I relied, therefore, on extensive telephone interviews with the headteachers and four nominated teachers, within each of the two elementary schools.

I began the interviews with a systematic series of questions as part of "ethnographic interviewing" (Gray, 2018, p, 443). My analysis of interview data has been inductive (searching for patterns of meaning, and links between people and events – Gray, 2018, p. 18). In this process my "understanding or *verstehen*" of the interview material (and the direction in which I led the interviews, or allowed the conversation to flow) stems from my position as a former Gazan resident, a teacher, a mother, a Muslim, and as one deeply concerned about trauma inflicted upon Gazan children. This raises questions of both validity and reliability of the interview material I have elicited. Of course, my position is value-based and "biased" in that I have elicited a unique set of accounts and reactions to trauma, based on questions which reflected my own experiential position. But at the end of the day a child killed by shrapnel or gunfire is a "social fact", as are the accounts by myself and others of the frequency of such deaths. What is subjective and controversial is how I and those I have interviewed react to these "social facts" and describe how injured and surviving children cope with the events of warfare.

A series of standard questions led to more discursive accounts of coping with children's trauma, and acting as both teacher and therapist. Interviews lasted from 30 to 60 minutes and were transcribed from Arabic to English. The validity and reliability of such interview data relies on the internal logic or inherent "truthfulness" of the case study, which ideally "speaks for itself" (Yin, 2018, p, 43),

The case studies of two types of elementary school in Gaza were planned to follow the standardised models of Case Study Research in education, using contextualised knowledge in offering value-informed accounts of how teachers may be struggling to cope with, and offer therapy for, pupils suffering from PTSD symptoms. How do teachers for example, merge the two roles of being both instructors (conveyers of knowledge), and being counsellors or therapists?

6. Findings from the Case Studies

All interviews were conducted by telephone, since the researcher is a refugee from Gaza, and was not allowed to return to Gaza for any purpose. The interviews were what Yin (2018) describes as "shorter case study interviews … the interviews may still remain open-ended and conversational." (p. 119)

Brief background will now be introduced for each of the two primary schools, followed by discussion and analysis by the writer, who was herself a teacher in Gaza (and taught in one of the case study schools prior to 2008), offering the findings from data analysis of each case. The main themes 'naturally' emerging in these 'research conversations' were:

The nature of external threat and its impact on children's emotional and behavioural development; and the impact of these threats on children's learning.

The role of the school in addressing and trying to solve problems of individual children; and the particular roles of women teachers in this process. On reflection and analysis of texts, these themes emerged both from the leading questions I asked, and from the emotionally strong and detailed responses of the teachers with whom I spoke. (Accounts of some particularly traumatic events I have had to leave out, in order not to identify the school involved).

How teachers develop modes of Islamic feminism in finding strength to continue in their difficult and stressful roles of offering support to each other, and to traumatised children and their families.

The two schools studied were not chosen at random: I have known both headteachers since I was a child. I know both of the schools personally (and taught in one of them prior to 2008), and have visited them several times, experiencing the tragedies of pupils who have been killed or maimed. Even as I write, in 2018 another phase of conflict is beginning to happen, and more than 100 children and adolescents have been killed (Elessi, 2018; SCF, 2018).

Background of the First Primary School

This school, in Northern Gaza is one of around 400 public primary schools in the Gaza Strip, located in an area which has been under heavy bombardment during the three recent punitive attacks by Israel (2008, 2011, 2014). Dozens of children attending the school have been killed, dozens more have permanent scarring and handicaps because of warfare, and all have experienced the killing of a family member, or have friends with such an experience.

The school is governed by the Ministry of Education, using the same teaching materials and methods used in other government schools, and is supported financially in terms of teacher salary and teaching materials by the government. Such a financial support is limited, as Gaza's economy declines under the conditions of chronic economic blockade since 2007. Despite their very low salaries, all teachers are professionally qualified, with college degrees. The school has more than 1000 children from year one (aged six) to year six (aged twelve) and is staffed by some 50 women teachers and their assistants. The five teachers selected for interview included the headteacher and four teachers whom the headteacher recommended as having special experience in helping children with behavioural and emotional challenges.

Table 4.1 Details of the Teacher Informants in the Government School

Participant code	Marital status	Experience	Gender
Teacher 1	Mother of 4	5 years	Female
Teacher 2	Mother of 3	5 years	Female
Teacher 3	Mother of 5	7 years	Female
Teacher 4	Mother of 5	8 years	Female
Teacher 5	Mother of 4	7 years	Female

Theme 1: The Impact of War on Children's Learning

Numerous examples were offered by all of the teachers interviewed of how traumatic stress interfered with a child's motivation to learn or to study, and illustrated the massive impact of war upon children behaviour and learning process such as the following:

> *"Farah" was an intelligent and dedicated student before she lost her whole family due to bombing. She lost the will to live, or speak, and she remained inside her cousin's home for two years in a very depressed state, barely able to move. She came back to school after two years, but has not recovered her grade level or study skills. She remains depressed and frightened. (From interview with Teacher 3)*

> *"Said" was a pleasant and well-mannered, smiling boy and one of the best students in his class in year 3, at age 9. After he witnessed the killing of his*

> *mother (who was holding his hand) by an Israeli sniper, he become an aggressive person in school, and was always hitting and punching his classmates. He is a very difficult child and challenging for the whole school. He is said to hate everything, himself and all other pupils in the school, and he refuses to study. No programme of therapy, counselling or help has been able to reach him. (From interview with Teacher 2)*

> *For this 10-year-old boy, only two siblings and his grandfather survived the Israeli bomb which hit their apartment. The face of the boy was badly burned, and scarring remains. He has become very isolated and is difficult to befriend. He rarely engages in social or group learning activities. He remains solitary and depressed. (From interview with Teacher 4)*

There were so many similar stories offered by the teachers that I interviewed, and I cannot bear to report all of them. Overall, my informants estimated that at least half of their pupils were suffering long-term psychological trauma which resulted from their homes being bombed, seeing family members and siblings killed or maimed, and their neighbourhood destroyed. Many children had lived through more than one episode of war. The affected children manifested a whole range of symptoms, including acute anxiety, acute depression and extreme aggression to self and others; post-traumatic stress disorder with different manifestations; problems of neurological origin, following head trauma; and psychological problems resulting from facial scarring, burns, and impaired movements through limb injuries.

Very often these disturbed children were lagging behind their expected learning progress at particular Grade levels. The picture which emerges from the case study evidence indicates a picture that is *more severe* than that presented in the clinical studies cited in the literature review summarised in Table 4, Appendix 1.

The experience and case histories offered to me by these five teachers was however resonant with my own experience as a teacher in Gaza.

> *I devoted extra time and effort to three very traumatised children, who before the warfare of 2008 were my brightest students. But during the war all three children experienced the killing of one or both parents. Following this, all three girls were depressed and confused, bewildered and lost, unable to study. I worked intensively with these three girls for a year, effectively re-parenting them. (Teacher 1)*

The situation was somewhat hopeful however, since many children who did recover a modicum of emotional stability and academic motivation. All participants agreed with the view, offered by Teacher 1, that:

> *Many children after they recovered, became very strong and were doing very well in school: for many this was to satisfy the dream of their parents who had died in war... this motivation is from ALLAH who gives them the power to survive, and to fulfil the dreams of their deceased parent ... they are keeping that dream alive.*

Theme 2: The Role of the School in Solving Children's Problems

There was clearly a great burden of work on teachers as instructors of learning, leaving them little time for individual or group counselling to aid children with extreme problem behaviours and emotionally disturbed states. The school did however have a social worker, engaged on full time support and therapy for traumatised children. A teacher stated that:

> *We are so lucky we have one social worker working only to our school, not for two schools [a second school population occupied the building in the afternoon]. In most schools there is only one social worker who is responsible to do work for two schools, each with more than 1300 children. (Teacher 3)*

Themes emerged from the interviewed teachers about lack of psychosocial resources in school, for traumatised children – this supports some earlier studies in which there is a lack of financial or organisational support in this area in most government schools in Palestine (Roy, 2013). The education system clearly needs further improvement in terms of reducing the average number of children in each class, and increasing the number of social workers and teachers in each school. Several teachers interviewed stated, for example:

> *There is limited resource and support in this regard from the Government. We cannot depend upon the Government for support for the social worker to solve the problems of our children - we as teachers try to work in looking after children and try to find outside institutions like Al-Mezan or Save the Children to help and support us". (Teacher 5)[2]*

In addition to lack of financial resources and recruitment of social workers, this informant identified the dependence of public schools on voluntary organisations to support the efforts of beleaguered teachers who struggle to meet both learning and emotional needs of pupils. Some limited programmes are offered by school teachers and social workers which could be effective in reducing the negative effects of war upon children. These programmes included group work, drawing and painting, and special

---

[2] Al-Mezan Center for Human Rights, based in Jabalia Refugee Camp, Gaza.

psychological therapies of the type pioneered in Gaza by Thabet et al. (2016).

> *We have been offering many social and psychological programs in the last three wars on Gaza and they have often been effective in getting many children back to normal and engaging in the learning process ... more than 50 children have been treated intensively because of depression and isolation, or extremes of aggressive behaviour. We are quite eclectic, trying to find the best programme or model that fits a child's needs, including group work, sharing of memories, cognitive behaviour therapy, and other approaches. If one approach doesn't work, we try another. Perhaps the passage of time and being in the presence of a caring community is the final cure ... (Teacher 2)*

> *Many children were treated by individual and group therapy, and they effectively recovered, but not necessarily very quickly... some children were under treatment for more than two years before recovering in any way from horrible incidents such as witnessing violent death and injury in their family home. (Teacher 1)*

Some of these programmes were derived from those described in the literature review above, and have sometimes been used to achieve an effective outcome. But their effectiveness depends, according to the five informants, on a number of different factors which vary with each child: the survival of the family home, and of adult carers in that home; and a supportive extended family. Often the school and its teachers served in place of fragmented family relationships, as several of the teachers I interviewed observed. I gained a picture from these interviews (which supported my own experience) that the elementary school is a caring environment, in which children tolerate and help their disturbed peers (knowing that they themselves have been subject to the same stresses). Older children too, assume responsibility for caring and nurturing their younger peers, in the same way in which they tolerate and care for their younger siblings. Indeed, this ethic of human relationships is an integral part of Islam.

There was too, a clear sense of chronic insecurity. No-one is sure when the next bombardment will take place, and indeed 2018 has seen more than 100 teenagers killed when they protested the blockade, and further lethal rockets were fired from Israel into Gaza (Abu-Shaban, 2018; Summerfield et al., 2018). The programmes of social and psychological help given in this elementary school risk being undermined by further conflict and insecurity, as well as by the new cuts in international aid to Gaza, for education, health and welfare.

Theme 3: The Power of Muslim Women Teachers

The teachers I interviewed in this case study were all strong women, profoundly anchored in the faith of Islam, as carers for their own children and families: and as both teachers and carers for children in the schools in which they worked. This school had been under bombardment, with the teachers shepherding their children into safe places.

> *We were moving from one child to another and sitting next to a child and then to another to support them emotionally when the air strikes were dropping bombs close to the school (we were hit by a bomb only once). We were like mothers caring for our children (and of course worrying about our own families). I was so scared myself, and I felt that I needed someone to support me! (She laughs) (Teacher 1)*

This supports other accounts of the courage and power of women surviving and helping others in times of acute stress, including warfare (Diab et al., 2017 & 2018). These teachers were the source of physical and emotional support, and extended their maternal and caring roles into work into the school's wider community. The history of Gaza tells the story of many brave women and their roles and strength in caring for women and children in a society under siege (Arrigoni, 2011). The accounts of the five teachers give pictures of women who are brave but modest about their efforts on behalf of traumatised children. The teachers themselves are traumatised, and support one another, linked together in their Islamic faith and its message of peace and caring for others.

One of the teachers in the telephone interviews had lost her 8-year-old daughter and her husband in the Israeli bombardment:

> *We are Muslim mothers, and believe in God . We believe that anything that happens to us is known to ALLAH, who is constantly looking after us and who gives us SABUR ["Wonderful Patience"] ... There is not anything that happens to us without ALLAH'S permission. Everything from ALLAH is perfect. (Teacher 4)*

The power of these Muslim women comes from their belief in God and in Islamic principles. There is a belief that ALLAH gives the patient ones *as-Sabur* for any bad occasion – this is 99th name of Allah, meaning "The most patient, the patiently enduring." When someone, such as a child dies like, this means that ALLAH has chosen him or her to be in Paradise, and the mother should be happy because it is ALLAH'S decision. This is part of Muslim culture described by Hofstede (1997). This idea of the will of God, and the caring nature of God's intervention in daily affairs exists in all

Muslim cultures, and has been a particular strength for the women of Palestine, as exemplified by the teachers in this case study.

The Background of the Second Primary School: The UNRWA Schools Programme

Since 1948 a special UN agency has been established for assisting the many Palestinian refugees: *The United Nations Refugee and Welfare Agency* (UNRWA). Currently in the refugee camps in Gaza UNRWA provides education for some 240,400 6 to 14-year olds (about a half of all the age group in Gaza – Roy, 2013), with 10,220 teachers and teaching assistants (student to teacher ratio is around 42:1). In addition UNRWA provides four Vocational Training and Education Centres, and supports professional training of around 2,000 college and university students, including trainee teachers.

The UNRWA website on Gaza states (2018):

> *Years of underfunding have left the education system in Gaza overstretched, with 94 per cent of schools operating on a double-shift basis, hosting one 'school' of students in the morning and a different group in the afternoon. As a result, children's education is severely truncated. In 2016 examinations, nearly 80 per cent of students failed mathematics, and more than 40 per cent failed Arabic ... Given the particularly challenging context in Gaza, UNRWA introduced a standard human rights course based on materials developed through our human rights, conflict resolution and tolerance programme.* (UNRWA, 2018).

The school that I have studied is one of around 350 UNRWA primary schools in the Gaza strip, and these schools serve about half of those aged 6 to 12 in Gaza. They are less well-equipped and staffed (with a poorer teacher-student ratio) than Government-funded schools. The school is located in Northern Gaza, directly in the path of the onslaught of the wars of 2008-2014.

A higher proportion of children in the UNRWA school had been killed or seriously injured in these attacks than had occurred in the Case Study One government school, reported above. While the teaching goals and materials, and the examination preparation are similar to those of government schools, UNRWA schools are decreasingly well-funded, largely due to the failure of certain countries with UN representation (particularly America) to provide continued funding. In January 2018 on the direction of its President, the U.S.A. withheld $305 million in funding from UNRWA for political reasons (Emmott, 2018). Many UNRWA programmes are suffering severe shortages and cutbacks, including schools where teachers face lay-offs, or work without pay. UNRWA health programmes for infants, mothers and children have also suffered severe cutbacks in Gaza in the past year. These new cutbacks have meant that many UNRWA programmes for health and education in Gaza were already closing by September, 2018 (Blanchet et al., 2018; Devi, 2018a & b), and these events were likely to make the lot of Gazan children and adults worse.

The UNRWA case-study school has more than 1200 children from years 1 to 6, and 53 women teachers. The headteacher (Teacher 1) identified for this research four teachers who were experienced and had practised various kinds of approach in helping traumatised children. Each teacher gave a telephone interview of between 30 and 60 minutes, and what I thought to be key passages have been transcribed into English. I had taught in this school myself, prior to 2008.

Table 4.2 Details of Teacher Informants in the UNRWA School

Participant code	Marital status	Professional experience	Gender
Teacher 1	Mother of 6	12 years	Female
Teacher 2	Mother of 5	11 years	Female
Teacher 3	Mother of 3	10 years	Female
Teacher 4	Mother of 4	8 years	Female
Teacher 5	Mother of 4	9 years	Female

As with the teachers interviewed for the first school, three major themes in the narrative emerged, partly because the researcher directed conversations into areas in which the respondents were clearly knowledgeable.

Theme 1: The Impact of Traumatic War Experiences on Children's Learning

As in the first case study, there were many examples of the negative impacts of intermittent warfare, bombing and blockade upon children's behaviour and learning such as the following:

> *This 9-year-old girl was an intelligent and dedicated student before she lost her whole family during bombing. For several months she entered a very depressed state, wanting to die, not eating, remaining mute, not wanting to*

interact with anyone, or attend school. After a year she began studying again, but not at her previous level. She remains depressed, and no form of counselling or social support has been of much use ... (Teacher 1)

After this 10-year-old girl witnessed the killing of all of her family by Israeli soldiers, she become an isolated, aggressive person, indifferent to learning, without the ability to concentrate on any school work. She is permanently angry, hates herself, hates school, hates the world ... we have several similar cases, and these children are very difficult to reach ... (Teacher 2)

All of the teachers interviewed produced similar cases, which involved the following sequence: child sees family member(s) killed, and often they are themselves wounded; they manifest a variety of symptoms, anxiety, depression, extreme anger, exact patterns probably reflecting their prior personality; observing the violent death of their mother was particularly traumatic; school work and achievement motivation is negatively affected; ad hoc support and counselling sometimes worked, but the process of recovery takes years rather than months; some children never recover. And in Gaza there is the constant threat of further violent warfare in which the school and the children's homes may again be targeted.

While this picture is consistent with previous studies in Gaza, the evidence from the Case Studies suggests that the situation is *significantly worse* (in terms of child trauma) than previous studies have indicated, and long-term outcomes are worse too, in terms of psychological adjustment. There is a lack of systematic training for teachers in coping with war-traumatised children, and although some of the programmes described in previous work on Gaza (Veronese & Barola, 2017) may work, trauma are so profound that conventional programmes of therapy often fail.

The situation of chronic warfare traumatises the teachers also:

The negative impact of war was harsh on children and on us... We are not surviving in a healthy environment, but we are doing our best to get children to learn and study...but it is so difficult within an unsafe environment. (Teacher 4)

Teachers attempted to meet the learning goals of children, all of whom have been threatened or traumatised by chronic blockade and bombardment, to a greater or lesser degree. There was a consensus among the teachers interviewed on the desperate and depressing nature of the chronic situation of war and the threat of war. I gained the subjective impression that this UNRWA school was coping less well than the Government school studied in Case 1. The school is understaffed, and even jobs of the existing teachers are in jeopardy through UN cuts to UNRWA, because of international politics. The ethos of the UNRWA school was one of a depressed institution, with teachers struggling to do their best in meeting learning goals, and helping traumatised children to study. These teachers needed better support, better training for coping with traumatised children, and helping them to recover a degree of psychological dignity.

Theme 2: The role of school and teachers in addressing the emotional and behavioural problems of children

All participants made comments on cuts to UNRWA's programming, along the following lines:

> There are cuts to the funding of all of the UNRWA facilities, and this includes the reduction in the number of teachers, and school social workers... we used to have 3 social worker in each school who were responsible for looking after children's needs, but at present we have only one social worker and this post could disappear very soon ... (Teacher 3)

The decline in UNRWA services, and the low morale of teachers in its schools was not a finding that I had expected, since previous studies had praised the high quality and effectiveness of UNRWA schools in Gaza, in comparison with government-funded schools[3].

The above theme was a common one amongst the teachers interviewed. These pressures seemed to impact negatively on the ability of the teachers interviewed to move from purely teaching tasks, to counselling ones. Many participants offered comments similar to the following opinions:

> We cannot depend upon the UNRWA support, or on the limited number of their outsourcing institutions which run some social programmes in school. We as individuals try to help and support children and this should be accepted and supported by the UNRWA... UNRWA is not a flexible institution which allows us to initiate some programmes that we think could be of benefit for children. (Teachers 4 and 5)

The teachers interviewed commented on the lack of organised or systematic programmes of help and therapy for the many traumatised children in the school. Programmes were, instead, offered on an *ad hoc* basis, in ways which seemed to address the needs of an individual child, and other (often

---

[3] Even the funding for the government schools is not guaranteed, since the local authority in Gaza has no independent source of income. All financial flows are monitored by Israel, and can be suspended at any time.

older) children as well as other teachers were often co-opted into these individualised programmes, which amounted to the development of a caring and understanding community: everyone knew why certain children were behaving in certain ways, and there was a network of sympathy and understanding within the school.

There was clearly a tension, according to my five informants in this school, between what UNRWA advocated as "therapeutic" interventions – group work to discuss common concerns, and drawing or painting, and then talking about, traumatic events. The teachers were unanimous that these strategies were often *ineffective* as therapy for deeply war-traumatised children. Drawing a picture of a soldier who is killing one's mother is likely to make the child's memory and reliving of the trauma worse, rather than better.

The five teachers were desperately seeking for new, more radical therapies for children whose chronic symptoms of post-traumatic stress disorder (depression and withdrawal; and/or acute and chronic anxiety; and/or violent acting out) do not 'remit spontaneously', and require long term psychiatric therapy – therapy that is completely unavailable for the more than 100 children in this school who manifest such symptoms to a marked degree. Moreover, there is the risk of repeated trauma from warfare, and vulnerable children are at risk of deep and profound psychological *further* trauma, for which none of the authors I have reviewed have offered any viable model.

The women teachers I interviewed are truly brave: traumatised themselves, they offer basic help and comfort to their bitterly traumatised pupils. But:

> *We have been offering social and psychological programmes in the last three wars on Gaza and they have been effective in helping to get a number of children back to normal, enabling them to engage in the learning process. We have helped dozens of children using the UNRWA methods, but we are unable to reach many more .... (Teacher 2)*

> *Many children were treated effectively, and to a large degree did recover psychologically but often not very quickly... some children were under treatment for more than two years in attempts to recover from horrible incidents such as losing all of their family members. (Teacher 1)*

Some of the programmes described in the literature summarised in Tables 4.A1 and 4.A2 had been adapted for use in this school, such as using cognitive reinforcement for improved self-concept, in group settings. But their effectiveness varied for each child, depending on parallel family support for the child, and the passage of time since the last months of warfare. Some children, traumatised in 2008 and beginning to recover, were retraumatised in 2011-12. Some children had become resilient due to teacher and social work support; but others remained vulnerable, and their second experience of trauma led them into a deeper state of trauma. These ideas which have emerged from the open-ended interviews with teachers, require further investigation with skilled clinicians.

Theme 3: The Power of Muslim Women Teachers

Muslim women of Gaza (like everyone else in Gaza) are under constant threat of war, and imminent air strikes and other kinds of bombardment by the government of Israel. Often these attacks are difficult to predict, in that the politics of conflict is difficult for ordinary people to read, predict or understand. Muslim women must remain strong under all these uncertain circumstances, maintaining the role of strong family managers, protecting and caring for the whole of their family, including the wretched male adults who have no job and no meaningful role in an economy decimated by eleven years of economic blockade. Teachers especially, exemplify the role of "the strong family manager", the Muslim woman who has special roles, rights and duties within Islam, and is frequently stronger and more responsible than her male counterpart. These teachers had all worked in the school when it was threatened by bombardment (and partially destroyed). They described situations in which they covered classroom windows, and helped children to hide under desks, waiting for the next Israeli bomb.

> *We were moving from one child to another and sitting next to one child after another, supporting them emotionally as the air strikes got closer and closer. We were acting like mothers for these children – even though we were scared ourselves, and had to support one another. (Teacher 1)*

This is consistent with studies of the power of women and their strength in war, and situations of high stress (Ahmed, 1992; Diab et al., 2017 & 2018; Ezzat, 2007; Lovat, 2012). These five teachers (and of course many other teachers in the school) were the source of much physical and emotional support which they offered in the combined roles of teacher and mother-figure. Some comments illustrating this were:

> *We are a Muslim mothers and believe in God – We believe that anything that happens to us is from ALLAH who is looking after us, and who gives us SABUR [Grace and Power of Patience when tested]: "There is not anything that happens to us without ALLAH'S permission. Everything from ALLLAH, however trying, is a perfect gift." (Teacher 4)*

> *'Aminah' was aged 6 in 2014 during the Israeli bombardment. She and her twin brother were playing at home, which was struck by an Israeli rocket. Her brother Ali was killed instantly; she had a penetrating cheek wound from shrapnel, and permanent facial scars. For two years she kept searching for her brother, dreaming of him, having nightmares, flashbacks, terrors, weeping, depression. She insisted that they were still playing hide and seek, he would appear again soon. After four years she now accepts that ALLAH has chosen her brother to enter Paradise. With the continued support of everyone in the school, she is now more settled, but still sad ... (Teacher 1)*

The primary power of Muslim women comes from their belief in God, and Qur'anic principles. There is a believe that ALLAH gives the patient believer tests, and also the means to overcome them (SABUR) in a variety of ways, both negative and positive. When children are killed, that means that ALLAH has chosen this child to be in paradise, and a mother should be happy because it is ALLAH's decision. The Islamic principles of nonviolent acceptance of the violence of others (following The Prophet's example) assumes too, that ALLAH has given free will to everyone, and those who murder children will bear a heavy burden in the next phase of their existence (Pal, 2011). Furthermore, many participants insisted upon the following point:

> *We follow Islamic principles as a mothers, and as professional teachers - and we are always looking at being responsible professionals in achieving our assigned tasks in the best way. (Teacher 1)*

It is a principle of Islam that the role of mother is the basis of women's power in leading not only her family, but also in achieving important roles of power both within the family, and in the wider society as well. This principle is powerfully exemplified by the women teachers I have interviewed. Women of Gaza also play a lead in the Arab world as both professional and responsible persons. This is mainly in Arab masculine cultures where men traditionally, had more power than women.

The crisis of both government and UNRWA funding has meant a reduction in counselling and educational services, meaning that the teachers who survive have had to innovate their caring and helping strategies, often in creative ways. They offer such programmes in addition to their teaching responsibilities. As one teacher stated:

> *In addition to our teaching responsibilities, we are working hard to bring children to a state of happiness, and after each war offering them intensive emotional support, often on an individual basis ... We are doing this because we love our job and our children. (Teacher 5)*

Effectively, the most powerful and intuitively appealing strategy was for teachers to "reparent" traumatised children, especially when the parents of the child had themselves suffered severe psychological trauma, or had actually been killed. This is consistent with the literature review showing that women are becoming professional persons, powerful within Arabic cultures effectively extending their strengths as "strong and stable" family managers. Women in Gaza have a strongly developed sense of responsibility for others, even under conditions of permanent blockade and warfare.

7. Conclusions and Summary

Two case studies were undertaken of contrasted elementary schools in Gaza, one government-funded, the other funded by the UN Relief and Works Association, which has been aiding Palestinian refugees since 1948. I conducted telephone interviews in Arabic with five teachers in each school, including the headteacher, initially following pre-set questions.

Both schools, despite having different funders and foundational values, emerged as very similar in terms of the crucial issues which imposed themselves on the daily routines of both schools. These 'overwhelming issues' concerned reaching learning and achievement goals by pupils, when so many were suffering from the chronic stress of resource blockade (which undermines both nutrition and health care).

I had expected the UNRWA school to have significant advantages for pupils, but cutbacks have undermined both staff morale and the level and kinds of services offered, including therapeutic interventions on behalf of war-traumatised pupils. Both schools were doing their best to offer inclusive and theoretically-informed programmes, but at the end of the day these interventions amounted to sympathetic reparenting, accompanied by some cognitive reconstruction and creative expression to "transcend the trauma". In both schools, teachers and older students worked together in order to care for their many unhappy pupils. Teachers and pupils acted as parents and siblings, often in place of those who had been killed.

Three dominant themes emerged in the accounts of the ten teachers in both schools. These were:

> *One: Teachers struggle to help children achieve "average" achievement levels in school subjects, following war-trauma experiences.*

Two: Teachers use a variety of strategies to help traumatised pupils. A core focus of these programmes is that of reparenting children within the caring environment of the school. These approaches sometimes, but not always, draw on professionally-developed modes of therapy. But lack of resources means that professional help was rarely available.

Three: The teachers themselves exemplified the model of strong, family-centred and caring Islamic feminism. The religious beliefs of Islam were an essential part of this commitment to caring.

I have attempted to illustrate ways in which schools in Gaza may help pupils in the tasks of learning and adjustment, following war trauma which causes marked PTSD in up to a half of children experiencing warfare which kills a family member, causes personal wounding (from burns, shrapnel, and crush injuries when their home is bombed), and leaves the psychological wounds of post-traumatic stress disorder. The literature reviewed suggests that programmes of assistance are fragmented and inadequate, and this is illustrated by the telephone interviews with the ten teachers in two elementary schools studied.

The professional literature on child trauma in Gaza, which has been examined in detail, does not discuss the additional stresses of children's physical injuries which can impact on psychological adjustment. Nor does this literature adequately address the extreme trauma of seeing a parent and/or a sibling killed. The professional literature does not adequately address the chronic nature of extreme stress, and the problem of children who never recover psychologically.

The professional theories on psychological therapy draw on Western models of a single trauma which is unlikely to be repeated. These models do not have elements to help children whose psychological trauma is accompanied by profound physical injury to the child, in a traumatic event that may have killed his or her siblings or parent. In a Western context, such models are theoretically sound, but when introduced into the situation of Gaza: by American clinicians and researchers (Barbara & MacQueen, 2004; Gordon et al., 2014; Vostanis, 2014); by British clinicians and researchers (Vostanis, 2016; Mohammad, Hannington & Jones, 2016; Samuels et al., 2017); by Italian and Danish clinicians and researchers (Fassetta et al., 2017; Pepe et al., 2017) - these 'imported solutions' which incorporated elements of cognitive behaviour therapy, group therapy, and extended social supports involving family, peers and school, sometimes worked well with children for whom they were offered on an intensive basis, even though at least a quarter of children in Gaza experiencing these imported programmes of therapy retained strong elements of PTSD.

The teachers in my research incorporated elements of these programmes into their work with very disturbed children, and were often successful – but they lacked the resources to cope with the most disturbed children, who also ran the risk of re-traumatisation through further episodes of warfare.

In the qualitative interviews, three main themes emerged: how trauma interferes with children's learning tasks; how teachers develop innovative strategies for helping children cope with trauma; and how the teachers draw on cultural and religious strengths in coping with challenges which affect them both personally and professionally.

The most salient finding in my study was how the teachers in each school *reparented* traumatised children, drawing on the entire school community – a community which itself had experienced the trauma of the chronic threat of warfare and destruction of home and family.

The teachers draw on the strengths of Islamic feminism (Khankan, 2018), in seeking psychological and spiritual sources of help for traumatised children. But it is clear too that the continued blockade of Gaza, and denial of funding for UNRWA means that specialist medical help is frequently not available, when so many children and adolescents need intensive professional help. It is at the level of teacher training that courses need to be developed which will enable teachers to provide enduring and successful programmes for traumatised children (Pepe et al., 2018). The same observation applies to the online teacher training programmes available for Gazans (Fassetta et al., 2017).

The two schools in the present study were selected on an 'opportunist' basis from my previous professional experience in Gaza: I knew the two headteachers personally and professionally for many years. I had visited the government primary school, and taught in the UNWRA school studied prior to 2008. It was extremely unlikely that I would have gained telephone access, and the confidence of the teachers with whom I spoke for up to an hour, without these prior contacts. I hoped therefore to offer unique, qualitative accounts which might lead to a fuller understanding of challenges to teaching and counselling in both types of elementary school.

The case study research findings have some biases, since I have strong emotional and value investments in finding the best and strongest efforts which teachers can devote to their often traumatised pupils. Set against this seeming bias, is the strength of being an *autoethnographer,* one whose knowledge comes from within, since she paints a picture based on deep knowledge, and this 'subjective account' has a validity in and of itself.

I 'know' that the picture I paint is true because my consciousness is embedded in it. Even though as a refugee from Gaza I can longer interact physically with schools, I am in daily telephone contact with Gazans, including my sister and sister-in-law who remain as teachers in Gaza. And as a Muslim, I think, feel and connect in particular ways with my Muslim Sisters, as we seek for solutions on behalf of our children and families.

The qualitative design of this work has been framed within the critical realist assumptions of Alderson (2013 & 2016) in identifying the hidden strata of alienation, which in Gaza takes the form of a seemingly permanent state of 'post-traumatic distress disorder' which affects so many Gazan children. The next stage is what Archer (2014) describes as *morphogenesis*, the dialogue of social change.

The road to positive social change in Gaza will be long, and it will be hard. In addition to new incidents of death of innocent civilians imposed by the occupying power in 2018, a significant part of funding has been withdrawn from the United Nations relief agency. A group of 163 physicians, diplomats, paediatricians and public health specialists wrote in a joint letter to *The Lancet* in September, 2018:

> *The United Nations Relief and Works Agency for Palestine Refugees in the Near East (UNRWA) provides lifesaving humanitarian aid for 5·4 million Palestine refugees now entering their eighth decade of statelessness and conflict. About a third of Palestine refugees still live in 58 recognised camps. UNRWA operates 702 schools and 144 health centres, some of which are affected by the ongoing humanitarian disasters in Syria and the Gaza Strip. It has dramatically reduced the prevalence of infectious diseases, mortality, and illiteracy. Its social services include rebuilding infrastructure and homes that have been destroyed by conflict and providing cash assistance and micro-finance loans for Palestinians whose rights are curtailed and who are denied the right of return to their homeland. Yet UNRWA is now fighting for survival. On Aug 31, 2018, the Trump Administration confirmed that the USA, previously UNRWA's largest donor, will no longer fund UNRWA. Funding crises are not new to UNRWA. This crisis, however, is unprecedented. An abrupt cessation of UNRWA services will create humanitarian emergencies that will burden host countries that are already overburdened. It will exacerbate existing conflicts, disrupt fragile peace, create new displacement, and generate disaffection and anger.* (Blanchet et al., 2018)

Added to the UNWRA cutbacks is the fact that US$300 million a year, payments made to Gaza by the West Bank Palestinian Authority were stopped, for political reasons. The role of Israel in this activity is unclear, but at the present time (2018) the effects on health, welfare and educational service delivery in Gaza are dire (World Bank, 2018).These pressures make the call by Tareen & Tareen (2019) for the treatment of psychological distress in conflict zones, by local volunteers in the absence of specialist care, very relevant for Gaza.

Sami & Hallaq (2018) who screened 889 Gazan adolescents and young adults found that 14 percent had engaged in non-suicidal self-injury, with up to a half of those with symptoms of PTSD expressing strong suicidal ideation. This may be manifested in the growing number of Gazan adolescents who mutely approach the barrier with Israel, heads bowed, waiting to be shot by Israeli snipers. In 2018 more than 100 young Gazans, 37 of them children as young as 12, were executed by Israeli soldiers for the crime of unarmed protest (Trew, 2019). Medical aid workers who try to help the young people injured by gunfire, appear to be targeted in particular by the Israeli snipers (Smith, 2018a & b). We cannot condone the despairing acts of self-sacrifice by these adolescents, but do point to them as one outcome of Israeli violence imposed on a defenceless nation.

I give a final word to Farah Baker, 17-years-old, who tweeted to the world in 2014 about her protests against Israel (and was quoted in David Patrikarakos' *War in 140 Characters*, 2017):

> *I live in #Gaza and Hamas is not using me as a human shield.*

Al-Jazeera commented: "She has become the sudden Gaza spokesgirl."

Farah, like Malala Yousafzai (2019) in other contexts, belongs to the new generation of brave young women in the Islamic world who speak out against injustice both within society, and that involving imperialist sexist attacks on the sovereignty of their existence.

The tiny enclave of Gaza and its 1.8 million citizens, is subjected to a merciless and continued system of economic sanctions, including blockade of people and goods entering and leaving; and intermittent episodes of murderous warfare. Gaza is too weak to strike back with any effectiveness, and the pacifist solutions (based on Qur'anic and Sunnah teachings and examples) advocated by Ali (2011) and Abuelaish (2011) appear to be the only viable (and Islamically justified) strategies. These ideas are strongly supported in Amitabh Pal's 2011 book: *Islam Means Peace: Understanding the Muslim Principle of Nonviolence Today*.

Appendix: Summary of Studies of Psychological Trauma in Children of Gaza Following Blockade and Bombardment; and of Studies for Therapeutic Intervention with these Children

Table 4.A1 Studies of Psychological Health in Children and Young People in Gaza

Study	Sampling & Variables Studied	Results
Abdeen et al. (2008)	Screening sample of 1135 West Bank & 724 Gazan children	PTSD & Somatic Disorder 31% in Gazan children, twice the prevalence found in West Bank
Abu-El-Noor et al. (2016)	Study of 324 children <18 admitted to ER after 2014 Gaza bombardment	90% (291/324) clinical PTSD at follow-up
Abu-El-Noor et al. (2018)	Further ER screening, and follow-up studies	PTSD in earlier sample from ER shown to be a chronic condition
Abu-Zaineh et al., (2018)	Representative sample of 4329 individuals aged 15-29 in Gaza & West Bank	Health impairments (physical & psychological) due to lack of access to good health care, regardless of income.
Altamimi, M. (2018)	Tests for anaemia & vitamin deficiency in large sample of pregnant women & infants in Gaza	Severe nutrient deficiencies possible cause of increase in 'autistic withdrawal' in young children faced with extreme stress

Barber et al. (2016)	Qualitative study of 68 young men enduring prolonged conflict.	Self-concept of "feeling broken & destroyed" emerges in adolescence.
El-Habil (2018)	Clinical data on 3362 patients seen for 'acute poisoning' in Gaza, 2010-15.	50% increase in acute poisoning in 5 years, with possible link to increasing despair in young people.
Giacoman et al., (2007)	Questionnaire completed by 3755 high schoolers in West Bank.	Feeling 'humiliated' because of occupation 2.5 times rate of expected mental health problems. Results may apply, with greater magnitude, to Gaza.
Lacey (2011)	Social psychological analysis of the relative positions of Israel & Palestine in generating apparently insoluble conflicts.	Themes of 'victimhood' are shared by both Israeli Jews and Palestinian Muslims. Themes of revenge & rage haunt the identities of both groups, contributing to chronic despair of Palestinians & chronic anger of Israelis.
Manzanero et al. (2017)	1850 6-15 year olds 6 months after the 51-day blockade of Gaza of 2014, completed Harvard Trauma Questionnaire.	73% trapped in dwellings for long periods; 67% saw conflict & destruction; 60% saw corpses. 27% had severe & chronic PTSD, incidence similar between sexes.
NRC (2018)	Surveys of 100,000+ children in Gaza, 2012-18	60% had 'disturbing nightmares', linked to prior conflict experiences, sometimes years before

Peltonen et al. (2017)	240 10-12 year-olds, 50% boys, interviewed in Gaza with standardised & open-ended measures.	Earliest memories for 30% were war trauma (including losses of known others) & were linked to poorer mental health, especially in boys.
Punamäket al. (2017)	511 mother-infant pairs studied in Gaza during pregnancy & 4 & 12 months after child's birth.	Mother's emotional trauma because of war conflict linked to less positive mother-infant interaction.
Qouta et al. (2007)	65 adolescents (50% male) sampled from 1082 in Gaza refugee camps, studied at 3 points in time over 7 years.	High score on PTSD measure at Time 3 predicted by high score at Time 2, being male, and prior school failure.
Thabet et al. (2008)	Study of 100 families with 200 adult parents and 197 children aged 9-18, using PTSD & other mental health measures..	PTSD scores in adults & children twice the level expected in untraumatized population. 74% of children had experienced tank fire close to/at their home.
Thabet et al. (2011)	Study of 780 males aged 9-18 spending more time in paid menial labour tasks than in school.	Mental health poorer than in "normal" children. Psychological problems predicted by both economic deprivation & war trauma.
Thabet & Thabet (2015)	Random sample of 502 adults from 5 sub-regions of Gaza completed standardised measures of stress & adjustment.	Chronic war trauma & its psychological sequels built into the psyche of most adult Gazans, whose resigned despair is dignified by the comforts of religious belief.

Thabet et al. (2016)	251 children aged 6-16 at Gaza summer camps completed standard measures of stress & adjustment.	Each new generation of children recalls bombing, shelling, drones, sonic booms, tank and machine gun fire. 51% had PTSD, often linked to severe depression and/or anxiety.
Veronese & Pepe (2017a)	1376 children 6 to 11 in Gazan refugee camps assess for the utility, validity & reliability of a short scale of negative & positive emotions.	A 20-item measure was developed for assessment of stress reaction, need for & potential for coping & support.
Veronese & Pepe (2017b)	Further analysis of data on 1276 Gazan children aged 6-11 in refugee camps.	Statistical modelling confirmed that each child, despite war trauma & stress symptoms, has positive strengths which can be reached by counsellors.
Veronese at. al. (2018)	Gazan children who witness or experience warfare have rates of clinical PTSD of 58% to 86%, confirmed in this 1276 Gazan sample.	Highly intrusive PTSD memories mediated or lessened by parental and school supports.

Table 4.A2 Therapeutic Interventions for Traumatised Children in Gaza: Theory and Practice, and Evaluation

Study	Sampling & Variables Studied	Results
Abu-Zaineh et al. (2018)	Representative sample of 4329 individuals aged 15-29 in Gaza & West Bank.	Recovery from trauma based on 3 strengths: education, income, & health knowledge. Holds for West Bank, less so for Gaza with blocks to good health care.
Barbara & MacQueen (2004)	Theory, based on key examples, on 'evocation & extension of altruism' through comprehensive health care leading to conflict reduction & resolution.	The model is proposed for Gaza so that both sides in conflict come to view health & growth as preferable to continued conflict.
Diab et al. (2018a)	Describes comprehensive public health program to treat & prevent post-violence trauma.	In 10 years 38878 individuals treated, many of them young people. 11713 treated in groups "to restore the psychological well-being in citizens of Gaza."
Diab et al. (2018b)	454 women studied at 3 points: when pregnant, when child 4 months, and then 12 months old. Experiencing warfare especially traumatic for mothers trying to protect infants.	Focusing on this high risk & high need group "increased social affiliation, spiritual awareness and psychological strengths" so that the woman was a strong carer, preventing & healing trauma in family.
Fassetta et al. (2017)	Description of online courses for teachers from UK via Islamic University of Gaza.	Establishes a model for 'critical pedagogy' including the role of 'strong & smart'

		teachers involved in stress reduction modules.
Gordon et al. (2004)	Application of Gordon's US model for reducing PTSD using 6-week groups with meditation, bio-feedback, mind-body control & guided imagery.	139 high schoolers in treatment & control groups, who had experienced war trauma & PTSD in Kosovo. Treated group significant reduction of PTSD symptoms.
Gordon (2014)	US-developed group model for stress reduction & promoting self-confidence uses 'self-awareness' mind-body techniques, with linked peer support.	Concurrently, Gordon et al., have introduced this model for PTSD treatment for children & adolescents in Gaza.
Marie et al. (2016)	Observational study of practice of *as-Sabur*, steadfastness in the face of chronic adversity, by psychiatric nurses in West Bank & Gaza.	This powerful & culturally appropriate model based on the non-violent struggles of The Prophet & his Companions, can be used by teachers in Gaza.
Hashemi et al. (2017)	Rapid screening of 6-18 year olds following 2014 war on Gaza, using mobile electronic devices.	Children's Relief Fund found high levels of PTSD post-conflict, information used for rapid referral & treatment.
Lange-Nielsen et al. 2017)	116 Gazans aged 11-17: 58 to 'writing therapy', 58 to waiting list control group.	Writing advice for a 'friend like me' experiencing war trauma did reduce PTSD, but also increased depression, with some recovery in longer-term.

Pepe et al. (2017)	Teacher 'focus groups' (N=104) in Gaza, West Bank & Arabian Israel produced textual themes.	Gaza teachers' themes, unique focus on: Quality of teaching; Social supports for self & others; and Religious steadfastness enduring war.
Qouta et al. (2007)	65 17 year olds studied at 3 points in time across conflict situations at 3 points in time: T1, T2 & T3.	Severe PTSD at 17 (T3) predicted by: medium PTSD at T1 due to war trauma; further trauma at T2; & destruction of fabric of ordinary living from bombing; strong maternal support reduces PTSD.
Qouta et al. (2012)	Post 2008-9 bombardment of Gaza, 242 11-yr-olds & 242 waitlist controls enrolled in teacher-led group training workshops (15 in each group) on gaining 'mastery & coping skills', with shared art and dream work.	Significant reduction in PTSD symptoms after 6 months, mostly in very traumatised boys. But a quarter of children still had PTSD symptoms, despite participation.
Samuels et al. (2017)	Comparative, feminist qualitative study of adolescent women in Gaza (N=89), Liberia & Sri Lanka, using themes emerging from focus groups.	Gazan girls emerging into adulthood must cope with gendered devaluation of their professional careers. War conflict aids the continuation of despairing male sexism.
Thabet et al. (2009)	Study of PTSD in 412 children following conflict trauma in Gaza.	Advocates treating parents & children together, with parents co-opted as counsellors for their children.

Thabet et al. (2015)	Survey of 381 Gaza students from 4 universities, post 2014 bombardment. 90% at least 1 traumatic event, including seeing someone killed/injured 10%; being assaulted/arrested by invading forces (18%).	50+% had chronic PTSD symptoms. Protective/recovery factors: Spiritual strength/growth (mostly females); Feelings of being strong/powerful (mostly males).
Thabet & Thabet (2015)	Reports by 502 adults (aged 20+, 50% male) enduring siege and bombardment in Gaza.	90%+ experienced war trauma. Personal resilience often based on religious beliefs.
Thabet et al. (2016)	"The violence & cruelty of conflict are associated with a range of emotional & behavioral problems … PTSD, suicidal behaviors …".	Since trauma of blockade & bombardment in Gaza are chronic, UNRWA schools may develop coping curriculum *in advance* of anticipated conflicts, to reduce effects of PTSD.
Veronese & Pepe (2017a & b)	Development of Arabic version of PANAS-C (Positive & Negative Affect Scale – Child Version) developed in 1376 children 6-11, in Gazan refugee camps.	This valid & reliable 20-item measure may be used for interventions for war-stressed children. Hypothesis: strengthening positive affects helps stress-coping retrospectively, & proactively.
Veronese & Barola (2018)	Controlled experiment to increase PANAS-C 'positive feeling' scores in Gazan school classes.	Experimental groups had increase of positive feelings concerning self, school, family and friends. *But* negative affect in many areas *not* reduced.

Veronese et al. (2018 a & b)	1276 Gazan children in refugee camps studied within 2 months of experiencing the 2012 war trauma.	"When children perceive themselves to be highly satisfied with home & school, peers & parents … effects of war trauma are less severe."
Vostanis (2014 & 2016)	These 2 books draw on the experience of a child psychiatrist in treating various traumatised groups, including refugees & children of Gaza.	No model of intervention is superior, but all approaches should have a sound theoretical base, and be regularly evaluated. In Gaza, programs must be culturally relevant, & not be naïve cultural imports.

Chapter Five

Muslim Youth in Britain: Becoming Good Citizens in the Age of Islamophobia

Christopher-Adam Bagley and Nader Al-Refai

Charity is incumbent upon every human limb every day upon which the sun rises. To bring about reconciliation between two contestants is charity. Helping a person to mount his animal or to load his baggage onto it is charity. A good word is charity. To move obstacles in the street is charity. Smiling upon the face of your brother is charity. Hadith of The Prophet Muhammad (Sardar, 2012, p. 40).

1. Introduction: Issues in the Education of Muslim Youth in Western Countries

One of the many exciting things about Islam is its emphasis on both men and women becoming educated to the utmost of their ability. This process of Islamic learning began when both Adam and Hawa were given the task of recording the names of all living creatures and everything in the natural world, together with the stewardship of all the world (Qur'an 2:31). Today boys and girls everywhere learn Arabic in order to read the Qur'an for themselves, "Read!" is the injunction from Allah (Quran 96:1-5). Right from the beginning of Islam, Muslims established schools within Mosques called Madrasahs, and often these schools have expanded as places of scholarship - for example the world's first university was founded by Fatima Al-Fihiri from her Mosque in Fez, Morocco in 859CE, a university which still thrives today.

Madrasahs reflect regional interpretations of Islam, and curricula and teaching methods change with the advanced educational technologies of the globalised world. Today there is a flux of change in Madrasah education, in countries both East and West, in which scholars seek to retain faithful links to the ground of Islam, while making Islamic education relevant for today's world (Abu-Baker, 2019). Schools which embody Qur'anic learning are agents which both preserve the traditions of Islam, and are also "agents of change", both in their methods of teaching and in the ideas they generate (Boyle, 2004).

Educational and social institutions have a role in developing communities in terms of both cultural belonging and citizenship. In Britain there is a growing energy and commitment among Muslim schools and other Muslim associations to ensure that a cosmopolitan view is taught to pupils, which is seen as a necessary stage in the acquisition of legitimate rights, and in the formation of duties and obligations within a cooperative social contract with the wider society (Badawi, 2003a & b; Waller & Yilmaz, 2011). And according to the literature we have reviewed, in British schools today commitment to a religious faith - any faith - can make a positive contribution to identity, citizenship and the common good. Additional studies, from England and France, support this view while acknowledging the many challenges which Islamophobia offers to Muslim educators (Everett, 2018; Bourget, 2019).

We argue that Citizenship Education not only serves a political function by addressing levels of political apathy and alienation but may also address certain aspects of injustice and social discontent in British society. It is notable, for example, that well-educated young people (that is, older teenagers and undergraduates) are those most accepting of ethnically and religiously diverse communities, rejecting the xenophobic selfishness of the reactionary movement to recover Britain's "greatness" at the expense of shedding a European or international identity (Lister, 2011; Whiteley, 2014; Kaur-Ballagan et al., 2018).

The nature of citizenship in the democratic political communities of the future suggests a world where citizens (including migrant communities) enjoy *multiple identities*. In local communities (the blocs of the emerging multicultural societies, in the model of Modood, 2013) ethnic and religious minority communities accept some of the general values of the state, while preserving their own identity (Merry, 2007). Each person in any state may have to learn to become a 'cosmopolitan citizen' who is capable of mediating between the rootedness of national traditions, and parallel forms of religious and ethnic identity (Held & McGrew, 1999). For Muslim youth who have settled in Europe the negative challenges to their traditional religious identity are strong. They seek empowerment, but at the same time many wish to retain a traditional set of Muslim values (Malik, 2006; Lewis & Hamid, 2018).

Educational and social institutions should have a role in developing the communities of faith, and they are challenged to give answers and solutions to the questions and problems arising in their communities, regardless of the particular nation state in which the person is born and brought up (Held & McGrew, 1999; Merry, 2007; Halstead, 2018; Everett, 2019).

2. Muslims in the United Kingdom

The Muslim population of the four countries of the UK numbered 1.6 millions in 2001 – some 3.1 per cent of the total population - but because this is a largely youthful group with many still in their child-bearing years, their proportion of the total population is increasing substantially. And new Muslims are created not only through birth, but also through conversion, about nine percent of UK Muslims being converts from other religions. Zebiri (2011) found that white, English women who convert and wear the hijab often have to endure both the usual social and physical assaults of Islamophobia, and also the scorn of non-Muslim feminists who are opposed to Muslim women's modesty.

Sahin (2008) estimated that in the United Kingdom (England, Wales, Scotland, Ulster) the Muslim population then numbered more than two million, of whom at least 450,000 were aged less than 18. By 2018 (ONS, 2018) the Muslim population of the UK was 5.17 percent of UK's total population of 65.3 million. The majority of Muslims live in London, and many English towns and cities contain very few Muslims. The general population of non-Muslims greatly overestimate the number of Muslims in the UK: "white" residents estimated that the Muslim population (of the UK, and of their local region) was six times the actual number (Kaur-Ballagan et al., 2018).

This imaginary inflation seems to be part of ethno-religious prejudice, called Islamophobia. In the IPSOS-Mori public opinion surveys summarised by Kaur-Ballagan et al. (2018), those overestimating the actual number of Muslims in their community were also those most likely to agree that "Islam is not compatible with British values". When pressed, most respondents were unable to give any coherent account of what "British values" might be. Those most tolerant of Islam tended to be the younger and better-educated sectors of the non-Muslim population. Generally similar findings were obtained in parallel surveys in Germany, France, Netherlands and the Nordic countries.

Between 2010 and 2017 there have been 14 general populations surveys in Britain which have identified Muslim respondents, asking them specific questions; and asking non-Muslims about their understanding of and attitudes to their fellow Muslim citizens. The results of these surveys using reliable and valid methodologies, have investigated large, representative sections of the UK population. A very useful overview and integration of these surveys has been undertaken by the Social Research Institute of Ipsos-MORI (Kaur-Ballagan et al, 2018), and it is appropriate to present some of these results here as a prelude to understanding how Muslims experience and relate to British society, including the important issue of education.

Discrimination and Islamophobia

Muslims have been the target of religious discrimination in Britain, as well as persecution on grounds of "race" and colour for the past three decades. Discrimination can be identified in schools and in the work place, such as lack of time-off for religious festivals; refusal to allow time for daily prayers; difficulties in obtaining planning permission for mosques, schools and burial sites; conflicts about dress and language in a range of settings, especially the wearing of the *hijab* in schools and the workplace; and the refusal, despite legal statute, to provide financial support for Muslim schools (Anwar and Bakhsh, 2003; van Driel, 2004; Abbas, 2013; Breen, 2018). These discriminations reflect Islamophobia, which is defined as dread or hatred of Islam and fear or dislike of Muslims (Modood, 2018).

Islamophobia in many areas of interaction was expressed in Europe immediately after the events of September 2001 in America. In the UK there were attacks on mosques and Asian-run businesses; firebombs were put through letterboxes; and death threats were made against Muslims. Sikhs and Sikh temples were (and continue to be) attacked by those who mistakenly believe that Sikhs are a kind of Muslim,

Sheridan (2006) interviewed a random sample of 222 British Muslim adults, and reported that they experienced significant increase in abusive attacks since the 9.11 terrorist action in America. At least a quarter had experienced some kind of personal abuse or attack, and many experienced an increase in fearfulness, anxiety and tension because of this manifest Islamophobia. The media's widespread usage of words such as 'terrorists' and 'fundamentalists', associating these labels with *all* Muslims, perpetuated the stereotype that Islam and Muslims are violent and dangerous.

In a survey of the coverage of Islam and Muslims in the British media before and after September 11, 2001, persistent stereotypes relating to Muslims were that they were 'intolerant', 'violent', 'cruel', 'strange' or 'different' (Sheridan, 2006). Since that study was published, Islamophobia in Britain and Europe has according to several authoritative studies, become increasingly worse (Abbas, 2011; Abbas & Awan, 2015; APPG, 2017; ENAR, 2016; Fekete & Sivandan, 2009; Lean, 2012; Meer, 2013; Zebiri, 2011).

Despite (or because of this growing) climate of Islamophobia in Britain, young Muslims are re-establishing their Islamic identity. In the surveys reviewed by Kaur-Ballagan et al. (2018), on personal identity 74 percent of Muslims saw religion as being part of their core identity, compared with 23 percent of Christians, in 2015. However, despite Islamophobic discrimination 83 percent of Muslims still saw "being British" and "being Muslim" as equal parts of their identity

Young Muslims in Britain (in the Ipsos MORI surveys) were significantly more likely to grow up in an intact home with both parents present (85% vs 63% in non-Muslim households). Muslim adolescents recalled significantly less quarrelling between parents. A half of Muslim households are bilingual or multilingual. While Muslim parents attach great importance to their child having a Muslim marriage partner, they have little bias (compared to the general population) concerning the colour or ethnicity of that partner, provided they are Muslim. (A visitor to a Mosque in Britain will be impressed by the range of ethnicities in those attending. "Inter-ethnic" marriages in Islam are common in many cultures).

Anthony Heath (2018) in his extensive review of *Social Progress in Britain*, gathers together and interprets official data, and national and longitudinal studies which show the degree to which Britain had "recovered" from the international recession of 2008. While there had been much progress involving many sectors of the community, the profile of disadvantage in Britons with Pakistani and Bangladeshi ethnicity stands out (this ethnic group is not identified by religion, but we can assume that the large majority are Muslims – Heath & Li, 2015a). By 2017 Pakistanis and Bangladeshis had mean income levels which were 70 percent of the income of the "white population" despite the fact that this minority group's educational attainments were *higher*. Unemployment rates at 40 percent for young people in this Muslim minority group were twice as high as in the mainstream "white" ethnic group. Housing quality was poorer, with 37 percent of Pakistanis and Bangladeshis living in "overcrowded dwellings" compared with 5 percent of the majority ethnic group. Many Pakistanis and Bangladeshis, suffering the yoke of employment discrimination were often too poor to move out of the zones of poor housing into which poverty had pushed them. But as Peach (2006) showed, when incomes rose, so did geographical mobility.

Heath & Li (2015b) confirmed the results of the Ipsos-MORI survey data: despite their higher levels of educational achievement, Muslims of Pakistani-Bangladeshi ethnic origins, including those born in Britain, have significantly less annual income that non-Muslims, and live in poorer quality housing. Nevertheless, according to Kaur-Ballagan et al., (2018) a high percentage (more than 90%) of educated, younger Muslims are proud to have been born in Britain, and overwhelmingly identify themselves as British: only one percent showed any sympathy with terrorist acts committed in the name of Islam.

Muslims of all ages frequently volunteered in a club or agency serving the community, at a higher rate than non-Muslims. (This ethic of community service is built into Islam and follows The Prophet's teaching on how we should interpret The Qur'an: this service is given to Muslims and non-Muslims alike). Annual giving to charity is an integral part of Islam, called *zakah,* in which the faithful Muslim is required to give 2.5 percent of net wealth each year to established charities (which may benefit both Muslims and non-Muslims). The average annual donation of Muslim adults in this regard was in 2015 about £345. Practising Christians in the UK gave about £230 per annum to charity. Others, on average, gave much less.

According to the national surveys of majority and minority groups in Britain summarised by Kaur-Ballagan et al. (2018) the large majority of Muslims are satisfied with how Britain at an official level tolerates Muslim worship and religious practices (e.g. fasting during Ramadan; availability of Halal foods). 83 percent felt that practising their Islamic faith was compatible with being 'a good citizen' of Britain. But less than half felt that the general population of Britain treated them tolerantly, or with respect. Being faithful to Islam's requirements (e.g. for daily prayers, giving to charity, avoiding alcohol, attending Friday prayer, fasting) had *increased* in British Muslims between 2006 and 2015. Now 79 percent of 13 to 15-year-old Muslims said that religion was very important for them. Only four percent of the total population of self-declared Muslims did not pray regularly. Today's second and third generation children of immigrants who are self-declared Muslims appear to be firmly committed to their faith, and this according to the survey data is entirely compatible with their positive feelings about being good British citizens, findings confirmed by Lewis & Hamid (2018).

Particularly during the last fifteen years, Muslims in Britain have become more involved in a number of spheres in politics, social action and organisation. There are a number of important factors central to the entry of Muslims in Britain into arenas of social and political mobilization, and subsequent state responses (Anwar and Bakhsh, 2003; Abbas, 2011 & 2013; Abbas & Anwar, 2015). For example, over the last two decades there has been increasing debate on how British Muslims should regard the national schooling system, and the special role of mosques and Muslim organisations in providing supplementary education (Breen, 2018; Halstead, 2018). Today, Muslims after Anglicans and Catholics are the third largest practising religious group in Britain. Muslims who are growing up in Britain, are having to face the challenge of defining their identity in peaceable, productive and law-abiding ways, in a society that is increasingly Islamophobic (Sheridan, 2006; Sahin, 2013; Tyrer, 2013; Kunst et al., 2016; Sadek, 2017; Lewis & Hamid, 2018).

Important information on the school achievements of Muslim minority children in the UK comes from the Millenium Cohort Study (Skopek & Passeretta, 2018), a longitudinal enquiry into the health and welfare of a representative, random sample containing some 18,000 children born in 2000. About 10 percent of the cohort were born to immigrant-descendant parents, the majority from Pakistan, India and Bangladesh, 75 percent of this immigrant-heritage group being Muslim: 32% of the "immigrant" group parents had education beyond the secondary level, compared with 21% of all other parents – a large and statistically significant difference (nevertheless, the occupational status of the minority parents was lower than that of the 'indigenous' group).

Standard measures of achievement were completed by the children from aged 3 to 14. In the preschool years the ethnic minority children *underperformed* on tests (probably because the first language at home was often not English). But after this they made *rapid progress*, outperforming their peers by a significant margin. This led the authors to comment:

> *Although, on the one hand, migrant families on average are poorer in income they have frequently more education than native families ... early disadvantages in achievement of children of these migrants vanish entirely once children enter the formal school system ... there is an astounding*

catching-up effect – children from most minority groups over-proportionately gain in achievement compared to children of majority status ... there is an achievement 'premium' for minority groups. (Skopek & Passaretta, 2018, p. 150).

The large majority of these children, reflecting their parents' education in rapidly catching up and achieving well in the British school system, are Muslims. How will the wider society regard this highly motivated, achievement-orient minority group?

The question of the identity of young people such as these affects second and third generation Muslims, who have to balance their religious upbringing and traditions with the demands of the culture surrounding them. Demands for Muslim "integration", thinly cloaked in the language of Islamophobia, present the new generation of British Muslims with a dilemma: how can we become fully British in a society in which hatred of our religion, and of ourselves, flourishes (Kunst et al., 2016)?

As Bagguley & Hussain (2017) put the matter in their writing on "late modern Muslims" of Britain, the new educated class of Muslim men and women experience "liquid identity changes" within the context of "the ever-unfolding hegemonic securitisation of Islam". Now the government agency called PREVENT may report to the police any suspiciously devout Islamic practice (such as praying aloud, within the hearing of non-Muslims) which is seen as a possible warning sign of a terrorist threat to society (Awan, 2012; Lewis & Hamid, 2018).

For us as Muslims, Islamic dignity is under attack in what we see as the official "Prevent Islam" strategy, and Muslim Britons need the example of Prophet Muhammad to guide them with quiet dignity through this persecution.[1] The need for such spiritually-guided patience is demonstrated from the extraordinary events in Birmingham, where a fugue of anti-Muslim hatred led to the dismissal of school governors (of state schools with a high proportion of Muslim students) on the *entirely false* grounds that these governors were introducing a secret curriculum to "brainwash" all students

---

[1] For example the conservative UK newspaper *The Daily Telegraph* carried a page one story on 19.1.19 on action by PREVENT concerning a Scout group run by a Mosque in London: "Police have been called ... because children as young as 5 were shown videos advocating the wearing of the hijab ... the Scouts were divided by sex, contrary to Scouting guidelines ... and contrary to the Scouts' own commitment to British values, children were encouraged to be 'Muslims first'."

with the hidden values of Islam. The falsity of these claims is ably demonstrated by the study of Holmwood & O'Toole (2018).

Some 80 percent of the current generation of young British Muslims have been born in Britain, compared with most of their parents who migrated to the UK in the 1950s and 1960s. These young people are increasingly asserting themselves in various ways in society (Lewis & Hamid, 2018). For them, issues of racial prejudice and discrimination based on religion are often fused, and the growing element of ethno-religious racism in British society is clearly directed against Muslims, forcing them into a greater sense of religious consciousness and Islamic social identity (Anwar and Bakhsh, 2003; Sheridan, 2006; Meer, 2014; APPG, 2017).

The rate of religious observance had up to 2002 had been relatively low among young British Muslims (Merry, 2007), which meant that for many 'integration' into their host countries had actually meant degrees of assimilation, of which there are several types (Merry, 2007; Modood, 2017 & 2018). On the other hand, the renewed commitment for religious observance among a significant number of Muslim parents in England has led to the creation of a number of independent Islamic schools (Halstead, 2018). Ironically, the manifest presence of Islamophobia in British society may be causing young Muslim's to re-evaluate the bases of their identity, moving to being "Muslim first" rather than "basically British" (Basit, 2009; Lewis & Hamid, 2018).

3. Educational Challenges for Muslims in Britain Today

Educational and social institutions, including Muslim schools in Europe have a role in developing communities in terms of belonging and citizenship (Parker-Jenkins, 1995; Merry, 2007). There is a growing energy and commitment among Muslim schools and other associations to ensure that a cosmopolitan view is taught to pupils. All schools now have to place greater value on civic education and citizen participation, which are seen as necessary stages in the acquisition of legitimate rights, and in the formation of duties and obligations within a co-operative social contract with the wider society (Sahin, 2013; Berglund & Gent, 2019).

Furthermore, the ongoing faith schools debate in Britain has opened up into various discussions which focus on the implications and effectiveness of single-faith and multi-faith schools, and the importance and general effectiveness of independent Muslims schools (Parker-Jenkins et al., 2005; Halstead, 2018). Reflecting this increasing number of independent Muslim schools being established in Britain, this Chapter will discuss the ways that the subject of Citizenship is taught in Muslim-run schools, as compared with state schools, and also attempts to assess the adequacy of such Citizenship teaching for preparing young Muslims for a productive and moral existence in a society in which religious groups recognize each other's differences and strengths.

Muslims have felt discomfited in the British school system (Anwar & Bakhsh, 2003; Abbas, 2011), but have also struggled to gain funding for their own schools. In the 1960s the British school system was significantly restructured, including the removal of most single-sex schools, just when Muslim parents were examining them with interest, since they met Islamic requirements for 'modesty' in education. In the 1970s, England began to contemplate some practical concessions to make Muslims more comfortable with British education, and in a system which funded Anglican, Catholic and Jewish schools there were clear cultural and legal precedents for supporting state-funded Muslim faith schools. At that time, and still today, the large majority of children of Muslim parents are enrolled in state schools, including many designed as 'Church of England' schools.

The fact that in some urban centres more than two-thirds of pupils in Anglican schools are actually Muslim has challenged educational scholars - for example, Wilson's (2015) account of an Anglican primary school in England with an enrolment of more than 80 percent of pupils who were Muslim. The school, under Wilson's leadership developed a theology of "translation" in which Christian ideas of hospitality and accepting "strangers" led to the acceptance of Islamic ideals of being tolerant. At the secondary level Wilkinson (2015a) using a critical realist perspective, uses Islamic concepts of "spiritual success" in developing a model of secondary schooling which envelops and enhances the values of both Muslim and Christian pupils.

Although Muslims generally accept the British view regarding the basic purpose of education, for Muslims the idea of 'good citizenship' is also synonymous with being a 'good Muslim' (Haines, 2000). In this regard, Al-Refai (2011) argued that Muslim parents want schools to produce good citizens through the exercise of religious authority and the understanding of sacred texts – epitomised in learning The Qur'an, which has many symbiotic benefits in terms of both character development and success in a broad range of intellectual tasks (Berglund & Gent, 2019). Muslim parents have negotiated many changes in state schools, including prayer rooms in schools with a large Muslim population, excused absence for children attending

Friday prayers and major religious festivals, segregated swimming and PE lessons, and *Halal* provisions in meals. It is argued that although these changes are specific to Muslim pupils, they are not intended to be divisive with other faith groups and implementing them has little impact upon the rest of the school organisation (Shah, 2016; Halstead, 2018).

Reflecting the commitment of Muslim parents to educational and spiritual "success", three types of Islamic educational institutions have developed in England: there are the mosque schools; second, there are full-time schools that are run in private homes or in rented places; and, third are full-time primary or secondary schools, such as Al-Isra Islamic College in Malvern, Worcestershire and the Islamic College in east London (Anwar, 1993; Al-Refai, 2011).

Thus Muslims in Britain in addition to or alternatively to state-run schools, often have a dual system of schooling - supplementary schools represented by weekend and evening schools; and independent full-time faith schools. There are many opinions which support the establishment of faith schools: these arguments are based on the fact that faith schools have the potential to promote (through the study of Qur'anic sciences, and Qur'anic learning – Shah, 2016) spiritual and moral values as well as cognitive skills, leading to improved reasoning skills, a more rounded sense of identity, and better academic performance (Tinker, 2009; Halstead, 2018; Berglund & Gent, 2019).

The arguments in favour of Muslim schools are also like those in favour of any religious-foundation school (Oldfield et al., 2013), and the controversies surrounding faith-foundation schools (e.g. Gardner et al., 2005; Breen, 2018) will continue, since there is a strong secular lobby which argues that it is the state alone, and not the religious faith of parents, which should order how children are educated. But we note that in the present century UK government provides funding for an increasing number of full-time schools run by Hindus, Sikhs, Quakers and Seventh Day Adventists (attended by mostly Caribbean-heritage pupils), and these along with the schools founded by Anglicans, Catholics, Jews and Muslims form part of Britain's multicultural heritage in the sphere of education.

Full-time or day-time independent Muslim schools are of two types, in terms of their curriculum. First are religious schools which are founded on the bases of Islamic Education, which teach inter alia the understanding and tolerance of Christians and Jews, as The Qur'an instructs. The second type of Muslim schools are those that teach National Curriculum (NC) subjects alongside other religious and cultural subjects such as Urdu, Arabic, Islamic Studies and Qur'anic Science (Al-Refai, 2011).

In the 1980s the Muslim community began to set up both types of Muslim schools. The first was in London, and now there are over 140 schools educating approximately 13,000 pupils. Legally, religious schools may seek full public funding, but for reasons which are unclear successive British governments have been very slow to give such approval, despite the success of other religious minorities. In comparison, the success of the Jewish population of Britain is notable, and there are now 38 publicly funded Jewish schools, reflecting a significant increase in that number in the past 40 years (Staetsky & Boyd, 2014).

Comparing the 2011 UK Census with Staektsky & Boyd's (2014) figures, we can see that there are 38 state-funded Jewish schools for a population of 59,252 five to 18-year-olds (ratio of schools to population 1:1,559). For the 386,967 Muslim children in this age group the ratio is 1:32,247 - a 21 times advantage in favour of Jewish parents. We wish the Jewish community well in their educational projects, but are puzzled at this difference. Is there some government policy which is (illegally) denying Muslims equity in this matter? We hope that in time the Muslim community of Britain can be as advantaged as our Jewish brothers and sisters in this area of public education funding.

4. Teaching Citizenship: Development of the UK National Curriculum, and Citizenship Education

The importance of teaching citizenship in parallel to or in conjunction with religious education for children of Muslim settlers in Western countries has been commented on by several educational researchers and philosophers (Held & McGrew, 1999; Crick 2000a & b; Osler & Vincent, 2002; Merry, 2007). These include helping pupils to become informed about Islam, promoting spirituality, encouraging pupils to play a helpful part in everyday life, teaching pupils about the economy, democratic institutions and values; encouraging respect for different national, religious and ethnic identities; and developing pupils' ability to reflect on issues and take part in value-based or politically oriented discussions (Kisby, 2009 to 2017; Lister, 2003 & 2011; Waller & Yilmaz, 2011; Moorse, 2015; Whiteley, 2014).

Until the 1988 Education Reform Act and the introduction of a National Curriculum in the 1990s, the UK government had limited control over the content of the curriculum, especially with regard to religious education. Up to that time the Local Education Authorities (LEAs), individual schools and some teachers' associations, tried to promote Civic Education - but these efforts were largely unsuccessful (King & Reiss, 1993). While guidance was non-statutory, the themes were intended to address Section One of the Education Reform Act 1998, where notions of balance and breadth were seen to be important, alongside the requirement for schools to address the social, cultural, moral, spiritual and physical aspects of children's education. This became a statutory requirement of the formal curriculum.

An *Advisory Group on Citizenship* reported to the DES in 1998 (Osler & Starkey, 2001). This group chaired by the philosopher Bernard Crick proposed a national programme of Citizenship Education for English schools, in its final report ('The Crick Report') which crafted a curriculum programme on Citizenship Education (CE) (QCA, 2000). 'The Crick Report' had three main strands - *Social and moral responsibility* - children learning from the very beginning self-confidence and socially and morally responsible behaviour both in and beyond the classroom, both towards those in authority and towards each other (this is an essential pre-condition for citizenship); *Community involvement* - pupils learning about and becoming helpfully involved in the life and concerns of their communities, including learning through community involvement and service to the community; *Political literacy* - pupils learning about and how to make themselves effective in public life through knowledge, skills and values. (QCA, 1998 to 2000).

These developments encouraged the continuing debate about the meaning of nationality, national identity and citizenship and the extent to which individuals and groups from both majority and minority communities feel a sense of belonging to the nation and state (Osler & Starkey, 2001; Adjegbo et al., 2007; Merry, 2007; Lewis & Hamid, 2018).

According to the Crick Report, there are two main reasons why citizenship education was introduced to schools: firstly to counteract a widespread feeling of disinterest in the political process and in community life as expressed by a high levels of voter abstention in elections; and further, to address 'social discontent' in terms of conflict (e.g. prejudice and discrimination) with fellow citizens: and finally to address 'political alienation', a disinterest in or hostility to becoming involved in democratic processes, and values and behaviour supporting a social contract of mutual tolerance.

Citizenship Education (CE) was also as an attempt to deal with *institutional racism*, which had become a serious concern of for governments after publication of the Stephen Lawrence Inquiry Report (on a murdered, black teenager), and other research on the survival or racist attitudes and behaviour in Britain (Home Office, 1999; Lawton et al., 2000). CE was seen, in idealist terms, as part of the movement towards "global education", as part of a movement in which young people in every culture learned more about themselves, and about the international communities of which they are increasingly a part (Banks, 2004).

While CE was developed in an era of confident British multiculturalism, darker clouds of populism were already spreading. A survey of the attitudes of the citizens of the European Union towards minority groups showed that multicultural optimism was *decreasing* in the UK. According to Osler & Vincent (2002), only around 22 per cent of British people could be classified as 'actively tolerant', in understanding and opposing racism in their society, while a further 36 per cent were classified as 'passively tolerant'. By 2008 according to a MORI poll carried out for the Equalities and Human Rights Commission (EHRC, 2009) the number of actively or passively tolerant individuals in the general population had decreased from around 58 percent to 50 per cent. By 2017 attitudes had shifted and consolidated, according to a survey of 10,000 English adults (Walker, 2018). At a time of Brexit those most in favour of leaving the EU were also those strongly opposed to the idea of multiculturalism. Such individuals were often strongly Islamophobic, with more than a half of the population holding reactionary views on at least two of these issues (anti EU, anti-multiculturalism, rejecting civil rights for Muslims). These findings are confirmed by the longitudinal studies of Abrams et al (2018).

These 'prejudiced' individuals were often disadvantaged, had achieved poorly in education, and had poor current or future job prospects. And many of these men and women lived in the northern half of England (where our research on education and employment discrimination reported in this and other Chapters, was conducted). 'Confident multiculturals' tended to live in the larger urban centres of southern England (particularly in London), where more than two-thirds were *not* Islamophobic, or overtly racist in any sphere.[2]

---

[2] However, in NE Leeds (where CAB lives) 62% voted "remain", with over half of Leeds voters choosing to "remain" in the EU.

Findings such as these point to the urgency of seeking ways not only to create occupational advantages and reduce inequalities in England (see Sawyerr & Adam-Bagley 2017 for data and policy discussion on these issues), but also to find pathways in creative education for fostering interpersonal and intergroup tolerance. Citizenship Education is one such pathway (Adjegbo et al., 2007; Lister, 2011).

Successive governments since 2000 have made some efforts to enhance the relationships between pupils of different ethnic origins in terms of citizenship awareness, social relationships and academic achievement, by introducing key policies, one of which was seen as Citizenship: "The teaching of citizenship in all primary schools and as a statutory subject in secondary schools will develop and encourage pupils' understanding and mutual respect of each other's differences." (Home Office, 2002b).

Racism in all its forms had been identified as threatening democracy and the civil rights of minorities in Europe, and needed to be addressed through programmes in schools and in teacher education (Verma, 1989 & 2007). Citizenship Education in England was therefore seen as a means of strengthening ideals of justice, equality and democracy, and challenging racism as an anti-democratic force (Osler & Vincent, 2002; Huddleston & Kerr, 2006).

Citizenship became a required subject in English secondary schools (years 7-11: ages 11-16) from 2002. However although Citizenship was taught in many primary schools as part of the statutory Personal, Social and Health Education (PSHE) curriculum, it had no status as a subject in its own right (Baker, 2013). In 2002 the government Quality and Curriculum Authority (QCA) launched guidelines and an interactive website for teachers to show how schools might value diversity and challenge racism within the framework of the National Curriculum (Osler & Vincent, 2002).

The Crick Report declared ambitious goals:

> *We aim at no less than a change in the political culture of this country both nationally and locally; for people to think of themselves as active citizens, willing, able and equipped to have an influence in public life and with the critical capacities to weigh evidence before speaking and acting; to build upon and to extend radically to young people the best in existing traditions of community involvement and public service, and to make them individually confident in finding new forms of involvement and action among themselves.* (QCA, 1998, pp.7–8)

British citizenship is presented here as inclusive of national and regional differences between England, Scotland, Wales and Northern Ireland, and throughout the report an inclusive and co-operative approach to the various nations which make up the UK was sought. A main aim for the whole community should be, according this government policy:

> ... *to find or restore a sense of common citizenship, including a national identity that was "secure enough to find a place in the plurality of nations, cultures, ethnic identities and religions found in the United Kingdom. Citizenship Education should be able to create a common ground between different ethnic and religious identities.* (QCA, 1998, p.17)

In this idealistic (but largely unfulfilled vision), teaching citizenship in schools was seen as a tool for change. It was about a sense of belonging and also about political participation (Osler & Vincent, 2002).

Kisby (2017), reviewed CE in the English context cites Bernard Crick's dictum which led to the beginning of such education in England (and in the UK), and observed that "Politics is ethics done in public." First, in this model, we teach our students the ethical basis of responsible living, and then through experiential education (Kolb, 1984), enable them to practise these value-based skills. But in Kisby's (2017) analysis, CE curricula in England have been too instrumental, too much of a means of social control, without releasing the creative energies of the individual pupil. CE has not focussed enough on the unequal status of women (Lister 2003 & 2011), and at the present time is in danger of evolving into a curriculum agency of indoctrination and social control whose narrow focus on "British values" denies the validity of Islamic values, and is merely an arm of the government's Prevent strategy, which seeks to suppress (or at least cloak) the spiritual identity of Muslims (Gholami, 2017).

At the same time, we observe that despite its manifest success in increasing civic engagement; interest, knowledge and activity in politics; and a firm understanding of ethical behaviours (according to the controlled, longitudinal study of Whitely, 2014) – the UK government in 2014 withdrew CE from the required curriculum, moving instead to a form of "values education" linked to the Prevent strategy aimed at "countering extremism in British schools" (Holmwood & O'Toole, 2018). "Prevent" is for us, a national tragedy, illustrating the ignorance and fear which has infected even those in high office who misunderstand the aspirations of Muslim citizens. However, the Islamic model of citizenship in Europe (and across the world) is a transcendent one, built on "the Muslim social contract", and will survive (Ceric, 2008; Ramadan, 2010; Maulawi, 2012).

In the Islamic model of citizenship, the child first becomes a citizen of the garden which Allah has created on earth, at the moment of birth when his or her father whispers the *azan* (the call to prayer) into the new born child's ear – an exquisite and moving ritual through which the father bonds to his infant, and promises care, love and leadership throughout life. Muslim citizenship is focussed on this caring relationship which involves mutual support and respect of all family members, reinforced through the family's daily prayer, and learning about the life of The Prophet, and the Message he received. Being a good citizen to everyone, Muslim and non-Muslim alike, should be a way of life. Muslim migrants hoped that the citizenship education of European state schools could support this ideal of citizenship (Maulawi, 2012).

The Social Context of Citizenship

In challenging negative stereotyping, schools continue to have a critical role. Faith-based schools should be permeated by a religious ethos founded on a firm and coherent set of values. Tolerance, for example, is one such value, and such schools have striven to produce materials to communicate their beliefs in a secular society. Tolerance of diversity is a further aspect which faith schools foster and recognize: society is multicultural, multilingual and multi-faith; tolerating such diversity proposes that one's own diversity should in turn be tolerated (Ramadan, 2010). There are a multitude of ways of having faith, of which Judaism, Hinduism and Catholicism are some examples. Indeed, apart from religious pluralism in society, there is also much diversity *within* religious groups and they should be, as communities, excellent examples of tolerant diversity within themselves (for example, the debates and compromises between Protestants and Catholics; between Conservative, Orthodox and Liberal Judaism – Stone, 2003; and between various groups within Islam – Al-Refai, 2011).

As Parker-Jenkins et al. (2005) observed, the citizenship education framework offers faith-based schools the opportunity to explore wider issues and to encourage pupils to perceive themselves, not merely as members of their own religious community but also as citizens of the world, aware of the wider issues and challenges of global interdependence and responsibility. In a plural society of diverse beliefs and practices, Citizenship Education cannot offer one vision of what constitutes a good or moral life. This is also true for Muslim schools, where Islamic teaching encourages culturally diverse beliefs and avoids a one-sided approach to citizenship. The report of the UK government Advisory Group (1998) on citizenship sought to place Citizenship Education within the context of a pluralist society that requires basic but robust civic and political foundations. A key passage in the report states:

> *A main aim for the whole community should be to find or restore a sense of common citizenship, including a national identity that is secure enough to find a place for the plurality of nations, cultures, ethnic identities and religions long found in the United Kingdom. Citizenship Education creates common ground between different ethnic and religious identities.* (QCA, 1998, p. 14)

Education for citizenship has in fact become a leading concern for educational policy and debate in the advanced economies of the English-speaking world, where education systems. researchers and agencies have produced valuable reports, evaluations and reflections on curriculum guidelines, and school programmes in surprising numbers (Osler & Vincent, 2002; Huddleston & Kerr, 2006; Keating et al., 2010; Lister, 2011; Halstead, 2018).

The UK Department for Education (DES) advocated that teaching citizenship was a *whole-school issue* declaring that the ethos, organisation, structures and daily practices of schools have a considerable impact on the effectiveness of Citizenship Education. Adopting a whole school approach to provision should ensure that citizenship runs through everything schools do. According to the National Curriculum Handbook for teachers (Huddleston & Kerr, 2006), schools have had a crucial role in providing opportunities for all pupils to learn and achieve, and in promoting children's spiritual, moral, social and cultural development; as well as preparing them for the opportunities, responsibilities and experiences of life.

Delivering Citizenship Education

The Citizenship Education curriculum has been divided into several stages: the Foundation Stage, where the curriculum for primary school children is meant to make a positive contribution to children's early development and learning that is critical to their perception of themselves and their relationships to others; and Key Stages one and two, which aim to promote pupils' personal and social development, including health and well-being. The programme of study described in the non-statutory guidance manual for PSHE and citizenship covers the knowledge, understanding and skills that prepare pupils to play an active role as citizens (Huddleston & Kerr, 2006). This aimed to promote pupils' personal and social development, including health and well-being: evaluation studies have shown these goals can be successfully met (Baker, 2013; Whiteley, 2014).

In Key Stages three and four (middle and final stages of secondary schooling), statutory requirements were set out in the National Curriculum. Planning of provision was intended to reflect the need to ensure that pupils have a clear understanding of their roles, rights and responsibilities in relation to their local, national and international communities. The three strands in the programmes of study were: knowledge and understanding about becoming an informed citizen; developing skills of enquiry and communication; and developing skills of participation and responsible action (Whiteley, 2014).

The Scope of Citizenship Education

In September 2006 OFSTED published a major review of the teaching of Citizenship Education (CE) in secondary schools (OFSTED, 2006). The report was based on inspection of a large number of schools and observed that despite "significant progress", there was not yet a strong consensus about the aims of citizenship education, or about how to incorporate it into the curriculum. "In a quarter of schools surveyed, provision is still inadequate reflecting weak leadership and lack of specialized teaching." However, in another quarter of schools, it was judged that satisfactory progress in the understanding, organization and delivery of citizenship education had been made. Probably, the report infers, the 'failing' schools were those experiencing stress for a variety of reasons. Profiles of such failing schools have been presented by Sawyerr & Adam-Bagley (2017).

The OFSTED report found that schools had responded to the goals of Citizenship Education (CE) sometimes in very different ways. "Some, a minority, have embraced it with enthusiasm and have worked hard to establish it as part of their curriculum. Others, also a minority, have done very little." The inspection report found contrasted methods of delivering CE, though most offered it as part of PSHE classes. Many teachers were unclear about the standards by which CE should be assessed, and written work in CE was poorer than that produced by the same pupils in other subjects. Standards were best when CE was included in GCSE subject teaching. However, in 2018 only 18,704 pupils were entered for GCSE examinations in Citizenship, compared with 260,300 who were entered for Religious Studies.[3]

---

[3] The Religious Education curriculum, which takes various forms according to the religion of focus but also containing elements of comparative religion, also has some focus on social ethics and citizenship behaviours.

Given the initial difficulties in establishing Citizenship Education as a viable part of the core curriculum of primary and secondary schools, the evaluation of CE by Whitely (2014) did offer encouraging findings. Whiteley's random sample of 1,510 young adults enabled him to compare the political consciousness, political participation, group and community engagement, and understanding of political and personal values across groups according to their exposure to CE. In all of these areas those who had experienced the full amount of CE had significantly *better* outcomes (in terms of achieving CE curriculum goals) than those who had only partial, or no Citizenship Education at all.

However, other factors contributed to good outcome scores on the measures used: currently being a college student and/or having graduated and now in full-time work; not unemployed, regardless of educational level; being male; and amount of parental education. The best long-term CE outcomes then, were in young men with significant amounts of 'social capital'. They began as advantaged students, and the CE lessons helped them flourish as political animals, and increased their 'social capital' (Kisby, 2009). But, as Lister (2003) has argued, there may be a pro-masculine bias in how CE lessons have been presented. And CE may be less well-delivered in schools suffering high levels of deprivation, or with multi-ethnic populations (Keating & Benton, 2013). But these are schools which have the *greatest* need for good citizenship education programmes.

Whiteley's (2014) sample was too small to partial out the effects of religious status (e.g. being Muslim) on how pupils absorbed and acted upon citizenship instruction. Our own study, drawn from schools in Northern England (see Sawyerr & Adam-Bagley, 2017, for further details of our samples), does allow us to do this. The research question, which Dunhill (2018) poses is this: "Does teaching about human rights, encourage pupils to practice, protect and promote the rights of others?". Put another way, should citizenship education for *all* pupils be part of the promotion of the social contract which will bind together a plural society, based on the equality of rights and duties for all citizens?

5. Objectives of our Research on Citizenship Education and Muslim Students in English Schools

Our aim has been to investigate differences between Muslim and state schools, contrasting ways of delivering Citizenship Education in Muslim schools, and examining the role of Muslim schools in preparing pupils for a role in British society by focusing on both Islamic education, and education for being a good citizen.

This study of young adolescents has further aimed to explore ways of delivering citizenship in Muslim schools in terms of the National Curriculum guidelines, the differences in teaching citizenship between Muslim and state schools, the attitude of pupils in Muslim schools towards the teaching of citizenship, the attitude of educational professionals, parents, and community leaders towards the teaching of citizenship; examining the role of Muslim schools in preparing pupils for a role in British society; investigating the relationship between Islam and citizenship; and demonstrating the possible contribution of Islamic Studies to the teaching of citizenship.

In the urban areas from which schools have been sampled, the 2011 census has identified the social geography of the ethnic and religious diversity of the North West of England from which the sample was drawn: Blackburn had the highest proportion of Muslims in the North West (27% of Blackburn's population); Pendle came second (17%); then Oldham (16%); Rochdale was fourth (14%); and Manchester fifth (11%). Many Islamic organisations have emerged in these urban centres to meet the needs of the new minority - mosques, youth clubs, weekend schools and, latterly, independent Muslim schools. There are now 15 Muslim schools within the areas in which our research was undertaken. Thirteen were secondary schools - seven of them are for girls-only, and five for boys-only.

The study not only a selected sample of pupils, but is also a case study of Muslim schools, which were accessed because of their willingness to participate, and their geographical location in northern England. The final selection of Muslim schools for study is biased in that it reflects our perception (from initial field work) of what is "best practice", in which Citizenship Education was delivered in contrasted but always in enthusiastic ways by the schools selected. In policy terms, we are seeking to describe what appear to interesting and indeed exemplary ways in which religious principles inform Citizenship Education, and vice versa.

The final sample chosen for intensive study included five Muslim secondary schools which were confident and active in their delivery of citizenship education, from different regions in the North of England. Three were girls' schools and two were for boys. These were five schools which felt confident or satisfied with how they were delivering CE, and thus the researchers were unlikely to have accessed the 25 percent of schools whom OFSTED (2006) had judged to be failing in their delivery of citizenship education. The principal researcher (N.A-R) of course, unlike the OFSTED Inspectors, had no right of access to a random sample of schools. The five comparison state schools all included Muslim pupils, and their willingness to be included in the research also reflected their enthusiasm for delivering Citizenship Education.

Pupils had the right to decline the completion of the questionnaire or the interview, since this often took time from other activities, such as voluntary sport. The final samples then are likely to be biased in favour of the most confident schools, and included those pupils who found CE particularly interesting or important – it is interesting in this context to note that 88 per cent of pupils in Muslim schools agreed to complete a questionnaire or interview, compared with less than 60 percent of all pupils in state schools, and the one faith school (Anglican, which resembled state schools in terms of ethos and curriculum). The state schools and the Anglican faith school were selected because the head teachers were enthusiastic about their CE programmes which they felt to be successful; because these schools had a significant number of Muslim pupils; and because they were usually situated within the catchment areas of the Muslim secondary schools.

Table 5.1 Gender and Year of Study in Students Responding to Questionnaires in State and Muslim Schools

	State Schools	*Muslim Schools*	*Chi-squared, & Cramer's V*
Female	43 (38.7%)	90 (51.1%)	Chi-squared 3.72 (1d.f.) V= 0.121, NS
Male	68 (61.3%)	86 (48.9%)	
Year 10	55 (49.6%)	102 (57.9%)	Chi-squared 1.62(1d.f.) V= 0.092, NS
Year 11	56 (50.4%)	74 (42.1%)	

Total number of questionnaire respondents: 111 from State Schools, 176 from Muslim Schools. NS = not statistically significant. Cramer's V is a non-linear measure of association between two variables.

In the 5 Muslim schools 176 pupils (90 females and 86 males) responded to the questionnaire, and 23 pupils (11 females and 12 males) responded to the extended interviews. There is a slight gender bias in the samples, more females completing questionnaires in the Muslim schools than in the state schools. This is because three of the five Muslim schools contained only girls. There is also a slight age bias, with more respondents from Year 10 in the Muslim schools. However, results did not differ significantly between Muslim and state schools when separate analyses by gender and year of study were undertaken for both questionnaire and interviewee respondents, and therefore results in the following tables and discussions have not been presented separately by gender, age or year of study.

The sample from the state schools included 111 pupils who responded to the questionnaire, and 29 pupils who were interviewed personally, answering not only the topics covered in the questionnaire, but also giving their opinions on a range of relevant topics. As with the Muslim schools' sample, the ages, gender and other demographic profiles of those interviewed personally were similar to those completing questionnaires.

6. Research Findings: The Citizenship Curriculum

Findings from Muslim and Non-Muslim schools revealed three categories of information: how citizenship is timetabled in schools; topics within the teaching of citizenship; and the content of citizenship education. Citizenship was represented in the timetable in two different ways: citizenship as a subject; and citizenship taught within other subjects such as PSHE, History, Geography, English, Islamic Studies or Religious Education. The table below indicates that only two out of ten schools presented citizenship as a completely separate lesson.

Table 5.2 Manner in Which Schools in the Study Teach Citizenship

School code	The way they present citizenship in the school timetable
State 1	through PSHE and History
State 2	through PSHE
State 3	through History and Religious Education
State 4	through English, History and PSHE
Faith 1	through Geography, History, RE and Assemblies
Muslim 1	through a separate lesson
Muslim 2	through Islamic Studies and PSHE

Muslim 3	through Islamic Studies, Assemblies and Form time
Muslim 4	through a separate lesson as well as PSHE
Muslim 5	through Islamic Studies and Assemblies

In these Muslim schools it was very clear that teachers did not want to impose a different model of citizenship to replace the existing one that is inherent in traditional Islamic education. What they were attempting to do was to satisfy the religious and cultural needs that had been neglected by the NC. Therefore, there are two models of teaching citizenship in Muslim schools: the first is teaching the same topics of the National Curriculum (NC) alongside the Muslim perspective where this was considered necessary. Secondly was teaching some of the NC themes, and adding the Muslim perspective within it.

The scarcity of time in the school timetable was apparently the only reason for not teaching the full NC of citizenship. In Muslim schools in general there is very limited extra timetable space because of the several extra subjects they teach, such as two weekly lessons for the Qur'an, three for Arabic, two for Islamic Studies and two for Urdu (in schools where the majority of children have Pakistani ethnic heritage).

7. Citizenship Topics: Pupil Responses

Data were collected from the pupils through 339 questionnaires and interviews: pupils were first asked to list the topics they studied in citizenship. Their responses have been categorised into twelve logically different fields. These are: Health, Rights and Responsibilities, General Attitudes, Personal Concerns, Religion, Economic Issues, Community Spirit, Tolerance, Social Issues, Political Issues, Education, and Environment.

There are some clear and statistically significant differences in the topics within the civics curriculum experienced or recalled by pupils in the comparisons between the Muslim and the state schools, regardless of gender and age differences between the two samples.

In state schools the most frequently occurring topics were 'health and safety' focussing on drugs, sex, alcohol and smoking. Secular teachers considered these issues as ones which young pupils might need to understand in their wider social participation, but also often approached the issues in terms of health and safety (e.g. 'safe sex') and postponement (e.g.

delaying sexual activity, and delaying use of alcohol, until the age of 18). In the Muslim schools, pupils were taught about Islamic doctrines of the sacredness of marriage, and the importance of not being promiscuous or having sex before or outside of, marriage.

The second most frequent category for Muslim schools is that of 'rights and responsibilities'. This field was less frequently mentioned in state school responses. This demonstrates a significant difference between the two systems, in terms of following or interpreting the National Curriculum. Pupils in Muslim schools most frequently mentioned the following responsibilities: obeying and following rules and laws; respecting the rights of parents and neighbours; displaying awareness of rights due to women.

The third most frequently recorded response in Muslim schools, and the second ranked set of problems in state schools is that of 'social issues'. Pupils in Muslim schools highlighted four main aspects of such attitudes: crime, bullying, good manners, and law-abiding behaviour. Similarly, in state schools, bullying and crime were frequently addressed issues. The fourth most frequent area of study mentioned by pupils in Muslim schools was that of 'personal issues', while in state schools such issues were only atypically mentioned.

In Muslim schools where the citizenship study programme had Islamic input, pupils were able to identify topics such as Islam's world view, the sanctity of life, being good Muslims, and life after death. One of the interviewees stated that in citizenship lessons they study "how to be good Muslims in society". However, in state schools few pupils referred to studying about God, or about religions. Pupils in both types of school highlighted many topics relating to 'community spirit'. In Muslim schools these topics were: respect for others, social problems, social and racial harmony, and caring for the community. In state schools salient topics were: living in cities, looking after the community, giving to charity, and having good relationships. In terms of tolerance, pupils in both types of school mentioned that they studied racism, prejudice and attitudes towards others. However, pupils in Muslim schools most frequently highlighted discrimination as one of the leading topics they had frequently covered.

Table 5.3 Perceived Issues Addressed in Citizenship Education: Comparison of Questionnaire Responses in State and Muslim School Samples

Issue	State/Faith Schools All pupils	Muslim Schools	Chi-squared with 1 d.f.	Cramer's V
Health & safety issues	68 (61.2%)	80 (45.4%)	4.06 p=.000	0.13
General issues	39 (35.1%)	72 (40.9%)	0.73 NS	0.06
Educational issues	34 (30.6%)	14 (7.9%)	23.53 p=.000	0.3
Social Tolerance	26 (23.4%)	21 (10.0%)	5.75 p=.016	0.15
Economic issues	21 (18.9%)	30 (22.2%)	0.52 NS	0.04
Social issues	20 (18.0%)	20 (11.4%)	1.99 NS	0.09
Community issues	16 (14.4%)	34 (19.3%)	0.82 NS	0.03
Political issues	8 (7.2%)	19 (10.8%)	0.65 NS	0.06
Religious issues	9 (8.1%)	25 (14.2%)	1.87 NS	0.09
Environmental issues	8 (7.2%)	0	6.52 p=.012	0.18
Rights & duties	6 (5.4%)	71 (40.3%)	40.20 p=.000	0.38
Personal issues	2 (1.8%)	47 (26.7%)	28.08 p=.000	0.32

Note: NS = not statistically significant. p = probability of a chance result. Total number of pupils completing questionnaires for state schools, 111; for Muslim schools 176. Cramer's V is a correlational measure for use with non-linear data.

Table 5.4 Perceived Issues addressed in Citizenship Education: Comparison of Questionnaire Responses of Muslims in State Schools, and in Muslim Schools

Issue	Muslim pupils in State schools	Muslim pupils in Muslim schools	Chi-squared with 1 d.f.	Cramer's V
Health & safety issues	20 (70.0%)	80 (48.4%)	5.51 p=.019	0.16
General issues/attitudes	13 (44.8%)	72 (40.9%)	2.47 NS	0.09
Educational issues	15 (51.7%)	14 (7.0%)	23.50 p=.000	0.32
Tolerance	4 (13.8%)	21 (11.9%)	0.10 NS	0.02
Economic issues	5 (17.2%)	39 (22.1%)	0.13 NS	0.04
Social issues	12 (41.3%)	20 (11.4%)	14.83 p=.001	0.29
Community issues	4 (13.8%)	34 (19.3%)	0.20 NS	0.05
Political issues	6 (20.7%)	19 (5.7%)	1.48 NS	0.10
Religious issues	6 (20.7%)	25 (14.2%)	0.39 NS	0.06
Environmental issues	4 (13.8%)	40 (4.9%)	1.39 NS	0.15
Rights & responsibilities	5 (17.2%)	71 (40.3%)	5.69 p=.005	0.17
Personal issues	0 (0.0%)	47 (26.7%)	8.59 p=.001	0.22

Note: NS=not statistically significant. p = probability of a chance result. Total numbers of Muslims in state schools, 29; in Muslim schools, 176. Cramer's V is a correlational measure for use with non-linear data.

Table 5.5 Perceived Issues Addressed in Citizenship Education: Comparison of Questionnaire Responses of Muslim and Non-Muslim Pupils in State Schools

Issue	Muslim pupils in state schools	Non-Muslim pupils	Chi-squared with 1 d.f.	Cramer's V
Health issues	20 (70.0%)	48 (58.5%)	0.85 NS	0.09
General issues/attitudes	13 (44.8%)	26 (31.7%)	1.62 NS	0.12
Educational issues	15 (51.7%)	19 (23.2%)	8.93 p=.008	0.27
Tolerance	4 (13.8%)	22 (26.8%)	2.03 NS	0.14
Economic issues	5 (17.2%)	16 (19.5%)	0.03 NS	0.03
Social issues	12 (41.3%)	8 (9.7%)	12.44 p=.000	0.35
Community issues	4 (13.8%)	12 (14.6%)	0.01 NS	0.01
Political issues	6 (20.7%)	2 (2.4%)	8.12 p=.004	0.31
Religious issues	6 (20.7%)	3 (3.6%)	6.12 p=.013	0.25
Environmental issues	4 (13.8%)	4 (4.9%)	1.39 NS	0.15
Rights & responsibilities	5 (17.2%)	1 (1.2%)	7.85 p=.005	0.31
Personal issues	0	2 (2.4%)	0.00 NS	0.04

Note: NS = not statistically significant. p = probability of a chance result. Total number of Muslims in state schools is 29; total of Non-Muslims in state schools is 82. Cramer's V is a correlational measure for use with non-linear data.

Tables 5.3 and 5.4 compare the perceptions which pupils in state and Muslim schools have of topics experienced in citizenship education. Overall, state school pupils (including those in the one secularized Anglican school) were significantly more likely to recall health and safety issues, educational issues, social tolerance, and environmental issues as topics within their citizenship classes. In contrast, Muslim pupils were significantly more likely to recall an emphasis on rights and responsibilities, and on personal issues.

Table 5.5 compares responses of the 29 Muslim pupils in the state schools with the questionnaire responses 176 Muslim pupils in Muslim schools. Muslims in state schools were significantly *more* likely to recall health and safety issues, educational responsibility issues, and important social responsibility issues, in comparison with their Non-Muslim peers in the state and faith schools. Thus pupils in Muslim schools were significantly more likely to recall the topics of rights and responsibilities, and personal responsibility issues. On first reading, these findings indicate that within state schools, Muslim pupils are simply absorbing the ethos of citizenship education which is offered in their particular school.

But inspection of Table 5.5 reveals that *within* state schools, the 29 Muslim pupils do experience citizenship education in somewhat different ways than their Non-Muslim peers. The Muslim pupils were significantly *more* likely to recall or to have been interested in educational responsibility issues, important social issues, political issues, religious issues, and rights and responsibilities within their citizenship classes in state schools, compared with their Non-Muslim peers. The reasons for this are not entirely clear, but it may be that Muslim pupils bring to citizenship education their own ethical, moral and spiritual outlook which leads them to experience citizenship instruction in particular ways. It may be that their life as Muslims has created a special type of "moral person", who more readily absorbs the prosocial messages of Citizenship Education in state schools. The differential responses of Muslim pupils in state schools could not be accounted for by any differences in age, year of study, gender, or individual school attended.

These findings imply then that Muslim pupils in Muslim schools may bring to their citizenship education a set of values derived from home and Mosque, which means that they would experience *added benefit* from the teaching of citizenship topics. In contrast to state schools, the Muslim schools had an Islamic input and contribution into the citizenship curriculum regardless of the form through which they teach citizenship.

Findings from Muslim schools suggested that their citizenship lessons placed significantly more emphasis on rights and responsibilities, and on matters of personal conduct, while state school pupils were more likely to recall issues such as personal health and safety.

8. Pupils' Views on the Good and Bad Citizen

The data for this section were collected from the open-ended questionnaires and interviews in both types of school, Muslim and State. Pupils responded to this part of the questionnaire and the interviews positively and generously, and a wealth of data was gathered for this topic. The data fell logically into the following fields: behaviour, law and order, politics, community spirit, environment, religion and tolerance.

Good Behaviour

From the perspective of many pupils, good behaviour is the main quality which differentiates between the good and bad citizen. Pupils highlighted a set of manners and morals that the good citizen should possess and another set of negative attributes that summarise the bad citizen. One of the Muslim single-faith school pupils interviewed declared that the good citizen is the one who is "clean, tidy, someone that upholds the law, willing to help others and has an open mind about things". In contrast, the bad citizen is one who is "uncooperative, dysfunctional, dishonest, impolite, and rude. He is also a citizen who is not altruistic by nature, and breaks the law and most likely causes others harm." According to another Muslim pupil, the good citizen is the one who is "caring, responsible, confident, lawful, kind, and generous", and the bad citizen is the one who is "uncaring, unlawful, selfish and chaotic". Another Muslim student said that the good citizen is: "helpful, enjoyable, can be trusted, thinks before he/she reacts", while the bad citizen is the "trouble maker, criminal, alcoholic and has bad behaviour".

The opinions of many pupils revealed that the good citizen must if possible, be kind to everyone in society, school, home and the street. 'Being kind' was important because it presents a good impression and about the ideas and thoughts one carries. Muslim pupils in particular mentioned that the good citizen has to be well-mannered in general because such behaviour indicates that you are carrying a set of values that enables you to interact with others and deal with them appropriately. As a good citizen you have to display respect for others as well as yourself, your family and your friends. Some pupils noted that the good citizen must have respect for parents, and he must maintain amicable relations with them. Also, you had to learn to be trustworthy amongst your family, friends, and colleagues. Another Muslim pupil observed:

> *A good citizen is one who is himself a better person and then utilizes his personal qualities in order to help others and make the environment better for others. While a bad citizen is one who neither cares for himself nor the environment, a person who does wrong themselves but also encourage others to do wrong. I would also consider a person bad if they may be doing good themselves but not encouraging others to do good.*

Many pupils mentioned that you should also be generous in spending from your own funds or other things you possess such as time, in order to aid other individuals and organisations. You have to care for those with whom you live such as siblings, parents and elderly family members such as grandparents:

> *A bad citizen is someone who is arrogant, proud, bad mannered, and a hazard to society or a menace, full of selfishness and they will not abide by any laws or morals.*

Many pupils, both Muslim and non-Muslim in both types of school said that this 'bad citizen' is one who has no respect for anything or anybody around him. He is selfish and nobody can benefit from him within the home, or in the wider environment. According to pupils, bad citizens are those who commit crimes and harm others. They may additionally find themselves involved in drugs and addicted to alcohol. They are those who steal, are arrogant, offer bad role models, are disruptive, bully fellow pupils, backbite, lie, cheat, and fight with others.

Law and Order

Pupils identified adherence to law and order as the second most important measure of the good or bad citizen. Knowing your rights and fulfilling your responsibilities is part of being a good citizen, according to pupils from both Muslim and state schools. Pupils believe that the good citizen is the person who obeys the laws and rules of the land. One of the interviewed state school pupils noted:

> *Good citizens abide by the law; they try not to hurt anybody's physical or mental state ... Bad citizens are troublemakers, criminals, alcoholics, have bad behaviour, cheat, thieve, are bad and feared.*

Another said of the 'good' person: "They know their responsibilities. They are law abiding, will do their best to make their country safe". Another pupil maintained that the good citizen is the one who: "... follows the law of the land". Pupils made it very clear that the citizen, whether a student, parent, teacher, politician or footballer, must abide by the law of the country to which he or she belongs.

Pupils noted that the good citizen should know his or her various rights in society. They knew too that the citizen who has a set of rights also has responsibilities and duties that they must fulfil. From the data emerged some responsibilities obligatory for the good citizen. These included awareness of health and safety issues for others in one's environment, since everybody is obliged to take care of their family members' health and safety. Moreover, it is the responsibility of the good citizen to act as a positive member in society through paying one's bills, making tax contributions and not seeking benefits if able to work.

Conversely, failure to adhere to law and order was seen by many as a characteristic of the bad citizen. Pupils define the bad citizen as the one who does not respect the law and breaks it at any opportunity. An interviewee stated that the bad citizen is the one, "who understands but chooses to be deviant towards society's law and norms. He breaks laws, is irresponsible and uncivil."

Community Spirit

Pupils in Muslim and state schools were of the opinion that the good citizen is one who helps other people in the community where he or she lives. They generally added that helping society and the community in general is a positive characteristic of the good citizen. One of the Muslim pupils observed:

> *A good citizen would be someone who helps their community, people and the environment. It would be someone who socializes with others and creates friendship with people. A bad citizen would be someone who stays reserved and doesn't take part in community activities.*

According to pupils' views each individual citizen should be actively involved in the community in terms of helping it to excel. A good citizen should be:

> *Loyal to their nation, willing to contribute to society, abiding by the law, respectful to others, helpful and works hard in society.*

Pupils also perceived such a citizen as being kind to all members of his or her community including neighbours, friends, family and colleagues. For example, neighbours might be of a different religion or ethnic background, and being good to them demonstrates sensitivity to the theme of citizenship. An interviewed pupil said that the good citizen is the one who is "kind, helpful and does things which benefit the community". As a good citizen you ought to care for the community and you should be aware of what is happening within it. Furthermore, you have to take part in ongoing activities in a positive manner. One state school pupil observed that:

> *Good citizens respect other people in the community; get involved in the community, such as charity work. They help each other and do not act with prejudice or racism to others. A bad citizen is someone who classifies people according to their colour, religion.*

Tolerance

Living in a multi-ethnic, multi-faith society requires a high degree of tolerance on the part of the individual, at the personal and as well as at group level. A number of pupils from Muslim and state schools considered the good citizen to be one who is tolerant when dealing with anyone in society. Being tolerant, from the point of view of pupils, requires respect for fellow citizens of divergent cultures, ethnic backgrounds and religions. One of the Muslim pupils stated that the good citizen is the one who "respects other people in the community, helps others, does not show prejudice and is not racist to others. Also he is involved in the community." Another said:

> *Good citizens are those who know their responsibilities. They are law abiding. Bad citizens are those who discriminate. They may be racist and bully others.*

In the pupils' views, the tolerant citizen is the one who treats everyone in society equally and is against discrimination and racism. An interviewed pupil stated that the good citizen should "accept all races, treat each other as equal, fights against racism. Helps others who are in trouble, tries their best to protect the environment". Several pupils spontaneousl cited racism and discrimination as the most unacceptable behaviour within society. Another said that: "... a good citizen helps to raise money for charity and respects people and their ethnic origin".

Political Participation

Pupils, both Muslim and non-Muslim highlighted many qualities for the good citizen in terms of political activities. The good citizen should be a staunch supporter of his or her country and contribute to the political life in a positive manner. Participating in political life by minorities was a crucial issue from the Muslim pupil's point of view. Many highlighted other issues such as being patriotic. The bad citizen, from a political perspective, according to pupils, is one who does not care about their country. One Muslim pupil claimed, "A bad citizen is someone who is disloyal to his nation, unwilling to contribute to society and refuses to work for the nation."

Findings from the questionnaire study indicated that 78 per cent of pupils in Muslim schools observed that studying Islam was similar to studying citizenship, while about half of pupils in state schools had the same view on the relation between Religious Education and citizenship. These differences are statistically significant. According to some Muslim pupils one of the similarities between studying citizenship and Islamic studies was that both were teaching a variety of social issues such as parenting, raising children, social harmony and socialising with others. One of the questioned pupils stated that both RE and CE are about: "parenting, socialising, equality, social harmony, bringing up children and duties". Moreover, some Muslim pupils (10 per cent) referred to the connection between Islamic Studies and citizenship as being due to both subjects instructing pupils about equality between different peoples in society.

9. Summary of the Study of how Adolescents Experience Citizenship Education in Muslim and State Schools

The findings of this study of "best practice" secondary schools reveal that pupils from both types of school, Muslim and Non-Muslim, are aware of their rights, and their responsibilities to the wider society. They would also like to contribute towards improving society when they become adults, through many different routes. The responses of the young people are for the most part, refreshing in their enthusiasm.

The majority of Muslim pupils for example, saw Citizenship Education (CE) as interesting and important. They saw such education as helping them understand and live in the wider society: "... it teaches us how to live in a multi-ethnic, multi-faith society". Many pupils thought that CE could help them to relate to the wider community in harmonious ways, and had taught them good values, in terms of right and wrong. It had taught them to respect others not only in school, but also in the wider society. CE was seen by many pupils as a factor in self-development – for Muslim pupils in particular it was a way of acquiring a meaningful social identity in a complex and sometimes hostile culture.

Muslim pupils in particular said that their citizenship classes had helped them understand both their rights and their responsibilities, and had also enhanced their understanding of the moral directions of their faith. "We can now see the big picture." In this 'big picture' many of the young Muslims interviewed or answering questionnaires, saw themselves both as striving to be good citizens and to be good Muslims, as integrated and complementary tasks.

An intriguing set of responses has been elicited by questions and interviews about the nature of a 'good' and 'bad' citizen. Most Muslim and Non-Muslim pupils who responded appeared to be both knowledgeable and enthusiastic about the characteristics identified. The good citizen is seen as someone who is kind, helpful and altruistic not only in his or her school or local community, but in the larger society as well; they are someone who obeys and respects the law; someone who is tolerant, and a productive member of the community; and someone who cares for the environment. One may ask: are these the responses of idealistic youth which would have emerged even without CE; or has the education in citizenship tasks given pupils a frame of reference with which to elaborate this idealistic view of 'the good citizen'?

It is apparent that a large part of the sample in both Muslim and state schools, including pupils, teachers, as well as religious and community leaders believe that teaching citizenship in schools was important to pupils' education. Most of the pupils in the sample believed that studying citizenship helped them to become aware of their role in society, and to become good citizens. Citizenship lessons were enjoyable for the majority of pupils, although these views may be based to a certain degree on sample selection, which was biased both towards "best practice" schools, and to the most enthusiastic students who agreed to take part in the research.

Given this, Muslim pupils do appear to have a preference for instruction on citizenship to be given by a teacher who reflects Islamic values. In Muslim schools pupils are subject to religious influence in terms of prosocial behaviours and positive attitudes towards others, whatever their ethnicity or faith. These schools were rather successful in building their pupils' value systems. Islamic Studies and lessons in the Qur'an and the life of The

Prophet, are often used to support the teaching of citizenship, and this too appears to be quite successful. Muslim schools are therefore judged to have the potential for the development and evolution of a new form of Muslim national identity within Britain through citizenship education, in useful and meaningful ways.

The large majority of pupils regardless of religious affiliation, felt that they "belonged" to British society. The main reason given was being born or permanently residing in England. Another reason given was pupils' understanding of the concept of equality. They considered that everyone in Britain, their motherland, should have the same opportunities, follow the same rules, receive the same respect, and have the same rights in society regardless of his or her culture, religion or ethnic origin. Having English friends, according to Muslim pupils, enhanced their feeling of belonging. It is emphasized here that it was considered important by Muslim schools, organisations and institutions to encourage Muslim pupils in single faith schools to interact positively with pupils of other cultures and backgrounds. Furthermore, religious freedom in Britain was one of the issues that was highlighted by pupils in Muslim schools. Muslim pupils especially said that they belonged to British society because they could freely practise their religion.

The reason why some Muslim pupils expressed a sense of alienation reflected their perception of widespread racism and discrimination in English society. As for some of the non-Muslim respondents in state schools, their reason for a sense of alienation was their perception (however mistaken) that liberal governmental polices regarding immigration and asylum seekers were "disadvantaging white people".

One of the most significant aspects of this study has been to try and answer the question of whether Muslim schools and their teaching of citizenship could be a tool for inclusion, or conversely whether such teaching in Muslim-led schools serves to isolate Muslim pupils from the wider community. Muslims in Britain are keen to remain recognised and valued members of society. According to Muslim belief, one of the main aims of Muslim schools is to foster an Islamic identity and to help transmit Islamic belief systems and values for the future generations, through the education system. Many Muslims feel that faith-based schools are the best way to achieve this aim, and the evidence from this study supports this view.

While full-time Muslim secondary schools are valiantly trying to incorporate CE within their curriculum in various ways, they still face a number of problems. Firstly the amount of work required to develop not only the National Curriculum subjects, but also religious education and the integration into wider society of pupils, is a major challenge. Secondly, financial problems minimize the ability of these schools to enact their plans, and can restrict them from the use of new and effective resources. The reason for this is that most of these schools are dependent on pupils' fees and contributed donations from the Muslim community. At present few receive any funding from the government, despite the legal right to seek such funding under the 1944 Education Act. Currently less than 10 percent of Muslim secondary schools in England are grant-aided in this way, compared with several thousand Anglican, Catholic and other religious schools in Britain.

It appears that we enlisted into the research confident and co-operative schools who are particularly likely to have been successful in their Citizenship Education. Clearly, the curriculum and model of delivery of CE in Muslim schools is changing and evolving, and from this and other research new models of practice can be proposed. Our findings support those of Reza Gholami (2017), who argues for a more creative form of citizenship education, which fosters individual identity "liberation" in both Muslim and non-Muslim pupils.

Muslim secondary schools, as our study shows, can be very successful. Despite some problems, their citizenship curriculum can effectively educate young people in expressing confident and tolerant values concerning other religions, and the wider society. Many of the pupils drew on Islamic values too, in presenting a multicultural identity that is optimistic and idealistic in the expression of a set of prosocial values (Halstead, 2017).

The need for a well-funded, vigorous Islamic secondary school system is emphasized in the study carried out in Redbridge, London by Bakhsh and a community action research team (Bakhsh, 2007) on drug use amongst young Muslims. Key workers estimated that some 20 per cent of Muslim adolescents in the Borough of Redbridge (which has a Muslim population of about 23 per cent) had taken illegal drugs at some time, and many had become regular users. This is an astonishing statistic, given Qur'anic proscriptions against alcohol and by inference, other drugs. The secular secondary schools which these young people attended had entirely failed to provide anti-drug education; on the contrary, Asian youth became absorbed into local subcultures in schools, many of which offered drugs of various kinds. The Muslim parents of Redbridge remain chronically poor, largely because of ethno-religious employment discrimination, and in the absence of state funding these parents cannot afford to set up their own Muslim-foundation secondary schools.

It is very clear from the five Muslim schools in the British North West in our own study that illegal drug use was something that young people saw as a form of retreat which undermined the actions of a good citizen. We must conclude that Muslim secondary schools of the kind we have studied need to be much more widely available for Muslim youth.

The continuous presence of Islamophobia inevitably influences the lives of Muslim adolescents in Britain, and the struggle to provide Muslim schooling. For example, an examination of Muslim school websites by a group called Civitas produced the spurious assertion that Muslim schools were fostering extremism (e.g. praying five times a day) in a way which "prevents integration". This led the Secretary for Education in 2012 to "check on the spiritual and cultural ethos" that is fostered by Muslim schools. But since that time Islamophobia in Britain has grown apace, evolving into the government's Prevent programme, a fugue of anti-religious spite which resulted in events such as the removal of Muslim governors from Birmingham schools (Holmwood & O'Toole, 2018).

We conclude that our study has shown how valuable British Muslim secondary schools can be in enabling the roles of young people, whose attitudes to the wider society are magnanimous and enlightened, and who have used their Islamic education to take maximum advantage of their Citizenship Education. These results do as Dunhill (2018) expected, support the idea that citizenship education (generously and comprehensively applied) can make a valuable contribution to the social contract which is an essential element of a successful plural society. The idealistic youth we interviewed, now in their early 'twenties, give us hope for the future of Islam in Britain, and for the evolution of a co-operative and stable multicultural society.

But we must all weather a plague of current events which undermine multiculturalism, as populism takes its toll. Since 2014 Citizenship Education is no longer a required part of the secondary school curriculum, and the new secondary academies have been given free reign to design new curricula.

10. Summary and Conclusions

Islam urges that all individuals, male and female, should be educated to the fullness of their capacity, in ways that reflect Qur'anic teaching, in order to become both spiritual beings and good citizens, magnanimous to their family, to their fellow Muslims, and to the wider community of Muslims and non-Muslims alike. From the very beginnings of Islam, religious schools (Madrasahs) were set up in Mosques, and this educational model has grown, changed, developed and expanded. Now the model has grown beyond the Mosque, and there are now established Muslim secondary schools, colleges and universities.

In Britain too there are established Muslim secondary schools and colleges offering quality education. Yet in the past decade such institutions have been under pressure from the rising tide of Islamophobia, which now floods not only sectors of public opinion, attitudes and behaviour, but also seeps into sectors of government. This may be the main reason why Muslim schools fail to receive financial support from public funds, unlike schools provided by Catholic, Anglican and Jewish religious groups.

We marshal available evidence on the status and progress of the Muslim community of Britain. This community, mainly of Pakistani and Bangladeshi cultural origin live in urban centres in London, Glasgow, The Midlands and Northern England. The evidence paints a picture of an often well-educated community, with firm goals for the upward mobility of their children, loyal to their new country, while also remaining faithful to Islam's basic purpose for humanity. But this community is well aware of the hurts of Islamophobia which infect both the media and everyday interactions. As subsequent Chapters will show, employment discrimination is a factor in the lives of Islamic minorities in Britain, and this community suffers significant amounts of poverty and poor housing as a result (Heath & Li, 2015b).

As negative pressure grows and ethno-religious discrimination increases, the Muslim minority in Britain expresses a greater need for the establishment of Muslim schools, as a way of fostering the Islamic dignity and identity of youth. Contrary to Islamophobic fears, such educational projects do not undermine "integration": rather, they provide an education which produces confident adolescents who are proud of being Muslim and proud of being British. Their confident identity allows them to be excellent citizens who contribute to the wellbeing of British society in important ways.

In this model of "integration" all majority and minority groups are secure in their own identities, and tolerant of each other within a mutual social contract, which orders the rights and duties of both minority and majority groups. However, the growth of Islamophobia has led to attempts to impose an "assimilationist" model on minorities such as Muslims and Jews.[4]

The persistent rise of Islamophobia in the present century has made it challenging for Muslims to identify fully with Britain as their "mother country", and it is surprising that empirical studies have shown their strong and enduring allegiance to the country in which they live, despite the insults and petty persecutions built into the government's Prevent programme, aimed particularly at young Muslims who boldly practise their faith.

The institutional racism of Britain's Prevent programme has been chronicled and exposed by the lobby group Human Rights Watch (HRW, 2016). Government anti-terrorism legislation, imposes on teachers the responsibility of spotting and reporting to the police anti-terror units, "suspicious behaviour" in pupils. Thus a teenager was reported, interrogated, his house and computers searched, his parents and siblings questioned because he arrived at school one day with a badge displaying the words "Free Palestine". Bizarre examples are documented by the report, including a 4-year-old Muslim boy at nursery school who told his teacher he was drawing a "cucumber". The teacher heard this word as "cooker bomb", so the terrorist police were called, the boy's family and house searched, and the adults interrogated until it was finally decided that the family did in fact buy cucumbers at the local market.

Several thousand innocent Muslim children and their families in Britain have been interrogated by the counter-terrorism police (HRW, 2016; Grierson, 2019) including families known to us, such as our nephew who was unfortunate enough to declare "Allahu akbar" when hitting a six in a school cricket match. The Prevent message has been picked up by non-Muslim bullies in some 'sink estate' schools, who know they can verbally and physically abuse Muslim children with little fear of retaliation. We have

---

[4] Concerning Jewish minorities in Britain and Europe the model is not so much assimilationist, but rather one of absolute rejection, based on the politics of paranoia, denying or minimising the Holocaust (in 20% of respondents to research questions across Europe), and assertions that Jews 'have too much power and are manipulating politics and the economy,' with estimates of the actual number of Jews in society which far exceed reality (Allen-Greene, 2018; Baynes, 2019). As the Holocaust has taught us, even Jews who hide their religious identity through "assimilation", are liable to be sought out, persecuted, denied civil liberties, and even killed.

cases on file of families known to us, giving evidence for this assertion: if the Muslim child fights back, they and their family run the risk of being labelled as potential terrorists. Many Muslim adolescent girls dare not wear their hijab in school.[5]

In fact, young Muslims in Britain, who are second and third generation children of immigrants are increasingly committed and fully practising Muslims, and only about one percent show any interest in, or support, for violent action against Islam's enemies. Muslim parents remain interested in and committed to Muslim schools (full or part-time) for their children, and we have examined this movement in historical detail, focussing in particular on the Citizenship Education (CE) curriculum in Muslim and state schools. We explore the basis of the CE curriculum in relation to religious education (RE), and the Islamic ethos of Muslim schools, and report a study of ten secondary schools (5 Muslim, 1 Anglican, 4 State) in North West England, in areas with high proportions of Pakistani and Bangladeshi ethnic populations.

We have chronicled the history of what seems to us be the admirable endeavour of successive governments (before 2010) to design a Citizenship Education curriculum for schools, which aimed to increase pupils' political literacy and prosocial behaviours. Some schools (it is uncertain how many in the country) have been enthusiastic and successful in introducing this curriculum (Whitelely, 2014). In the 10 schools in our own study in North West England, half of them faith schools for Muslim pupils, we have shown how successful CE can be in producing optimistic and idealistic young people (both Muslim and non-Muslim) who have a clear identity and set of values which should make them ideal citizens who would fit into a social system described by Modood (2013) which incorporates "multicultural integration".

However, the rider should be added that our evidence is based on schools selected *because* they appeared to be successful in delivering CE before the research began, schools which welcomed the researchers. Other schools, less confident in their CE programmes, did not allow the researchers to have research access. As we know from Whitely's (2014) research, it is likely that up to a half of all schools have neglected CE teaching, or had not offered it at all, despite it being a national curriculum subject. And in 2014,

---

[5] One 'game' practised by teenaged, Islamophobic girls is to slap a Muslim boy across the face in the playground, confident that the boy dare not fight back. Verbal protest will be met with a torrent of obscene abuse.

government withdrew CE as a compulsory subject, allowing new academies to design their own curricula.

The important point which emerges from our research concerns Muslim pupils in both Muslim and state schools. Muslim pupils, according to our results, absorb the lessons of CE more readily, and on the face of things emerge as more rounded citizens, more prosocial in their attitudes. Just as CE had enabled students from advantaged backgrounds to "flourish" as well-rounded, good citizens in Whitelely's (2014) cohort, so Muslim students in our study (and that of Wilkinson, 2015a) have flourished in their absorption of the ideals of the good citizen in English society.

These young Muslims need, too, the patience of The Prophet, in enduring the burdens imposed by Islamophobia and discrimination, as they make their way through life, as good multicultural citizens.

CHAPTER SIX

MUSLIM WOMEN (AND MEN) AND YOUTH SEEKING JUSTICE: ENGLISH AND DUTCH CASE STUDIES OF PREJUDICE, RACISM, DISCRIMINATION AND ACHIEVEMENT

CHRISTOPHER ADAM-BAGLEY AND MAHMOUD ABUBAKER

1. Introduction and Overview

The measurement of discrimination in employment is a key variable in understanding dynamics in the nature of and change in 'race relations', ethnicity, Islamophobia, alienation and multiculturalism. Measuring such discrimination using 'situation' and 'correspondence' tests was influenced by John Rex's sociological analyses (Rex, 1970), and was pioneered in England in the 1960s, and then replicated in Europe and America in later decades.

Logically, underlying discriminatory *action* (denial of access to employment, promotion, housing, or services; only allowing access to a diminished degree, such as offering lower wages; asking for higher rent; and direct verbal and physical abuse of minority people) is the holding of prejudiced *attitudes*. But not all prejudiced people have the opportunity, or the bravado, to put their prejudiced and stereotyped views into practice, except perhaps, in the anonymity of the voting booth.

Attitudes – positive or negative – are generated at three levels:

Culture, in which a set of values are shared by the majority of people;

The Social System, in which roles and status in society influence attitudes, beliefs and norms;

Personality, through which early temperament interacts with systems of family, school and peer group in creating a stable set of attitudes towards oneself (self-concept) and to others.

This theoretical system of how attitudes are generated, and how these are translated into discriminatory action, is inspired by the work of Talcott Parsons and Thomas Pettigrew, and elaborated in our previous research (Adam-Bagley & Verma, 1979; Adam-Bagley, Verma, Mallick & Young, 1979).

More recently we have added a fourth level of action, that of *free will*. This is because although individuals are tempted to act wrongfully because of the pressures and dispositions of their personality, values, and place in a social system (variables acting in concert, or even synergistically) almost always individuals have the possibility of choosing *not* to commit bad or evil actions. This is clearly implied by Islamic theology, which holds that Allah tests each individual (Muslims and all others in whom rests a divine spirit, or soul) each day, with new choices. The choices we have to make are influenced by all of our previous choices, so that the available matrix of choice options is determined by the social situations which we have created for ourselves. There is a fascinating similarity between this idea, and Hume's 'compatibility' idea of free will (Russell, 2007; Adam-Bagley, 2015b).[1]

Understanding cultural influences on prejudice requires a *cross-cultural approach*, and our chosen countries for comparison are England and The Netherlands, with work begun in the late 1960s and continued to the present time, with new studies of ethnic and religious discrimination in employment, presented in the next Chapter. The present Chapter offers an overview and analysis of Dutch, English and American studies of employment discrimination, as well as the evolution of prejudiced attitudes - from being 'merely' towards people of colour, developing into strongly held beliefs of dislike, opposition and even hatred expressed towards a religious group (e.g. Muslims), who are often also people of colour, with Muslim women experiencing the most hatred in two seemingly civilised European countries, The Netherlands and England.

---

[1] Freely willed choice, and freedom to choose social actions, are essential components of dialectical critical realism (Bissel, 2019).

2. Multiculturalism, Prejudice and Plural Societies: Dutch and English Comparisons

We focus on the theme of the *plural society*, and the different blocs or pillars (*verzuiling* in The Netherlands) which make up the plural society, arguing that Britain has the possibility of adopting the model of "plural multiculturalism", in which all ethnic and religious groups have equal status, based on a system, an implicit social contract, of mutual tolerance. We explore too the "Muslim social contract" through which Islamic minorities in Europe seek to be not 'newly arrived' groups seeking tolerance, but instead seek acceptance as permanent and equal partners with all other groups of society. 'Integration' in this model means becoming a loyal group within society, mutually tolerating all other groups in a peaceful manner, but refusing to be 'assimilated' if this means a compromise of religious principles, dress and diet, and the use of a traditional language in private settings.

Ideological and Religious Pluralism - The Case of Islam

Writing about Europe, Mustafa Ceric (2008) points to the mutuality of rights and duties which make up the plural society in spiritual (and social) terms, drawing on Qur'anic sources. The scholarship of this pluralistic position is soundly based in both Qur'anic and Hadith analyses (Eaton, 2008). Historically, Islam has been much more tolerant within a national state, of other monotheistic religions than Christianity has been of Islam and Judaism (Lewis, 1984; Esposito, 1998). Islam has indeed the distinction of being the world's oldest value tradition in which a coherent set of ideas and practices have laid the foundations of ideological pluralism, and the mutual tolerance of different Abrahamic religious traditions within the same state. This was established early in Islamic history through Qur'anic revelation. Abrahamic religions of Judaism and Christianity have traditionally been tolerated as minority groups within Muslim-majority societies (Armstrong, 2002; Lewis,1984; Karabell, 2007).

All that was required of such minority groups in Muslim states was that they should reciprocate this tolerance, follow their own religions faithfully, obey general laws, and if a working adult pay a basic tax. Their rewards were protection and tolerance (including support from Islamic welfare systems) but without the obligation of military service. Jewish groups fleeing from religious oppression in Spain were offered sanctuary and protection in Muslim countries (including Palestine) for many centuries (Lapidus, 2002).

This harmonious balance was undermined when Western colonialism suppressed the Muslim polity of North African and Middle Eastern countries (Lewis, 1984), and more directly in 1948 with the founding of the State of Israel, which was imposed on Palestine without that nation's consultation, or material assistance from the major powers.

Our reading of this history is that international powers, in horror at the revelation of the Nazi holocaust, washed their hands of the so-called "Jewish problem" by resettling Jews in a land long occupied by Arabs, to the profound disadvantage of the latter.[2] As the American Muslim scholar Mehnaz Alfridi (2014) puts it: "The Holocaust was a crime inflicted by Europeans for which Palestinians paid the price." By this she meant that Christian ideas about Jewish responsibility for Christ-killing provided the ideological foundation of National Socialism's holocaust of Jewish people.

Once "Israel" was created, the Palestinian problem was conveniently forgotten in the West's "orientalist" agenda, which relegated Muslim nations to a discarded fragment of forgotten colonial history, just as Western anti-semitism was largely unremembered (Said, 1978; Penslar & Kalmar, 2005; Karabell, 2007). The rejuvenation of the West's orientalist agenda is seen in the rise of Islamophobia in the 21st century (Zebiri, 2011).

Maryum Mehmood (2017) in an ingenious research design, compared Islamophobia and its victims in modern England with antisemitism and its victims in Weimar Germany of the 1930s, using interviews with a cross-section of Muslims (in England), and diaries and published accounts of Jews, on their experience in Germany. She explores the concept of "collective self-esteem" in trying to understand the varied responses of victims of ethno-religious discrimination, and shows some important similarities between Jewish and Muslim reaction to ethno-phobia - prejudice ranging from degrees of abuse and hatred up to an actual holocaust.

Gijsberts & Hagendoorn's (2017) exploration of Tajfel's social identity theory (Tajfel, 1981; Abrams et al., 2005) in understanding the generation of, and reactions to inter-group prejudice leads to a further hypothesis:

---

[2] But see the final Chapter, in which we make the case, based on Qur'anic sources, for an "Islamic Zionism", arguing that Jews and Muslims should occupy Palestine together, on equal terms. This position has surprisingly strong support from Jewish scholars who offer a "Post-Zionist" model. As Spangler (2019) puts it: "The Zionist dream comes true [but] be careful of what you wish for." The Zionist politics of Israel are in a morphogenic state, and the final chapter is not yet written.

creating persecuted outgroups enhances the group self-esteem of economically disadvantaged majority groups. Antisemitism and Islamophobia are useful elements for the functioning of society, in which the alleged faults of targeted outgroups enhance the self-concept of the majority. In writing about European Antisemitism and Islamophobia, Topolski (2018) draws a conceptual comparison between the idea of 'the good Jew, the bad Jew' and 'the good Muslim, the bad Muslim'. The bad "others" are those who refuse to live quiet, subordinated, non-visible lives. Creating images of 'bad other's is a necessary part of maintaining the majority's sense of power and sense of control.

3. Racial, Religious and Ethnic Discrimination: Historical and Sociological Perspectives

In the sociology of "race relations", discrimination in access to employment, housing and services has been of central importance (Rex, 1970). Discrimination on grounds of race, ethnicity and religion is deeply rooted in all human societies, and countering it must involve social, economic, political and psychological understanding and strategies (Banton, 1996). In this sociological model attitudes drive actions in various ways. Measures of prejudice seek to measure the *knowledge* (biased or otherwise) which various role-holders have about minorities (cultural, religious and racialized groups) – and even about people with 'disabilities' such as those with epilepsy, or psychiatric illness (Adam-Bagley & King, 2004; Adam-Bagley, 2015b).

This knowledge is often stereotyped, reflecting the views of media and various arenas of "false news". Biases are often deeply held, and barely conscious to the actor (Deitch et al., 2003), who nevertheless acts upon them if he or she is in a position to deny access of a stereotyped minority to goods, services, employment, salary awards, or promotion. Prejudiced attitudes are held with varying degrees of strength, and may not be acted upon when there are clear rules and procedures by which such bias could be exposed. Prejudiced but powerless persons (e.g. 'poor whites') may not be able to deny employment to minorities, but they can at least engage in verbal abuse and physical attacks on 'weak targets' such as Hijab-wearing women (Busby, 2018).

The 'prejudiced but powerless' mainstream populace (with poorer self-esteem, poorer psychological adjustment, and less cognitive capacity or educational achievement) may be able to gain subjective or symbolic social power by voting for reactionary politicians, or by supporting reactionary positions in referenda. Although this social psychological model was established with English and Dutch data in the 1970s (Adam-Bagley, 1973; Adam-Bagley & Verma, 1979; Adam-Bagley et al., 1979) we have not come across studies in the intervening years which offer evidence contradicting our model of how prejudiced attitudes are formed, and are directed at particular cultural targets.

Prejudice and discrimination remain the same: only the generation who engage in racist attitudes and behaviour have changed. Now the objects of their prejudice, once the hated "coloured immigrants", then the generalised group of "Pakis" (including Sikhs and Indians), are now (in addition) the Islamic menace which allegedly threatens the stability and well-being of the British and Dutch people and their culture. North American studies of Islamophobia and its effects paint a similar picture to that of Europe (Lean, 2012; Esposito & Kalil, 2011).

We follow the model of the American sociologist Talcott Parsons (Lidz, 2009) on understanding ethnic relations, with the original thesis that all human actions can be understood and explained by the interaction of three levels of analysis: the cultural (hence the need for cross-cultural and transnational studies); the social (hence the need for understanding rules, roles and relationships in social systems); and the personal (hence the need for personality and self-other studies in understanding prejudiced attitudes). The methodology of cross-cultural and personality analysis we take from Thomas Pettigrew, who has recently reappraised his six decades of work in this field (Pettigrew, 2019).

The Continued Thread of British Racism: Prejudice, Xenophobia and the Hatred of Islam

There is, despite a façade of a liberal society and its legislation, a persistent thread of racism, xenophobia and Islamophobia in British society, which is only partially checked by any legislative social action. Earlier studies of attitude cohorts showed that about a quarter of Britons were firmly racist in their attitudes to various groups (Rose et al., 1969; Adam-Bagley, 1970). More recently a major surveys of public opinion (Abrams et al., 2004 to 2018; Lowles & Painter, 2011) have shown that around a quarter of Britons still hold very negative attitudes towards ethnic and religious minorities, including Muslims, as well as towards those challenged by disabilities.

This 'prejudiced' population tends to be less qualified, more often blue collar or lower white collar in status. On the positive side, more than two-thirds of those questioned in the most recent surveys believe that religion was a private matter, and should be tolerated; and that minority groups should be protected in this regard, with only about a third of respondents being markedly Islamophobic (Abrams et al., 2018).

Even prior to 9/11 in 2001, a strong current of anti-Islamic ideology pervaded Christian countries of Europe and North America (Strabiac & Listhaug, 2006). In Britain a long-standing prejudice against foreigners in general, and Arabs in particular, evolved into a more coherent Islamophobia, even before 9/11 after which it increased markedly (Poynting & Mason, 2007). The purveyors of extreme prejudice in most Western countries are typically the "white" third of the population who are nominally adherents of Christian "values", and have lower social status in society (Fetzer & Cooper, 2003). UK research has shown that in fact adherents of extreme right-wing parties, those most opposed to the "Islamic menace" have little coherent Christian or religious identity, and rarely attend any place of worship (Coid et al., 2016).

One of the cries of rage by the xenophobic third of Britain's population is that ethnic and religious minorities are failing to "integrate" (effectively, failing to become subordinated to the nominally Christian values of their new culture). These critics of "integration" argue also that too often minority groups (particularly Muslims) live in ghettos, "no-go" areas of cities. But analysis of British Census data in which religious affiliation is recorded, showed that the group most often living in tight residential clusters were Sikhs, followed by Jews and Hindus. Muslims were less likely to live in such "ethnic clusters" (Peach, 2006). Thus the evidence from social geography indicates that in Britain "ghettos" rarely exist, and upwardly mobile minority immigrant groups and their children tend to spread out rather than cluster together, unless there are special reasons for not doing so (e.g. when walking to a synagogue is a religious necessity).

Legal Checks to 'Incitement to Racial and Religious Hatred 'in UK

Britain, for all its confusion about what consists "British values" and how citizens should acknowledge and live these values[3], does have a

---

[3] A recent attempt by the so-called Prevent Strategy initiated by the UK national government to "prevent" Muslim youth being radicalised, adopting instead

comprehensive set of laws which can prevent discrimination of various kinds, as well as legislation regarding the protection of minority and multicultural rights. This is relevant regarding the spate of scurrilous cartoons, which sought to depict The Prophet in an insulting and obscene manner[4]. It is likely that few people in Britain (unlike the general population in the rest of Europe) will have seen these cartoons. This is because of 2007 legislation in Britain, *The Incitement to Racial and Religious Hatred Act*. An editor or publisher in Britain (or any media distributor importing print or broadcast materials) who displays such cartoons or similar material is liable to an unlimited fine, and indeed imprisonment, for distributing such media. This might be one factor influencing individuals in Britain with strongly held negative attitudes to minorities, from using these prejudices as guides for actual behaviour (Abrams et al. 2005 to 2018).

The key British value which for us is salient and seems worth preserving is that of "critical multiculturalism" as Farrar (2012) terms it, the value premise that we are all - men and women, Muslim and non-Muslim, and of whatever "racial" origin - equal, and our principle value is that of pursuing our own interests through a *social contract* with other groups in society within a framework of mutual tolerance, respect and support (Crick, 2001a). In this "post integration" model, Islam is a basic religion of Britain, one which fosters inter-ethnic and inter-religious tolerance, and good citizenship (Ramadan, 2012).

Nevertheless, the twentieth century demand that newly immigrant groups to England (Irish Catholics, European Jews, African-Caribbeans, Indians and Pakistanis, and various Muslim minority groups) should "integrate" was (and remains) effectively a demand that they should accept a subordinate role in society, giving up their 'alien lifestyles', manifest for example in dress, and public religious observance.

At its base, the call for minorities to "integrate" is fundamentally racist or Islamophobic, since the corollary is that those who fail to "integrate" should be subject to control, discipline, and exclusion (Adam-Bagley, 2008a;

"mainstream British values" has been a notable failure, since it is not clear what British values actually are (Tyrer, 2013).

[4] For example a 'Charlie Hebdo' cartoon which portrayed The Prophet prostrated in prayer, his backside uncovered, from which emanates a speech bubble uttering obscene phrases, implying gross hypocrisy etc. We were reminded of the incident in Medina, in which the decayed entrails of a camel were thrown on to our Prophet's back, as he was prostrated in prayer (Safiur-Rahman Al-Mubarakpuri, 2008). The Prophet, characteristically, forgave his persecutors.

Fekete, 2008; Kundari, 2007; Lowles & Painter, 2011; Farrar, 2012; Law, 2013; Tyrer, 2013). If immigrants are indeed to "assimilate", the loss of identity which the dominant majority requires, if accepted will leave very little of the immigrant's identity left, except his or her skin colour (Parekh, 2001). This, like the core of Jewishness or Islam in the individual, just will not go away, however hard the individual tries (Modood, 2017 & 2018).

Indeed, as Sian at al. (2013) argue, ethno-religious racism is a factor which threatens a pacific world order in many countries, England and The Netherlands amongst them, and offers a major political challenge to every culture. Phases of economic deprivation, and the rise of populist ant-ethnic sentiment and extreme right-wing or nationalist parties, tend to go in parallel. In the present world we are entering a new phase of hatred of minorities.

4. The Plural Society Concept and the Tolerance of Integration: England and The Netherlands Compared

The idea of *pluralism* is socially and politically important, and in current British society has been expressed as multicultural pluralism (Modood, 2013), a concept which sometimes engenders fear and loathing amongst sectors of the British population and their political leaders, since the concept implies that minority groups have rights to retain cultural and religious values, while subscribing to a social contract which involves the toleration of the rights of other groups within the plural society. We define a plural society as:

> *A nation or society which in its legal, social and constitutional arrangements supports the existence of distinct blocs (defined by such factors as ethnicity, values, religious observance) whose rights and freedoms are legally guaranteed in ways which mutually respect the rights of other blocs. Inherent in these arrangements is a social contract between members of any bloc with the state, and with members of other blocs, to foster tolerance, and equality of rights and aspirations, with legal protections from all forms of discrimination.*[5]

Ramadan (2010 & 2012) for example, draws on both theological and political concepts in his proposals for a liberal social contract which accepts

---

[5] Other forms of 'plural society' have existed in the recent past, often resulting from colonialist imposition of arbitrary national boundaries across linguistic and ethnic divisions – the inclusion of 'Bangladesh' within the country of 'Pakistan' in 1948 is an example. Such 'plural societies' are inherently unstable.

the integrity and moral aspirations of Muslim minorities as plural blocs in Western societies.

The sociological concept of pluralism emerged from British anthropological studies which described political societies or countries containing highly contrasted cultural groups (in terms of ethnicity and religion), but which had reached modes of accommodation in which each group tolerated the existence of the other group(s) from self-interest, as a way of protecting the individual aspirations of their own group in way which did not clash with those of other blocs. Overarching co-operation in these cultures usually took the form of economic exchange, and political arrangements in which governing parties acted in the interest of all cultural groups. The prime example of such a plural society in Europe in the past century has been that of The Netherlands (Adam-Bagley, 1973).

The purpose of studying Dutch society at that time was to try and understand, by means of a Weberian cross-cultural analysis (Banton, 2013), why The Netherlands, superficially similar to Britain, had successfully absorbed a refugee population (from former colonies in the Indonesian archipelago) in a span of less than five years, that amounted to more than 10 percent of its total population, into a society that tolerated a variety of minority groups. This was in marked contrast to Britain, in which some mainstream politicians promised "rivers of blood" if "non-white" immigration continued (Rose et al., 1969).

One answer seemed to lie in the Dutch plural society model of social structure in which well-developed "blocs or pillars" (*verzuiling*) absorbed immigrants according to ethnicity and religion, and traditional political arrangements ensured degrees of balance and harmony between the blocs. Britain, without such constitutional arrangements, tended to reject commonwealth immigrants and refugees who were perceived as being unable to "fit in" to British society and its values (values which were then, as now, only vaguely defined).

We have also argued that pluralism in society is, under conditions of mutual tolerance and cultural exchange, likely to change its character over time, and this has proved to be the case in The Netherlands, which has become an increasingly secular country. An indicator of blocs of a plural society "withering away" is the amount of marriage *between* (compared to *within*) members of such blocs, in the form of inter-religious and inter-ethnic marriages (Adam-Bagley et al. 2018). Another, ironic, indicator is the degree to which "minority" youth are absorbed into mainstream categories of deviant behaviours (Adam-Bagley, 1983; Baksh, 2007).

Analysis of the Dutch 'plural society' system identified separate cultural and religious blocs engaged in legal and social interactions that ensured mutual respect and tolerance between the blocs. Immigrants from the former colonies were usually absorbed into these blocs, with minimal tensions. The exception was the case of Muslim immigrants from North Africa and Turkey, who, not fitting into any of the existing blocs, were often subject to hostility and discrimination.

By 2000, the crumbling of the blocs of the Dutch plural society (Kremer, 2013) coincided with an increase in immigration of Muslim minorities, also associated with an increase in anti-Islamic prejudice (Bracke, 2013; Fetzer & Soper, 2013). This has continued, and was paralleled by the emergence of a far-right party, the PVV which prior to the Dutch general election of March 2017 was supported by more than 15 percent of potential voters (Corde, 2015).

This party advocated the banning of all future immigration of Muslims, closing of mosques, imprisonment without trial of "radical" Muslims, and forbidding distribution of the Qu'ran, seen as a seditious text (Wilders, 2012). However, the supporters of this party tended to live *outside* of Randstad Holland, the commercial, manufacturing and financial core of The Netherlands, which includes major Dutch cities, The Hague, Rotterdam, Utrecht and Amsterdam. Voting for both centre and radical parties in the Randstad area in 2017 was strong, pushing the PVV vote into third place in the March 2017 election. This has not stopped the far-right party supporters from infecting larger cities however, and they are thought to be responsible for the vandalism of Muslim schools in major cities. This may be one reason why Dutch mosques are rarely labelled as such (in Dutch, at least).[6]

Despite the surge in anti-minority attitudes (Van der Valk, 2015), research on those living in Randstad Holland indicated that they had on average, more favourable attitudes to Muslim minorities than those living in other parts of The Netherlands (Zick et al., 2008; Gonzales et al., 2008; Gieling

---

[6] The Mosque attended by one of us in Amsterdam is located on the floor above a Turkish grocer's store and warehouse, identified as a mosque only by a small sign in Turkish. Two notable exceptions, of visibly magnificent mosques, are the Essalam and Mevlanen mosques of Rotterdam.

et al., 2010)[7]. The apparent reason was that since most Muslims lived in the Randstad area, familiarity with and interaction with Muslims had influenced favourable attitudes—a well-known thesis developed in the work of Thomas Pettigrew, and shown to be valid in various contexts in America and Europe (Pettigrew & Tropp, 2008). This idea is borne out by Dutch research on multicultural classrooms (Bakker et al., 2007). However, this finding was not replicated in Adida et al.'s (2016) French research, which indicated a strong cultural aversion to Muslims in interpersonal situations which was not reduced by prolonged interaction. What is crucial here is the strength of pre-existing prejudice prior to interethnic interactions: equal-status contact can overcome weak or moderate prejudices, but not strong ones.

Some Dutch sociologists, such as Essed & Hoving (2014) have argued that, despite an official claim of "tolerance", there is an undertow of racism in Dutch culture. This we had observed in fieldwork in The Hague; in an overtly tolerant society, we described "race riots" in which Moroccan migrant workers were attacked and their homes burned, by mobs of the white, working class (Adam-Bagley, 1973). Our argument then was that this kind of "discipline" imposed on a strange minority, outside of the blocs of the plural society, was part of the strict social control by which bloc pillarization was maintained. Now several decades later the blocs have crumbled, but Islamic minorities have to face continued forms of Dutch racism in seeking a stable identity within a rapidly changing society (Essed & Hoving, 2014)

There is, despite a façade of liberal legislation, a persistent thread of racism, xenophobia and Islamophobia in both British and Dutch societies. Earlier studies of attitudes showed that at least a quarter of Britons were firmly racist in their attitudes to various groups (Adam-Bagley & Verma, 1979). More recently, major surveys of public attitudes (Abrams et al. 2005 to 2018; Lowles & Painter, 2011) have shown that up to third of Britons hold generally negative attitudes towards ethnic and religious minorities, including Muslims. According to the most recent evidence (Abrams et al., 2018) about a quarter of Britons continue to be strongly Islamophobic.

As The Netherlands' social structure became less defined by plural blocs (e.g. Protestant, Catholic, Secular), so Britain had until about 2002 moved

---

[7] In Dutch elections for the EU Parliament on May 23, 2019 (42% turnout of voters), PVV's share of the votes fell to 3.5%, compared to their 13.3% share in the 2014 EU elections. As a result, PVV lost all of its 4 seats in the EU parliament.

in the opposite direction, towards a greater degree of plural multiculturalism, in which newly arrived groups (e.g. Asian refugees from Uganda in the 1970s) were accommodated by the UK government in a purposive manner which allowed them to retain a protected ethnic and religious identity within British society (Marett, 1993)[8]. At the highpoint in British multiculturalism (circa 1980), the Rose et al. (1969) principle of multicultural integration (taken from a speech by Roy Jenkins, a Labour Home Secretary) appeared to be achievable (Farrar, 2012). That principle had declared:

Integration should be defined not as a flattening process of assimilation but of equal opportunity, accompanied by cultural diversity, in an atmosphere of mutual tolerance.

This idea had also been reflected in the European Union's "basic principles" (cited by Fekete, 2008):

Integration is a dynamic two-way process of mutual accommodation by all, both immigrants and residents, of Member States.

But, as Fekete (2008) and others have shown, current policies in most countries of the EU vary from this principle to a greater or lesser degree (Renton & Gidley, 2017). The Netherlands is no longer a paragon of tolerance, and there is great pressure on for example, Muslim minorities, to "assimilate" or at least to remain a silent religion, with no public manifestations of dress, worship or public behaviour (Van der Valk, 2015; ENAR, 2016; Jung, 2016; Vellenga, 2018). Similar points are made by Abrams et al. (2016, 2018) who point to the failure of successive British governments to implement equality policies which could benefit access to employment by Muslims, and by Black and Ethnic (BEM) minorities – two overlapping groups.

In Britain as well as in The Netherlands (and in other European countries), Muslims in Europe have become like "the new Jews", convenient scapegoats whose suppression may divert energies from criticizing the true state of inequalities in society (Greenslade, 2005; Bunzl, 2007; Meer, 2013 & 2014; Vellenga, 2018). In The Netherlands today Jews are a very small minority, a reflection of collaboration of a war-time Dutch government with

---

[8] This is illustrated by the rather high proportion of the residents of the Midlands city of Leicester who have the Gujerati surname of 'Patel'. Leicester was the principle city for government relocation of refugees expelled from Uganda. Though penniless at that time of expulsion, these Gujerati immigrants are now frequently represented among the ranks of successful professionals and business people.

Nazi policies for their removal. Despite the virtual absence of Jews, anti-semitism parallels Islamophobic sentiment amongst sectors of the Dutch populace (Vellenga, 2018). And as in other European countries including the UK, anti-semitic acts of violence have increased, in parallel to the rise of "populist" movement (Porat, 2018).

With the crumbling of the blocs or pillars of the Dutch plural society has come a certain mood of national anxiety as The Netherlands struggles to find an equitable policy for accommodating non-European *allochtonen* (a pejorative but commonly used word implying 'otherness' in people from afar) including the increasing number of Muslim immigrants who come mainly from North Africa, and Turkey. Violent events in 2004 led to conflicts in popular opinion on how to handle *allochtonen*, leading to a mood of "social anxiety" in the Dutch nation as a whole (Doppen, 2010; Brocke, 2013; Slootman & Duyvendak, 2015) and even led, in a sociologist's term, to a kind of "national aphasia" (Weiner, 2014) a forgetting of a colonial past and the involvement of The Netherlands with social movements, good and bad, in many parts of Europe and the world.

Liberal and social democratic governments have tried to stress a certain form of Dutch identity through the introduction of a prescribed "canon" (or special curriculum) focussing on Dutch history and citizenship (Doppen, 2010; Bron & Thijs, 2011). And at the classroom level, at least, indigenous Dutch youth in metropolitan areas relate in largely non-biased ways to their peers from different faith or ethnic backgrounds (Verkuyten 2005; Verkuyten & Thijs, 2013).

The ultimate success of these Dutch educational programmes is unknown, but it is fair to say that international surveys (from UNICEF and OECD) of social health, welfare and adjustments (analysed and summarised by Sawyerr & Adam-Bagley, 2017) place Dutch adolescents at the positive end of the measures of healthy adolescent development. Britain has poor scores on these rankings (e.g. of children leaving secondary schooling early; failing to enter further and higher education; premature sexuality; drug involvement; self-harm). These disadvantaged outcomes are apparently linked to Britain's markedly unequal division of national income, in comparison with most other European countries.

The evidence from England suggests that it is the children of "poor whites", the traditional underclass or 'reserve army of labour' (Engels 1845/1978) who are most likely to hold reactionary attitudes towards a stereotyped lower status group (immigrants and ethnic and religious minorities). These social psychological models which we based on data from the 1970s (Adam-Bagley et al., 1979) on status, self-evaluation, relative deprivation and prejudiced attitudes appear to hold true today, and have some valence in the understanding of the social psychology of prejudice in Europe (Abrams et al., 2005; Verkuyten, 2005; Pettigrew & Tropp, 2008; Pettigrew 2017 & 2019),

5. Muslims in Europe as a Minority Group, and the Continued Plural Society Debate

Besides accommodating and tolerating Jewish and Christian groups in countries where it was a majority religion, Islam has a long history as a minority group itself, beginning with the movement from Mecca to Medina where, as refugees Muslims were a minority and worked out ethical standards and procedures for conduct in relation to the majority population. Thus was born the *Fiqh of Minorities*, or law of minorities (Al-Refai & Adam-Bagley, 2012). Since then in nations where Muslims have been minorities they have tried to apply these principles, emphasising that in return for tolerance they will work hard to be self-sufficient and law-abiding.

Muslims expect that the outcome of their offered tolerance and respect for the host culture will be that they are allowed to worship and engage in the multiple religious practices of Islam, be allowed to dress modestly as their religion requires, and have their children educated either in Muslim-run schools, or in schools which respect their religious aspirations. These include principles of modesty, so that pupils will not be required to undress or change clothes other than in private, that girls may wear religious dress (e.g. hijab), and sit separately from males if they so choose.

These straightforward expectations of Muslim minorities in Britain are rarely considered by those who require the "integration" of Muslims in British society – and such critics usually fail to define what they mean by integration. Sociologically speaking, "accepted integration" means that the minority group are tolerated in their customs of religion, dress, diet, clothing and personal language – and are legally protected from discrimination in access to services and employment, and from acts of religious and racial hatred. In return the minority group will live peaceably with neighbours, according them the tolerance which they themselves enjoy. And the minority group will maximise their talents through education and training, working hard to support their families and making (as all citizens should) minimal demands on state aid.

Classic studies of "race relations" in Britain pointed to Jews as an "ideal" minority group in this regard (Rose et al., 1969). In more recent decades, Muslims now seek this ideal form of integration. Like Jews, Muslims seek upward mobility on the basis of stable adaptation, as well as retaining traditional languages for use in home and mosque, wearing traditional religious dress, and seeking protection from discrimination through legal means. Like Jews, Muslims are hard working and law abiding, and draw on a set of values which are expressed as being ideal citizens, helping everyone regardless of their religion, who occupy their local community. That is an ideal, but xenophobic forces in British society often make it difficult to achieve. Much public dislike and even hatred seems to be expressed against Muslims simply because they are different, not Christian, often newcomers, and who are ideal scapegoats in times of economic stress (Greenslade, 2005).

The British sociologist Tariq Modood (2013) has carefully analysed the paradoxes and dilemmas embodied in British multicultural and social control policies: it is clear from his analysis that these policies are still evolving, and multiculturalism is "far from dead".This multicultural ideal differs from "interculturalism" which involves mutual interest in values and religion between seeming disparate groups (Meer & Modood, 2011; Modood, 2017). Rather, multiculturalism involves "collectivities of complex identities" which interact, on equal terms within a political state which tolerates and protects such diversity.

However Joppke (2004 & 2009) also shows that despite an official policy of multiculturalism which should in theory ameliorate feelings of alienation in religious and ethnic minorities, the current fugue of Islamophobia in Britain may have resulted in a significant degree of alienation of the Muslim population, especially as right wing elements, including the press, denigrate multiculturalism as involving the accommodation of an "alien" religion.

How profound this alienation is, in a general sense, is difficult to judge. Certainly the evidence reviewed by Modood & Ahmad (2007) suggested that the large majority of young Muslims accepted five salient features of 'British values': Freedom (to pursue career, express ideas, practise religion); Democracy (the right to choose and dismiss leaders); Sexual Equality (the absolute equality of women, which is a fundamental part of Qur'anic revelation); and Secularism (the right not to have a state religion such as Christianity, govern one's personal affairs). In this model the majority of Muslims are 'moderate', since a fundamental principle of Islam is indeed that of moderation and modesty, the middle path. The task of Muslims in Britain and The Netherlands is to demonstrate the practical ethics of Islam, through everyday interactions with their non-Muslim peers.

In his analysis of Dutch (and European) multiculturalism Bader (2005 & 2007) offers a useful political analysis of the concepts and problems involved, in ways which show how democratic states (including England) might accommodate the aspirations of religious and cultural minorities. This is clearly an ongoing political debate, and several different models may be explored as we seek to fulfil Tariq Ramadan's (1998 to 2012) ideal of Islam as the province of a new, confident and respected minority in western societies (Law, 2013). Nevertheless, we must listen to Kalin's (2011) opinion that the extent of Islamophobia in a nation places severe limits on its ability to maintain successful programmes of multiculturalism, in North America, England, Netherlands, Austria and Germany (see Abbas, 2011; Cherribi, 2011; Casari, 2011). Abdelkader (2017) summarises evidence that Islamophobia and prejudiced actions towards Muslims are increasing in all nations of Western Europe. According to Adida et al. (2016) the greatest amount of Islamophobia is encountered in France, with almost-apartheid like aversion to any contacts with Muslims.

However some notable Muslim theologians in different continents continue to elaborate with eloquence doctrines of religious tolerance and pluralism which are to be practised by Muslims in Europe, whatever the degree of persecution they endure (Karabell, 2007; Pal, 2011; Ramadan, 2012). Foremost are those inspired by the Algerian Mohamed Talbi (1998) who goes to the roots of Islam, to its earliest practices in Makkah and Medina: out of that puritan piety came great wisdom, great tolerance, and much spiritual joy. Tariq Ramadan, another advocate of religious pluralism also goes to the roots of Islam in his biography of The Prophet, and advocates the role of an Islam that is faithful to its roots (the authority of The Qur'an and The Hadith), and the five pillars: but designs a new and powerful role for the positive dignity of migrant Muslims in Europe and America (March, 2010a & b; Ourghi, 2010; Ramadan, 2009 to 2012).

Europe Today: Further British and Dutch Comparisons

Government support for liberal multiculturalism in Britain has since 2000, been eroded by an increasing xenophobia, and a desire to control "immigration". Nevertheless, Britain has developed a comprehensive set of laws (evolving since 1975 into the 2010 Equality Act) which outlaw discrimination and hate propaganda in the areas of "gender, disability, race and religion".

And despite the emergence of a far-right party in The Netherlands which advocated both political and cultural violence against Muslim minorities, in key Dutch cities (Amsterdam, Rotterdam, Utrecht, and The Hague) there is (apparently) a stronger ethos of tolerance than in Britain (Zick et al, 2008; Sevelkoul et al, 2010). This is not of course to assert that there is no overt 'cultural racism' amongst the Dutch populace: rather there is an element of "smug ignorance" as Essed & Hoving (2014) put it.

Curious manifestations of racism such as "blacking up" to represent the African slave helper of *Sintaklaas* each year is widespread, and regarded by many Dutch people (including children) as "harmless fun" (Mesman et al., 2017). It is also deeply offensive to our Jamaican-descent family who live in Amsterdam.[9] In a penetrating essay Anne de Jong (Jong, 2019) links the intersectionality of "blackface fun", Dutch Islamophobia, and Western indifference to oppression in regions such as Gaza.

Tariq Ramadan (2011), reflecting on his experience of The Netherlands, and commenting on a European-wide survey which showed that the Dutch expressed lower levels of direct prejudice and racism than adults in many other European countries (Zick et al., 2008), observed:

> *I would say the Netherlands should really start reassessing their own attitudes towards their own values – not even just towards Islam. It's about their own values: how do we deal with pluralism, how do we deal with mutual respect and mutual dignity.* (Ramadan, 2011).

This perspective argues that the Dutch, despite much interactional tolerance, have not adjusted their traditional "plural society" values to accommodate the aspirations of Muslim minorities to become equal partners in a Dutch plural state (Bader, 2005; Fenetke, 2009; Ourghi, 2010; Sloootman & Duyvendak, 2015). Yet despite the emergence of a popular right-wing party with an explicit anti-Muslim agenda, surveys of several thousand indigenous Dutch respondents showed that in the urban areas most settled

---

[9] The daughter of one of us caused some consternation and offence in Amsterdam when she "whitened up", covering her African face with white paint, in mockery of the "Black Piet" face-painted-black Sintaklaas clowns. In the past century in Austria (according to an Austrian Quaker colleague) *Schwarzer Piet* was also a satanic imp who punished the bad boys and girls, and withheld their presents.

by Muslim populations, direct contact with Muslims resulted in significantly *higher* degrees of acceptance of this religious minority, despite lack of official policies fostering political or value accommodation (Gonzalez et al., 2008; Sevelkoul et al, 2010).

Tariq Ramadan's observations (applying both to Britain and The Netherlands) on Muslim "integration" are highly relevant here. Ramadan (2007 to 2012), a leading scholar on the adaptation of Muslims in Europe stresses that Muslims have choices in this matter. What Ramadan offers, with much brilliance, is a "post integration" role for Western Muslims who have:

> ... *multiple, moving identities, and there is no reason – religious, legal or cultural – a woman or man cannot be both American, or Muslim ... Millions of individuals prove this daily. Far from the media and political tensions, a constructive, in-depth movement is under way, and Islam has become a Western religion ... Of course there is only one single Islam as far as fundamental religious principles are concerned, but it includes a variety of interpretations and a plurality of cultures. Its universality indeed stems from this capacity to integrate diversity into its fundamental oneness.* (Ramadan, 2010).

6. Summary and Conclusions

This chapter has argued that prejudiced attitudes and opinions precede actual acts of discrimination. We don't know how to counter prejudiced attitudes in any fundamental way, except though specific interventions using school curricula (e.g. Adam-Bagley & Verma,1972 & 1975). More recent programmes of Citizenship Education, discussed in the previous Chapter have a broader focus and have not attempted experimental studies of attitude change. Nevertheless, this new curriculum is warmly accepted by many young students, and should be explored further as an agency of positive attitudinal and behaviour change.

In considering the studies of racial discrimination in employment, including our own new studies in the following Chapter, we are deeply concerned with the problem of alienation, in which minority students and young people are so hurt by their experience of racial, ethnic and religious discrimination that they rebel violently, either individually or in riotous groups (Bagguley & Hussain, 2016). The street level rebellion these researchers describe in the northern English city of Bradford, featured angry or despairing youth, mainly Muslim, a reaction against the multiple ills of their lives including

Islamophobic denial of the rewards of employment following educational achievement.

In the Netherlands, youth with Turkish heritage survive, with the cultural and religious support of their parents in a subtly racist culture, as they face significant challenges to their dignity and identity (van Bergen et al., 2017).

CHAPTER SEVEN

DISCRIMINATION IN ACTION: THREE CASE STUDIES OF MUSLIM WOMEN SEEKING WORK IN ENGLAND AND THE NETHERLANDS

CHRISTOPHER ADAM-BAGLEY AND MAHMOUD ABUBAKER

1. Comparing Racial Discrimination in English and Dutch Cultures

Attitudes (biased, prejudiced, or otherwise) underpin actions, such as the denial of access by minorities to housing, employment and service (Abrams et al., 2005 to 2018). The only previous attempt at systematic comparison of attitudes linked with ethnic discrimination between England and The Netherlands has been Adam-Bagley's (1973) fieldwork in 1970, to replicate an English study (Daniel, 1968) using young, professional men both as "actors" in applying for vacancies; and also as genuine applicants, accepting a vacancy when it was offered. The three Dutch professionals, with qualifications in industrial management in this 1973 study were "indigenous white", "black colonial immigrant" (Surinamer), and "foreign" (Yugoslavian). Their experience in seeking a response to advertised vacancies, and submitting to interviews when offered, was contrasted with three "similarly qualified" English actors applying for jobs and housing (Black Jamaican, Hungarian immigrant, and indigenous white).

In the 60 "situation tests" of advertised employment, the Dutch West Indian was discriminated against in 30 percent of his applications, while the English West Indian was rejected in 75 percent of the cases in which the white tester was offered an interview. Similar levels of discrimination pertained for applications for accommodation. In the Netherlands the "foreigner" was rejected as an applicant for employment *more* frequently than the black applicant, quite the opposite of the English situation.

Changes in Dutch society, including the fading of the "bloc" system, which absorbed certain kinds of immigrants such as black Surinamers, have been rapid, and by the year 2,000 it was difficult to find any remaining semblance of bloc culture: the religious sentiments supporting these 'pillars' of society had melted within a generation, as outlined in the previous Chapter. At the same time, by the 1990s, Dutch evidence of greater levels of discrimination against minorities was beginning to emerge, and this has clearly been mapped in the work of Andriessen and her colleagues (Andriessen et al., 2010, 2012, 2015, 2018; Nievers & Andriessen, 2010).

The changes in Dutch social structure had resulted, paradoxically, in an increase in hostility towards ethnic minorities such as settlers from the former Dutch colony of Suriname. Nevertheless, today in The Netherlands as in other parts of Europe, the most stigmatised minorities are Muslims, who, as migrant workers and their descendants, have cultural origins in Turkey and North Africa (Fekete & Sivandan, 2009; Van der Valk, 2015). In Britain, Muslim minorities are mostly the descendants of settlers from the Indian Sub-Continent, with substantial numbers also from former British colonies in East and West Africa, the Middle East, and Malaysia.

According to the 2011 National Census, some five percent of the British population were Muslims, most in younger age groups, either still undergoing education or in the early stages of working careers or family development. In The Netherlands, Muslim minorities (some four percent of the population) are, like their co-religionists in Britain, victims of Islamophobia. Dutch Muslims have always stood outside of the *verzuiling* system of protective tolerance (Kremer, 2013), Indeed, Frank Bovenkerk and colleagues (1995) in comparing methodologies for studying racial discrimination in Dutch, French, Swiss and Austrian cultures, found that Dutch Moroccans were subject to considerable degrees of rejection (in 56% of employment applications), compared with other ethnic minority groups.

2. Development of Testing to Measure Degrees of Racial and Ethnic Discrimination

'Prejudice and racial discrimination' in a population has most frequently been inferred from attitudinal data which elicits agreement with statements about 'behavioural readiness' in response to questionnaires aimed at measuring prejudice attitudes to different groups. While one would expect a person who declares the intention of discriminating against a particular kind of individual to actually discriminate when the occasion arose, there is no guarantee that he or she would actually do so (Abrams et al., 2016). An alternative (although logistically difficult) strategy is to see if prejudiced intentions lead to prejudiced action, having individuals (e.g. actors) apply for advertised jobs, vacancies or services.

This design was employed in Britain by Daniel (1968) who showed that in about half of the situations (for an employment or housing vacancy) an African-Caribbean applicant was discriminated against, compared with the acceptance of the white applicant. Jowell & Prescott-Clarke's (1970) "correspondence test" study indicated significant discrimination against visible minorities, but it did nevertheless show that about half of the British employers approached were, initially at least, non-discriminatory. The authors speculated that recent publicity surrounding the Race Relations Act could have influenced initial responses, while the actual interview process might include implicit or explicit biases whose subtleties of rejection would be hard for any legislation (or applicant) to detect.

At least there had been some advance from the frequently seen public advertisements in Britain of the early 1960s prior to the 1965 Race Relations Act, with advertisements boldly declaring: "Accommodation Available: No Blacks, No Dogs, No Irish" (Lydon, 1993; Nwanokwu, 2016).

Pager & Shepherd (2008) have surveyed mainly American studies of the measurement of racial discrimination, which they report is still "subtle but strong" following minority gains stemming from the Civil Rights era up to the 1970s, concluding that such discrimination remains "a major problem in the USA". The sociological evidence on discrimination which they collected came from three sources: (1) studies of the agents of discrimination, using qualitative or concealed methodologies; (2) statistical analyses of income and employment profiles of minorities, controlling for educational achievements, to judge whether systematic discrimination has taken place; (3) quasi-experimental studies using "situation testing" (e.g. actors, playing the role of minority applicants; and/or applying for advertised jobs using "correspondence testing" by submitting job applications in which the ethnicity of the applicant, e.g. European-American, or African-American) was manifest.

The empirical study of racial discrimination using "situation" and "correspondence" testing was, according to the review of Riach & Rich, 2002, pioneered in the United Kingdom, and the degrees of discrimination identified have been paralleled by studies showing lower earnings and occupational achievements of ethnic minorities which reflected discrimination, when differing levels of age and educational achievements are taken into account (Wrench & Modood, 2000; Khattab & Modood, 2015).

In the Netherlands Iris Andriessen and colleagues (2010 to 2019) in government-sponsored research have examined discrimination surrounding perceived Muslim minorities in Randstad Holland (the urban core of the nation), by submitting resumes for advertised job vacancies, indicating that the applicant was either of "purely" Dutch origin, or had Islamic antecedents. This extensive Dutch research has shown that racial discrimination in The Netherlands was actually increasing in the age of Islamophobia, even in the Randstad region (including the cities of Amsterdam, The Hague, Utrecht and Rotterdam) which traditionally had contained more liberal elements of the Dutch population.

Andriessen and her colleagues used various methodologies to measure amounts of discrimination over several years, including the use of actors applying for advertised jobs, and the submission of CVs identical except for the name (and implied ethnicity) of the candidate. Either the "twin" CVs were virtually similar, or the minority candidate had enhanced qualifications and experience. Several thousand of these "situation tests" were made, using varying methodologies. These tests showed that the well-qualified Dutch, "white", candidate was successful in gaining access to an interview in up to a half of their applications, while the Moroccan or Turkish "Muslim" candidate was successful in a little under a fifth of applications. These results give a net figure for discrimination of around 20 percent, which is approximately the same as that obtained in the English "correspondence testing" for ethnic discrimination by Wood and colleagues (2009).

The results of these various studies in England and The Netherlands showed then, that there remained significant potential job discrimination against ethnic and religious minorities. In the Netherlands this seemed greater than that in earlier work in Amsterdam and The Hague, although differences in methodology make accurate comparisons difficult. We have hypothesised, as have others, that the levels of employment discrimination for minorities may have been worsening with the collapse of the Dutch plural society system (Bracke, 2013).

In a depressing study from Amsterdam, van den Berg et al. (2017) showed that a young male Muslim (with no offence history) was significantly more likely to be discriminated against in "correspondence testing" in application for an entry level post, compared with a young Dutch non-Muslim applicant, who revealed a conviction for sexual offending when a juvenile. This study of 520 hypothetical applicants found that employers strongly preferred young Dutch applicants, regardless of any declared prior offence history of theft, physical or sexual violence, over the young Muslim male applicant with no criminal history.

Legislation to Diminish Ethnic and Racial Discrimination, and the Problem of Institutional Racism

Political understanding of the reality of discrimination in the UK led to the passage of the first Race Relations Act in 1965 which made various kinds of discrimination illegal, but with certain concessions to the embedded sensitivities ("prejudices") of small groups. Thus in the early versions of the legislation, small businesses with ten employees or less were exempted, as were small boarding houses or hotels with less than ten beds. Later versions of this Act (now subsumed under broader 'Equality Legislation') included no such sensitivity, and indeed prosecutions by government, and individual litigation by workers on grounds of 'racial discrimination' has disappeared from the 'equality' lens, as we discuss below in a case study of Britain's so-called Equality and Human Rights Commission.

In the Netherlands there is legislation (the Equal Treatment Act) which forbids discrimination on grounds of many minority statuses, including ethnicity or religion. But, according to the contributors to collection of papers on *Dutch Racism* edited by Essed & Hoving (2014), this law is frequently ineffective. Very few examples of this Equality law in action, exist.

The largest group of so-called *allochtonen* ('foreign others') in The Netherlands have ethnic origins in Turkey (Yilmaz & Schmid, 2014). The large majority are Muslims, and most mosques in The Netherlands have a Turkish foundation, with a Turkish-speaking imam. The research on employment discrimination against applications for employment by ethnically-Turkish Dutch applicants reported in this Chapter was undertaken both during and after a major diplomatic quarrel between The Netherlands and Turkey which focussed among other issues, on press freedom (Yazil, 2017). Stoter (2017) argued that a coup in Turkey had imposed 'loyalty pressures' on Dutch Turks who generally supported President Erdogan, whom the Dutch government saw as unacceptably authoritarian. This clash of views led to public demonstrations by Dutch Turks, and some very negative press concerning 'Turks', now often seen as indistinguishable from citizens of a backward nation which The Netherlands had criticised. This led, according to community-level reports, to angry reactions amongst young Dutch Turks. Stoter commented:

> *For their part, Dutch-Turkish citizens, especially the younger generation, often feel excluded by mainstream society. They often complain of being viewed as second-class citizens at school or in work. This is because they are still being addressed as an outsider ('foreign', 'Turk' or 'Muslim') or even discriminated against, as research shows.* (Stoter, 2016, p. 4)

Zihni Özdil, an Erasmus University historian and analyst of The Netherlands colonial and slave-owning past, commented with irony, "Racism is an American problem" - that is how the Dutch polity perceives race and ethnic relations in The Netherlands, seeing racism as part of the grosser forms of public disorder, which was certainly not a problem for the Dutch. In this analysis, institutional racism such as the everyday acts of discrimination involved in the denial of employment to minorities, are ignored (Özdil, 2014). Özdil, a Dutch Turk is a leading advocate of Turks finding a belonging *within* Dutch culture, the form of integration which Ramadan (2004) advocates. Studies of Dutch-Turkish youth have shown them to be rather conservative and religious, compared with non-migrant Turkish youth (Schmitt, 2014). Strong cultural and religious socialization of Dutch-Turkish youth by their parents was associated, in a study of 14-18 year olds, with prosocial behaviours, compared with non-minority youth (van Bergen et al., 2017).

3. Studies of Racial and Ethnic Discrimination in Britain since 2000

Wrench & Modood (2000) identified a move away from government concern with ethnic discrimination in the workplace, with the Commission for Racial Equality leaving responsibility for the expensive litigation under the Race Relations Act to individuals, if they were able to obtain trade union support. They suggested that governments were now relying on the "natural benevolence" of employers, and an innate sense of British fair play to prevent racial discrimination occurring. Successful litigation using the Race Relations Acts is now extremely rare. But the failure of the "natural benevolence" argument is amply demonstrated by research studies, reviewed below.

Heath & Cheung (2006) offer a useful review of the British employment situation, including experience of racial discrimination experienced by Black and Ethnic Minorities (BEM) adults, using a variety of data sources, and try and partial out the degree to which employment status and income reflect either low educational achievements, or discrimination by employers. Their results showed that Pakistani, Bangladeshi, Black Caribbean and African men were failing to gain levels of monetary reward in various occupations, in ways which could only be explained through racial and ethnic discrimination. Reviewing time trends in relation to economic cycles, Li & Heath (2008) found that Black and Ethnic Minority (BEM) men's unemployment levels were significantly higher than those of British-born whites in the period 1972 to 2005, results which held even after effects of their educational qualifications were taken into account.

These findings indicate widespread denial of employment access because of ethnicity (BEM) when age and education of individuals was accounted for. The situation for men and women of Pakistani and Bangladeshi origin was, amongst the BEM group, particularly disadvantaged. Their continued employment in low-skilled work, and their frequent spells of long unemployment could not be explained by age, educational attainments, and recency of immigration. There was a tendency for older Pakistani and Bangladeshi workers to adopt "the sick role" as an alternative to the fruitless research for adequate work, trying to exist on disability benefits. The situation had improved only marginally for the adult children of migrants, and seeking and finding employment was particularly difficult for young Muslim women in Britain, despite their British birth and local accents. The only ethnic minority groups not severely disadvantaged economically were Indian and Chinese males (Li & Heath, 2008).

BEM workers tended to seek employment in governmental and health service sectors, probably because of government monitoring policies (following the MacPherson Report on institutional racism, in 1999, which highlighted and tried to minimise) discrimination in public institutions; and also because low pay in these sectors made these posts relatively unattractive to whites. For women "ethnic penalties" (lack of hiring, or employment on lower pay than whites) was according to Heath & Cheung (2006), "marked". Using various data sources to support these arguments, these researchers found that these "ethnic penalties" pertained in manufacturing, distribution, private transport companies, and banking: "Getting a good education is not, on its own, enough."

The authors observe that the Race Relations (Amendment) Act of 2000, which followed the Macpherson Report, shifted the focus from legal interventions on discrimination by private companies, to quasi-legal appraisal of public institutions. Heath & Cheung (2006) advocated the addition of systematic monitoring of racial discrimination by the private sector (e.g. through the Equality and Human Rights Commission, and the Confederation for British Industries). This had not, by 2019, occurred.

Brynin & Guveli (2012) analysed the British Labour Force survey data for 1993-7, contrasting this analysis with the data for 2004-8, looking for changes in patterns of ethnic disadvantage, and whether income disadvantage for BEM groups was due to failure to enter certain occupational sectors, or whether once recruited, pay differentials were imposed on BEM individuals. The former appeared to be the case, since the data indicated patterns of employment segregation, reflecting entry-level discrimination in denial of employment. Moreover, the picture in the later years (to 2008) was as bleak as in the earlier period. Looking at income differentials in more recent data, Brynin & Longhi (2015) show that BEM workers were the most disadvantaged of any group of British workers, more than half not achieving the Rowntree Foundation's "minimum living wage" level.

Following Clark & Drinkwater's (2007) account of the complex of interacting factors which diminish wage levels and status of employment in ethnic minorities, Dyke & James (2009) studied, using telephone interviews, 634 English women of Pakistani or Bangladeshi origin: all were Muslim. The motivation for this research was the finding from literature they surveyed that South Asian, Muslim women were the most discriminated against group in access to employment in the UK. While 57 percent of the women contacted said they would like to work outside of the home (and indeed some were already doing so), 49 percent could not seek work at that time because of child care responsibilities. The researchers did not attempt to estimate the degree of rejection which these Muslim women were experiencing in the search for employment, but observed that many had become inhibited in seeking work because of the fear of discrimination.

The authors of this study advocated the setting up of special placement agencies in British cities, which would liaise with employers, establishing potential avenues of work, and of training opportunities for Muslim women. So far as we can establish, such agencies have not been set up. Further research on employment, education and income data for more than 750,000 British households by Khattab & Modood (2015) showed that Muslim women were the most disadvantaged in terms of income and employment, despite their levels of education. Islamophobia and ethno-religious discrimination in access to employment are linked, and are not diminishing.

The most comprehensive experimental study of racial discrimination in England using 'correspondence testing' in job applications comes from a report by Wood et al. (2009) who examined the acceptance or rejection of *curriculum vitae* which implied an ethnic minority origin, compared with the acceptance of a similar CV when it was clear that the applicant was 'an indigenous white'. Three similar CVs (varying only by ethnicity) were submitted for posts advertised in seven major British cities, in nine categories of occupation. One CV was always on behalf of the 'white British' candidate; the further two CVs included, randomly, CVs contrasted by presumed ethnicity (African-Caribbean; Chinese; Indian; Pakistani/Bangladeshi). Pre-testing showed that for example, the average white adult was able to identify 'Andrew Clarke' as white, and 'Eroll Griffiths' as black. Religion of candidate was not made explicit in the CVs. All candidates claimed to be born and educated in the UK.

Overall, 2,961 "applications" were made for 987 advertised vacancies (84% on a 'job-search' web site, the remainder in newspaper ads), in 2008-2009, a period of recession in the British economy. 'Success' was judged to be if an employer responded to an applicant with a request for an interview, or asked for further details. Overall, only 16 percent (155 out of 987 advertised posts) responded to *any* of the applicants. 'Net discrimination' was the negative difference between a 'white' applicant being contacted, versus a 'non-white' or 'minority ethnicity' candidate being contacted for interview or further particulars. The net difference – the index of discrimination - of 29 percent across all seven cities studied, was a highly significant, in statistical terms. But degrees of discrimination varied between the cities, being lowest in Bradford and Leeds (at 20% net discrimination) and highest in Manchester (at 42%). The authors of the report do not calculate significant differences between individual cities, but their data allow this to be done: when Manchester is compared with the other six cities (Bristol was the next highest in net discrimination, at 27%) the difference is highly significant: that is, in statistical terms, Manchester employers were significantly *more* rejecting than employers in any other city. No factors in the test situations could be adduced to explain these differences, and we have to entertain the hypothesis that factors within Manchester's social system make life more difficult for some ethnic minorities.

Other findings emerging from this study were that employers advertising higher status jobs (requiring professional qualifications) were more accepting of ethnic minority candidates; employers posting jobs on a website were less discriminating than those advertising in the local press; and public sector employers were more accepting of minority candidates. Nevertheless, even when combining these 'favourable' factors, employers' discrimination in favour of white candidates remained statistically significant. Overall, the "ethnic minority" candidates had to submit more than twice as many CVs as their "white" counterpart, in order to gain an interview.

Martin, Heath & Boswell (2010) draw together the literature on disadvantages in the labour market which being both an ethnic and a religious minority entail, using a variety of data sources:

> *The results demonstrate a strong 'Muslim penalty' for women from different ethnic groups. There were also ethnic penalties which persisted despite allowing for religion, in particular for Black Caribbean and Black African women.*

Thus for some women there was a triple disadvantage: being female, being 'of colour' (with Pakistani, Bangladeshi or African origin), and being overtly Muslim. Women who had "obviously" been born in Britain experienced slightly less discrimination in employment.

In Britain, some studies show that BEM workers who obtain high level professional and university qualifications actually encounter more discrimination, as being 'suspiciously overqualified' (Rafferty, 2012). Setting up a small business is an alternative for ethnic minorities when faced with discrimination in employment: but small manufacturers are likely to meet discrimination in their supply chain and sales outlets (Ram et al. 2011). Small business development by British Pakistanis and Bangladeshis does not appear to reduce "the ethnic penalty", or raise the individuals involved out of the ethnic bands of poverty (Modood & Khattab, 2016).

Research from the House of Commons Women's and Equalities Committee (Miller, 2016) established that unemployment rates in Muslims in Britain were twice as high as those for any other group: 65 percent of Muslim women who wished to work, remained unemployed. Research for the Committee indicated that some "situation testing" had shown that hijab-wearing women were particularly likely to experience discrimination in job-seeking. Employers were four times as likely to ask Muslim women candidates about 'family obligations' which, inferentially, might interfere with their commitment to employment. Of the employers interviewed in this study, 25 per cent said that they would be "hesitant" about considering a Muslim woman for employment. The Parliamentary Committee found some evidence that Muslim women were removing hijabs (head covering), and adopting Anglo first and/or second names, to obtain employment. Parallel to this report, the Trades Union Council (TUC, 2016) found that Black and Ethnic Minority women were a third more likely to be unemployed than were their male counterparts. Once employed, they earned less for the same work than did male counterparts, and were more often required to accept fewer hours of employment.

4. The Role of the Equality and Human Rights Commission in Britain in (not) Preventing Racial, Ethnic and Religious Discrimination

This important but apparently ineffective publicly-funded organisation grew in part from the Race Relations Board (RRB), which was set up to monitor (and improve) the workings of the Race Relations Act of 1965 (Britain's first legislation in this area). The RRB's first report for 1966-7 presented to the Home Secretary indicated that "the Board" constituted nine part-time members, with some secretarial support, but they were unable to initiate prosecutions under the Act. Their role was simply that of monitoring and advocacy. The RRB became the Commission for Racial Equality (CRE) in 1976, following the passage of a somewhat strengthened Race Relations Act of that year. This "non-departmental public body" was better funded that the RRB, but in 2004 its function regarding "race" was ended, when it was merged with a newly created Equality and Human Rights Commission (EHRC). The CRE's extensive library on "race and ethnicity" was donated to a university, and many of its specialist staff left or were dispersed into other roles.

The EHRC simultaneously absorbed the Equal Opportunities Commission (concerned with sexual discrimination) and the Disability Rights Commission. Initially it had a much larger budget than the CRE, but also a much broader mandate. This involved being responsible for monitoring, advice and policy on lack of equality (because of, inter alia, discrimination) in the fields of: "Age, disability, gender, gender realignment, sexual orientation, and race." (Bourne, 2015). Religion was not included in this remit unless (as in the case of Jews and Sikhs) religious beliefs coincided with a "racial" (sic) category. This meant that Muslims, who can be of any ethnicity, were not directly covered by the EHRC's concerns with equality and discrimination.[1]

Action on discrimination is not initiated by the EHRC: it is left to individuals, to bring their case to an "Employment Tribunal", which has a quasi-legal, mediating role in cases of alleged discrimination or other unfair practices - it can order payment of significant financial redress for successful claimants. But without Trade Union support, Black and Ethnic Minority individuals rarely seem to bring claims of discrimination to these Tribunals. We have been unable to obtain any publicly available information on the nature of cases brought, since the Tribunals almost always seek to achieve compromise between the contesting parties, and these kinds of decisions are *de lege*, unavailable for public scrutiny. The most recently available comprehensive report of the UK Employment Tribunals (OITFET, 2014) indicated that only 163 of the 12,781 cases presented alleged "racial discrimination". Because of UK government policy no further public reports on "fair employment" tribunals have been issued since 2014, so far as we can discover.

No information was given on the nature of cases in the 2014 report, though for all cases 43% were withdrawn; "conciliation" was obtained between the parties in 37%; and up to 20% of complainants "did not attend" the Tribunal. A complainant had to pay a fee of £250 to file a complaint, and a further £950 to the Tribunal if the case was proceeded with. The lone worker, believing that he or she has been the victim of racial, ethnic or religious discrimination has many difficult hurdles to overcome in seeking redress, and it is not surprising that so few seek compensation through an Employment Tribunal. The fee requirement was rescinded in 2016, but even if the litigant is successful they will still have to meet all of their own legal costs, which could be considerable.

The worker who feels that they have been discriminated against will rarely have access to evidence which might prove that rejection was on grounds of race, religion or ethnicity, rather than on lack of merit, since they are

---

[1] The dynamic energy of the Equal Opportunities Commission seemed to have been lost when it was absorbed within the body with the broader remit. Initiatives such as the valuable, sponsored research of Bradley & Healy (2008) on ethnicity and gender at work – giving qualitative accounts of struggle against discrimination – have not been paralleled or replicated in the larger EHRC. Research sponsored by EHRC has focussed on attitudes to minorities, but not on the actual practices of discrimination (Abrams et al., 2018).

unlikely to have access to information on the *internal* decisions made by the company in question. A brief report from the Tribunals office (Moss, 2015) reported a 38% fall in claims once fees were introduced. Most successful awards were in the field of sexual discrimination in hiring, pay, and dismissal: race and ethnicity were not mentioned in this report.

The Equalities and Human Rights Commission (EHRC) issued a major report in 2015 with the perhaps ironic title *Is Britain Fairer?* The answer seemed to be: almost certainly not. The EHRC's ever dimming vision was meant to focus on the following tasks: (1) Improve the evidence base for judging how fair society is; (2) Raise standards and close attainment gaps in education; (3) Encourage fair recruitment, development and reward in employment; (4) Support improved living conditions in cohesive societies; (5) Improve access to mental health services and support for those experiencing poor mental health; (6) Prevent abuse, neglect and ill-treatment in care and detention; (7) Tackle targeted harassment and abuse of people who share particular protected characteristics. In all of these areas, except the first, Britain had manifestly failed.

This failure of the EHRC to check ethno-religious discrimination in access to employment in England was further demonstrated by the work of Heath (2019) who submitted 3,200 "paired" applications for advertised employment for manual and non-manual jobs. Arab-Britons had to apply for 90% more posts before being given an interview; Asian-Britons (mainly Pakistanis) had to apply for 70% more posts. Overall BEM applicants had to apply for 80% more posts before any interest by an employer was shown. The authors comment:

> The absence of any real decline in discrimination against black British and people of Pakistani background is a disturbing finding, which calls into question the effectiveness of previous policies. Ethnic inequality remains a burning injustice and there needs to be a radical rethink about how to tackle it.

There was a sufficiently developed body of statistical data through which the EHRC commentators could accurately describe the manifest *unfairness* of British society in general, and of its racist/ethnicist nature in employment practices in particular, as evidenced for example in the series of monographs issued by the Rowntree Foundation in 2015 (JRF, 2015).[2] These data show

---

[2] Policy Exchange, another independent pressure group, also gathers together current data on income and employment disadvantage experienced by UK ethnic minorities: www.policyexchange.org.uk

that substantial numbers of BEM individuals earned less than Rowntree's estimate of "a living wage"; these levels of relative poverty have remained largely unchanged during the present century; and levels of discrimination in access to employment have remained substantial, and largely unchanged[3]. The EHRC's identification (in their report of 2015) of unfulfilled equality goals seems to have been something of an idealistic swan song, impossible of realisation in a Britain in which inequality, and relative poverty, especially for ethnic minorities, are actually increasing (Unwin, 2013; JRF, 2015; Sawyerr & Adam-Bagley, 2017).

Following the election of a coalition (Conservative-Liberal) UK government in 2010, the EHRC's annual budget was cut from £70 million (in 2009-10) to £12.1 million (in 2014-15), at the time that its remit was becoming ever wider. Several hundred of EHRC's employees became redundant or left over five years, and there were no signs that the trend of reduced funding would not continue (Pring, 2014). In its annual report for 2016 EHRC reported a focus on "hate crimes" against three groups: the disabled, LGBT people, and Black and Ethnic Minority groups. Racial discrimination in the workplace was very far from the horizons of this diminishing group. Any connection which the EHRC had with black and ethnic minority communities seemed now to have been lost (Bourne, 2015). The EHRC had not been able to grasp the poisonous snake of Islamophobia, despite (or because of) its widespread and many-headed nature (Fekete, 2008; Bourne, 2015).

By 2018 the EHRC had continued to grow smaller, reflecting reduced government funding, and reduced staff numbers. But in 2018 it did issue a report *Inequality in the United Kingdom*, which argued that the national government was in breach of the UN human rights convention, of which the UK was a signatory. The Report showed that the poorest 20 percent of the UK's families had suffered a significant decline in income in the previous seven years. Black and ethnic minority workers, over-represented in this poorest class, had endured the greatest income decline in the nation as a whole. But EHRC has not in its Annual Reports made any public comments on the continuation of discrimination against BEM workers in the sphere of

---

[3] It may be that employment gatekeepers are not amongst those whose opinions have become more liberal; or else that facile liberalism hides implicit prejudice. It is for this reason that Quillan (2008) in a review of the American evidence suggest the "implicit prejudice measures" should be operationalised in understanding the continuation of racial discrimination in employment.

employment, nor on the ethno-religious discrimination which Islamophobia represents, and which may be a driving force in employment discrimination.

5. Methodological Issues in Correspondence Testing

Constructing CVs for correspondence testing can be challenging, since the researchers must ensure that "fake CVs" appear genuine to a potential employer, and the CVs submitted must be identical, apart from the crucial variable of the applicant's ethnicity, which is implied by their name, or othe information. The following two quotations from the major study by Wood and colleagues in 2009 (Wood et al., 2009) of employment discrimination in several English cities, making inferences from employers' response to submitted CVs, illustrate some of these methodological challenges:

> *In principle, for a given number of vacancies, the more applications sent per vacancy the greater the statistical power of the study, but there are some practical limits. Certainly, if too many forms were to be sent after each vacancy then some employers might suspect they were part of an experiment, with the risk that all the forms are rejected. There is also the question of whether sending more than three or four applications is too great a burden on smaller organisations in particular ... Qualifications had to be closely matched between the templates, but also sufficiently different to avoid suspicion. For instance, efforts were made to understand the structure of professional accounting qualifications and to ensure that different awarding bodies were similarly regarded. Constructing work histories was the most complex element. Real organisations that could be verified by employers were listed, although these were generally based outside the local area in case the recruiter knew about them. Years of experience were kept similar between templates, as were the types of organisation and roles carried out".*
> (Wood et al., 2009, pp 16 & 22).

The description of methodologies employed Wood et al.'s 2009 study of 2961 CVs submitted to 987 job advertisements (3 for each advertisement, for the different ethnicities described by the CV) did not discuss what seems to us to be a problem: would not an employer detect, in some cases, that three of the vitas submitted simultaneously were suspiciously similar? This could result in all three vitas being rejected. Wood and colleagues attributed the relatively low response of employers to the applications to the economic conditions prevailing following the economic recession of 2008, with strong competition for a declining number of jobs; but there could have been other reasons, such as the confounding effect of vitas being too similar.

In exploring these methodological issues, we submitted (in our first two case studies, in Manchester and Rotterdam, but not in the third case study reported below, which employed a more traditional 'correspondence testing' methodology), only a single vita (either an 'English/Dutch Christian-name' candidate or 'Muslim-name candidate') to advertisements, until we had sufficient numbers of applications to ensure that the two candidates were applying to organisations whose 'modal' characteristics were similar.

Similar methodological problems may have affected the Dutch work of Andriessen and colleagues, and by Nievers and Andriessen between 2008 and 2015, discussed later.

6. The Manchester Case Study with a 'Real' Job Seeker

The whole assemblage of buildings is commonly called Manchester, and contains about 400,000 inhabitants, rather more than less. The town is peculiarly built, so that a person may live in it for years ...without coming into contact with a working people's quarter. (Engels, 1845, p. 85).

While the back-to-back housing described by Engels has now been demolished, some zones of deprivation Engels identified, in Salford, Hulme, Pendleton, Chorlton, Ardwick, Cheetham Hill and Broughton remain today, despite massive "slum clearance" and shipment of the poor to large areas of council-house deprivation in Wythenshawe, and Handforth. Manchester was the city manifesting the highest levels of "racial discrimination" in the correspondence-testing of employment applications administered by Wood et al. (2009). Why is not clear. Greater Manchester's population is now 2.68 million, of whom about 8.6 percent are Muslims, mainly Britons of Asian and Middle Eastern origin. Manchester has 62 listed Mosques. Islam in Manchester compared to, say Amsterdam[4], is confident and outgoing and dominates much of the restaurant trade in the university districts.

The study reported here was planned in one of Manchester's finer suburbs, Didsbury (discretely separated from the white working class zones

---

[4] The proportion of Muslims in the Amsterdam population is around 14%, higher than the proportion in Manchester. There are "only" 29 listed Mosques in Amsterdam, and for the visiting Muslim they are often difficult to find, and poorly signed. Islam in Amsterdam seems to be trying to stay "under the radar" in a society which increasingly requires conformity to some kind of secular civic standard which has emerged from the post-pillarization process (Bracke, 2013). This has coincided with a rise in Dutch Islamophobia (Van der Valk, 2012 & 2015).

identified by Engels), where in the local mosque attended by one of the researchers, collaboration with a Sister who was planning to return to work after completing her family, provided the essential "subject" whose curriculum vitae formed the bases for a "correspondence test" in applying for mid-level accounting vacancies. Our Sister, Aminah's ("Ami") history is this: she was born in Manchester, to immigrant, Pakistani parents, and attended an all-girl's local authority high school with a high proportion of Muslim pupils, and achieved good GCSE results. Leaving school with two A-levels, she obtained a junior administrative position with a Housing Association, and took courses at Manchester College part-time, specializing in accountancy.

Towards the latter part of her 3-year employment, she concentrated on accountancy tasks. Ami married at 20, her husband working in his father's travel agency (specialising in Hajj and Umra tours, and travel to Middle Eastern countries, and Pakistan). She left employment in the fourth month of her first pregnancy, and in the following eight years had three children.

In the letter accompanying her vita she wrote:

> *Now that my three children are attending school, and my mother-in-law who has recently retired, can take on child care arrangements, I am seeking to return to full time employment. I have, since leaving employment with [the Housing Association] worked occasionally in my husband's business, handling the accounts of a busy travel agent, including client accounts, payment to airlines, tax calculation, and liaising with HMRC.*

The reason for this (accurate) statement was to reassure potential employers that Ami's family demands would be unlikely to conflict with the demands of work. The e-mail address she gave in her applications was: *aminah.husain.muhammad@* so that employers might clearly know her religious and ethnic background. The second CV for "Emily Woodward" (a fictitious name) was identical in every respect to Ami's vita, including birth date, school attended, school and career examination successes and grades obtained, accounting qualifications, and occupational history.

Ami's qualifications in accountancy (including those resulting from home study using on-line and correspondence instruction with commercial education providers) achieved NVQ (National Vocational Qualifications) Level 4, the equivalent to a Foundation Degree level. She was successful in the first part of the Advanced Diploma in Accounting offered by the Association of Accounting Technicians, with whom Ami achieved provisional registration. This British qualification is recognized by bodies such as the Institute of Chartered Accounts, and achievement of levels 5 and 6 allows the individual, after successful professional experience and submission of professional case studies, to full recognition as a chartered accountant. Level 4, achieved by Ami during her part-time study while at home with children, enabled her to claim skills in final accounts preparation for sole traders and partnerships, management accounting and costing, calculation and payment of direct and indirect tax liabilities, and facility in computer software in preparing and balancing accounts, and managing employee expenses and payrolls.

In submitting pairs of CVs (one for a real job-seeker, the other for a fictitious one) the researchers faced the dilemma, which previous researchers using correspondence testing have not mentioned: submitting two identical CVs (apart from differing ethnic names) might alert potential employers to the oddity of this coincidence, making it more likely that *both* CVs would be ignored. Making the CVs unalike in some way to avoid this possibility might introduce uncontrolled variables into the experiment. To avoid this problem, we submitted the CVs *singly*, to employers who gave details of vacancies in the Manchester area on a web-based advertising system: that is, only *one* CV was submitted to each employer.

The employers approached were advertising intermediate level accounting positions, with tasks which Ami was certain she could perform, offering annual salaries of about £19K p.a. (in 2015 to 2017).[5] We continued submitting CVs until we had sufficient employers who were similar (in modal or average terms) in salary offered, size and function of the organisation, type of employment, specific job requirements, and skills required: thus we submitted (on Ami's behalf) the ethnic minority CV to 516 employers, and the "white, Christian" candidate (Emily) to 527 advertisements, ending the experiment when the two sets of employers appeared to be identical in their overall characteristics.

The final results can be simply stated, and confirm the image of Manchester as a city whose outgoing Muslim community is not, by some employers at least, well accepted: Ami received a positive phone call or e-mail for 151 of her 516 applications (29.23%), compared with Emily's success rate of 306

---

[5] There is an ethical issue here of course, in that some potential employers will be momentarily deceived in considering false CVs. An ethics committee agreed with us (as had ethics committees for previous researchers) that this brief confabulation was justified, provided employers offering an interview were advised immediately of the applicant's decision.

of her 527 applications (58.06%), a net difference of 28.8 percent. Chi-squared analysis with one degree of freedom yields a value of 87.85, the probability of a chance result being virtually zero.[6]

7. Case Study Two: Comparing Employment Discrimination for Muslim Candidates in Manchester and Rotterdam

Since we were puzzled by a problem in the methodology of correspondence testing for ethnic discrimination in employment in which virtually identical CVs are submitted to the same employer (thus inviting the rejection of both "suspiciously similar" vitas), we explored a new methodology: that of submitting vitas similar in every detail except the ethnicity implied by a religious (Muslim) name to two *different* sets of employers. We submitted the vitas individually until the contrasted groups of companies were similar, on average, on a variety of factors such as the company's size, trading purpose, geographical location, and role requirements for the advertised vacancy. In both the English and the Dutch situations the Muslim candidate was a real person, applying for accountancy positions, and each of these testers did take one of the posts offered. In the two cultures the "indigenous" candidate was in fact a fictitious person with an identical CV, except that they were manifestly of English or Dutch ancestry.

"Muhammad", the real-life correspondence tester in Rotterdam, was in his early 30s, and had worked for six years as a management accountant with the same wholesale supply chain company, and was now earning 55,000 Euros a year. He had BSc and MSc degrees in economics, accounting, auditing and cost control, and was a fully qualified RA (Registered Accountant) in the Dutch system. He was of Turkish ethnic heritage, but had been born in The Netherlands. The company that employed him was small in size, and he had reached the peak of his income level in that organisation. He submitted an online vita for positions paying 70,000 Euros a year or more in 2016–2017. A dummy tester ("Hank Van der Waal") submitted an identical CV for advertised positions, but to different companies, very similar to those to which Muhammad applied. The companies approached (207 for Muhammad, and 214 for Hank) were, overall, similar in profile (location, function, employee numbers, financial

---

[6] On a positive note, hijab-wearing Ami accepted one of the positions offered, and after a year was promoted to a post earning £23K p.a., with added responsibility as the firm's accountant.

turnover). Muhammad was called for further information or interview in 39 per cent of applications; Hank was contacted in 53 percent of submissions, indicating a net discrimination index against the Muslim candidate of 14 percent.

These findings, using regionally limited case studies, with relatively small samples of employers, suggest that a methodologically revised method of correspondence testing for ethnic discrimination in employment practices showed the persistence of discrimination, possibly avoiding the confounding effects of employers rejecting both the mainstream and minority candidate CVs because they were suspiciously alike.

However, we must concede a number of criticisms that have been made concerning this approach: that sending CVs singly to different employers may lose an important amount of information on employers who are accepting or discriminating; that, in reality, large employers will always receive many CVs which are almost identical, given the nature of the position advertised, so a revised design is hardly necessary; and in fact the most rigorous tests of discrimination would involve submitting different "ethnic" CVs to the *same* employer—thus also avoiding the problem that submitting a single CV to each employer could not control for the qualifications and experience levels of competing candidates.

A further critique of our "opportunistic" methodology (using real-life applicants) is that we limit the sociological scope of explanations for discrimination. For example, responses to an applicant with a Turkish-surname may be more favourable than reactions to an applicant with a Moroccan-surname in The Netherlands, in a manner similar to that observed in other cultural settings (Booth et al., 2012; Blommaert et al., 2013; Carlsson, 2010).

In exploring the sociological richness of data on discrimination, we must also take into account the "intersection" of statuses (e.g., gender, ethnicity, religion, educational background) in explaining the phenomenon researched more fully (Veenstra, 2013). There may be, for example, less discrimination against well-qualified ethnic minority applicants, who have skills that are in short supply (Baert et al., 2015); this may have been the case with regard to their study of a well-qualified, Muslim, Dutch accountant applying for a senior management position. In contrast, a young man from an ethnic minority without qualifications who applies for a basic-wage job may experience considerable discrimination; this was shown in Dutch work in which a young, unskilled "Dutch" male with a declared history of child sex offending was significantly *more* likely to be offered unskilled employment than a young "Moroccan" male with no history of offending (van den Berg et al., 2017).

The English and Dutch results presented in Table 7.1 are not directly comparable, since, although both minority group applicants were overtly Muslim, in the English case the applicant was female applying for a junior position; in the Dutch case, the applicant was male, older, and applying for a relatively senior position. Differences in acceptance could therefore be related to gender and qualifications of the applicants. Our method of testing using real applicants who actually were looking for employment, each accepting one of the posts offered, also seems to be unique in the literature on measuring ethnic employment discrimination.

Table 7.1 Comparison of Positive Responses to the Submitted CV of the Muslim Applicant, in British and Dutch Settings

Manchester, UK	"Christian" female: 306/507 positive responses (56.06%)	Muslim female: 151/516 positive responses (29.33%)	*Net discrimination* 29.53% (Chi-squared (1, $N = 1023$) = 95.22, $p < 0.000$.
Randstad, Netherlands	"Christian" male: 114/204 positive responses (53.27%)	Muslim male: 89/226 positive responses (39.6%)	*Net discrimination* 13.67% (Chi-squared (1, $N = 430$) = 11.71, $p \leq 0.000$.

Note: Net discrimination, English results compared with Dutch results: Chi-squared (1, $N = 1,453$) = 7.35, $p < 0.007$ (i.e., significantly higher levels of net discrimination in the English situation.

There was significantly higher "net discrimination" against the Muslim woman in Manchester than for the Muslim man in Rotterdam, who accepted a senior accounting management post at 70,000 Euros per annum in his home city of Rotterdam.

The tentative Dutch results from this case study support the findings of Andriessen and her research group, although the discrimination against the Muslim Dutchman was somewhat less than we had expected; nevertheless, it was of sufficient magnitude to suggest that racial discrimination is a persistent problem in The Netherlands.

A critical methodological issue is that the "single CV" method must be compared with the "multiple CV method" (i.e. more than one contrasted CV submitted to the same employer) if we are to draw firm conclusions about the reliability and validity of the new method of enquiry that we offer in the first two case studies.

8. Case Study Three: Testing for Employment Discrimination against Muslim Women in England and The Netherlands

This third case study builds on the first case study carried out in Manchester, and focuses on a (hypothetical) woman aged 30, who had college education and employment as a junior accountant before leaving the external workforce at age 24 to be a full-time homemaker and carer of her two children, seeking to return to entry level positions in accountancy and management. According to their CVs the Muslim woman candidate was born in England or The Netherlands, with full high school education and good A-level/Baccalaureate results. No direct indication of religious affiliation was given in any of the "fake CVs" submitted.

The British applicants were *Fatima Husain* or *Emma Johnson* ("Fatima" is a common Muslim first name, chosen in honour of The Prophet's daughter; "Husain" is a common surname with origins in Pakistan). "Emma" is a common first name both in England and The Netherlands. Both stressed that their mother was now caring for their two young children, and they were now ready to re-enter the employment market full-time, on a progressive career track. Both claimed to have degrees in commerce and accountancy (lower second class, from a local metropolitan university by the UK candidate), and intermediate qualifications in professional accountancy (but were not yet chartered accountants). Each claimed three years' experience in a medium-sized company.

The 'company of record' in which the candidates claimed to have experience was randomly rotated between the two applicants, but was never the same firm on the "twinned" applications submitted for a single vacancy. Local residence addresses and schools were relevant to the city of residence (Liverpool, Manchester, Leeds, Newcastle) in which online advertisements for relevant accountancy positions were responded to. Fatima made it clear that she was UK-born, but Emma did not state birthplace, which would probably have been out of place for an applicant with an English name.

The Dutch CVs (in the Dutch language) were of *Fatima Aksoy* or *Emma De Vries*. ("Aksoy" is a common Turkish-origin surname, and "De Vries" is a common Dutch surname). Their "fake CVs" followed the protocol of the two hypothetical English candidates, in terms of age, experience, family background and education. Both Dutch candidates claimed to have attended Rotterdam University of Applied Sciences successfully graduating with a degree in "accountancy & control", with subsequent work experience under the supervision of a qualified Chartered Accountant, and then gaining intermediate professional qualifications. Fatima declared her Dutch birth; Emma did not. Fatima made no reference to Islam or Turkey. Family circumstances of the hypothetical candidates were the same. Applications were made online to advertised positions in Rotterdam and Amsterdam, with candidates' addresses and earlier schooling made locally relevant. In both cultures, the twinned applications were submitted separately, either on the first day the advertisement appeared, or on the closing date, or after 7 days if there was no closing date (in random order by ethnicity). It was felt that two almost identical CVs arriving simultaneously might have resulted in both being rejected. Relevant posts applied for were offering salaries of between 3000 & 3500 euros a month.[7]

The English testing was begun in May, 2017 and ended when what seemed to us to be 500 relevant advertised vacancies were found, 14 months later. Submission of CVs began in The Netherlands in July, 2017 and ended in November 2018, when 500 submissions were achieved. This research although technically easy to undertake from the researcher's office, is nevertheless time-consuming, and our goal of completing a parallel study

---

[7] Some advertisements asked for a 'personal statement' on how their qualifications and experience would fit with the advertised post. We are grateful to our Dutch collaborator for assistance in crafting such statements.

of male applicants in the two cultures for comparative purposes, is not yet complete.

The results in Table 7.2 indicate significant amounts of bias against the ethnic minority candidate in both English and Dutch settings. The bias was significantly greater in England than in The Netherlands. The English minority candidate had to apply for a post three times as often as the 'mainstream' candidate in order to gain an interview, or to be called for further details. The Dutch minority candidate had to apply around twice as often as the mainstream applicant in order to receive a response. Calculating an index of "net discrimination" faced the issue that some employers expressed interest in both candidates, leaving us with the dilemma of whether to exclude these "positive" employers from the analysis. Calculating "no positive response" for two cultures indicated net discrimination of 31% (England) and 19% (Netherlands). Excluding the positive responses for both candidates gave discrimination indices of 34% (England) and 20% (Netherlands), indicating that the English employers contacted were about 1.6 times more likely to ignore an ethnic minority candidate – a Muslim woman.

These results confirm those of the first two case studies, showing significant bias against the apparently Muslim minority candidate, and confirm too that although such bias exists in The Netherlands it is (at least in the Randstad Region) of a lesser degree than in Northern England.

In both cultures we explored acceptance/rejection by type of employer (size and function where such information was available; salary offered; and whether the employer was part of a national or local government, or a non-profit foundation – specifically 'ethnic' employers were not approached). For these different types of post or employer, no statistically significant variations were obtained in either culture. Nor in the English sample, were we able to show that Manchester employers were significantly more rejecting, in contrast to the findings of Wood et al. (2009). There was greater discrimination by employers in Newcastle and Manchester, compared with employers in Liverpool and Leeds – but not to a statistically significant degree.

Table 7.2 Results of Situation Testing Comparing Employment Discrimination against Muslim Women in England and The Netherlands

Name or type of applicant(s)	Both had response (% of 500)	Only one had response (% 0f 500)	No response (% of 500)	% of positive responses to all; & % unique, positive responses
UK: Fatima	49 (9.8%)	20 (4.4%)	431 (86.2%)	69/500 (13.8%); & 20/451 (4.4%)
UK: Emma	49 (9.8%)	173 (34.6%)	278 (55.6%	222/500 (44.4%); & 173/451 (38.3%)
England: Net discrimination			30.6%	33.9%
NETH: Fatima	67 (13.4%)	38 (7.6%)	395 (79%)	105/500 (21.0%); & 38/433 (8.8%)
NETH: Emma	67 (13.4%)	123 (24.6%)	310 (62%)	190/500 (38%); & 123/433 (28.4%)
Netherlands: Net discrimination			17%	19.6%

Significance of differences: In the English applications, bias in favour of "Emma", chi-squared (1,999) 154.2, p.<000. In the Dutch applications, bias in favour of "Emma", chi-squared (1,999.) 55.1, p<.000. English & Dutch biases compared: chi-squared (1,1999) 29.1, p<001, showing significantly more bias in the English setting.

An important conclusion for both England and The Netherlands is that at least some employers do not initially discriminate, and do show interest in ethnic minority candidates. And such candidates will find an appropriate post in course of time – unless, discouraged and exhausted, they prefer to stay at home and care for children. We do not have data on variables such as salary increments, additional responsibilities, and prospects for promotion for those actually hired: but we know from the review of data on women's employment in general that there is often discrimination in these aspects of employment.

The data from our case studies have examined employment discrimination involving a male professional applicant in only one culture, the Netherlands. But the studies reviewed lead to the certain conclusion that Islamophobic or ethno-religious discrimination in employment access still exists in both cultures. Certainly female Muslim applicants are likely to experience discrimination in Britain, as the third case study shows. This means that there is very likely significant discrimination in many spheres of life against young Muslim males also.

This leads us to consider the possible outcomes for such *alienation*, which results from the blocking of legitimate aspirations in employment, and fair reward for honest labour.

Khattab & Modood observed in 2015 that:

> *If you are a Muslim in the United Kingdom, you are likely to face a penalty regardless of your culture or geography. If you are a Christian in the United Kingdom you are not likely to face any penalties unless you are black. If you are white you will be protected unless you are a Muslim or to a lesser extent atheist ... The penalty will peak if you are a Muslim and black.* (Khattab & Modood, 2015, p. 529).

The work we have undertaken since 2015 reinforces this conclusion, and also suggests that it may true (perhaps to a lesser extent?) in the Netherlands as well. We urge repeated use of the "situation test" methodology in these two cultures, in order to have indicators of whether ethno-religious discrimination is changing to any degree, with parallel studies of how such findings can influence public policies for diminishing such discrimination.[8]

---

[8] Abrams et al (2018) offer findings from England on the extent of prejudiced attitudes concerning BEM groups, Muslims, and the developmentally challenged. They argue that this "barometer of prejudice" should be systematically replicated

If unchecked, such discrimination can have strongly negative consequences both for the victims, and for society at large. This theme of alienation from oneself (from one's true identity) and from society (from one's socially just identity) is one of the themes of this book.

9. Conclusions: Dimensions of British Racism and Islamophobia Reflected in Employment Discrimination

We have reviewed English and Dutch research on how Islamophobia is often translated into denial of access to essential services such as housing and employment. We urge the importance of such research, both in England and The Netherlands, by declaring the hypothesis that if employment discrimination against young Muslims is widespread (and, implicitly, is known to occur by those who are denied jobs for which they are in fact qualified), degrees of alienation will occur that may lay the seeds of profound personal disaffection, with the potential genesis of violent disorder. The overt and profound hostility to hijab-wearing women in England in street-level interactions has been described by ethnographers (Zempi & Aswan, 2017); public hostility, combined with "private hostility" on the part of employers, may have profoundly negative consequences for "quiet civility", the manners that Muslim immigrants and their children traditionally bring to British and Dutch society (Al-Refai & Adam-Bagley, 2012; van Bergen et al., 2017).

Conformity (in terms of dress, diet, public and private language discourse, and religious values and practice) is demanded of the "immigrant" (including those born in the Western country) in ways which imply the abandonment, in public at least, of traditional values. But even those that do conform are nevertheless often discriminated against because of their manifest ethnicity. This is most true of the "highly visible" minorities from Africa, the West Indies, and parts of Asia who, however much they conform to the demands of the indigenous, white community are still subjected to significant discrimination. This form of alienation has been particularly true of African-Caribbeans who despite being mostly Christian and desiring to assimilate (including frequent intermarriage), nevertheless still encounter significant amounts of self-reported racial discrimination (Astell-Burt et al., 2012; Sawyerr & Adam-Bagley, 2017).

---

every few years – we certainly agree. Unfortunately, their work did not examine, objectively, employment discrimination experienced by minorities.

For those who have internalized the message of the demand for conformity to majority values, but who are still blocked in their goal achievement, a profound degree of *alienation* may result for some in self-blame. Alienation manifests itself in a variety of ways, including entering drug-using subcultures, gang membership, and mental illness (Adam-Bagley, 1983; Baksh, 2007; Adam-Bagley, 2008).

The victims of racist or religious stereotyping may ritualize their individual alienation (sometimes termed *anomie*) in different ways: ritual conformity, accepting work in the lowest status occupations, often engaging in self-blame for lack of achievement; they may rebel within the existing political frameworks as activists; they may even join counter-cultural groups, and become non-violent rebels both inside and outside of existing social structures; or in a state of rage and powerful derangement they may engage in individual or group acts of violence against innocent, but symbolic targets. We will return to this theme in the final Chapter, referring to studies which suggested that socially isolated, depressed minority group individuals without good links to their Muslim heritage, but who have recently experienced acts of discrimination may see this final act of rejection as justification for a violent (and often suicidal) acts of terrorism (Bhui et al., 2016; Corner & Gill, 2015; McGilloway et al., 2015; Misiak et al., 2018).

We offer the critical realist comment that the "hidden racism" is the *absent* part of the social system of employment discrimination which if "unmasked" (to use the Marxian term) could show that capitalist societies continue to be institutionally racist: the failure to reward legitimate aspirations of minorities has the potential to push ethnic minorities into a permanent precariat (the precariously employed underclass described by Standing 2014, and Savage, 2015).

10. Final Reflection: The Hidden Wound of Racial Discrimination

Racial discrimination in employment in Britain and The Netherlands is widespread, although it has changed in nature in the past fifty years, taking new forms in targeting ethno-religious minorities, in addition to people of colour. 'Visibly Muslim' women are particularly likely to be targets of discrimination, both in Britain and The Netherlands. Such discrimination is a hidden crime, "absent" from public understanding, as critical realists would term it (Alderson, 2013). It is a deeply embedded, hidden, festering part of modern capitalist society in North America and Europe. Insofar as racism helps to mould a permanent underclass, it creates what Standing (2014) calls a "dangerous" sub-group, one liable at points of tension to violently rebel (Unwin, 2011; Bagguley & Hussain, 2016).

In terms of alienation theory, when legitimate aspirations are blocked, individuals may blame themselves, and retreat into ritual or escapist modes; or they may rebel, in both legal and illegal ways. We hypothesize that the alienation imposed by a racist social structure is far more dangerous for society, than is the alleged radicalisation of youth by some violent, islamist sects, who violate the fundamental principles of Islam. Countering this radicalisation, Muslim educators must draw on the material and spiritual "success" that is inherent in Islam (Wilkinson, 2015a).

The British establishment purports to uphold a set of artificial British values, which it imposes on schools and colleges through a system of education and social control, by means of its "prevent" strategy, authorised and funded by the regulations of the Counter Terrorism and Security Act of 2015, nominating "non-violent" extremists (with severe civil penalties). There is inherent hypocrisy in the official position, when British values by default, at the same time support widespread racial discrimination in employment. Similar hypocrisy occurs in The Netherlands, as for example when the moderate Muslim, Tariq Ramadan (2012) was deprived of his university position, and forced to leave Rotterdam for maintaining that Islam could become a separate pillar of Dutch society (Van Sandwijk, 2014).

The British establishment urges ethnic and religious minorities in Britain to "integrate", meaning that they should assimilate, giving up alien features of dress, religion, language, etc. Morally implicit in this assimilationist position is a social contract in which the minority group, as a reward for conformity, would be offered tolerance and acceptance. The evidence we have reviewed, and our own empirical studies in Northern England shows how false that promised social contract is. However much minorities conform, become educated, fill employment niches, apply again and again for jobs easily offered to indigenous white "Christians", they continue (as a group) to be discriminated against, with long-term negative consequences for income and welfare. Siddique & Hanrahan (2018 & 2019) report that discrimination against minorities in Britain has remained pretty constant in England over a 60-year period. Only the targets of discrimination have, to a certain extent, changed.

A former prime minister of Britain and now a leading international diplomat and politician, Tony Blair, issued a report in 2019 from his Institute for

Global Change in which he blamed "those who fail to integrate" for the rise of "far-right bigotry" (Savage, 2019). Blair writes in this report:

> Over a significant period of time, including when we were last in government, politics has failed to find the right balance between diversity and integration. On the one hand, failures around integration have led to attacks on diversity and are partly responsible for a reaction against migration. On the other hand, the word multiculturalism has been misinterpreted as meaning a justified refusal to integrate, when it should never have meant that.

Blair, who initiated the Prevent programme when in government, blames Muslims and other "immigrants" for this "failure to integrate", and advocates policies discouraging certain "unintegrated" minorities from setting up their own schools, and practising certain forms of "gender segregation". Blair advocates that these groups should by law, be forced to learn "British values".

Blair ignores entirely the continuing insults to the dignity and welfare of minority groups that Islamophobia and employment discrimination poses (Chakrabortty, 2019). The fundamental British value that Blair and other politicians implicitly defend is that the needs, wishes and interests of the majority white population shall take precedence over the aspirations of ethno-religious minorities for equity in employment and in the other institutions of society. Blair and his group have also condemned "non-violent but extremist" Muslims (e.g. political activists of whatever type) as "potential terrorists" who are "failing to integrate" (IHRC, 2019).

Chapter Eight

Exploitation of Girls and Women Through Enforced Prostitution in the Culture of Bangladesh: Denial of Islamic Moral Principles

Christopher Adam-Bagley, Sadia Kadri and Afroze Shahnaz

1. Summary of Findings, and Synopsis of our Argument

From a review of literature and from our ethnographic field work, we present an analysis of the sexual abuse of children, girls and women engaged in "sex work" in Bangladeshi brothels. We argue that *commercially sexual exploited women and children* (CSEWC) often involves a variety of abuses, sexual, physical, emotional, and economic. "Sex work" is a major industry in Bangladesh, and up to 1% of girls and women in the population aged 12 to 49 are subject to being CSEWC, for shorter or longer periods.

Men of all ages and classes use CSEWC. Although rates of HIV/AIDS remain relatively low in the overall population, HIV is estimated to have a lifetime prevalence of up to 5% in long-term CSEWC, while STIs (sexually transmitted infections) affect about 40% of CSEWC, and up to 15% of men who regularly use them. There is some evidence that men's widespread use of CSEWC spreads STIs to their wives, so that rates in women in the general population are high. The women subject to CSEWC themselves suffer numerous physical and sexual abuses, and have poor physical and mental health. In addition, the trafficking of children (to countries of the Middle East, and India, for purposes of labour and sexual exploitation) is entirely contrary to principles of Islamic morality and jurisprudence (Alshareef, 2018).

Police and local officials in Bangladesh are involved in the toleration of this abuse, and about a third of money paid by men for sexual services passes to corrupt officials (Redfern, 2018). We advocate support for the growing movement of adult women who campaign against the abuse of CSEWC, as a means of ending at least the exploitation of children and adolescents. We advocate also programmes of preventive education for high school students, as well as the reiteration of the norms of an Islamic culture which should end the sexual abuse of women and children. We also advocate, following Indian examples, the introduction of a basic income which would give women choices, enabling them to escape the life of CSEWC.

2. An Economically Poor Nation, with Widening Gaps Between Rich and Poor

Farley et al. (2015) categorise those who do research on prostituted women and children into two camps: those who view such "sex work" as labour, which implies some degree of voluntary entry; and those who see such activity as part of the broader spectrum of "sexual exploitation", of children, adolescents and women, a status over which the individuals involved have few choices, and would exit if they could. We belong, firmly, to this latter group of scholars and activists. The nature of "sex work" (or CSEWC: *commercialised sexual exploited women and children*, as we prefer to call this group) varies in different world cultures, reflecting different traditions, moral values, and legal systems (Adam-Bagley, 2017 & 2018).

One important variable described in the literature is the role of "sex tourists" who visit countries such as Thailand and The Philippines (Jeffrey, 2003; Law, 2003; Urada et al., 2014). In other countries of Asia, such as Pakistan, India, Nepal and Bangladesh the men who access sexually exploited girls and women are almost entirely from *local* cultures (Emmanuel et al., 2013; Nessa et al. 2005; Sarkhar et al., 2008; Simkhada & Adam-Bagley, 2008).

Bangladesh provides an extraordinary case study of *commercialised sexual exploitation* (CSE), which is enforced through bonds of poverty, and sanctioned by a corrupt legal and administrative system (Islam & Smith, 2016). This country is one of the world's poorest, with an average income of US$1,440 per annum. However, national income is unevenly distributed, and 13% of Bangladeshi adults have an income that is less than US$2.50 per day (less than $1000 per annum) (Misha & Sulaiman, 2016). Most girls and many boys do not complete primary education, and 18% of women have little option but to marry before the age of 15, usually to men at least a decade older (Rashid, 2006).

Although an increase in average wages (mainly in workers in textile industries) puts the average wage of the Bangladeshi worker above that in Nepal and Pakistan, the gap in child health indicators between the wealthy classes, and the mass of the population who are poor is *increasing* in Bangladesh (Rabbani et al., 2016).

Some reasons for this are offered by Nurazzaman (2004) in his argument that chronic poverty, which is increasing in relative terms, results from the imposition on Bangladesh of neoliberal policies of international aid bodies; and international monetary policies which have mainly enriched the 50 very wealthy families who control capitalist enterprises in Bangladesh. Rahman shows that small farmers, labourers, small traders and business people, service workers and the intermittently employed rural poor – all have incomes which have declined since 1980, in relative terms. The main employers of labour are now the clothing mills, which engender large profits for a group of capitalists, and very moderate rewards for those who actually make the clothing for Western retail outlets. These enterprises reflect the move from state control of industry and enterprise to complete privatisation (as required by those giving aid and loans to Bangladesh), since 1980. By 1990 these privatisation policies were in full flow, and the large-scale acquisition of commercial ownership by "the 50 families" began.

Rahman (2001) found that by 2000:

> *Hundreds of thousands of workers are now becoming unemployed due to the closing down of both state-owned and private industries, but government is doing nothing to help these workers. The workers who have lost their jobs are now living a sub-standard life. Many of them have been compelled to withdraw their children from schools. Their children have become child labour, sex labour, breaking bricks on the streets* ... (p. 21)

Children as cheap labour are preferred by employers regardless of the difficulty or dangerousness of the tasks they perform. The village brothels of Bangladesh also provide a useful form of child labour, from whom impoverished adults may benefit. Underage street prostitution is another form of labour which may benefit impoverished families – or at least it provides a subsistence income for homeless children. Shahjahan et al. (2016) in their study of child labour in Bangladesh found that about 12% of these children had never enrolled in schooling, while 59% failed to complete primary schooling. 1.4 million children aged less than 15 were engaged in "hazardous work", with about 150,000 employed in roles which involved "sexual abuse and exploitation".

Labour laws to prevent such exploitation are weak, and rarely enforced effectively. The cause of such child labour, according to Shahjahan et al. (2016) was extreme poverty of parents, who themselves had rarely completed elementary schooling. Figures may be underestimates, because of lack of registration of children's births amongst the very poor. Causes of poverty were seen to be the extremes of inequality in society, which perpetuated poverty and exploitation.

Service provision for treatment of childhood diseases is poor, and Rahman & Rahman (2018) estimate that on current trends (other things being equal) Bangladesh will fail to meet the WHO *Universal Health Care* goals of achieving free and universal coverage of child and maternal health care by 2030, although up to 80% of infectious diseases and malnutrition-caused conditions will be addressed by that year. However, predictions such as these do not factor in the effects of climate change, which in Bangladesh are likely to be dire, with many areas flooded because of rising seas, and patterns of agriculture changed or permanently failing because of glacial melt reduced river flows, and more erratic monsoon seasons (Glennon, 2017). An important question on the profoundly negative effects of climate change on the economy (and health) of Bangladesh is not how much, but how soon.

Looking to the past, we argue from the available evidence that exploitive capitalism in Bangladesh is a spinoff from global neoliberalism, specialising in producing cheap garments for Western countries, by the five million workers in this sector. Such work is carried out in poor safety condition, and although profit margins for employers are high, occupational mortality rates in garment factories (by Western standards) are also high (Safi & Rushe, 2018).[1] At the bottom of the employment strata are the men and boys who do difficult and dangerous work such as cleaning human waste out of the sewers of Dhaka, work which has a high fatality rate (McPherson, 2018); and the girls who endure commercialised sexual exploitation. This is despite

---

[1] Another task which Bangladesh performs for the international capitalist system is shipbreaking, in which dozens of beached cargo ships foul the shores of Chittagong with leaking materials, while thousands of men undertake the breaking down and cutting up of the vessels for scrap under extremely hazardous conditions without safety gear, ingesting a variety of substances including asbestos; their fatality rate is high, their wages low (Gibbs, 2019). A similar type of shipbreaking beach exists in Gadani, Pakistan. Here too workers' mortality rate is high (HRCP, 2017).

that fact that the exploitation of girls and women for sexual purposes is *haram*, profoundly forbidden in the Islamic moral system.

3. 'No Place is Safe': High Prevalence of Rape and Murder of Girls in Rural Bangladesh

Islam (2015) in reviewing both Islamic moral codes and Bangladeshi laws with regard to the exploitation and abuse of children and minors, observes that:

> Bangladesh has experienced a growth in child killings and abuse in recent years; most of the sufferers have been lowly and poor children. Islam strictly prohibits all sorts of abuse towards the child. Islamic basic norms to the child are love, mercy and compassion which are uniquely practiced by the Prophet (s.m). ... Islam forbids abuse of children; their exploitation is excluded and child labor is prohibited ... buying or selling children for purpose of prostitutions are prohibited under the Bangladeshi laws.

Nevertheless, Islam concludes, in modern Bangladesh Islamic guidance is frequently ignored, and secular laws concerning child abuse and exploitation are rarely applied.

Naznin Tithi (2017) has written (from a journalist's viewpoint) a penetrating expose of the ever-present danger of sexual assault and rape and sexual assault of girls in rural Bangladesh. We reprint this excerpt with permission, for it seems to us to be an essential complement to more detailed ethnographic accounts. This Dhaka *Daily Star* journalist wrote on October 25th, 2017:

> On October 21, one of the most depressing news reports was of the rape of a seven-year-old girl by her 45-year-old neighbour in Jessore. The less than one hundred word report was published in an inner page of the daily. And not all newspapers even reported the incident. Not surprisingly, the news escaped the eyes of many ... but we may get a glimpse of the horrific crimes committed against children in the country from the reports of NGOs. According to Bangladesh Shishu Adhikar Forum, a total of 494 children were raped in the eight months from January till August this year—among them 58 were gang-raped. According to their statistics, 37 disabled children were raped during this time, while 46 were victims of attempted rape. And as Manusher Jonno Foundation (MJF) has reported, at least 15 children died as a result of rape in the nine months since January to September this year.
>
> A Daily Star *study in 2015 found that 82 percent of the rape victims in the country were under the age of 20. Children are sexually harassed and raped*

by their neighbours and close relatives, schoolchildren are raped by their teachers and school staff (A study by The Daily Star *found that 52 percent of rape victims are schoolchildren), domestic workers have been raped by their employers—a sickening rape culture seems to have engulfed the whole society. The situation is so horrifying that even babies are not spared. According to a study by BRAC, around 1.7 children were raped on an average every day in Bangladesh last year. Let's look at some recent newspaper reports. On October 9 this year, a 12-year-old girl was gang-raped on her way home after she fled her employers' house where she had been tortured regularly. A seven-year-old girl was raped by her neighbour in Savar's Begunbari area on September 26. A three-year-and-nine-month old girl was raped and murdered by a neighbour at the end of July. A seven-year-old girl was found raped and killed in Dhaka's Jatrabari on October 1. ... some cases of child rape have received media attention, especially after outcry on social media, but sadly [because of under-reporting] these are only a fraction of the officially processed cases of rapes of children. When crimes against children are all pervasive in our society, our efforts to fight these crimes should be persistent ...*

Naznin Tithi references a BRAC study. BRAC stands for Bangladesh Rural Advancement Committee, an internationally regarded NGO famous for giving small, no-interest loans to rural people for business and agriculture. BRAC now sponsors a bank and a university, and is famed for its freedom from corruption, an issue which may plague some NGOs. BRAC's efforts to bring quality education to rural primary schools are also noteworthy (Nath, 2008 & 2017).

The BRAC study reported by Fattah & Kabir (2013) reviewed all 1,117 cases of rape and sexual assault against minors (aged less than 18) known to BRAC's community action teams in an area of rural Bangladesh in the previous 5 years, and gives a detailed analysis of the 713 cases (99% female victims) involving actual rape (thus excluding most cases of within-family sexual assaults which involved victim-grooming). The rapes most frequently occurred in public spaces or buildings (including schools and madrasahs). In 80% of cases the rapes were perpetrated by individuals previously known to the victim. Only 27% of those reporting received any medical or psychological support from any agency.

The majority of rapes were of girls aged 7 to 15. In rural Bangladesh 65% of girls will marry before the age of 18: once married, the girl was much less likely to be raped, since she was then publicly "owned" by one man, and not by the male community in general. Gang rape occurred in 8% of cases, and in another 4% the victim was murdered during the course of the rape; 2% of girls killed themselves soon after a violent and public rape. A girl whom the community knows to be a rape victim will lose status, with diminished marriage prospects. It is likely, then, that many rapes go unreported. In only 10% of reported cases was an alleged offender(s) subjected to legal arraignment, most often when the victim was publicly murdered. The perpetrators were most likely to be unmarried men in their 'twenties, but older men and boys also perpetrated rapes.

The sociological context of this "rape culture" is important. Many men and boys apparently feel a sense of natural entitlement to have free sexual access to unmarried females, and there is an implicit tolerance for boys and men who rape in a countryside in which "no place is safe" for unmarried girls and women. Nothing in the religious or secular education of boys has addressed the issue that the rape of a child is morally and spiritually wrong. We can find no evidence that these cultural norms are changing, or that the rape of girls is diminishing. But understanding these cultural norms regarding the degraded power and sexual status of girls gives us a better understanding of Bangladeshi culture, and its tolerance of Brothel Villages.

An incident occurring in April, 2019 received considerable publicity (Sabbir, 2019). A teenaged girl, Nusrat Jahan Rafi complained to police that the head teacher in her madrasah had sexually assaulted her, and she also complained of sexual assault by male students. These students set her on fire in the madrasah, but before she died the girl spoke into her phone naming those who had doused her in kerosene, apparently creating a 'fake suicide'. Following media exposure, there was a mass demonstration of mostly women and girls demanding the end of sexual crimes against girls and women. Whether this is the beginning of a "Me Too" movement in Bangladesh is too early to say.

4. The Brothels of Bangladesh

Bangladesh is an overtly Muslim society (a religion which offers, in the conduct of everyday life, strict rules forbidding 'fornication', and the rape and murder of children): nevertheless 'brothels' – entire villages clustered within urban centres – are legally tolerated, and widely used by men. *The Guardian* newspaper of London has taken a special interest in these 'sex villages', and the feature articles and filmed reports by its correspondents are worthy of consultation by those who seek ethnographic insights into life in these villages, and the men who frequent them.

"Prostitution" (legally defined as penetrative sexual relations between a man and a woman aged 18 or over, in which money has been paid for this sexual access) is generally legal in Bangladesh, but statutes specify fines, and periods of imprisonment for sexually using, or trafficking for sexual purposes, those aged less than 18, and for being an intermediate person in sexual transactions involving persons of any age. We have been unable to locate any reports of prosecutions in this regard, however.[2]

"Operating or working in a brothel" apparently has an ambiguous legal status, which police and local officials exploit, allowing women to continue in sex work only if they pay "fines" (i.e. bribes, to corrupt police and officials) (SWN & SWASA, 2016). Police also have the power to arrest any woman on arbitrary grounds, as "a public nuisance", a strategy which ensures that they can pocket bribes from the sex worker, or from the person who "owns" her, in this form of bondage or slavery. To use a sex worker, the customer will pay around US$3 (three dollars). A third of this will go to corrupt officials, a third to the "owner" of the sex worker, and a third to the worker herself: unless she has been sold by her family or by kidnappers, to the brothel, in which case the bonded or enslaved individual (almost always a child or adolescent) will receive nothing (Shamim, 2010). The exact number of CSEWC is unknown, but it may be as high as 1% of the total population of impoverished girls and women aged 10 to 39, including those who manage to escape these sexually exploited roles (Vandepitte et al., 2006). At any point in time about a quarter of this 1% will be actively exploited in commercialised sex.

Younger CSE people are in greater demand than older females, and may have to service up to 20 males a day. Shamim (2010) who studied these brothel villages, estimated that more than 40% of the CSEWC (commercially sexually exploited women and children) were aged 13-17. By the time, she is 30, a woman is much less attractive to customers, so she relies for her meagre existence on the earnings of her younger sisters, and her children. Some too will become "managers", a desperate survival strategy in the perpetuation of this commercial sexual exploitation.

Our informants, who gave detailed information concerning daily life in the Bangladesh brothels were women who had left sex work in order to organise

---

[2] See the articles and short films which are available online from www.theguardian.com in the issues of: April 5, 2010; March 14, 2014; November 2, 2016; May 17, 2017. See too Al-Jazeera (2017) for a filmed documentary (available on YouTube) on 'Bangladesh's biggest brothel where 1,500 women work as prostitutes, some as young as 10.' See also Fortin's (2015) photo-journal essay on Binshanta Brothel.

collectives of women who campaign for better treatment of those who are forced to perform CSE roles, as well as workers from NGOs working in the brothel-villages (Eva et al., 2007; Sultana, 2015; SWT & SWASA, 2016). Most of the male "clients" are Bangladeshi, with a few Indian migrant workers (truck drivers, seamen, bargemen). Bangladesh is not a country which Western sex tourists visit.

The government, at the ministerial level, condemns such trafficking and points to the six "rescue centres" across Bangladesh.[3] These centres take in juveniles, but the numbers who are "rescued" is small, relative to the total number of juveniles coerced into sex work, well over 100,000 at any point in time (Shamim, 2010; Zareen, 2014; Shahjahan et al., 2016). One factor hampering the reintegration of rescued children is the continued stigma against CSEWC of any age. Paradoxically perhaps, significant numbers of men who use "sex workers", simultaneously despise the girls and women whom they exploit (Corraya, 2015). Perpetuating this stigma is part of the process which ensures that little official action is taken on behalf of the vulnerable population of CSEWC.

Bangladesh is unique in being a Muslim majority (89%) country, in which institutionalised commercial sexual exploitation is a visible, public institution. In Bangladeshi cities, there are (known to us) 20 brothel-villages each containing between 800 and 1,600 sexually exploited women and children, and their dependents, living in one-storey shanty dwellings. Families of women, from grandmother to grandchild, live in these villages – the children usually being conceived through commercial sexual exploitation, or by their controllers.

In perpetuation of this exploitation, the women who bear children in the brothels are rarely married, and their children are stigmatised from birth. Many of the female children are inducted into sexual exploitation at around the age of 12, while a small number of younger male children may be sold to international traffickers.[4] This may be the only way in which a woman can earn enough capital to escape from the slavery of the brothel. Interviews

---

[3] The reader who is fluent in Bangla, may gain a sense of Ministerial views from several YouTube films, for example: *A Documentary of Prostitution Area in Bangladesh: The Documentary Channel*. Posted to YouTube on May 10, 2016. https://www.youtube.com/watch?v=gMiObyyoNZY There are several videos, in Bangla, on YouTube on sex work in Bangladesh which provide details of the views of officials, NGOs, and of the women themselves.
[4] The fate of these male children is unknown. Reviews of research have not located any relevant studies (Joffres et al., 2008).

with the young children who had not yet become "sex workers", are presented in the film made by Silverman and Tait (2016).

In addition to these brothel-villages, sectors of cities include 'red-light' streets and tenement areas, each housing hundreds of women who are commercially sexually exploited "sex workers". The total number of these areas is unknown, but they are widespread. In addition, in several areas of cities there are low-rent "hotels", where the "customer" will pay a somewhat higher fee than in the brothel (Haseen et al., 2012). There are also an unknown number of women and children who are "street prostitutes" (Rahman et al., 2000). In the brothel-villages children are born, become objects of sexual exploitation early in life, and they will also be likely to die in the brothels, often at a young age. An organisation of sex workers has been campaigning, so far without success, for the right to bury their dead within the confines of these brothel-villages (SWN & SWASA, 2016).

Brothel managers now frequently require younger teenagers (aged 12 to 17) to take the steroid drug Oradexon (or Dexamethasone), a hydrocortisone medication (also used for fattening cattle, being low cost when purchased in bulk) whose side effect causes plumpness of body, so that a fragile 12-year-old can be passed off as a plumper or more "attractive" girl. It appears that a plump prepubertal child is more attractive to the male who pays a small amount of money in order to rape her.

This drug also causes hyperglycaemia, hormonal dysfunction, diabetes type 2, raised blood pressure, weakened immune system (with emergence of latent diseases such as TB), kidney disease, and reproductive disorders (low birth weight or malformations in infants). Girls may be forced to take this drug for several years, with unknown effects on their long-term health, but early mortality seems a distinct possibility. How this drug may affect the acquisition and immune response to STIs is unknown.

It was clear from a comprehensive health assay by Wahed and colleagues (2017) that the sexual and reproductive health of 'brothel village' women aged 15 to 49 is very poor: 15% had an abortion by various and often unsafe means in the previous year (abortions usually forced on them because pregnancy reduced their availability for "sex work"); those who carried a pregnancy to term had poor prenatal care; 42% had a sexually transmitted infection (STI); unmet physical health needs were "substantial".

A psychiatric survey of 224 inividuals aged 11 and over in a Chittagong brothel village by Hengartner et al. (2015) found 86% would "quit if they could". Poverty and coercion were the main reasons which kept them trapped in "sex work": 39% had a serious psychiatric illness; "dangerous drug use" (a means of psychological escape from the daily impact of sexual slavery) was common. "Suicide" was usually effected by means of drug overdose, but was rarely entered into official records as completed suicide. Aldama (2017) re-interviewed women in the Faridpur brothel after five years, and reported a number of deaths in CSE women he had seen earlier: "For sex workers in Bangladesh the future is as bleak as the past."

Men enter brothel villages not only to purchase sex, but also to buy drugs and alcohol which they consume in the brothel, since this kind of purchase and use is legally forbidden elsewhere. Many CSEWC use methamphetamine (*Yaba*, methamphetamine cut with caffeine, costing in 2019 about £2.30 for an addict's daily dose), in chronically high doses. 'Users' are likely to be 'spaced out', in a psychotic-like withdrawal from their experience of a debased reality. Women in this state can rarely insist that customers use a condom.

The youngest of the commercially exploited population in Dhaka are the homeless street children, aged 5 to 12. They can earn up to US75 cents a day doing odd jobs for traders, but can make more from being objects of sexual exploitation, often as much as five dollars a day for servicing customers in dark corners. Boys as well as girls are subjected to this exploitation (29% of those studied by Uddin et al., 2014a). Condoms, according to Uddin et al. (2014a & b) of 493 street children, are never used, and boys as well as girls are subject to oral and penetrative sex. This study found that 9% of the children were drug injectors, sharing needles. Health care for this group was non-existent, but significant numbers described symptoms suggesting STIs. These children are clearly at risk of contracting, and spreading, HIV/AIDS. If they survive to 18, 80% of male street youth will have themselves used CSEWC, or will have been so used themselves (McClair et al., 2017). Overall, the rate of HIV/AIDS in street level CSEWC at any point in time may be in excess of 10% (Shannon et al., 2015). Many street children are addicted to Yaba, and engage in sex work to support an addiction which costs about £2.30 a day to support.[5]

---

[5] Yaba (methamphetamine and caffeine) addiction, affecting about 4 million Bangladeshis has allowed a drug-peddling mafia to thrive, and also gives the police an excuse to shoot suspects (and others) both before and after arrest (Khan & Jinnat, 2019; Presley, 2019).

The most recent estimate of the number of CSEWC comes from the UN AIDS prevention agency (UNAIDS, 2016). This estimate was of about 140,000 women at risk through "sex work" at any point in time. This estimate does not account for hidden populations, such as the 'invisible' street children who hustle sex in order to survive; those who have died before age 39 as a result of sexual exploitation; and the numbers who manage to escape, perhaps for a temporary period, from these exploited roles. The population of CCSEWC are, perhaps, a 'stage army'. This is why researchers have estimated that the numbers of girls and women involved may involve, over a 10 year period, up to 1% of all girls and women enduring chronic poverty.

5. Men and STIs (Sexually Transmitted Infections)

The feminist researcher Elizabeth Pisani (2008) has raised an angry voice against the "AIDS bureaucracy", the volume of medical researchers whose growing interest in sex workers is funded by granting agencies fearsome of the possibility that women in sex work may be infecting "ordinary" men with HIV/AIDS. Surprisingly, several studies have shown the rate of HIV disease to be relatively low in Bangladeshi CSEWC (national rate 0.15% in 2014), although rates of Sexually Transmitted Infections (STIs) (chlamydia, syphilis, gonorrhoea and other infections) exceed 40% in CSEWC (Azim et al, 2008; Baral et al., 2012; Eva et al., 2007; Hosein & Chatterjee, 2007; Hossain et al., 2014; Islam & Conigrave, 2008; Nessa et al., 2005; Mondai, 2008; Nessa et al., 2008; Rahman et al., 2000; Uddin et al., 2014a & b).

HIV rates are certainly elevated in injecting drug users (mostly males) who share needles (Azim et al., 2008). But HIV/AIDS in the general population of Bangladesh is less than 0.2% (Nessa et al., 2005). Epidemiological research suggests that rates of various STIs (but not of HIV, which technically is not a sexually transmitted disease) are high in Bangladesh, not only in CSEWC, but also in women in the general population (Hawke et al., 1999; Nessa et al., 2005; Bogaerts et al., 2001; Rashid, 2006; Baral et al., 2012; Nessa et al., 2008). This implies that the use of commercially sexually exploited women and children has become to some degree normalised among sectors of Bangladeshi men, both married and unmarried, who pass infections on to their present and future wives.

Although rates of HIV/AIDS in the general population are "low" compared with some other developing countries, in all type of CSEWC HIV may have a lifetime prevalence of up to 5% (Shannon et al., 2015). The possibility exists therefore of the spread of HIV infections to the wider population, given the widespread use by "ordinary" men of commercial sex.[6] Noor & Munna (2015) describe new groups of microbiological disease associated with lack of condom use, which are difficult to treat, may be fatal, and increase the risk of HIV transmission.

A crucial issue is not that point-prevalence rates of HIV/AIDS are relatively low in CSEWC in Bangladesh (compared, say, with Africa): rather, the conditions of such exploitation could mean that *an epidemic of HIV transmission could occur at any time*. Early screening for those at risk of HIV/AIDS is atypical, and the infected individual may only go to a public hospital when they are extremely ill with an infectious disease (most typically, TB) which is caused by their weakened immune system. Late diagnosis of HIV/AIDS in Bangladesh accounts for the fact that according to one study, 19% of those hospitalised had died within six months (Shahrin et al., 2014). A major source of HIV transmission in Bangladesh is in men who return from work in other countries, having acquired the infection through the use of commercial sex providers: they may then pass on the infection to their wives, local CSEWC, or both (Urmi et al., 2015).

Rob & Mutahara (2000) in a study of 2,600 Bangladeshi male adolescents found that 5% were sexually experienced (15% prior to the age of 16), usually with CSEWC. In older slum-dwelling adolescent males, 80% will be sexually experienced, mostly with CSEWC. A unique study from Bangladesh (and indeed, a rare kind of study in the world literature on STIs) comes from Haseen et al. (2012).[7]

These researchers asked 1,013 young men (aged 15 to 25, mean 21.1 years) to provide blood and urine samples, and to complete a short questionnaire when they visited "hotel brothels" in Dhaka, Bangladesh. A quarter of these males were aged 18 or less, and of the whole group 46% had their first sex in such a hotel, usually before the age of 21. Of the young men studied, 15%

---

[6] HIV is mainly a blood-borne disease, but can be transmitted sexually via semen, especially in those who have an STI, such as syphilis (Chaillon et al., 2017). "Pre-exposure prophylaxis" (medication taken by the HIV-infected person) appears to be very effective in preventing sexual cross-infection of HIV (Blackstock et al., 2017). However, the current cost of this drug is around US$50 a month, per patient, and is unavailable for most of those with HIV infection in Bangladesh.
[7] Note also the valuable study of Qudus (2015) of the sexual histories of some older 400 men living in slum areas of Bangladesh. According to his informants, 80% of men said that they had engaged in completed intercourse before or outside of marriage, the majority with CSEWC. Similar findings were made by Jha et al. (2014) in India.

were married. Most held office or service sector jobs, a half having completed (or were still attending) high school: 52% had "good" knowledge of how sexually transmitted diseases were transmitted, and most of this group used condoms. Nevertheless, 37% never used condoms. 50% used CSEWC at least once a month, and 25% did so weekly. Almost all of this latter group used condoms. In the whole sample 15% tested positive for one or more of: gonorrhoea, syphilis, genital herpes, or another type of STI. One phenomenon noted were the reports of young men (9% of sample) joining together (probably for financial reasons) in a group, having serial sexual relations with one woman: in such situations, condom use was atypical.

It is notable that only 52% of a sample of male high school students had acquired reliable knowledge of HIV/STI transmission from their school curricula, such as the need for condom use when using "sex workers" (Huda & Ferdous, 2018). This raises the issue of the degree to which such curricula should educate young people of the problems of such promiscuity not merely for public health purposes, but from an ethical, moral and religious perspective as well.

6. Male Sexuality and Moral and Religious Dimensions of Bangladeshi Culture

Haseen et al. (2012) and Huda & Ferdous, 2018) make worthwhile proposals: in addressing CSEWC, a good place to start is the education of high school boys. We would add that not only should such education address the "dangers" of such sex, but it should also address the rights of women not to be sexually exploited, and the teachings of Islam forbidding such behaviours. Of course, issues of consent, equality and respect for women are contained in the religious values of all world cultures, and are often reflected in legal statutes, including Bangladeshi and Shari'a laws. The issue is one of value change with regard to the dignity and equality of women, and the application of existing moral values and statutes.

We must ask: why in predominantly Muslim societies (such as Bangladesh and Pakistan) are Islamic norms concerning sexual purity and expression so frequently violated? Bradley (2010), Gohir (2010) and Qudus (2015) in surveying sexuality the Islamic world, point to Middle Eastern countries as well as to Pakistan, Bangladesh and Afghanistan as countries where child marriages are tolerated, commercialised sexual exploitation of children is common, and daughters may be prostituted by their fathers through the institution of "temporary marriage (*mut'ah*)".

Child marriage is sometimes used in Bangladesh as a means of acquiring a girl who can then be sold to a brothel, for two or three years (Redfern, 2018). During this time, the girl receives no income from her enforced work, since she is "paying off her debt" to the man who exploits her, and regards himself as her "owner". Police are usually aware of this sexual bondage of children, but may accept payments which allows them to profit from this form of slavery (Redfern, 2018).

Several informants also gave accounts of the trafficking of Bangladeshi girls into brothels in India and further afield, often with the false promise of marriage or employment. It is clear from the literature surveyed, and from our informants, that child bondage, trafficking, violence and rape are common in the brothels of Bangladesh, and also for the Bangladeshi girls trafficked to India and elsewhere for sex work (Hengartner et al., 2015; Hudy, 2006; ILO, 1998; Alshareef, 2018). Another form of trafficking involves the sale of adolescent girls to traffickers for purposes of "marriage" to Indian men. Blanchet (2005) followed up 112 of these girls, and found them living in conditions of servitude, often unable to speak local or national languages of India. Maltreatment was frequent.

Our informants gave vivid accounts of recent cases of such child slavery, and trafficking of girls into brothels, and the violence imposed on them to ensure sexual conformity. Clark (2015) writes of a world which has ignored the plight of Bangladeshi sex workers, focussing more frequently on the world of sex tourism in Thailand and The Philippines, and the threat of HIV infections to the white men who visit as sex tourists. But there are now welcome signs in Bangladesh and elsewhere of women becoming more militant and organised in their struggle to achieve 'better' conditions in commercialised sexual exploitation (SWN & SWASA, 2016).

Among the several brave women rising above the sexual exploitation of the brothels of Bangladesh is Hazera Begum, one of our informants. Now aged 46, Hazera escaped brothel life at the age of 23, and began rescuing 'at risk' street children - becoming foster mother to 40 of them, and helping many others. Several of the children she fostered are now attending university, and all have remained in high school. In March, 2019 Hazera was nominated as one of seven women who are "unsung heroes of Bangladesh", including some brave women who were active in Bangladesh's liberation in 1971 (Bari, 2019).

Ethnographic work has identified an interesting phenomenon, of girls from middle class families who spurning arranged marriages, now give mutual support as independent "sex workers," in higher income apartment blocks. These women include several college students, and graduates. This is an interesting form of a feminist collective which rejects the sexism inherent in men's approach to women in Bangladesh. Lysistrata-like[8], these women deny men sexual access, unless they pay for it (and also use condoms; and eschew verbal and physical violence). This development is paralleled by interesting movements both within the brothel villages, and in the wider society, by older women organising collectively for better treatment, a fairer reward for their exploitation, and for a heightened respect for the service they perform (Alam et al., 2013; Eva et al., 2007; Jenkins et al., 2002; Khan, 2013; Pisani, 2008; Salim, 2004). But our fieldwork suggests that this beginning movement has an uphill task.

7. Conclusions

The ending of child and adolescent sexual exploitation in the Bangladeshi brothels must be a major priority if the moral principles of Islam are to be followed. The rise of militant Islam in Bangladesh may not be helpful in this regard however: it has, for example, resulted in the burning down of a 'red-light' tenement, endangering lives and impoverishing further, hundreds of girls and women. We note too, with dismay, the actions of a mob in tearing down the structure of one of the brothel villages, and beating and injuring the women there (SWN & SWASA, 2016). We were unable to get a sense from NGOs, media and government that there is any official impetus to end this exploitation (Corraya, 2015).

Our conclusion from this overview of commercially-exploited sex work in Bangladesh must be one of pessimism. The United Nations Office on Drugs and Crime as well as various media are well aware of the problems of children and adolescents who are treated as sex slaves. Yet we can find no evidence of progress in ending their exploitation, at an official level. Our argument is that *all* of sex work involving minors is a form of slavery, and its continuation can no more be justified than could the slavery of Africans by Europeans in North America.

The institutionalisation of sexual exploitation of women and children both creates and reinforces the general value that women are creatures who may be violated in brothels, controlled and abused outside of the brothels and the

---

[8] Lysistrata is the title of a play by Aristophanes in ancient Greece, where women denied sexual access to men unless they ended an internecine war with a neighbouring state.

red-light zones of cultures east and west, and abused in society at large (Adam-Bagley, 1997; Adam-Bagley & King, 2003; King, 2016). We must acknowledge that modern sexual slavery is often consumer-driven and dependent on inequalities of gender, ethnicity, and social class (Farley & Kelly, 2008).

The sexual abuse of children, adolescents and women is built into the general ethos of male hegemony within the culture of many countries. Parallel to the value change required, world poverty and its ending must be a major goal. Thus, we advocate the enhancement and growth of both traditional, and new values (religious and secular) on the rights and dignity of women (Salim, 2004). And offering programmes which develop skills training in adolescent females (and in sexually-exploited women and their children) can be a relatively effective way of increasing choices for these girls (Shohel et al., 2012; Amin et al., 2018).

One viable solution for enhancing women's options which we advocate is the introduction of a "Citizen's Income" available as a basic right to all.[9] Experimental work in India (Davala et al., 2015; Safi, 2017) has shown that guaranteeing each citizen a basic wage (in the Indian context of about US$80 a year, and half that sum for any child), decreases malnutrition and increases productivity and school attendance, and for women in particular allows them options of delaying marriage, choosing educational pathways and careers, as well as increasing choices on when and if to have children. The economics of the citizen's basic income have been extensively discussed by economists and political scientists (Davala et al, 2015; Jameson, 2016; Standing, 2011; Torry, 2015) and it would certainly fit well with a free market economy. But of course, ending the commercialized sexual abuse of women and children involves much more than economic issues: fundamental value changes are necessary.

Nevertheless, if international capitalism which ultimately controls the economic welfare of Bangladesh can countenance the idea of a "citizen's income" (which enables families to keep girls in education for longer, and reduces reliance on child marriage, and other forms of sexual exploitation) then there would be many gains, and Bangladesh might emerge as a truly moral, Islamic culture.

---

[9] Another possibility is "microfinance", small loans which enable women to start businesses. These may have had some success in enabling women to avoid the violence of commercial sexual exploitation, and STI risk, in Bangladesh and elsewhere (Schuler et al., 1996; Sharif, 2001; Dworkin & Blankenship, 2009).

Chapter Nine

Suicidal Behaviours in Bangladeshi Girls and Women, and the Oppression of Women in an Islamic Culture: Issues for Feminist Conscious-Raising and Intervention

Christopher Adam-Bagley, Afroze Shahnaz and Sadia Kadri

1. Introduction and Overview

Deaths by suicide in Bangladesh have an atypical sex ratio, with higher rates in females than in males, a characteristic shared with several countries in Southern Asia. Reasons for this are explored. An examination of social structure in Bangladesh suggests that girls and women are subjected to high rates of sexual and physical violence compared with males, especially in rural and urban slum areas. This violence is often linked to the enforced marriage of young girls to older men.

Our systematic review of 23 studies on suicide and suicidal behaviours in Bangladesh has shown that suicide death rates are exceptionally high in younger women, at a rate of about 20 per 100,000, more than twice the rate in males aged less than 49. In girls aged 15 to 17 the estimated suicide rate is 14 per 100,000, 50% higher than in males. Because of problems in obtaining systematic data on deaths by suicide, these rates are likely to be underestimates.

Extreme poverty and lack of education have been recorded as factors in deaths by suicide, although there are methodological problems in reaching such conclusions. We speculate that some of the "suicides" (especially those using poison) may in fact be cases of murder. A dowry system (not sanctioned by Islam) is thought to be a major cause of family poverty, and violence experienced by young girls. In proposing solutions, we argue the case (as Muslims) for the support of an Islamic feminism which urges better support for girls growing up in extreme poverty.

Suicide in young people in Bangladesh is a notable issue for public health suicide prevention strategies:

> *Every year on Sept 10,* World Suicide Prevention Day *is an opportunity to raise awareness and increase literacy on a highly complex and wide-reaching global health problem. WHO estimates that around 800 000 people die by suicide every year, but this number is likely to be just the tip of the iceberg: for reasons that include the stigma shrouding suicide in many cultures, the lack of adequate vital registration systems, or even the arduous administrative steps that go with the registration of a self-inflicted death, many suicides remain undetected or are routinely misclassified. Regardless of the limitations in the available data, suicides are without doubt among the top 20 causes of death worldwide, and the second leading cause of mortality among people aged 15–29 years, with great variations by region and population group. Perhaps surprisingly but also worryingly, close to 80% of suicides are thought to occur in low-income and middle-income countries (LMICs), where fewer public health resources and reduced access to mental health services limit prevention efforts.* Editorial Lancet Global Health, August 14, 2017.

2. Why are Suicide Death Rates in Bangladeshi Females so High, Compared with Those in Males?

The World Health Organisation in issuing periodic information on completed suicide (WHO, 2016) offers a warning to those who try and interpret the data presented on 183 world nations. The quality of the information on suicide rates (that is, the reliability and validity of the rates of suicide submitted by different countries) is not guaranteed by the WHO. Actual rates may vary according to methods of case finding, which reflect particular medico-legal systems, and cultural views concerning suicide, of contrasted countries. For this reason, Silverman & De Leo (2016) advocate much greater international co-operation in standardising the terms used in deciding on whether a death has been caused by suicide, including an agreement between different national jurisdictions of whether such a death is suicide, beyond reasonable doubt. Collaborating countries should also work towards standardisation of criteria for allocation of cases to the "undetermined" category which often display the same social and psychological factors as completed suicides (Shrivastava, Kimbrell & Lester, 2012).

Where systems of deciding cause of death are carried out systematically, by a legally-trained forensic pathologist following clear legal guidelines – as in, say the Medical Examiner systems in Europe and North America – there is reasonable certainty that most deaths by suicide are counted. However, in developing countries where registration of births and deaths is not standardised, and where stigma both social and religious is attached to the act of suicide, estimates emerging from national governments may seriously underestimate the rate of deaths by suicide (Pritchard & Amanulla, 2007; Colulcci & Lester, 2009).

Given this reservation, we approach the WHO data on international rates of suicide with caution, including the rate of suicide (especially that of youth suicide) in Bangladesh. We note that Wasserman et al. (2005) in their review of international data on youth suicide draw on WHO data for only 90 countries for whom reliable data seemed to be available: Bangladesh was not one of those countries.

Table 9.1, drawn from WHO (2016) data for 183 countries which reported rates of death by suicide, gives rates by gender for the most populous Western nations (i.e. those in whom a majority of the population are of European-ancestry), and of countries in Asia with populations of more than five million, which contain the leading nations in which the male:female suicide rates are, unlike those of the Western nations (in which the ratio is about three male suicides for every one female suicide reported), much closer to parity. In Wasserman et al's 90-country comparison, the average male rate was 10.4 per 100,000, and the female rate was 4.1. From the WHO 2016 data, Bangladesh has the *highest* ratio of female to male suicides of any world nation, followed by China, Pakistan, Nepal and India. China has one of the highest recorded suicide rates in females in any world country while Sri Lanka has one of the highest recorded rates for males, in any country with a population exceeding 5 million.

As Jordans et al. (2014) conclude from their scoping review of suicide in South Asia, rates in the Asian region are high compared with the rest of the world, but methods of case-recording are underdeveloped. This bias in statistical reporting most likely means that deaths by suicide are *undercounted* in these developing countries. "False positives" – recording a suicide death when it did not occur seems unlikely. We do however discuss below, the possibility that in Bangladesh, murders of young women are actually disguised as suicide.

This Chapter reviews the literature on suicide (and other forms of violent injury and death) in Bangladesh, searching for indicators of why, relatively speaking, the suicide rate in young Bangladeshi females is so high. We do so on the assumption that surveillance systems for recording causes of death in Bangladesh are not well-developed; and because of the stigma which attaches to self-killing in a mainly (89%) Muslim nation, suicide may be underreported (Carnetto, 2015; Arafat, 2018). We have therefore to look in detail at studies which have been published on suicidal behaviours in Bangladesh, for clues.

Table 9.1 (using World Health Organisation data for 2016-17) is divided into halves, the most populous Western nations (i.e. those with a majority of population of European origin), in the top half, and the Asian countries with populations of more than five million in the bottom half. The Western nations show a consistent pattern of suicide rates in males at more than 2.5 times the rate in those in females. In contrast the countries with the world's highest female to male suicide ratio (Bangladesh, Nepal, India, Pakistan) tend to form a contiguous cluster in South Asia, while China shows the unique pattern of a relatively high rate of deaths by suicide in both genders. South Korea and Japan also display a particular pattern, with very high rates in males, which are more than double the rate in females. Sri Lanka stands out as a puzzling case with very high rates in males.

Bangladesh is not one of the countries in which a well-established medical examiner or coroner system adjudicates on causes of suspicious death, and there are no readily available figures on how suicide rates in Bangladesh are actually determined, published by bodies such as the World Health Organisation (WHO, 2007-2017). There have been however a number of specific studies which have estimated suicide rates in regions, or in special populations, published during the past three decades which allow us to offer estimates of rates of suicide and self-harm (Shahnaz et al, 2017).

Table 9.1 WHO Data on Suicide Rates by Gender, Selected Countries, 2015

Country	Both genders, rate per 100K (rank out of 183 nations)	Males, rate per 100K (rank out of 183 nations)	Females, rate per 100K (rank out of 183 nations)	M:F ratio of suicide per 100K (rank out of 183 nations)
USA	14.3 (35)	22.1 (25)	6.6 (43)	3.35 (134)
Canada	12.3 (54)	18.1 (60)	6.5 (48)	2.78 (69)
Germany	13.4 (40)	19.9 (45)	7.1 (39)	2.80 (75)
France	16.9 (20)	24.7 (26)	9.4 (18)	2.63 (65)
UK	8.5 (115)	13.3 (109)	3.8 (116)	3.50 (148)
Australia	11.8 (65)	17.2 (65)	6.3 (54)	2.73 (67)
Bangladesh	5.5 (135)	4.6 (170)	6.5 (48)	0.71 (1)
China (PRC)	10.0 (92)	8.7 (143)	11.5 (15)	0.76 (2)
Pakistan	2.1 (177)	2.2 (179)	2.0 (153)	0.95 (3)
Nepal	6.0 (135)	6.5 (153)	5.5 (81)	1.18 (4)
India	15.7 (24)	17.1 (72)	14.3 (8)	1.20 (5)
Cambodia	11.9 (62)	16.0 (90)	8.2 (29)	1.95 (7)
Myanmar	4.3 (154)	5.4 (167)	3.2 (122)	1.69 (6)
Malaysia	5.8 (147)	8.6 (140)	2.9 (135)	2.96 (79)
Japan	19.7 (15)	27.3 (17)	12.4 (13)	2.20 (21)
Sri Lanka	35.3 (6)	58.7 (1)	13.6 (10)	4.32 (160)
Indonesia	2.9 (172)	4.2 (174)	1.5 (166)	2.80 (75)
Vietnam	7.4 (122)	11.2 (126)	3.7 (123)	3.02 (85)
South Korea	24.1 (10)	36.1 (10)	13.4 (11)	2.69 (66)

3. Suicidal Behaviours in Asia

Suicide is a major public health problem in Asia, where the suicide rate exceeds the global average, despite problems of underestimated rates in low-to-middle-income (LMIC) countries (Chen et al. 2012; Beautrais, 2006). Suicide rates are highest in the South Asian region (Jordans et al. 2014). In Sri Lanka, the rate is exceptionally high at more than 35 per 100,000 population (Krug et al. 2000; Khan & Reza, 2000). Similar high rates of suicidal deaths have been observed in Nepal with rates of 25 per

100,000, with the rates for men and women being 30 and 20 per 100,000. These are estimates from locally-based research, and greatly exceed the 'official' WHO rate[1]. It has been further observed that unmarried women aged 10-24 years are at most risk of suicide in Nepal (Simkhada et al. 2015).

In most high-income countries, mortality reporting systems are well established, but this aspect of health surveillance is generally not adequately addressed in public health systems in Lower and Middle-Income Countries - LMICs (Mashreky et al., 2015). Suicide deaths mainly occur at home, and indeed some deaths may be unreported so information about cause of death in official statistics is often absent or unreliable. In some rural areas or regions of LMICs suicide data are not available, and if available their validity may be questionable, especially when a suicide attempt is illegal, and self-killing offends religious values (Jordans et al., 2014; Varnik, 2012). It is likely that in LMICs, the actual completed suicide rate is significantly higher than the recorded one, while that in developed countries with their well-developed coroner and medical examiner systems is more likely to be accurate. If that is the case, reported differences in rates between developed and developing countries may be much higher than currently estimated.

4. The Cultural Context of this Review – Bangladesh

Bangladesh is a densely populated country, with 166 million people living in a space of 147,570 sq. km. The country is surrounded by India, with a small common border with Myanmar in the southeast, and access to the ocean in the Ganges delta. The majority (89%) of the people are nominally Muslim; the second largest religious affiliation is Hinduism. More than 75% of the population live in semi-rural areas (BBS, 2007). Income inequality is high, and is increasing (Lewis, 2011; Matin, 2014), and 31% or around 43.2 million people in the lowest income sector live in extreme poverty, with incomes equivalent to $2.50 a day, or less. Poverty is associated with poor maternal and child health, and the health gap between economically advantaged and economically poor children in terms of stunted growth in children is actually increasing (Huda et al., 2017). Tropical monsoons and frequent floods and cyclones inflict heavy damage on infrastructure and agriculture almost every year. Drowning is a major cause of death (Sharmin-Salam et al., 2017).

---

[1] http://apps.who.int/gho/data/node.main.MHSUICIDE?lang=en (accessed on the 11 February 2017).

As in many other developing countries, a patriarchal social system is dominant. Women are subordinated to men both within the household, and in society at large, often in contradiction of Qur'anic, Sunnah and Shari'a principles (Hashmi, 2000; Chowdhury, 2010; White, 2017; Alam, 2018). These folk-based (rather than religious-based) cultural normative structures surround the oppressive and unequal treatment of female children and women. Gender inequality and discrimination against women is a common (but rarely discussed) factor in Bangladesh society (Parveen, 2007). Barely literate men apparently repeat forms of folk wisdom, supposedly Qur'anic quotations and Hadiths (sayings of The Prophet) in order to justify their patriarchal rights: but these 'quotations' are in fact 'folk fabrications' (Arens, 2014).

Early marriage of female children is a major problem. Nearly 60% of girls are married before the age of eighteen and in many rural areas more than 15% of girls are married before they reach fifteen, the highest proportion of child marriages in South Asia (Islam et al., 2016). Effective legislation to prevent the marriage of very young girls is lacking (Dearden, 2017). The practice of child marriage is perpetuated by poverty, linked with a traditionally patriarchal society in rural areas, and in the rural to urban migrants living in slum dwellings in cities (Hossain, 2010).

The Dowry Issue and Violence Imposed on Females

Considering the issue of "dowry payments" offers an important case study in our understanding of how Bangladesh, a nominally Muslim nation, has not absorbed Qur'anic values with regard to the rights of women. *The Fiqh of Marriage,* the body of law derived from Qur'an and Sunnah (the latter referring to how Qur'anic principles are reflected in the life and teachings of Prophet Muhammad) is clear and unambiguous (Ghaanim al-Sadlaan, 1999; www.IslamsWomen.com, 2017). Surah 4 *Women,* of The Qur'an clearly states (verses 4 and 24) that the dower, or *mahr* in Arabic, is a gift from the groom (or his father) *to* the bride, minimally of goods worth about £20 (at today's values), or any larger amount that the groom decides to give his new bride. Even on divorce, a wife will rarely have to repay the basic dower; and after divorce the groom is obliged to maintain his former wife and her children at the same level she enjoyed during marriage. This Islamic law of marriage is unevenly applied and interpreted, and often ignored in rural Bangladesh (Suran et al., 2004; Chowdhury, 2010; Shahid, 2016; White, 2017; Alam, 2018). In contrast, in many Arabic cultures today, the bride will also receive an endowment of household goods from the male's family, which she will retain in the event of divorce.

For very poor families, female children are often considered to be an economic burden. Thus for families living in extreme poverty, marrying daughters to older men is a survival strategy, albeit one imposed by male hegemony. However, dowry payments (from the female's family to the husband, the *opposite* of what Islamic law requires) are common in Bangladesh (Chowdhury, 2010; White, 2017), but are lower when girls are younger (the closer a girl's age is to her eventual fertility, the higher the cost of the dowry required – for the husband, feeding a fertile wife and enduring the inconvenience of any female child she bears, will devalue her as a chattel of labour, and makes her a poor bargain). Younger, pre-fertile girls are sold to older men (whom the child has never met before) as chattels, servants, domestic and sexual slaves, and sometimes as goods to be traded in one of the many legal brothels of Bangladesh, or to be internationally trafficked into a brothel in India or elsewhere (Blanchet, 2010).

The un-Islamic "bride price" expected in rural Bangladesh when a female child is married, frequently results in continuous violence and abuse of the adolescent or young women, especially when the groom's family consider that the money given to persuade them to marry the girl, is too low. Only when a family insists on Islamic practice (no bride price) is the girl less frequently abused, suggesting that families well versed and steadfast in Islamic principles are much less likely to abuse females (Suran et al., 2004). White (2007 & 2017) reaches somewhat similar conclusions.

Despite Qur'anic principles specifically forbidding the killing of infant girls (because they would be an economic burden, emphasising instead Islam's focus on the sanctity of human life), female infanticide does occur (Blanchet, 2001). However, rates of female infanticide seem to be lower in Bangladesh than in another Islamic nation, Pakistan (Miller, 1984; Grant, 2017). Grech & Mamo (2014) estimate rates of female "gendercide" through census data: if both the genders are treated equally then their numbers in census data of older populations should be about equal (although because men are more likely to migrate for work, fewer males would be counted). However, the census figures identified an *excess* of males in 2010: Pakistan, 11% excess; India, 9.4% excess; and Bangladesh, 8.9% excess of males. "Sex-selective" abortion in China and Southern Asia has resulted in about 23 million girls being aborted each year, although policy changes in China may be reducing that number (Chao et al., 2019).

Large numbers of female infants continue to be subjected to sex-selective abortions, killing after birth, and/or death from neglect and malnutrition in their early years in Southern Asia. Grech & Malmo (2014) point to the consequences of this excess of males, including the known kidnapping of girls as 'forced brides' when a man cannot obtain a wife through his own endeavours – almost always these are prepubescent girls. The lack of females of marriageable age may also be a driver for men who use commercialised sex.

In Bangladesh the Qur'anic principle of the dower is often *completely reversed*. Patriarchy has such power that men claim (with no knowledge of Arabic, or of Qur'anic teaching) that Islam requires that the dowry should be paid by the woman's family to her new husband (Chowdhury, 2016). This theological falsehood is mixed with Hindu customs (in nominally Muslim households, in which the 'money child' is referred to as Laksmi, after a Hindu goddess bringing wealth and good fortune: White, 2015). Average levels of these 'reverse dowries' are unknown, but often involve considerable sums, forcing poor families to obtain loans from BRAC, the rural development bank – loans which are purportedly for agricultural development (Lewis, 2011). Sometimes however a family is able to barter down the 'bride price' for what is deemed to be a desirable girl (perhaps reflecting the overall excess of males). But this also has the consequence of punishments being inflicted on the newly-wed girl for having cheated the man's family of a 'fair' price.

Sometimes an impoverished family will agree to pay the new husband the dowry in instalments after the marriage takes place. If the family defaults, then violence may be inflicted upon the child bride. Amnesty International (2011) issued a special report on violence and denial of civil liberties in Bangladesh, and scanned newspaper reports and other records for cases in which violence occurred because of dowry non-payment: they located 3,434 cases of violent abuse, 21 of them resulting in the girl's death. Using this and other data they reach an approximate estimate of two deaths per 100,000 young women at risk, each year, because of dowry-based violence. One recorded death involved a girl of 17 whose 34-year-old husband forced her to swallow a bottle of household cleanser. This alerts us to the possibility that some of the cases of "suicide" involving ingestion of poisons in young women (discussed below) may in fact be cases of murder. Murders because of unpaid dowry debt are more frequent in India, where it is common for husbands to require payment from their bride's family – Wyatt & Masood, 2010).

White (2015 & 2017) offers valuable ethnographic data from a Marxist-feminist analysis, arguing that male hegemony in Bangladesh forms a class-for-itself (males) who retain and acquire wealth and power by their often violent control of, and theft from, women. But she also gives examples of devout Muslim families who refused to pay a reverse-dowry for their daughters on marriage. Khan (2006 & 2007), trying to explain 'honour killings' in Pakistan also identifies the male "class" as the dominant force which benefits in social (and economic) power from murders of young women.

Rural to Urban Migration

Rural to urban migration of the very poor is common, with millions living in makeshift dwellings on the periphery of Bangladeshi cities (Das, 2000; Hossain, 2010). These slums are marked by extreme poverty, lack of clean water and waste management, malnutrition, and high rates of disease and early death. The "infectious diseases of poverty" are economically devastating for economically poor families in which medical treatment is rarely free, and the death of a wage earner is catastrophic (Bangert et al., 2017).

Social integration in urban slums is poor, education and school buildings are lacking, and religious socialization in basic values is often absent, since there are rarely mosques or madrasahs (schools for religious instruction) in these slum areas. According to the ethnographic work of Das, lives are marked by pre-Islamic rituals grounded in despair and fatalism. Islam forbids the sacrifice of female children, but one means to family survival is to sell female children to one of the many urban brothels (Das, 2000; Blanchet, 2001). Up to 1% of the country's impoverished population of girls and women aged 10 to 39 will have been employed in these legal 'brothel villages' for shorter or longer periods, in which mortality (including that by suicide) is high. "Children's rights" in these slum areas may only be "imagined" (Blanchard, 2000; White, 2007)

5. Suicidal Behaviors and Violent Deaths of Girls and Women in Bangladesh

Suicide is one of the major causes of death in young adult females in Bangladesh (Mashreky et al. (2013): indeed, a well-conducted epidemiological study such as that by Mashreky and colleagues does lead us to conclude that the actual rate of deaths by suicide is much higher than that published in the WHO (2017) overview. Although the officially estimated average rate of suicide in Bangladesh is between 5 and 7 individuals per 100,000 of the population per year, the rate in adolescents (15-19 years) from local studies (e.g. Ahmed et al, 2004; Mashreky, 2013) is much higher: at least 17 per 100,000 in males, and 23 per 100,000 in females up to the age of 49. These figures are likely to be an underestimate, since most of these deaths occur in rural areas where procedures for legal and medical surveillance of premature deaths are not well-developed. "Bangladesh is an Islamic country and socially and religiously suicide is stigmatising, therefore suicide deaths might be hidden by the family." (Mashreky et al, 2013). This idea is supported by Caneto's (2015) international survey of suicide rates in women in Muslim countries.

It is notable that contrary to the global pattern, the suicide rate for females in all age groups is higher than in males in Bangladesh (Mashreky et al, 2013). Adolescent females (10–19 years) were found to be the most vulnerable with the rate of suicide of above 20 per 100,000 in rural areas. These rates resemble the age-sex specific suicide risk in Nepal (Simkhada et al., 2015). The suicide rate in Bangladesh is 17-fold higher (95% CI 5.36–54.6) in the rural population than in urban areas (Mashreky et al., 2013).

Mental illness and depression are widely cited as a potential correlates or risk factors for suicide in developed countries, and up to 90% of suicides are said to be linked to depression, substance abuse or psychosis (Vijayakmur, Pirkis & Whiteford, 2005). However, this link may in part be artefactual, in that a verdict of "suicide" may be reached only after *prima facie* evidence of mental disorder is available (Kreitman, 1977; Shrivastava, Kimbrell & Lester, 2012; Gjelsvik et al., 2017). Since in many other LMICs such as Bangladesh, mental health is not prioritized by the government (with only 0.5% of total health expenditure allocated to mental health, there being no specific mental health authority in that country), construing suicide as a sequel of mental illness may not dominate the conceptual frameworks of officials designating cause of death.

In LMICs, only some four percent of doctors and two percent of nurses are trained in mental health care (WHO, 2007). The situation in Bangladesh is not likely to be any better. In the general population and at the governmental level, being psychiatrically ill is likely to be a highly stigmatised status, associated with shame for the family, and neglect by health and social services. The extreme despair which drives the individual to self-killing may be linked to unrecognized or untreated endogenous illnesses (e.g. clinical depression, or psychosis); or it may have psychosocial causes within the social system, such as the very low status of girls and young women, and the frequent violence and forced marriage at a very young age, within families whose overwhelming problems are those caused by extreme poverty (Ahmed et al., 2004; Nahar et al., 2015).

6. A Scoping Review of Literature on Suicide in Bangladesh

We summarise here a scoping review of the available literature on suicidal ideas, self-harm, and completed suicide summarising relevant studies published up to January, 2018. For details of this methodology, and for a fuller account of findings, the reader is referred to Shahnaz et al. (2017. The objectives of that review were to explore through a scoping analysis of published literature, the prevalence of suicidal ideation, suicide attempts, and deaths from suicide, and the correlates and presumed causes of such behaviours, in order to develop a model of public health research and prevention. This type of review aims to contextualise existing knowledge, setting it within a practice and policy context, and making recommendations for health care service delivery and evaluation (Anderson et al. 2008).

Searching abstract databases for relevant titles and keywords, 85 studies were primarily selected, of which on consultation 44 were duplicates across databases. After abstract screening, 36 articles were selected for reading the full text: but the full text was not available for 3 articles. The remaining 33 articles were read and quality assessed. Of these, 10 articles failed to meet quality assessment and/or inclusion criteria, and 23 articles were finally selected for the review.

These 23 studies were based either on hospital or on epidemiological samples. Ten of the studies were cross-sectional, with six of these 10 carrying out follow-up work with similar populations at later points in time. One review of some earlier literature review was found. Ten additional studies were further excluded because of their clinical focus (e.g. single case reports), or because of inadequate methodology, and/or publication in unknown or non-standard journals. Community or population-based studies are predominant, in 14 out of 23 studies.

Prevalence of Suicidal Ideation and Attempts

All but one of the five studies which estimated prevalence were conducted in rural areas. One study investigated six countries including Bangladesh, examining both urban and rural populations (Ellsberg et al., 2008). Three studies included women of "reproductive age" (15-49 years). One study observed that amongst ever-married women in Bangladesh 21% who experienced sexual and/or physical violence in their lives (compared with 7% who did not) reported that they had considered committing suicide (Santos et al., 2007). These findings clearly implied that the experience of physical and sexual violence contributed to suicidal ideation amongst younger married women. The study of Naved & Akhtar (2008) investigated possible reasons behind suicidal ideation in women aged 15 to 49, and report that 12% of ever married women (in their stratified random sample of 2,702 individuals in rural and urban areas) reported the experience of suicidal ideas and thoughts in their lifetime – 5% in the previous month, a much higher proportion than in women in other developing countries considered. In this study women who reported physical violence by their husbands were twice as likely to say they had thoughts about killing themselves. These findings are consonant with the cross-cultural work of Ellsberg et al. (2008).

Completed Suicide in Community and Population-Based Studies

Ten studies of community populations identified deaths by suicide. Six of these were conducted only in rural areas, and the rest at the national level including both urban and rural areas. The study of Alam et al (2014) found that the proportion of all deaths attributable to completed suicide in two rural areas was 3.5% (in Abhoynagar district) and 1.5% (in Mirsarai district) among all adults. In both areas women had a higher proportion of deaths from suicide than men in their life-times, with proportions of 5.1% and 2.5% respectively.

A study in rural areas of North-West Bangladesh found that in women aged 15 to 49, 5.7% of total deaths were attributed to suicide (Labrique et al, 2013). A similar outcome, showing that 6.6% of all deaths (according to informants in the households surveyed) were due to suicide (Shahnaz et al., 2017). Another study which included nearly 62,000 women (15+) of "reproductive age" from 70 villages in 10 rural districts (Ahmed, et al., 2004). found that women were more than twice as likely to commit suicide than men (4.2% of all deaths in men, versus 8.9% in women).

Higher suicide rates were also found amongst women (13 versus 8 per 100,000) in an earlier study of Ahmed et al. (2004, which included data from 1982-98 in a rural area (Matlab) in Bangladesh. For the period 1976-86 in the same rural area (Matlab), Fauveau & Blanchet (1989) had observed that 4.9% of deaths among non-pregnant women aged 15-44 years were due to suicide, while 4.1% of post-partum deaths in the same age group were attributed to the same cause. However, suicide amongst women was mostly concentrated (54%) in the age group 15-19 years.

From the national level studies, we conclude that women were significantly more prone to death by suicide than were men, usually at more than twice the rate in males of similar age. These various Bangladeshi studies confirm the inverse ranking in gender ratios, i.e. more suicide deaths for females than for males (Beutrais, 2006).

Research by Mashreky et al. (2013) showed furthermore, that suicide as a cause of death was 17 times higher in rural than in urban areas. Younger females in rural areas were particularly likely to die from suicide compared with adolescents in other countries (22.7 per 100,000 population of females aged less than 20 in rural Bangladesh).

A comparative analysis of two national level surveys of Bangladeshi females aged 10 to 49 by Nahar and Colleagues (Nahar et al., 2015) compared data for the years 2001 and 2010, and estimated the prevalence of deaths by suicide to be 23 and 16 per 100,000 in the two years compared, which indicated a decrease in suicide in Bangladesh in the younger female population. On historical data, the *Health Science Bulletin* of ICDDR,B[2] (2003) reported that during 1983-2002 in two sub-districts in rural areas South-West Bangladesh, the suicide rate for all ages was 39.6 per 100,000 populations per year; amongst those less than 40 it was higher, at 42.0 per 100,000 populations. These are higher rates than those estimated by Nahar et al, (2015), and may reflect more careful case finding and diagnostic techniques concerning causes of death in rural areas. Another reason for a lowered suicide rate could be the lack of availability of the most lethal pesticides (Gunnell, 2017).

Completed Suicide Described in Hospital-Based Studies

We found six studies on completed and attempted suicide, conducted by psychiatrists and pathologists working in hospital settings. Two studies in a tertiary-level hospital found that 94.9% and 81.6%% of all poisoning related deaths were attributed to suicide (Quader et al., 2010; Khan et al., 2013). Another study in the same region investigated the cause of death of 2,534 individuals within the hospital's urban-rural catchment area, and estimated

---

[2] ICDDR,B is the acronym for International Centre for Diarrhoeal Disease Research, Bangladesh. This major NGO is now active in many areas of public health, including mental health, and is a major provider of both preventive and curative medicine.

that 18% were attributable to suicide, mainly by poisoning (Islam et al., 2003). That study also found that suicide victims among women increased by 8% per annum over the period 1988-97. Of the 467 suicide deaths, 45.8% involved females.

A study by Chowdhury and colleagues (2011) in a hospital of the southern region of the country found, in a review of hospital records that a surprising number - 68.7% - of total deaths had occurred due to suicidal actions. A large-scale study by Hussain and colleagues (2000) of 4,751 health facilities, including all of the 13 government medical college hospitals, five infectious disease hospitals, and 96 maternal and child welfare centres, found that 10.7% of all deaths in women aged 10 to 50 years were attributable to suicide. Amongst these women, deaths from suicide in the age group 10-19 years were the most frequent cause of death (21.7%). The rate of suicides in younger women was higher in the Khulna administrative division (27·0 per 100 000) than in the other four administrative divisions of the country (range 3·5–11·3 per 100 000).

Possible Causes and Factors Underlying Suicidal Behaviours

Some of the studies calculating suicide-related prevalence have investigated, explored or speculated about the causes and factors underlying suicidal behaviour. These studies have described 'emotional stress due to family quarrel' as the most common factor of aetiological significance (but these were usually *post hoc* speculations, without comparison with non-suicidal controls). Feroz and Colleagues (2007) reported that such emotional stress was frequent (in 60%) in the lives of people who later killed themselves. But again, how this was measured, and the lack of any non-suicidal comparison populations make this a tentative speculation concerning aetiology. Using the deceased's relatives as sources of information may elicit rationalisations from people who feel covertly guilty about the death of a family member. The second most common cause claimed by Feroz et al (2007) was poverty.

Three other studies found ''emotional stress due to family quarrel' as the most commonly alleged cause, with relatively high frequencies (50.7%, 65.5% and 57%) (Chowdhury et al., 2011; Reza et al., 2014; Feroz et al., 2012). 'Suicidal death in any relative' (23.0%, 48.7%), 'marital disharmony' (49.3%, 46.9% and 41.7%) and 'previous attempts to suicide' (43.3%) were also reported as prevalent causes or factors associated with suicide in several studies (Reza et al., 2014; Feroz et al., 2012; Sharmin Salam et al., 2017). Infertility was also identified as a possible causal factor in suicide

(Ahmed et al., 2004) in impoverished families, where the role of the young wife must focus on adequate performance in providing her husband with 'good food, good sex, and good children'. Failure' in such role performance can have serious consequences. Divorce and expulsion from the family home by husband is one possibility[3]; severe physical punishment is another; voluntary or involuntary death occurs at the extreme end of this spectrum of sexist maltreatment (Rashid, 2006).

Methods of Suicide

Poisoning was identified as the most common method for committing suicide among both males and females, followed by hanging. Mashreky et al. (2013) found in a national survey that 78% of suicides among males and 50% among females had used these methods. This study found that pesticide was the most frequently used poison (in 80%). By hanging themselves, 19% of males and 41% of females died by suicide in Bangladesh.

An urban hospital-based study in Dhaka city by Qusar et al. (2001) observed that most patients who attempted suicide used drugs (usually benzodiazepines or tricyclic antidepressants) and chemicals (kerosene, bleaching agents, organophosphorus) for attempting (and sometimes completing) suicide. Of the 44 attempted suicide cases 18 were male and 26 female; 95% of cases used drugs and chemicals. Only two males attempted suicide by hanging. (It is possible that self-poisoning in urban areas is more likely to result in resuscitation, since hospital emergency facilities are easily reached, which would not be the case in many rural areas).

A community-based study in a rural area by Feroz et al (2012) observed that hanging was the most common method (62.5%), followed by poisoning (31.2%). Rail and road injuries (deliberately standing before trains or traffic) accounted for 6.2% of completed suicide events. However, a comparative analysis of two national surveys in 2001 and 2010 found that poisoning was the most common method (68.2%) followed by hanging (19.7%) in the first year of focus (Nahar et al., 2015). In 2010 poisoning, while being the most common method, was used less often (53.1%), while hanging was increasingly common (40.6%). Given that drowning is the commonest cause of "accidental death" in a country with many waterways

---

[3] Qu'ranic law prescribes that if a man divorces his wife for any reason other than her adultery, he must maintain her and all of her children at the same material level that she and her children enjoyed in marriage. This Qur'anic principle is widely ignored in Bangladesh, however.

and frequent flooding (Along et al., 2017), it is surprising that so few officially recorded suicides have used this method.

The possibility remains that numbers of such drowning deaths are actually suicide, but are not recorded as such. Or it could be as Colucci and Lester (2009) observe in their cross-cultural work on suicide, that for some, suicide is a symbolically aggressive act, and slow or spectacular methods (poisoning, hanging oneself within the household) have important symbolic significance, unlike being "just another drowning death".

Socioeconomic Variation in Suicide, Suicide Attempts and Suicidal Ideation

Some of the studies reviewed measured rates of suicidal behaviour according to socioeconomic differences. Variables identified have been educational level, socioeconomic status and income level. Feroz et al. (2012) found that of those who committed suicide, around one third (33.3%) had some education at secondary level and another 28.6% up to primary level. People with fuller educational levels apparently had significantly lower rates: 45.7% of the people who committed or attempted suicide belonged to the least educated class, compared with 37.1% in the lower middle class, and the fewest (17.2%) in the middle and upper-class (these estimates did not calculate rates according to the populations at risk in each educational or socioeconomic category).

In the work of Feroz et al (2012) families with low incomes (3,000 to 5,000 Taka, about US$38 to $62 per month) had the highest rates of suicidal behaviour. Socioeconomic status, measured by a composite score of earning capacity, housing status, and possession of essential and luxury goods in the family, identified a clear socio-economic gradient in completed and attempted suicide cases: 68.4% of such cases occurred in the lowest classes, compared with 7.3% in those in the more complex definition of 'upper class'.

Reza et al. (2014) observed that 80.5% of all suicide and para-suicide cases were from lower (<3,000 Taka i.e. $38 per month) or lower-middle (3,000-5,000 Taka per month) income groups. Through a national survey in 2003, Mashreky et al. (2013) observed that the majority of suicide victims (55.0%) were economically very poor with a monthly family income of less than $50 a month; and more than 14% of the suicide victims' families earned less than $25 a month. The same study found also that literacy was a strong correlate suicidal behaviour (42% of the suicide victims were illiterate); less than 7%

had a higher secondary education or above.

In sum, the studies reviewed suggest the strong possibility that chronic poverty associated with poorer education and illiteracy, is a significant risk factor for suicidal behaviours in both genders. Despite some methodological problems in these studies, we feel that it is safe to conclude that completed suicide rates are significantly higher in the very poorest groups, and these economic circumstances may be of aetiological significance. Nevertheless, it is also true that the large majority of the very poor in Bangladesh do not attempt or complete suicide. This is a perennial problem in suicidology: why do so *few* people kill themselves when the conditions of life for so many are wretched, painful and uncertain? (Shrivastava et al., 2012; Lester & Rogers, 2013).

7. An Additional, Confirmatory Study

Since this scoping review was undertaken, focussing on literature published up to June, 2017 a further comprehensive study of fatal and non-fatal injury outcomes in Bangladesh has been published (Sharmin-Salam et al., 2017). In the same issue of *Lancet Global Health* for August, 2017 Gunnell et al. (2017) reviewed available studies on the effects of banning the most noxious pesticides on suicide rates. The majority of the 38 studies reviewed show clearly that removing from legal sale noxious pesticides (as defined by WHO) does result both in the reduction of the numbers who die by this method of suicide, as well as an overall reduction in actual suicide rates.

Chowdhury et al. (2017) showed that Bangladesh passed laws between 1998 and 2007 banning the sale of the most noxious pesticides, resulting not only in a reduction of deaths using this method, but a net reduction of about 10% in the actual suicide rate (the lack of availability of the most lethal pesticides did however see an increase in suicide due to hanging, which offset to some extent lives saved by lack of lethal pesticides). This finding could account for the decline in deaths by suicide in Bangladesh reported in the earlier work of Chowdhury et al. (2007).

The team led by Sharmin-Salam (2017) conducted sample surveys with 1.7 million adults living in 453 villages in rural areas of Bangladesh, and asked respondents about any deaths and serious injuries occurring in their household in the previous 6 months. Judgements were then made in a structured questionnaire, about the nature and causes of each serious injury and death (no external validity data were available, so these accounts could have underestimated rates of suicide).

Suicide was found to be a leading cause of injury-related deaths in those aged 15 to 24, with more than 50% of such deaths occurring in females. "Drowning" accounted for 38.3% of all deaths, but was rarely reported as a form of suicide.

Suicide death rates in *males* were:

> *Age 10-14, 2 per 100,000; Age 15-17, 9 per 100,000; Age 18-24, 2 per 100,000.*

In *females* suicide death rates were:

> *Age 10-14, 4 per 100,000; Age 15-17, 14 per 100,000; Age 18-24, 9 per 100,000.*

Overall, death from suicide in younger males (10-24) occurred in 5 per 100,000; and in younger females (10-24) at the rate of 9 per 100,000. These rates are much higher in both males and females, than those given in earlier WHO data (Wasserman, Cheng & Jiang, 2005), and in the WHO world comparisons. In these figures the male:female imbalance (compared with Western data) is even more marked than that implied by WHO (2012017). Hanging was the most frequent form of death from suicide in this Bangladeshi study (in 59%), followed by poisoning, usually from household substances at 31%. Thus although highly toxic pesticides are now rarely available, self-poisoning from bleach, ammonia, and other available substances in the household is still widely used as a method of suicide. Indeed, using such "less toxic" substances is likely to lead to a more lingering and painful death than a substance such as paraquat. 60% of suicides occurred in or close to the domestic dwelling.

8. Summary and Review of Findings, and Proposals for Intervention

The main findings from this literature review suggest that girls and young women (who often enter marriage prior to age 18 – Islam et al., 2016), and females aged 10-29 years in rural areas of Bangladesh are particularly at risk for suicidal behaviour, including completed suicide and suicidal attempts. Girls aged 10 to 14 (including some who were already married) also had high rates of suicidal behaviour. In contrast, in the world literature younger adolescents aged 10-14 have been identified as having much *lower* rates of completed suicide than older individuals (Hawton & C'Connor, 2012). In contrast to this mainly Western pattern, the self-killing of young

Bangladeshi females occurred both prior to, or soon after their being married to older men.

These adolescents also had an unexpectedly high death rate from violence that was apparently *not* self-inflicted (e.g. domestic fires), an indicator of the very vulnerable status of these individuals whose levels of formal schooling were minimal, and who lived in impoverished families (Varnik, 2012). Another possibility is that some of these young women were in fact murdered, or were required by others to kill themselves, crimes passed off as suicide (Ronsmans & Khlat, 1999; Amnesty International, 2011)

Such young women often had experience of physical and sexual violence imposed first by their family, and then by their spouse. One study found that following marriage, adolescents were physically abused by *both* their original families, and their new husband, so that levels of abuse actually increased after marriage (Ahmed et al., 2004).

Poisoning was identified in earlier studies as the most frequent method for committing and attempting suicide, followed by hanging. Poisoning using pest control mixtures (following the banning of more 'lethal' forms) in the absence of medical help, was likely to be a slow and painful method of self-killing, and the possibility that this was an involuntary form of death cannot be discounted. Alternative methods of suicide, such as purposive drowning, or road and rail injuries could be rapidly fatal, but were atypically used, or at least were not reported as suicide (Feroz et al., 2012; Sharmin-Salam, 2017).

It was suggested by some studies that lower socioeconomic status in terms of lack of income, education or assets, were significant antecedents of suicidal behaviour (Reza et al., 2014); Feroz et al, 2012; Mashreky et al., 2013). One study when comparing suicide cases between two surveys in 2001 and 2010, found a decrease in such antecedents. However, further studies are required to arrive at definitive conclusions about social factors in the aetiology of suicidal behaviours (Nahar et al., 2015). It is clear from the research that most cases of completed suicide occur in rural areas, and unlike studies undertaken in developed countries, females outnumber males in completed suicide. These young women are poorly educated or are illiterate, live in families enduring extreme and chronic poverty in which the status of females is low, and in which violence against women is common.

The evidence suggests that married women aged 15-29 years with experience of physical and sexual violence, living in rural areas constituted the most vulnerable group for suicidal behaviour.

We observed some variation between studies in relation to methodologies employed. Most studies used cross-sectional surveys (11 out of 23 studies), but lacked information on control or comparison groups who had not completed suicide. Without such information, studies are confined to *post hoc* generalisations, which may reflect localised "cultural meanings" of suicide (Colucci & Lester, 2012), rather than more systematic estimates of antecedents of suicidal behaviour. Emotional stress due to quarrel in the family, marital disharmony, and suicide in any relative were often cited as predisposing factors in suicidal behaviours, but these could be *post hoc* justifications. There are no carefully controlled designs in the literature on Bangladesh which can pinpoint exact causes. But there is enough information on high rates of suicide in young, rural women living in impoverished families to give us confidence in identifying this as a group at high risk, needing programmes of public health intervention.

We note with interest the work of Ronsmans & Khlat (1999), which was not included in the studies in the above matrix of studies on suicide, since they conflated "unintentional deaths" in women aged 15 to 49 into a single rate, including deaths from suicide, murder, and failed abortions. They argue that these three kinds of death (particularly common in teenagers) are linked within a poverty-afflicted rural culture, in which unwanted females and unwanted children and/or pregnancies are sometimes subjected to extreme violence, including forced abortions, forced suicides, or becoming a victim of murder. There is a need here for qualitative and ethnographic studies on the social meanings of 'suicide', and other forms of death, and of the empowerment of women.

Hospital-based studies have provided important complementary information to that provided by the large-scale community studies, probably using better information sources, and more standardised methodologies. While the community-based studies have identified suicide cases using 'verbal autopsy', hospital-based researchers may have given more accurate accounts of events leading to suicidal death. In the community-based studies, data for verbal autopsies, screening very large populations, were primarily collected by research assistants with moderate-educational levels, and minimal knowledge of health research (Alam et al, 2014). In contrast, in hospital-based studies, medical records were reviewed and psychological autopsies were conducted by medically trained staff (Chowdhury et al., 2011; Hussain et al., 2007).

The review data indicate that in Asia, suicide rates are higher in the South Asian region than elsewhere in Asia and the rest of the world (Jordans et al, 2013), although Bangladesh has lower overall suicide prevalence than some other countries in the region. Nevertheless, localised studies eg of rural areas, show that suicide rates in Bangladesh are much higher than those recorded in WHO data (Sharmin-Salam et al., 2017).

Compared to many other world countries, Bangladesh experiences a considerable difference in the prevalence of gender-related suicide, with the unusual manifestation of suicide prevalence being much higher in females. Young girls both before and after 'child marriage', and younger married women contribute disproportionally to Bangladesh's suicide rate, and these rates of self-harm and self-killing appear to reflect both physical and sexual violence imposed by family and spouse Feroz et al. 2012; Ahmed et al., 2004; Ronsmans et al. 1999; Hadi, 2006). Sometimes this abuse is extended to effectively "selling" a young girl into bondage, which may result in brothel servitude, or sexual trafficking to another country (Das, 2000). There are certainly according to our ethnographic work, cases of "hidden suicide" within these brothels, usually from drug overdoses.

9. Development of a Public Health Prevention Model

First of all, the wretched status of female children, adolescents and young women in rural Bangladesh (and in the slum dwellings on the periphery of cities into which many of the rural poor migrate) compared with that of males cannot be overstated. The case for an Islamic feminism in Bangladesh has been eloquently argued by Hashmi (2000) in *Women and Islam in Bangladesh: Beyond Subjection and Tyranny*. Hashmi begins with a quote from The Qur'an: "And for women are rights over men similar to those of men over women." (2:228) - that is, Islam properly observed, guarantees women equality with men, except under Qur'anically prescribed instances: a woman for instance will inherit a smaller amount of a family's property. The same Qur'anic verse establishes the *duties* of men with regard to their spouses.

But in rural Bangladesh a woman will likely inherit nothing despite her Shari'a law entitlement, all property being claimed by those in the male line, whenever there is wealth or property to leave (Alam, 2018). Hashmi ends his study of Bangladeshi women with the gloomy conclusion:

... patriarchy has been the main stumbling-block towards the empowerment of Bangladeshi women. The marriage of convenience between patriarchy and popular Islam has aggravated the situation. (p. 209).

In the rural-urban slums described in the ethnographic accounts of Das (2000) and Hossain (2010), there is profound poverty, with the absence of schools, mosques, madrasahs (religious schools). Unremitting malnutrition, lack of medical care, and starvation-level employment means that "unwanted" females (including girls of 12 or younger) may be sold either for sex-trafficking, or for use in one of the many 'village brothels' which exist in every city of Bangladesh.

Preventing Suicidal Behaviours in Girls and Women

We propose a model for preventing suicidal behaviours which first of all, reflects existing epidemiological data and the identified risk factors from the literature review. It is clear that any programme must be focussed firstly on girls and women, and their rights in an Islamic society. This also means the initiation of programmes of education for both adolescent females and males[4]. In elaborating this approach, we have proposed a demonstration project in a rural area of Bangladesh, which will be contrasted with a "control" district of similar demographic and socioeconomic status (Shahnaz et al., 2017).

Combining this with an approach used in The Philippines (Adam-Bagley et al., 2017b) of giving financial support for secondary school students would mean that the pressures for adolescents to forgo education because their employment or marriage was necessary to support an impoverished family, would no longer prevail.

We advocate too that the students in the focus secondary institutions should receive an adequate education in Muslim citizenship, the universal values of Islam in which students absorb the high ideals of daily living of respect and equality between genders prescribed by the Qur'an and the Sunnah.

---

[4] Such educational programmes must, we argue, include a proper Islamic education which both restrains individuals from self-killing, and also requires individuals to fulfil the ethical obligations of Islam which oblige individuals to treat women with respect, in accordance with Qur'anic principles (Khan, 1998).

Suicide Prevention in Bangladesh: National initiatives

Our proposed national model, which would run in parallel to the experimental programme outlined above, reflects programmes of suicide prevention which have been offered and evaluated in other cultures (Hawton et al., 2016; Zalsman et al., 2016) and includes both general and specific interventions (e.g. counselling and mental health support following a suicide attempt).

The epidemiological data from the above review suggest that married women and adolescents aged 12 to 29 years who experience physical and sexual violence from husband, and from their family in rural areas are significantly at risk for suicide, suicide attempts and suicidal thoughts. 'Consciousness building' for young women should be considered as an important approach, concerned with how women of all ages recognise and resist the male hegemony which imposes violence (and suicidal despair) on women, and also instruct males in the Islamic ethics of interpersonal behaviour and respect for women (Parveen, 2007; Bickmore et al., 2018).

This can be approached through educational programmes in secondary schools, not only in the schools involved in the proposed experimental study. But the reality is that free basic schooling is available only at the primary level, and indeed only two-thirds of children will even complete this elementary schooling (Shajahan et al., 2016). Many parents cannot afford to keep a child in secondary schooling, and household duties, marriage, and basic-level employment are the fate of many young adolescents.

For those who have already left education, telephone help-lines are an interesting possibility, given the ubiquity of mobile phones, even in very poor families in rural areas. A national helpline has been established in Bangladesh for communication to an online support service for those who are enduring stress, despair, and suicidal thoughts – but this new initiative is not well-publicised, or well-funded, and the professional quality of the help offered is unknown. Such helplines are well established in many countries and are well-researched (Hawton, 2005; Zalsman et al., 2016).

The Hadith of the Prophet Muhammad (such as those related by his wife Aisha) on the care of, and respect for a wife should be more widely known (Eaton, 2008). We also advocate the growth of Islamic feminism which acts to intervene on behalf of oppressed women in Muslim majority cultures. There are a growing number of feminist voices in Arab countries and in Malaysia (see Chapters 1 and 2), and we will support Muslim women in

Bangladesh who draw on this active feminist movement within Islam to speak and act on behalf of their oppressed sisters (e.g. Hashmi, 2000; Parveen, 2007). As the Bangladeshi anthropologists Ahmed & Bould (2004) concluded from their study of women in the external labour force: "One able daughter is worth 10 illiterate sons."

Internationally, the dilemma is whether to advocate cross-national movements to improve data collection (and international action) on behalf of disempowered women *versus* local action campaigns on behalf of women (Raj, 2017). While we would like to see both movements going forward, at the present time we perceive the most utility in the localised campaigns such as those which we advocate in Bangladesh.

Finally, we note that Wasserman et al's (2005) international survey of youth suicide called for more prevention work on "these needless deaths". While there have been advances in programme development in more affluent countries (Zalsman et al., 2016), in low and middle income countries there seems to have been little progress, and in Bangladesh none at all (Jorm et al., 2018). Vijayakumar (2004) described the task confronting suicidologists in developing countries as "urgent". It remains so (Lancet, 2017). Novel approaches such as those we propose in rural Bangladesh and in its city slums may be unconventional; they may not work. But they are worth trying – as for example a novel programme of income support for rehabilitation of high school girls pulled into commercial sexual exploitation in The Philippines was, despite expectations, very successful (Adam-Bagley et al, 2017b). We have also initiated a similar programme in Pakistan, but on a smaller scale, described in the next Chapter.

We are keenly aware, too, of the problems that offering intervention in a newly emergent nation which expresses the political voice of "radical, feminist Islam" in a climate of fierce political and cultural debates in Bangladesh's plural society, is problematic. Finding a 'political space' between profoundly different religious and political voices on what constitutes 'a good Muslim' in Bangladesh (Siddiqi, 2018), is fraught with difficulty. There are indeed radical voices within Bangladesh which wish to *diminish* the status of women - the *Boku Haram* model (Rahman, 2018), which the alternative movements of Bangladeshi feminism seek to resist (White, 2010; Alam, 2018).

As Kaderi (2018) argues, peacebuilding (and Islamic justice) in this divided nation must begin within the enlightened madrasahs, and within the broader educational system. These enterprises should be linked to the Bangladeshi women's movement which seeks to "reshape the holy" in asserting the value of women, and the respective rights and duties of men and women stressed by Qur'an and Sunnah (Shehabuddin, 2008). Too often, the lives of girls and women in Bangladesh are ordered by acts of atavistic selfishness by men, who ignore or distort the message of peace and mercy, forgiveness and care, modesty and self-restraint which is the core of a proper Islamic conduct.

In sum, on the basis of the knowledge derived from this literature review, our knowledge of Bangladeshi culture, and our commitment to what we understand to be the highest ideals of Islam, we urge that more research in both urban and rural areas should be conducted which can form the basis for monitoring new prevention programmes aimed at reducing suicidal behaviour, and at raising the consciousness and status of women to that promised by Islam.

This issue is most urgent with regard to the degraded status of the young women driven by poverty into demeaning sex work in brothel villages and elsewhere. This will be a grassroots movement, beginning with women in rural Bangladesh who in the morphogenesis model of Margaret Archer's critical realism, (2014) enlarge their self-concept and local power as mothers, marital partners and workers in Islamically-grounded conversations of "Muslim women seeking power" (White, 2007, 2015, 2018; Sultana, 2015; Alam, 2018).

As Alam shows in her ethnographic study of women in rural Bangladesh, many men wrongly believe that The Qur'an sanctions the disempowerment of women, without having read The Message; these men are also unable (or unwilling) to read any translation of The Qur'an. The Hadith of The Prophet are almost certainly unknown to them. However, rural women (Alam, 2018) and the vocal former "sex workers" (Sultana, 2015) are gently but firmly rising up as Muslim women. This is the third force in the polity of Bangladesh, seeking dialogue with both secular and established religious power structures.

CHAPTER TEN

CHILD MARRIAGE AS TRAUMATIC RAPE: A CAUSE OF PTSD IN WOMEN IN BANGLADESH AND PAKISTAN?

CHRISTOPHER ADAM-BAGLEY AND WESAM ABUBAKER

1. Introduction

Bangladesh became independent in 1971 from Pakistan after a brutal war of independence. As the Pakistani army retreated they subjected many thousands of women to "the rape of war", causing both physical damage to the women, and the trauma of unwanted pregnancies (Neill, 2003). Despite this splitting of a nation, the two countries have much in common. They are both predominantly Muslim, and formally at least accept both Islamic ideals on women's equality and on the care and welfare of children (HRCP, 2018). Both countries are signatories to UN declarations on the rights of women and children.

In an article addressed to legal scholars in Pakistan Abba & Riaz (2012) begin with a joyful statement of Islamic ideals:

> The first Qur'ānic reforms and values concerning society were integrated [in the era of the First Caliphates], and they were practiced to raise the status of women and the family in the new Muslim society by establishing the rights of family members. After the advent of Islam, women were granted the right of marriage, education, inheritance, dower, divorce, work and various other rights. Islam came to correct misconceptions, implement justice and women's dignity ... Islam gave women dignity and raised their position to be able with men, to work for the development and prosperity of nations. (p. 174)

Abba and Riaz regret however, that the many laws, statutes and conventions which The Islamic Republic of Pakistan has adopted on women's equality are rarely implemented, or properly applied in practice. Pakistan, with its morass of competing cultures and interest groups is more like the tribal society to which Prophet Muhammad delivered the Final Message, than an Islamically reformed society. In other words, we assert that Pakistan despite its great promise, remains a pre-Islamic nation. We expand on this theme in the next Chapter.

Today in both countries child marriage (of a female minor between 10 and 17 years) is common. Bangladesh has the honour of being the leading country in the world, with 30% of all marriages still involving a minor female. Pakistan lags behind, with only 22% of being married whilst children or minors. Each country contains millions of women who were married at age 15 or less. There are now some laws which forbid such child marriages: they are not enforced.

2. Physical and Mental Health Consequences of Child Marriage

Obstetric and Traumatic Fistula: Clinical Description

The most frequently occurring fistula[1] in women is a breach of the upper level of the vagina (or birth canal) close to the neck of the uterus. Obstetric fistula occurs when the head or shoulder of an infant, during birth, breaches the wall of the birth canal (more frequently occurring, for example, in the firstborn of a very young mother). Sometimes in the immature, malnourished female the birth is stuck, and the child (and sometimes the mother) will die at this point. If the mother survives and there is no immediate surgical repair of the fistula, urine (from the bladder) or faeces (from the colon) may leak into the vagina causing chronic infection, and urinary incontinence, as well as bladder infections. Infertility may result from the chronic infection (which also increases the possibility of acquiring STIs). The woman so infected will be in chronic pain and discomfort without surgical repair of the vagina (relatively straightforward surgery) for the rest of her life.

In the West, chronic obstetric fistulae are a thing of the past. The successful surgical procedures for repairing fistula were pioneered by the American surgeon James Sims in the 19th century. Sims purchased African women with obstetric fistula from slave-owners, for purposes of experimenting with different techniques of fistula repair, in which he was finally successful. He

---

[1] A fistula involves a breach of any organ of the body which then links it to another organ, sometimes with pathological consequences.

did not use anaesthesia, and all of the women on whom he practised, died (Whyte, 2019).

Obstetric fistula is now almost never seen in Western countries in which perinatal care and birth monitoring procedures are of a high standard. In developing countries simple instruments could monitor birth stress which would precede a fistula, and an initial ureteral catheter applied. A caesarian section should then occur. Such procedures are rarely available in rural areas of Bangladesh and Pakistan, where only traditional birth attendants are available. However, even when a C-section procedure is available, maternal mortality rates are likely to be high, with death rates in the young woman a hundred times greater than in developed country medical systems (Sobhy et al., 2019).

Traumatic fistula can be caused by violent intercourse or gang rape, imposed on an immature female. The brutal insertion of large objects into the vagina may bring similar results. The first intercourse by a mature man with a minor female who is newly married may cause such vaginal tearing and damage. Sexual maturity (following menstruation for some months) might have allowed the young female to develop an immune system which could cope with some of the trauma and indignities of what we can only term as a form of child rape. The immature female (compared with a fully developed, healthy woman) is much more likely to acquire infections from such intercourse, including STIs and the risk of cervical cancer. The child may be doubly traumatised: she has been removed at a young age from her protective kindred, married to an older man whom she may well not have seen before, who rapes her immature vagina. There is likely to be considerable pain imposed on the unprepared child.

In reading literature and reports on the mental health of married women in Pakistan we were struck by the similarity of the symptoms presented by these women to those described in the PTSD (Post Traumatic Stress System) described by Vostanis (2014). This leads us to make the following propositions:

Child marriage (in Bangladesh and Pakistan) begins with two traumas: the breaking of emotional bonds to close kindred (mother and sisters) whom the child may never see again; and the physical pain and trauma of brutal intercourse. Built upon these initial traumas are the child's lowly status in the new family, the frequency with which she is verbally, physically and sexually abused by her husband and his family; and the burden of pregnancy which in a significant minority of cases may lead to a difficult, unattended birth (perhaps with obstetric fistula occurring); and the increased risk of low birthweight, and heightened risk of mortality and morbidity of her child in the first five years.

If she fails to produce a son, or is infertile the punishments imposed on her may be both chronic and severe. In extreme cases she will be battered and set on fire with fuel oil, her death being attributed to a stove's explosion. At least 5,000 such deaths occur in Pakistan each year, many of them reckoned to be cases of disguised murder (HRCP, 2017). The mental health evidence from Pakistan does build up a picture of helpless and hopeless traumatised women who despairingly accept their fate.

A Review of Obstetric Risks of Early Child Marriage

Nour (2009) has reviewed the world literature up to 2007 on the increased health risks of early child marriage, focusing both on obstetrical factors, and general health. He focuses on three groups: those aged 19 or more at marriage; those aged 16 to 18 at marriage; and those aged less than 15. Whatever the age of the girl, the man marrying her was (in 95% of cases) older. In the East Asia and Pacific region, about 5.6 million women were married at age 18 or less (we estimate that this number may have halved since Nour's review, with the lowest falls in Bangladesh, India and Pakistan). Girls married at ages 10 to 15 were, according to several studies, 5 to 7 times more likely to die in childbirth. Those aged 15 to 19 were twice as likely as fully mature females to die while giving birth. Nour comments:

> *Girls aged 10-15 years have small pelvises and are not ready for childbearing. Their risk for obstetric fistula according to several studies is elevated by 75% ... mothers under the age of 18 have a 55% higher risk of delivering preterm or low-birthweight infants than do older mothers ...*

Other risks of child marriage identified in Nour's (2007) review were elevated risks for chronic infections of the woman's reproductive system (independently of fistula occurrence), higher rates of cervical cancer, and inability of the immune system to resist various STIs. Throughout their lives very young mothers could experience pain, illness and reproductive inefficiency, which has many social consequences. These women were more likely to manifest profound depression and hopelessness throughout life.

Zakar et al's (2013) study from Pakistan gives an account of the psychological and physical health of women who were married in their early teenaged years, and what emerges is a chronic state of depressed helplessness, with

PTSD-like symptoms. Many women were cut off from their own kinship network which might have offered her support, and had to accept daily events of verbal, physical and sexual abuse. One surprising finding (for a Muslim culture) was that 3% of husbands increased their abuse after consuming alcohol. When the husband was absent, his relatives (father, brothers) would (in an unknown proportion of cases) persistently rape the girl (Ali et al., 2011 & 2013). Within the privacy of both rural and urban households, such behaviour seemed to be normative.

In a 6-year longitudinal cohort study of 133,156 Bangladeshi women of reproductive age (14-45) Labrique et al. (2013) found that 22% of all the 1107 deaths ascertained by the research team were due to complications of pregnancy and childbirth, with significantly higher rates of pregnancy-related deaths occurring in those aged less than 18.

We cannot find any overview of more recent studies focussing directly on health risks of child marriage, but note that individual studies of maternal health offering indirect evidence, continue to appear. Raj (2010) found that children born to young mothers were significantly more likely to be underweight at birth, and to have stunted growth as children. Mustafa et al. (2017) reporting on a national cohort of 5,046 mothers in Pakistan and their 10,164 children found a clear link between being a very young mother, and the morbidity and mortality of her first delivery (girls who had died in childbirth were not included in this cohort). The infants born to very young mothers had low birthweights, more often died (if they survived birth) in their first year, and had poor immunity to infectious diseases. Whyte (2019) estimates that there are more than two million women in Africa and Asia with untreated obstetric fistula, with 100,000 new cases (according to UN global health data) occurring each year.

Women who married in childhood or adolescence experienced elevated amounts of violence from their husband and his family, violence which did not end even when the women entered early middle age (Nasrullah et al., 2014 & 2015). These authors argue that the act of marriage imposed on a child whose consent is for logical reasons unavailable, is the first of the many acts of violence imposed on her.

Economic Aspects of "Child-Bride Marriage"

The evidence clearly indicates that such marriages are driven by extreme poverty, especially where the female's family are required by custom or tribal law to give to the male spouse a substantial gift, or dowry. Even in urban centres, such as the slums of Lahore, 'tribal' norms often prevail in which the female child is regarded as a chattel who may be disposed of, if it is economically beneficial for her often desperately poor family (Nasrullah et al., 2015).

The practice of disposing of females in this way is forbidden by Islamic Shari'a law. Such law, which protects the rights of women in many areas, requires that it is the *male* partner who must give to the bride or her family, a traditional dower. Nevertheless, Islamic moral and legal guidance is ignored in this and many other aspects of the lives of women and children, in Bangladesh and Pakistan.

Should, in general, laws on child marriage be more strictly or clearly enforced? Suarez (2018) analysed data from 50 countries in examination of this question, looking at information over several years to see what effects stricter enforcement of laws against child marriage might have. Suarez found that applying laws more strictly had the unintended consequence of making the support of female children more burdensome for very poor families. This in turn led to *increasing* rates of infanticide and/or sex-selective abortion as a means of disposing of "unwanted" females.

Neither Bangladesh nor Pakistan were included in Suarez' data-set, since neither had taken effective steps to end the marriage of prepubescent girls. But we know from other studies that selective elimination of young females (both before or shortly after birth) occurs in both Bangladesh and Pakistan (Grech & Mamo, 2014). In 2010 census data identified that there were about 50 million "missing females" in Pakistan due to various causes: infanticide; sex-selective abortion – expensive and unavailable for the very poor, who instead resorted to killing the female child after birth; and to poorer quality nutrition and medical care given to very young females (Bowcott, 2011).

In Zakar et al's (2016) random sample of 490 rural women, current levels of extreme physical, emotional and sexual violence expressed by men towards their wives was associated with extreme poverty, and having been a prepubertal bride. Such women had poor mental and physical health, and 30% had been required to terminate a pregnancy, probably for economic reasons. In a review of legal statutes, Abbas & Riaz (2012) show that in all Provinces of Pakistan there are comprehensive laws which could prevent both child marriages, and the violent abuse of women. But these are rarely enforced, and women have no institutional support for taking independent action under these laws: for example, less than 5% of abused women ever sought divorce. These women were living in a state of "enforced helplessness" which they had learned from childhood onwards, and had internalised feelings of "shame" simply for being female (Ali et al., 2015). And the step into divorce would likely bring profound poverty for the women and her female children (Shahid, 2013).

Their poor mental health may incorporate the syndrome of PTSD outlined above. Zakar et al. (2013) after interviewing Pakistani men on their ideas concerning the status of women (and their wives) develop the thesis that in economically poor families women are framed in the status of what Foucault called "docile bodies", fit only to be used and dominated by men – the most extreme form of sexism known to human civilisation, and very far from the ideals of Islam for the guidance of male conduct. It is the women rather, who remain truer to Islamic ideals, accepting their fate with an Islamic dignity, praying to Allah whilst their bodies and minds are violated (Zakar et al., 2013 & 2016). We are reminded of the women of Gaza who suffer, with quiet Islamic dignity, the murderous assaults on men, women and children by the Israeli army.

In Pakistan feminists argue that Islam gives women equal rights to men in many domains, but this interpretation of the Qur'anic message is not accepted by most men (Zakar et al., 2013). Men in Pakistan and Bangladesh have interpreted (and invented) Qur'anic precedent to justify the practice of having extramarital affairs, the rape of a brother's young wife in a shared household, and even the practice of sodomy on young boys of inferior rank (Ali, et al., 2011). In this latter case, Islamic codes forbidding such a type of intercourse were seen as applying only to the passive 'partner'.[2]

Police in both rural and urban centres are known perpetrators of this practice, involving arrested juveniles (HRCP, 2017). A girl or woman who complains to police about rape is likely to experience further rapes by police. Unsurprisingly, sexual and violent crimes against women and girls are under-reported, but to what extent is unknown (Sarwar, 2016; HRCP, 2017). A woman who complains of rape by someone who is not her husband, and is pregnant by the rapist, also runs the risk of being stoned to death because of the incorporation of Shari'a law into the penal code of

---

[2] Rules forbidding homosexual conduct only properly apply, apparently, when both parties are post-adolescent. This excuse for pederasty is profoundly un-Islamic.

Pakistan (Mydans, 2002; HRCP, 2004). Eye-witness accounts of such stonings are given in the next Chapter.[3]

Ali et al. (2013) in their review of 23 studies on Pakistani girls and women report the continued incidence (absolute numbers are unknown) of trading a girl child in payment for a debt, or a legal obligation in disputes. A girl of 8 could be traded for a year's supply of rice, her fate entirely unknown (HRCP, 2017). In addition there is an active market in the sale (and kidnapping) of young girls who have value for work in one of the many brothels in Pakistan's major cities (Coyle et al., 2015). The extent of this marketing is unknown; what is known is that more than a 500 young girls are kidnapped without trace in Pakistan each year (Ali et al., 2015; HRCP, 2017; HRW, 2018).

3. Conclusions

Many of the oppressive practices endured by women and girls in Bangladesh also occur in Pakistan (including frequent rapes, kidnapping, trafficking, commercial sexual exploitation of minors, violence against women and girls, both before and after marriage; and imposition of non-Islamic dowry systems, inheritance practice, and post-divorce settlements).

Ayesha Shahid (2013) in comparing how post-divorce settlements in both Pakistan and Bangladesh frequently violate principles of Shari'ah law in ways which leave divorced women in great poverty (contrary to Islamic principle), observes that:

> *In both Pakistan and Bangladesh, the patriarchal ordering of the state at judicial and societal levels exacerbates this situation ... patriarchy has silenced the more egalitarian aspects of Islam ... It is therefore pertinent to maintain a clear distinction between the normative teachings of Islam and the male-dominated patriarchal norms prevalent in Muslim societies.* (pp 211-212)

---

[3] Attitudes to rape victims in a contrasted Islamic country, Malaysia, are profoundly different and more in keeping with an Islamic culture which addresses the rights of women with justice, not persecution (see Jamaluddin et al., 2018).

CHAPTER ELEVEN

PAKISTAN: THE HARD STRUGGLE FOR THE ISLAMIC EQUALITY OF WOMEN AND GIRLS

CHRISTOPHER ADAM-BAGLEY

I am going to give you such a weapon that the police and the army will not be able to stand against it. It is the weapon of the Prophet, but you are not aware of it. That weapon is forgiveness and righteousness. No power on earth can stand against it. (Abdul Gaffar Khan, known as Bacha Khan)

1. Introduction: Pakistan's Islamic Promise

The journey from our home in Leeds in Northern England to Lahore, and then to Islamabad is long. But the journey from Leeds Grand Mosque to the wonderful Faisal Mosque in Islamabad requires just a breath of movement, in metaphysical time. This masjid was designed by a Turkish architect in an eight-sided form, representing a Bedouin tent, and was built with funding from the Kingdom of Saudi Arabia. The International Islamic University is focussed within this outstanding building. The two mosques in Leeds and Islamabad and the thousands who worship there each day, are the beginning and ending of my Pakistani journeys: we are part of the Ummah, the worldwide sisterhood and brotherhood of the believers of Islam. We are linked by the Qur'anic revelation, and by the Sunnah, the wisdom and action of our blessed Prophet Muhammad. Islamic is a strong and bountiful religion, full of wisdom and mercy.

The Islamic Republic of Pakistan is strong, tough and hard. Anatol Lieven (2012) describes Pakistan, in his masterful socio-political overview as "a hard country". And it is also the potential home, embedded in the *ruh* or soul of its Islamic people, to the fountain of wisdom and mercy inspired by Allah.

This Chapter (like the previous Chapter on Child Marriage) will however be highly critical of many of Pakistan's current social institutions, describing widespread corruption and the violation and murder of women and children, and the general denial of women's rights and their Islamic equality. My argument is that Pakistan can accept this criticism, and knows how to improve. The infrastructure of human rights in moral, theological, legal and constitutional terms is already in place in Pakistan's laws and constitution, to effect such changes.

Pakistan is poised for take-off. We know this from our Pakistani brothers and sisters in England, the Pakistani diaspora who in their moulding of an Anglo-Pakistani Muslim identity, are among the leaders of Pakistanis reaching out to the world, as they form new identities while remaining true to their motherland (Shaw, 1988). Mahmoud Abubaker and I joyously meet our Pakistani brothers in Leeds each day; and our extended family includes a Pakistani wing. My niece, and my adopted son are of Pakistani descent. A British Pakistani scholar, Tahir Mahmood has led Christopher into Islam, renamed him Adam, and has linked Mahmoud and Adam in their Islamically inspired journey.

2. Three Honourable People in Pakistan's Developing Identity: A Politician, a Scholar and an Activist

Bacha Khan

> *God makes no distinction between men and women. If someone can surpass another, it is only through good deeds and morals ... there were many scholars and poets among women, in Islam's history. It is a grave mistake we have made in degrading women ... Today we are the followers of custom and we oppress you. But thank God we have realized that our gain and loss, progress and downfall, are common. Bacha Khan, quoted by Manji (2011), p27.*

Our choice of heroes is of course partial, and subjective. There are many more brave men and women, political activists and scholars who strive for the realisation of Pakistan's identity.

Our first choice is that of *Bacha Khan* – the honorific title given to the Pushtan anti-colonial leader Abdul Ghaffar Khan. He was part of the triumvirate of heroes whom Malala Youzafzai mentioned in her speech to the United Nations, alongside Mother Teresa and Nelson Mandela. Bacha Khan was a contemporary of Mahatma Gandhi, and is often referred to as "the Gandhi of Pakistani". His Islamic philosophy of non-violence led to lifelong campaigns against British colonial occupation, and then against the militarism of the factions which formed the developing nation of Pakistan after 1947 (Pal, 2011). Because of this he spent most of his adult life either in prison, or under house arrest, until his death in 1988. Shamsie (2017) argues that "Pakistan must never forget Bacha Khan, its great unsung hero" who was:

> ... The man who gave his name to the latest educational institution to be targeted by terrorists and a champion of non-violence. No wonder the Taliban hates him. Attacks on educational institutions have become a hideous way of marking the start of a new year in Pakistan. On 5 January 2014, the heroic student Aitzas Hasan died while struggling with a suicide bomber to prevent him from entering his school. On 15 January 2015, armed men on a motorcycle opened fire near the front gate of a girls' school ... and 20 January 2016 has given us the attack on Bacha Khan University, with the death toll at 30. The attack has been claimed by a Pakistan Taliban (who are) behind the massacre at Peshawar's Army Public School in December 2014.

> Since 2011, there have been 29 attacks on schools and universities in Pakistan – 30 if you include the attack on the school van that was carrying Malala Yousafzai when she was shot. It's horrific but not inexplicable that schools should become frontline targets in a state in which terrorist groups operate – what more effective way to terrorise a nation than by killing its children in their playgrounds? But some of the targeted schools seem to have a particular reason for drawing the attention of the Taliban – the Army Public School was singled out for educating the children of the military; the van carrying Malala was attacked because its 15-year-old passenger had dared to challenge the Taliban's rule of fear; and Bacha Khan University is very likely to have been attacked because everything represented by its namesake, the anniversary of whose death was being commemorated on the day of the attacks, stands in opposition to the Taliban.

Bach Khan's energy (and the national Foundation[1] which carries on his work) was devoted to peace-making between oppressors and the oppressed. His Islamic pacifism declared that "We shall not take revenge. It is God who will impose punishment on the unrepentant aggressors."

---

[1] https://bachakhantrust.org

Tariq Ali

Tariq Ali was born in Lahore in 1943, and by the 1960s had begun his renowned international career as researcher and writer of both political analyses and commentaries, and of wonderful historical accounts of lives in the Islamic world since the foundation of Islam – most famously the books of his Islamic Quintet (1992 to 2015). We chose Tariq not for his theology (he is a mischievous agnostic who honours all Gods) but for his pacifism and his political common sense, which has groundings in the best traditions of Islam. His magisterial history of Islam and "its final resting place" in Pakistan (Ali, 2002) is titled *The Clash of Fundamentalisms: Crusades, Jihads and Modernity*. Tariq is often scathing about the pompous self-importance of the self-appointed scholars who emerged in the centuries after the first Qur'anic message.

He is scathing too about the distortion of the Qur'anic message through the fabrication of Hadiths (supposed sayings of The Prophet). He shares this view with the convert to Islam, Johnathan Brown. Brown (2015 & 2018) offers stern scepticism concerning the fabrication of the true words and actions of Muhammad. We too share this scepticism, arguing that a crucial criterion for assessing any Hadith is the degree to which it reflects and is harmonious with The Qur'an. We accept the words of Aisha (Muhammad's wife, who recorded about a third of all "valid" Hadiths) that:

> *On one occasion when Lady Aisha, the truthful (God be pleased with her) was asked about the morals and manners of the Prophet (pbuh), she replied: "His morals are the Qur'an."* This meant that the Prophet's actions and sayings were a practical commentary of the Holy Qur'an, or, in other words, the Prophet was the embodiment of action based upon the Holy Qur'an.
> (Noormuhammad, cited by Eaton, 2008).

Tariq Ali's historical analysis ends with an account of the surprising Islamic vigour of Indonesia, to which we would add our own delight concerning the Islamic flowering of Malaysian culture, which offers for us a brilliant way forward for an ethical Islamic state based on readings of Qur'an and Hadith which do justice to the message of peace and equality in Islam.[2]

Tariq Ali also writes in his many books and articles about the rise and fall of socialist ideology and socialist republics: always he writes with humour

---

[2] The student pictured on the cover of this book is Malaysian. On the challenges faced by Islamic feminism in Malaysia, see Schäfer & Holst (2014). Even when progress is made, there are always new barriers to be addressed.

and wisdom, forgiving and peaceful in his intellectual mien. Often he writes about his estranged (but beloved) Pakistan, such as *Uprising in Pakistan* (about Bangladesh's struggle against Pakistani colonialism), and the emergence of what Trotsky described as "permanent revolution" (Ali, 2015). He is scathing about pompous and hypocritically-held ideologies exposing "Prime Ministers without clothes", the governors and leaders whose secret pockets are lined with loot, and the anti-Islamist ministers of the West who are the engineers of Islamophobia (Ali, 2005). We enjoy Tariq's writings because he is an intellectually free spirit, a man who has emerged from the political maelstrom of Pakistan as a powerful intellectual who has earned an enduring place in the intellectual critique of socialisms, colonialism, and capitalist exploitation. Most of all, we love the sheer intellectual and aesthetic quality of his writing.

Malala Yousafzai

Like Tariq Ali, Malala is deviant from the mainstream norms of Pakistani culture: from the age of 11 she publicly campaigned for girls' equality in education, and by the age of 15 was an internationally known media figure, clearly a person of boldness and brilliance. This is why the Taliban tried to murder this 15-year-old adolescent. Malala's "night journey" began when she was shot in the head on her way to the school run by her father in Mingora in the Swat Valley in Kyber Paktunkwa, in October, 2012, waking up many days later in a hospital bed in Birmingham, England. The Taliban gunmen invaded the school bus carrying Malala and other students shouting "Which one of you is Malala Yousafzai? Tell us, or we will kill you all." Malala bravely identified herself, knowing her fate. She was immediately shot in the head, probably from above, since the bullet entered her skull at the side of the eye, travelled down through her neck and lodged near her spinal cord. Soon afterwards she was flown, still unconscious, to the Queen Elizabeth Hospital in Birmingham, along with her immediate family. She required surgery to reduce brain swelling, and later to repair some facial nerves, and hearing.

Malala recovered fully, though with residual scars and chronic pain. She attended high school in Birmingham, and after success in examinations was admitted to Oxford University to study PPE (Philosophy, Politics and Economics), with expected graduation in 2020. In 2017 she was awarded the Nobel Peace Prize, the youngest ever recipient of this award. In addition to her studies she has become an advocate for refugee families and children, and reflects in the introduction to her edited book on refugee children's accounts, on her own experience as an 11-year-old refugee from the Taliban, in the Swat Valley.

This widely publicised book *We Are Displaced: My Journey and Stories from Refugee Girls Around the World* (2019) aimed to give profits to refugee aid organisations in Pakistani, and the rest of the world. She had previously published books for girls on their rights to education, and an updated autobiography in 2018 titled *Malala: My Story of Standing up for Girl's Rights*. Malala has been inspired by the Islamic pacifism of Bacha Khan and also by the life of Benazir Bhutto, Prime Minister of Pakistan until her assassination by The Taliban in 2007. Despite her conservative economic policies Benazir Bhutto has become an iconic symbol for advocates of women's equality in Pakistan.

What is outstanding about Malala? She is firstly, a symbol of the rise of women's rights in Pakistan and elsewhere across the world. She is brave and intelligent and may enter the political affray of Pakistan. Or she may retain and develop her role as a world ambassador for the United Nations on women's rights. Go well, Malala, we pray for you.

3. Pakistan: Social Structure, Economy and Politics

Population, Poverty and Food Security

Pakistan is a big nation, twice the size of France and the UK, and has a population of more than 205 million. GDP per head in 2018 was about £150 per month, but very unequally distributed, with a small number of families controlling two thirds of all industrial and commercial enterprises (Junaidi, 2016). High birth rates (6.9 children, on average, born to each woman) mean that a rising population in a very poor nation have to exist on a national agricultural system which does not produce enough to feed even the existing population adequately (Kugelman & Hathaway, 2011). If high birth rates continue, with moderate decline (*more* infants surviving, to women having *fewer* children) Pakistan's population size will increase to about 245 million by 2025, which will require a substantial increase in food production, which agricultural economists (e.g. Malik, 2011) argue is not possible.

Chronic poverty (in more than 40% of all households, and in two thirds of rural households) is currently associated with high infant and child mortality (especially in girls), chronic malnutrition, and limited access to health care (Hazarika, 2011; UNDP, 2018). Despite small steps toward poverty alleviation, the wealth gap between rich and poor in Pakistan is increasing (Junaidi, 2016).

Sial et al. (2015) used a multidimensional measure of family poverty (no individual in household achieved more than 5 years of education; no perinatal care for mothers and young children; no immunisations for children; no safe drinking water supply; no electricity; crowding at 3+ per room; no spare income after basic food purchased). Applying these combined measures to large scale survey data indicated that 65% of rural Pakistanis were 'poor' on at least two of these indicators, and at least 40% were poor on all five indicators. Lack of education, and lack of safe drinking water were the strongest predictors of all of the other indicators, leading the authors to advocate policies to help children stay in school, and to improve water supplies.

On the bright side, Pakistan developed an independent nuclear weapons force in 1998, and maintains a large and sophisticated force of rockets, fighters and bombers, and a deep-sea navy of 70 ships, including submarines (Shah, 2014). Currently the number of armed forces personnel is now in excess of 630,000 with a further 480,000 paramilitary forces mostly based in Punjab, apparently to maintain internal security – this employment provides a form of income stability for many men and their families, mostly in the Province of Punjab (Lieven, 2012). Pakistan spent 11% of its GDP on armaments and armed forces, and also received substantial international aid for this purpose. Shah (2014) provides detailed data on these expenditures, but current figures on weaponry and its funding are not available.

In contrast Pakistan devotes around 3.9% of national wealth to education, and a further 2% to primary health care and welfare services (HRCP 2018 & 2019). Pakistan's proportion of national wealth spent on its military force is amongst the world's highest; expenditures on education and health are among the world's lowest: about 6% of a meagre GDP goes towards education and primary health care, and this is clearly inadequate for its purpose.

The Challenge of Climate Change

Low levels of industrial activity mean that although Pakistan has more than 200 million souls, she contributes less than 1% of carbon emissions to world levels. However, Pakistan will be a major victim of unchecked climate change and is listed as the seventh most threatened world country in this regard (Jaffery, 2018b). This is due to a number of factors: loss of glaciers in the Himalayas will mean reduced water flow into rivers, and the Indus River irrigation schemes will be threatened, with increasing crises in agricultural outputs (Jaffery, 2018a). Pakistan is already facing a water shortage, with depleted underground supplies which will be exhausted by 2040. Climate change also causes longer periods of drought, fire, and flooding, and washed away or non-growing crops (Jaffery, 2018a). Environmental degradation coupled with high population growth puts much strain on food resources, and it's likely there will be migration of many millions away from drought-stricken, arid regions putting severe strain on existing health and welfare services (Ijaz, 2017a). By 2040 environmental degradation may lead to a loss of more than 10% of Pakistan's GDP.

The annual reports of the well-regarded independent foundation, The Human Rights Commission of Pakistan[3] (2012 to 2019) point to the environmental challenges to an economy which struggles to provide adequate health, education, welfare and justice programmes. Already 80% of Pakistanis do not have easy access to safe drinking water; climate-induced environmental degradation coupled with an increasing population will make this problem worse, and HRCP report a deterioration in the quality of both urban and rural environments from 2016 to 2017. Arable and habitable land is scarce, and land theft (and violent quarrels which result) are common, but rarely policed. City air is very polluted, and an increase in urban heat stress is likely in future years (HRCP 2017 & 2018).

4. The Plural Society of Pakistan

Pakistan is a plural society, a nation state attempting to draw together many different regions and districts with different languages and cultural traditions, trying to meld a state which has to cope with many competing interests (Altaf, 2011; Moonis, 2014). These markedly different cultural groups are spread across 13 ecological zones with marked differences in traditions of agriculture and lifestyle, and with ongoing armed rebellion (Taliban-led) in some areas of rural Pakistan. In addition more than a million refugees have moved from Afghanistan to Pakistan.

The country is divided into seven provinces, each with much autonomy in administrative, legal and fiscal measures. Six main languages are spoken, with English as an additional official language. The dominant ethnic group

---

[3] Another of our "Pakistani heroes" is the human rights lawyer Asma Jahinger, a founder of HRCP. She died recently, aged 66, having achieved much on behalf of women, and persecuted groups.

are the Punjabi- and Urdu-speaking inhabitants of Punjab; there are six main ethnic groups in the nation defined by region and language. Pakistan includes 10 cities with populations of one million or more, Karachi (15 millions) and Lahore (11 millions) being the largest. Literacy rates are 70% in males, 46% in females; but there is considerable variation in these rates (and other indicators of progress) between rural and urban areas, and across provinces.

Government and politics in Pakistan are difficult and challenging tasks, and have evolved since emancipation in 1947 through various types of rule (Muhammad & Brett, 2019), including democracy and military dictatorship, into Pakistan becoming an Islamic Republic in 1977, with attempts to harmonise laws with the Shari'a codes prescribed by Islam: 96% of the population are nominally Muslim, mostly in the Sunni tradition. The harmonisation of secular and religious codes has also established the Zina ordinances in 2007, in which the Shari'a prescribed morality of sexual relations and marriage, derived from the Hudood ordinances have emerged as national codes, observed with varying frequency or severity across Pakistan's main regions.

Another strand in Pakistan's plural society are the (five or more) competing ideologies of Islam, taught by different madrasahs across Pakistan. Since these madrasahs are often the only sources of education and welfare for local populations, they can exert a powerful ideological influence (Khan, 2014). Some of this madrasah teaching does permit or advocate violence against women and female children, and the murder of political dissidents, scholars and journalists (Sadruddin, 2017):

> *Islam was the first religion to introduce human rights ... which is why we are unwilling to accept UN edicts as ideas dominating our value system. However ... multi-layered philosophies of human rights in Pakistan have heightened civil unrest and bred a culture of tension among teacher educators and their students ... traditional Islamic values such as integrity, freedom and human rights are seen by conservatives as incompatible with the philosophies of the radical right which now rules Pakistan through the means of a strong military.* (Sadruddin, 2017 pp 77-80)

On the issue of conflicting values in Pakistan, Haider (2013) observes:

> *The Islamic narrative in Pakistan has been hijacked by an array of groups who use religion as a means to diverse ends: to secure political and territorial power, exorcise corrosive Western influence, engage in class warfare, redress perceived injustices, and even overturn the state in the pursuit of a purer Islamic order ... Pakistan's viability as a state depends in*

large part on its ability to develop a new and progressive Islamic narrative. (Haider, 2013, p. 242-245)

Afiya Zia (2009a & b) appraising law and politics in Pakistan from the viewpoint of Islamic feminism focusses on the "enlightened despotism" of the Musharraf regime who, with the aid of military rule, reversed "misogynist" edicts put in place during the regimes of 1977 to 1988, partly revised by the more liberal Benazir Bhutto. Musharraf from 2002 to 2008, allowed a women's movement to develop provided that it supported current political regimes, and was compatible with Islamic principles. The "faith-based feminism" which emerged was, in Zia's analysis relatively successful in both supporting women in the polity, and rejecting some criticisms of Pakistani values concerning women. Zia argues that the Zina ordinances (much criticised in the non-Islamic west) actually helped women in establishing a Qur'anic critique of male conduct, emphasising women's right to be free from physical and sexual assaults, and to equality in divorce and property settlements.

To this analysis Durrani et al (2017) add the observation that: "The confluence of religion, national and ethnic identifications within a conflict-affected context produces strong gendered subjectivities." For advocates of Islamic feminism this as an important comment. The voices of women are but one of the many voices and interest groups fighting for power in a complex plural society in which "struggle" is framed in essentially male terms – reflected for instance in school curricula and textbooks (Emerson, 2017; Muhammad & Brett, 2017). Zia's (2009a) model for feminisms to work "from the inside" of key power groups in Pakistan is highly relevant here.

An important strand (or strata) in Pakistan's pluralism is the economy, divided between rural and urban wealth (or lack of it), and the needs, rights and interests of the desperately poor third of the nation. Pakistan "has done a very poor job of poverty alleviation" (Hussain et al., 2004). Baqir (2019) has shown that neither international aid nor internal policies have been successful in reducing chronic poverty which influences all aspects of life in Pakistan. It is reflected in high death and serious illness rates for children, lack of effective primary education, and multiple acts of violence of which women and girls are the most frequent victims. In Marxian terms consciousness and values grounded in poverty are, in the earlier stages of social development of a nation, generally reactionary. Males create for themselves a status group, "a class for itself" which sees women as inferior. Religious ideology (e.g. Islam) in this model is hijacked and distorted to serve this class interest. For the wealthy classes there is powerful interest in maintaining a class model of the perpetual poor.

Islam advises believers to observe the practice of *zakah*, giving 2.5% of one's asset each year, to the poor. This is a sound principle followed by many: but for the impoverished half of Pakistan's population, 2.5% of net assets amounts to zero. Reforms must be made to Pakistan's quasi-capitalist system before the poor can be lifted from the mind and value-eroding bonds of basic existence. Until absolute poverty is ended in Pakistan, we argue, not much else will change.

Numerous scholars have commented on the complexity of Pakistan's plural society, and the extremely challenging task of serving the human rights and needs of all sectors of the population. Majeed (2017) for example, offers an interesting and challenging psychological model based on "human needs theory", which might be incorporated in, or used to evaluate, other models of pluralism. Certainly, according to the Qur'anic guidance analysed by Musofer (2012) and Rais (2017), an Islamic state should adopt Islamically-guided models for a plural society. And as Zia (1994) cogently argues, the refusal to see women and their rights and needs as an essential element of Islamically guided pluralism has led in Pakistan to a "a vociferously anti-woman ideology … or silent compliance on violence against women."

One aspect of the "plural struggles" in Pakistan is the policy of decentralisation, in which each Province decides how much and in what manner it will fund and administer essential institutions such as schools and colleges, and how laws on female infanticide, child marriage, 'honour killing', rape and wife-burning shall be interpreted and applied (HRW, 2018). National government is reluctant to try and enforce such laws to a uniform standard (HRCP, 2017). But, as Haider (2013) asserts, The Pakistan state must evolve a set of moral imperatives which meld Islamic principles concerning human rights, and those standards of human rights, advocated by the international community.

5. Education Systems in Pakistan

Pakistan produces many brilliant scholars from its first rank universities, although social scientists and educationists must be careful about what they write, or lecture on. The bold scholar or journalist can be a target for assassination by one of several dissident groups (HRCP, 2017). In writing this account of Pakistan's educational and social progress, I draw strongly on the annual reports of the authoritative, Lahore-based Human Rights

Commission of Pakistan, an independent group of judges, lawyers, economists and other scholars who draw on a wealth of reliable data from local and international studies.

Literacy rates, and primary education systems especially in rural areas, are dismal. Pakistan leads the world in the proportion of children of primary age who are not in school. It is estimated that at current rates of improvement, universal enrolment in primary education will occur by 2060, and in secondary school (to age 18) by 2095. At present only 69% of children are educated up to age 12 (HRCP, 2017). These figures on age are estimates only, since the births of many children (about 34% according to one study) are not officially registered. Around 64% of males achieve some years in high school, compared with 14% of all females. About 5% in the age group 18+ are enrolled in some form of higher education (HRCP, 2018). A further study found that in rural areas 69% people of all ages were functionally illiterate, compared with 35% of urban dwellers (HRCP, 2019).

The proportion of the adult population judged to be "literate" *fell* from 60% in 2016 to 58% in 2017. At the same time, proportion of children attending primary schools was also *declining*, as was the proportion of 8-year-olds passing standard tests of reading and numeracy (HRCP, 2018): only 43% of enrolled boys could read by age 8, compared with 33% of girls. Only 13% of girls continue schooling until age 16, compared with 49% of boys (HRW, 2018).

Primary and secondary education is, in formal terms, free but many rural areas do not have schools available to attend. Mismanagement (and sometimes corruption) leads to some 900 "ghost schools", 15,000 "ghost teachers" and an estimated 300,000 "fake students", for whom money is allocated but is diverted to other purposes. Many teachers are not appointed on the basis of qualifications or merit, but because of a system of appointment which can only be described as corrupt (HRW, 2018). Long walks to school are hazardous for girls, who face the very real danger of rape, and even kidnapping for purposes of trafficking (HRCP 2017 & 2018). 236 rural children disappeared in rural areas in 2018, mostly during journeys to or from school (HRCP, 2019). In Karachi in 2018 more than 5,000 children were reported missing, but most of these are thought to have been recruited (or kidnapped) into various forms of informal labour, including sex work (HRCP, 2019). The number of children dropping out of primary schooling increased from 22.63 million in 2017 to 22.84 million in 2018, partly reflecting the increase in population size (HRCP, 2019).

More than 40% of rural schools are one-room buildings (and sometimes a fenced area, with no roof) with a single teacher for all age-groups, with no boundary wall or security fence, no toilets of any kind, and no supply of drinking water. Because of the strong decentralisation of government, each province is responsible for expenditures on education, and monitoring its quality. There is wide variation in educational quality and achievement between provinces, and some schools are merely enclosed spaces without a building or desks of any kind: children simply sit on the ground in order to receive instruction. (HRW, 2018)

Teachers are poorly trained, and often absent. Corporal punishment (sometimes causing permanent injury) is frequent, and the Human Rights Commission of Pakistan reports cases of teachers who demand money, external labour, or various gifts from pupils, in exchange for not being beaten. Beating of very young children with rods is common, and one known fatality occurred because of teacher punishment in 2018 (HRCP, 2019). Lack of security means that schools are vulnerable to murderous attack by groups opposed to any kind of education for girls. Indeed, many girls soon decide that school is not a safe or pleasant place. At least 100 children are raped and then killed in rural areas each year, and there is no sign that this incidence is declining (HRCP 2017 & 2018). In rural areas many parents also withdraw daughters from schooling as they approach puberty, preparing them for marriage (HRW, 2018).

Sociological studies of schools, their textbooks and curricula and social relationships within schools have concluded that most schools perpetuate the ethos and image of male violence. Girls are frequently harassed verbally and physically in sexual and other ways, by their male peers. On journeys to and from school boys poke, prod and feel the girls' bodies over their modest clothing in ways which violate Islamic dignity (Emerson, 2017; Muhammad & Brett, 2019; HRCP, 2018). Verbal and physical sexual harassment of female students in public universities is also common, and unchecked (HRCP, 2019).

School textbooks emphasise nation-building and praise of military heroes, emphasising the threat of India, the supposed enemy. These textbooks contain nothing on "peace-making, non-violence and reconciliation" (HRCP, 2018). Some madrasahs (the only source of education for many children) teach that: "Women's employment is ruining the family. Women should not seek employment outside of the home ... Dual career women injure both themselves and their families ..." (Wadud, 2005). Girls are socialised to accept that husbands have the right to beat them, that they must accept parental wishes for marriage in their early teenaged years, and that they must be exchanged in marriage for a substantial dowry paid to the prospective husband – quite contrary to Shari'a principles (Nour, 2009; Ali et al., 2011; Zakar et al. 2013).

6. Children's Health and Health Systems in Pakistan

In addition to the health consequences of child marriage discussed in the previous Chapter, Pakistani children and adolescents rank near the bottom on world statistics of infant and child mortality, infectious diseases acquired through contaminated water supplies, stunted growth due to malnutrition, and infections resulting from impaired immunity (Mustafa, 2017). In 2017 42% of households were enduring "food poverty", and 52% of under fives had stunted growth or were underweight (HRCP, 2018). Pakistani women and girls experienced on average, 6.8 pregnancies during their years of fertility[4]. Pneumonia and diarrhoea were leading causes of death for under-fives, followed by malnutrition. Death rates at birth were 66 per 1000; in children surviving birth, death rates in the first year of life were 19 per 1000. Life expectancy at birth was 59 years (HRCP, 2017 & 2018). In 2018 HRCP observed that:

> As in previous years, the healthcare provision in the country deteriorated during 2017 and failed to address the needs of the poorer sections of society ... Doctors are reluctant to work in rural areas ... there are few screening or prevention programmes in rural areas ... the World Health Organisation recommends that 6% of GDP should be spent on health. In Pakistan it is less than 1%.

One problem identified by HRCP was that of "fake doctors", "fake pharmacists" and "fake medicines". The actual extent of this problem is difficult to estimate, but many poor people spend money on fake medicines (e.g. so-called antibiotics). Prolonged drought in 2017 resulted in elevated child death rates in poor families in rural provinces (HRCP, 2018).

---

[4] Although there are conservative voices, contraceptive use is generally accepted in Islam, and is part of Pakistan government policy. In 2017 about 60% of women of fertile age used some form of medically approved contraception, although 40% did not for a variety of reasons including husband's wishes, and lack of available contraceptives, which are only atypically given by health centres to mothers without payment. Lack of available contraception is most prevalent in rural areas (GoP, 2018).

The Human Rights Commission of Pakistan (HRCP, 2019) concluded its overview of children's rights in 2018:

> *Overall, Pakistan failed to protect its children in 2018 with nearly all their fundamental rights and freedoms infringed or put at serious risk of violation. Lack of neonatal care, low birth registration levels, food insecurity, excessive violence and inadequate legal and social protection, hazardous labour, as well as child marriage were some of the recurring issues faced by children of the country. While the judiciary and law enforcement were seen to be more actively pursuing cases of crimes against children, the extent and severity of the violence against children did not see much improvement.*

7. Women and Children of Pakistan: Failure to Meet Human Needs

Child Labour

The employment of children and adolescents as labourers is common in Pakistan, not only in the brick kilns and farming, but also in areas such as ship-breaking where injury and even death are relatively common occurrences (HRCP, 2017). Twelve million children and adolescents have left school early, and then work for low wages in menial tasks (HRCP, 2018 & 2019). Children may be sold as "bonded labourers" to dangerous trades such as brick-making, meaning that they receive no wages at all (HRW, 2018). Employing children is a useful way for employers to avoid paying the official (but rarely enforced) minimum wage. The extent of child-selling is unknown, since most provincial governments have no interest in investigating this trade (HRCP 2017 & 2018). Another form of childhood exploitation, prostitution, is discussed later in this Chapter. Overall, including selling children for sexual purposes involving "Bonded, forced slave labour of woman and girls, has not improved." (HRCP, 2018). This includes the use of children as domestic servants, in which roles they are frequently physically and sexually abused.

In rural areas, women and girls make up about 70% of all agricultural labourers: only 60% of these female workers receive any monetary reward for this labour (UNWomen, 2018; HRCP, 2019).

Exploitation of Boys

Apart from bonded physical labour and other forms of employment under difficult conditions, boys in a culture which separates the genders in many social institutions, are subject to the indignities of sexual abuse in large but unknown numbers. This seems more prevalent than in Bangladesh (HRCP, 2017). The informal ethic of adult males seems to be that a minor who is a passive recipient of sodomy is, in Islamic terms, not sinful (nor is he causing the adult male to sin). Therefore a boy, not having reached puberty cannot be said to be a sinful homosexual (and neither is his adult male 'partner'), in this false interpretation of Islamic principles. It is alleged (HRCP, 2017) that using young boys sexually is widespread in some madrasahs, and is practised by both teachers and older boys upon younger boys.

Outside of the madrasahs, in larger cities sexual prostitution of boys is common, with numbers exceeding 250,000 in certain city areas, particularly around transport hubs (Aurat, 2011; UNAIDS, 2016). According to my informants, a boy may be bought for £2 or less, varying on the type of sex required, and where it takes place (e.g. type of 'hotel'). The boys are largely ignorant of modes of HIV transmission, and the elevated risks which unprotected anal intercourse poses. According to the Aurat Foundation (2011) a 10-year-old boy would yield when trafficked to a Middle Eastern country, as much as $1000 for his "owner". Police are not merely complicit in these crimes; they may actually be the pimps who own and traffic the boys (HRCP, 2017).

Stoning of Women to Death under Hudood and Zina Ordinances

The legal system of Pakistan is in disarray. There is a huge backlog of cases waiting to heard by the higher courts (HRCP, 2017 & 2019). Bringing cases to lower courts, and successful outcome of cases which meet the aspirations of litigants, defendants and witnesses seems to be the exception rather than the rule. Much "justice" is administered by police themselves, or by religious and tribal courts in remote regions, without the clear element of justice or due process we would expect from a clear and rational application of Shari'a law principles and procedures (Esposito & DeLong-Bas, 2018). Police often exercise a "shoot to kill" policy of suspects, before or after arrest – exact numbers killed by police are unknown, but likely amount to several thousand each year (Boone, 2016a and b; HRCP, 2017).

Arrested females and boys are likely to experience repeated rapes by the police. Complaints to police of having been raped are an invitation to be the victim of gang rapes by police. Torture and beating of suspects is routine. 87 suspects were formally hanged in 2016, several of them for alleged crimes committed as juveniles, being then held in prison until they were old enough to be executed (HRCP, 2018). A further 482 await their execution.

This is the violent world of Lahore and Karachi: in the countryside things are quieter and slower. Islamic religious law incorporated into the Pakistani constitution in 1977 legitimises or emboldens religious courts in rural areas, including the imposition of stoning to death of adulterers: but in practice it is only women who receive this fatal punishment. Why only females? The Qur'an requires four witnesses to adulterous sexual intercourse. A 'false witness' in this regard is liable to suffer severe penalty. Liberal interpreters of Shari'a law (e.g. Esposito & DeLong-Bas, 2018; Brown, 2017) argue that the prescribed stoning punishment has likely never occurred (because 4 witnesses are never available), and is merely symbolic. Clearly, these scholars are unfamiliar with Pakistani religious law customs.

A married woman in Pakistan who has been raped, and becomes pregnant when her husband is absent (e.g. as a migrant worker, on military service, or in prison) has, from the evidence of her swollen belly *obviously* committed a Zina crime. Many more witnesses than four can attest to this (her bodily state), and her guilt is obvious. Her accusation of rape against a named male is not accepted, because there were no independent witnesses, and she is doubly at fault, having made a "false" accusation.

Indeed, it is unwise for any Pakistani female to report her rape outside of the family: impugning the family's status could also lead to a death sentence, and 'honour killing" is much more frequent then stoning. For the religious court the matter is clear and unambiguous: she must be stoned to death, as soon as her child is born. Religious opinion is divided on the guilt or otherwise of the child, but it is known for a female infant to be stoned to death after her birth, since as a female she shares her mother's guilt.

The manner of execution by stoning is thus: a pit is dug, usually in front of the mosque, and the woman buried up to her neck, only her head exposed. The Imam (or another designated elder) will then stand over the woman holding aloft a heavy stone which he will aim at the top of the woman's head. At this point she is unconscious or already dead. Adult males will then throw token stones at the woman's head (rather like Hajj pilgrims throwing symbolic stones at the devil). I owe the details of this, and of several other stonings to my brave research students whom I will not name, in order to protect their safety.[5]

---

[5] My accounts of stonings in Pakistan are more than 10 years old, and were not collected by students at the University to which I am currently affiliated. Another student has collected fairly recent observational data on *suttee*, public widow burning in India.

We have no estimates of the number of stonings which occur across Pakistan at the present time: but we have enough evidence to assert that such activities were still, in 2018, continuing. This fear is confirmed by the Aurat Foundation's annual reports on women's rights and equality in Pakistan (Aurat, 2006 to 2018). Earlier evidence is confirmed by the report of National Council on The Status of Women on Hudood Ordinances (HRCP, 2004).

There is an informal tradition in many Islamic countries that an infant which a parent(s) cannot look after can be placed on the steps of a mosque before the first, dawn prayers. The infant will be taken into the mosque by those arriving for prayer, and the Imam will find a home for the infant from amongst his congregation. In Karachi at least, this practice has become dangerous, since some Imams see the infant as "the product of immorality" and will stone the female infant to death without requiring approval from any religious court. In 2018 the Telsur news agency reported:

> *A few people found a baby at the doorstep of a mosque in Karachi, and they handed the baby over to the prayer leader. The cleric decried that this is an 'illegitimate baby' and it should be stoned. Resultantly, the baby was stoned to death. "I tried to register a case against the cleric, but nothing happened," Anwar Kazmi, a senior manager at Edhi Foundation in Karachi, told the News International.*

In 2002 a case publicised by *The New York Times* (Mydans, 2002) led to worldwide and UN pressure on the government of Pakistan, and this may have influenced the national government's scrutiny and control of rural stonings, although we cannot ascertain any evidence of this. The case involved Bibi Zafran whose husband was absent, serving a lengthy prison term. Ms Zafran was raped by her husband's younger brother: the woman did not complain about this at the time, since such rapes by brothers- and father-in-law are common when husband is absent for a lengthy period (Aurat, 2006-2018). However, when her pregnancy began to show, the woman was required to give an explanation: her public explanation led to her arraignment in a religious tribunal (Shari'a court).

The judge said he had no alternative but to sentence her to death by stoning. Her story of rape was held to be irrelevant, and indeed the idea of "rape" has not much purchase in Pakistani legal systems. However, international publicity led to a higher court considering an appeal, and Ms Zafran was persuaded to say that the child was conceived by her husband during conjugal leave from his prison. All parties knew that this was untrue since such leave is never granted; nevertheless, the legal fiction enabled the court to free Ms Zafran, and restore the family's "honour".

Village or rural district courts continue to impose death by stoning for 'adulterous' women, and occasionally these verdicts leak to the national press with reports that require the national government to intervene prior to execution (Qarni, 2017). Aurat (Womens' Rights Foundation of Pakistan) commented at this time:

> *It is not only women but also young girls who are at risk, Aurat says. If girls report a rape, they face the same prospects of punishment as women. A man can deflect an accusation of rape by claiming that his victim, of any age, consented. If the victim has reached puberty, she is considered to be an adult and is then subject to prosecution for zina. As a result, the Aurat report says, girls as young as 12 or 13 have been convicted of having forbidden sexual relations and have been punished with imprisonment and a public whipping.*

As Qadir (2018) observes, the progress towards gender equity in Pakistan is slow indeed, and this country remains last but one in the ranking of nations on a number of measures of women's equality and health (Talib & Barry, 2017; Morin et al., 2018).

Rape as an Instrument of Social Control

For the masculine hegemony of Pakistan, rape (and violent sex imposed upon wives, and upon married women and girls) is a useful means of socialisation and social control, enforcing the subordinated roles they occupy as women. These rapes occur in the many child marriages in Pakistan, but are also imposed on unmarried girls whenever they can be cornered and overpowered, including on journeys to and from school (Bowcott, 2011; Kfir, 2014; HRW, 2018). A girl who complains of rape to the police risks two penalties: being subjected to further rapes by police officers; and being charged with engaging in self-confessed, immoral behaviour. Without four independent witnesses of her rape, the girl has no hope that her rapist(s) will be prosecuted. The whole concept of rape seems puzzling for the Pakistani judicial system; but the number of known rapes appears to be increasing year on year, perhaps as a result of population increase. Rape followed by murder cannot escape judicial investigation, and more than 100 of such cases in 2016 involved child victims (HRCP, 2017). Violence in marriage, and sex imposed on juveniles seems to be extension of Pakistan's rape culture, and is prevalent in a variety of institutions, including schools (Ali, 2011; Zakar, 2013).

This "rape culture" extends to the workplace as well, and Fouzia Saeed (2013) has written a brave account of working as a woman in United Nations offices in Pakistan: an educated, middle class women in an office full of educated middle class men must endure daily sexual harassment of a physical kind: without prostituting herself to superiors, she is unlikely to advance. Previously Saeed had studied female prostitution in Pakistan (Saeed, 2006) and draws clear parallels between prostitution and the degraded status of Pakistani women. The Aurat Foundation (2011) record that "casual sexual abuse" of girls and women by public officials, police and teachers is common.

While the sexual misuse of boys may be common in some settings, there is an implicit ethic in this type of abuse that the victim will in course of time, graduate to being an abuser if he so chooses. It may even be the case that confining sexual expression to all-male communities actually "spares" women and girls from heterosexual abuse.

"Honour Killing" and Woman Burning

What can be honourable about the widespread Pakistani practice of "honour" killing - in complete contradiction of Qur'anic revelation, the Sunnah, and Shari'a principles? This puzzle is partially solved by sociological writers who show that what is threatened by a woman's potentially independent choice of a marital partner, is the authority and status of her father, in a country where symbolic status is all that the wretchedly poor have – a kind of social capital, to borrow a term from Bourdieu (Bourdieu, 1989; Khan, 2006; Jafri, 2009; Cooney, 2019). In an "honour killing" girl or woman will be murdered by her father or brothers for a variety of reasons – looking at a boy of the wrong caste, or at too many boys; having a telephone conversation with a boy; touching the hand of the wrong boy. Sexual contact does not have to be proved, but there is evidence of girls who, having been raped in the community, are then killed by family members because her defilement has filled the family with shame, or dishonour (Luopajarvi, 2004).

Until a Federal Law of 2016 was passed, honour killings were treated as local or tribal matters, with maximum penalties of a year's imprisonment (but this was rarely enforced). This new law was passed in reaction to an award-winning documentary about the case of a woman "honourably killed", but who survived (Boone, 2016b; Clark, 2016). This documentary gave the extraordinary account of a woman who was shot and stabbed by her father and his brother and then thrown into a river. She survived, to give powerful testimony.

According to the Human Rights Commission of Pakistan in 2018, and other observers (Ijaz, 2017b) the national law has had little effect, and such killings continue unreported by media, and are unpunished. Woman burning is a convenient alternative to honour killing (knocking the women unconscious, and leaving her soaked in kerosene next to an 'exploding stove', death usually occurring after some days as a result of 3rd degree burns). This practice seems to be quite common in Pakistan, India and Bangladesh (Lakhani, 2005). But being reported as "accidents" they lack the satisfaction for family honour of the publicly declared and enacted, primitive ritual of controlling females by beating, stabbing or stoning, in ways which restore the status and "honour" of family males. The official record of deliberate killing through burning puts the number in Pakistan at between one and two thousand a year, a certain underestimate missing around 80% of all cases (Badings, 2017; HRCP, 2018).

I turn now to an extraordinary case of honour killing: exceptional in that it occurred within the boundaries of urban Karachi, and also involved the killing of two adolescents, a girl of 15 and a boy of 17, by the unusual method of burning through connection of the bound victims to the public electricity supply (Mann, 2017). The events reported took place in 2017, a year after a national law forbidding honour killing was established in the national legal code (Rasmussen, 2017). The boy and girl wished to marry but permission was denied, so they tried to elope. There was no evidence of any physical contact, apart from holding hands. The problem was that the boy came from a lower caste background than the girl:

The night Ghani Rehman was condemned to die, his father asked if they could share a last meal together. But Ghani excused himself, preferring to wait in his room. His sisters came to see him, and he gave them each a small token to remember him by: a plastic-wrapped mint drop. The 17-year-old boy knew what was coming. Less than 24 hours earlier, the neighbour's 15-year-old daughter Bakhtaja, with whom Ghani had tried to elope from Ali Brohi Goth, their poor neighbourhood of Karachi, had been tied down and electrocuted .... His father finished dinner, then returned. With the help of an uncle, he strapped his son to a rope bed, tying one arm and one leg to the frame with uncovered electrical wires. Bakhtaja had endured 10 minutes of searing electrical jolts before she died. The boy took longer, and eventually the uncle stepped in and strangled him. The couple were buried in the dead of night.

Ghani and Bakhtaja had known each other since childhood. She lived on the second floor of a newly built villa, overlooking the dusty patch of ground where Ghani's family had a brick home, and from where he would catch her eye when she stood on the balcony. Ghani had tried several times to get permission to marry her, but was rebuffed.... Bakhtaja and Ghani are buried 10 metres apart in the local cemetery, their graves dug between shrubs and covered with red cloth still not faded by the sun and dust. Ataullah, a gravedigger, said the bodies were charred from burns when they were lowered into the ground. Female relatives of the couple, who were not available for interviews, were "removed" from their houses when punishments were meted out, neighbours said. After the murder, Bakhtaja's mother told human rights defenders: "I forgive him," meaning her husband. (Rasmussen, 2017)

HRCP (2018) observed that:

An effort was made in 2017, through laws enacted in 2016, to bring 'honour' killings and rape/gang-rape outside of the control of 'traditional law' systems [into the sphere of Federal law] .... However, no marked improvement was observed or recorded in 2017 ... in fact, new loopholes emerged on what is an 'honour killing' ... many so-called suicides and accidents are in fact honour killings ... Powerful (but technically illegal) tribal courts rule on honour killings and the giving away of little girls to appease for 'blood crimes', land disputes, debts ...

In 2018 "only" about 200 honour killings were known to the authorities, a declining number of reports, which almost certainly underestimates the true incidence (HRCP, 2019).

8. Pakistan: The Problem of Caste

Caste is usually known as part of Indian culture, a reflection of Hindu metaphysics in which rebirth into a higher or lower caste, or into the "untouchability" of Dalithood reflects the individual's sins in a previous life. Being born female is also evidence of previous sin. I have offered a detailed account of the apartheid-like oppression of the "untouchable" Dalits of India, whom members of the four hierarchical castes will not touch (except in acts of rape) (Adam-Bagley, 2008c).

In the past century many millions of untouchables converted from being Hindu to being Christian, Sikh or Muslim in attempts to forge a new and freer identity. Unfortunately many Christian, Sikh and Muslim descendants of former Dalits remain desperately poor, and are looked down on by "true" holders of these faiths. This still applies in varying degrees in the three faiths to whom Dalits converted. In Islam all Muslims should be equal, whatever their ethnic origins. But this has not been the case in Pakistan and India, both before and after partition in 1947.

There exist in Pakistan today many millions of former Dalits, whose children are now Muslims, but who still experience discrimination at the hands of "true", higher status Muslims. This according to some sociological commentators, is a major factor feeding the violence of "honour killings", other types of murder, and accusations of blasphemy (a capital offence) (Patek, 2016). The leading scholar providing evidence for this argument is Faisal Devji (2018). Wishing to marry a Dalit-descendant may disgrace the honour of a family member.

9. The Commercialised Sexual Exploitation of Girls, Boys and Women in Pakistani Cities

In Bangladesh the brothel villages are legal entities. Pakistan probably has as many CSEWC (commercially sexually exploited women and children) as there are in Bangladesh: but these boys, women and girls work in a more clandestine fashion (Saeed, 2001 & 2006). Since intercourse outside of marriage is a Zina crime, punishable by beating and imprisonment (at least for the females involved), police have powerful agency in controlling, by threat of prosecution, the CSEWC. They use this power by acting as pimps, and gaining the right of sexual access to many females.

The urban sex trade is usually an 'after dark' activity, in which auto-rickshaw drivers also make a profit in taking a customer to a dark hotel. After various people have been paid off, the woman will receive about 10 UK pence (15 US cents) for submitting to intercourse. Children may earn more, except for those who have been sold as bonded labour, who will receive nothing. This an entirely local trade: there are no 'sex tourists' in Lahore or Karachi. Bangladeshi girls are trafficked into this trade, and in the past year Rohingya adolescents from the refugee camps in Bangladesh have also become available for Pakistani men.

Emmanuel et al. (2013) in a combined public health and ethnographic study of "female sex work" in Pakistan report that an extensive network of "sex for sale" exists in all of the 15 major cities. The trade is complex, with women working from home, in established brothels, or in small 'hotels' with a variety of intermediate pimps and adult males involved. Cell phone numbers are touted by some intermediaries. These researchers estimate that more than a million women and girls aged less than 39 (about 1% of women of this age in Pakistan) become CSEWC for shorter or longer periods.

Emmanuel et al.'s work indicates that about 7 in 1000 adult males use women in commercialised sex transactions on a regular basis.

Any kind of violent sex act can be negotiated through intermediaries, and imposed on girls and women whose status is that of bonded workers. Given the high rates of physical and sexual abuse imposed on young girls in rural areas, their sale as bonded sex workers in cities is not unusual (HRCP, 2017). Another way of assuring a fresh supply of young girls to the sex trade is to kidnap a lone girl on her journey to school in a rural area (HRCP, 2018; HRW, 2018).

Boys seem to have more freedom than girls as sex workers, but their commercial usefulness for police and pimps in the major cities ends when they reach puberty, and Islamic norms about the wrongfulness of homosexuality (involving two adults) begin to prevail. Anal rape imposed upon a prepubertal boy is not, according to the Islamic folk wisdom of Pakistan, a crime or a sin. According to fieldwork by one of my students, these boys graduate into lives of petty crime as well as pimping.

Knowledge about STI and HIV transmission is poor, and condom use probably occurs in less than half of transactions. Rates of HIV/AIDS are allegedly high, although Burgri (2006) casts doubts on the reliability of case-finding techniques. Many cases go undiagnosed, and deaths are often recorded as being due to secondary infections, rather than to AIDS itself. The matter is complicated by the still surviving practice of payment for tainted but unscreened blood donations, and the reuse of needles in poorly funded medical centres. Green (2019) reported "an epidemic" of HIV infections in children in Sindh Province detected by a WHO field team – 730 cases were identified, thought to be small proportion of the total number of cases, which likely stemmed from needle reuse in unregulated health clinics.

Ethnographic Study of a Type of 'Child Prostitution'

I hold a strong value position, based on evidence and argument, that all forms of commercialised sexual transactions are gross exploitations of the 'paid for' person, and amount to a form of commercialised rape (Adam-Bagley, 2017 & 2018). I also advocate the ethical principle that no research should be undertaken with commercially sexually exploited women and children (CSEWC) *unless* the researcher is able to offer the exploited individuals a realistic alternative to having to sell themselves sexually. This is the model we employed in Manila, Philippines in which scholarships were offered to enable young adolescents to leave sexually exploited roles, and return to high school (Adam-Bagley et al., 2017). We have with the aid of a Canadian Foundation, used this model for the 40 girls (working in pairs) whom we studied in Lahore – providing both moral counselling and funding to aid them to stay in school. In the Filipino case this proved to be successful in more than two thirds of cases. No long-term follow-up data are yet available for the Lahore study, however.

This study was undertaken by a female researcher, a Pakistani Muslim who spoke both Punjabi and Urdu. The student used observational methods to identify likely subjects, with some 'snowball' linking from the initial sample until 20 pairs of girls (40 in all, aged 10 to 18) were identified. All of the pairs involved in this particular type of prostitution were either sisters or cousins. The girls worked in pairs for personal protection, and because a pair of girls are known as likely candidates for sexual proposals. The girls would carry shopping bags, but would linger in a stationary position close to the door of a shop manager or security guard. Lunch time, following midday prayers, was a common time of recruitment. Once a contact was established the girls would call by every few days, and all had established a group of regular clients.

Typically, the manager would call the girls into his office or warehouse, often with the connivance of a security guard who would also be serviced. Usually the younger girl would perform fellatio upon the male(s), while he fondled her breasts or those of her sister. Because of the setting, intercourse was atypical but occurred in a quarter of cases, with the girl (almost always the older girl) kneeling on a chair or box. All of the girls accepting intercourse carried condoms with them, which they insisted the customer use. The girls worked without an intermediary (police or pimp), although one pair had been arrested and subjected to the usual police station rapes. The pair would earn about UK 50 pence (US 70 cents) per transaction, earning an average of about £12 a week.

These descriptions of "sex work" were given by the pairs of girls to the female researcher, who interceded to protect the girls from having to undertake further sex work; the worker also intervened immediately with the families (to the relief of the girls, and the women of the household). All of the families knew what the girls were doing, and in 12 cases the father had required them to undertake "sex work" because of his unemployment, debt, drug or alcohol habit.

The scholarships we were able to offer to the 40 girls following intervention, for the girls to return to school or college were up to £200, for each girl. Initial results were encouraging, and the researcher in her social work role was usually successful in persuading families that there were better (Islamic) alternatives to sex work. We concede that this study and rehabilitation project accessed only a small number of girls engaged in one of the 'milder' forms of prostitution in this city. But we are trying to save the world, one life at a time. "If anyone saves a life, it shall be as though he had given life to all of humankind." (Qur'an 5:32)

10. Islam Forbids the Murder of Female Infants: Pakistan Permits this Practice

On one occasion, a few companions saw Umar ibn al-Khattab (Allah be pleased with him) laughing and then crying; one after the other. They asked what reason made him laugh then cry. He said, "I remember that in the days of Jahiliyyah, I used to have this idol made of dates. ... And then, I cried when I remembered digging a hole and burying my daughter. While I was putting her in, she reached up and brushed dirt from my beard[6].

We are advised by Qur'anic revelation, that on the final day of reckoning we shall all be questioned about our earthly conduct:

... When the female (infant), buried alive, is questioned, for what crime she was killed ... (Qur'an 17:31).

This ironic question is part of an injunction which forbids female infanticide (prevalent in some pre-Islamic Arabian tribes), of men killing new-born females when they wanted a son rather than a daughter – a deed rarely approved by the girl's mother (Shehadeh & Maaita , 2000). Islam not only prohibits female infanticide: it forbids all types of infanticide, irrespective of whether the infant is male or female. Surah Al-Anam 6:151 declares:

Kill not your children on a plea of want. We provide sustenance for you and for them. Come not near shameful deeds, whether open or secret. Take not life which Allah has made sacred.

---

[6] This is a much repeated folk saying rather than an authenticated Hadith. Its rhetorical significance is that the man is shamed by the tender action of his daughter. In another version, a man weeps when he recalls that his infant daughter held his finger while he buried her, but as he scooped sand over her face, her grasp on his finger relaxed, and ended. Not killing daughters is part of the deeply embedded value system of Islam. Not killing girls is the first step for a society in which female and male are equals.

Before discussing Pakistan's female infanticide, we must mention the world literature on "gendercide" (Grech & Mamo, 2012; Channon, 2018) - the practice of diminishing female populations by means of sex-selective abortions, or post-birth "terminations" (Coyle et al., 2015). These practices are common in SE Asia, particularly in India, Bangladesh and Pakistan. The extent of these practices can be inferred from national census data. Under "natural" conditions with equity in health care females will be more likely to survive to a greater age than men, and men are more likely to absent as migrant workers – thus census data should show an excess of females in the population of about 4%. In the 'gendercide' cultures of India, Bangladesh and Pakistan, census figures up to 2010 (reported by Grech & Momo, 2012) showed the *opposite* trend, indicating that in Pakistan the ratio of females to males was 89:100, in India 91:100, and in Bangladesh 91:100 – compared to an expected ratio of about 104:100 (Chao et al., 2019).

Another study suggests that excess mortality of females at all ages means that there are at least 3 million more males than females in Pakistan (Sadiq, 2017). This reflects gender inequity in health care at birth and in the perinatal period: more violence towards women, at all ages; and "discarded daughters", the victims of post-birth infanticide. These figures raise the difficult question (for feminists) of how these female lives were terminated. One feminist argument is that a woman has absolute rights over what happens to her body, and she has the right to have a pregnancy terminated at any stage, for what ever reason. But what if the termination is based entirely on the child's female gender identified through prenatal screening (which can only be reliably done after about 20 weeks of gestation)?

Before I became a Muslim I was a Quaker pacifist, and felt that *all* human life was sacred, from the moment of conception. I argued that instead of abortion, women's right *not* to become pregnant should be promoted, and a range of supportive services for pregnant women be offered, to allow the pregnancy to become a living being (Adam-Bagley, 1976). After embracing Islam I accepted that at about 14 weeks of gestation, Allah breathes the light of the soul into the foetus, who then becomes a human being. Late terminations are then permissible only if the pregnancy gravely endangers a woman's health. Terminations due to female gender are not, in Islamic ethics, permitted. Of course, only wealthier mothers can afford the gender-determination scans. The very poor of Pakistan cannot afford such scans, so they contemplate the dreadful practice of killing the infant for the "crime" of being female. It is men who carry out these executions, not women (Qadir et al., 2011).

Ali et al. (2015) report numerous acts of violence against female children in Pakistan beginning with the possibility of being "buried alive" after birth, then the violent acts imposed on surviving female children, through to murder and honour killing of young adults. Ideologically, there is an equivalence in these actions. The prevailing culture of patriarchy and the un-Islamic dowry system are factors in this devaluation of female life. At best a woman who delivers several unwanted female children will be divorced, rather than she or her children being murdered (Zakar et al., 2013; Nasrullah, 2015).

Tanaka et al. (2017) report on alternatives to infanticide, such as "baby hatches" in which an unwanted child can be deposited, knowing that a reputable charity will care for the child. The lead agency in Pakistan dedicated to providing care for these 'unwanted' children (most of them female, or visibly handicapped) is the Edhi Foundation, begun in Karachi by Abdul Sattar Edhi in 1951. Edhi died in 2016 and is referred to as "The Mother Teresa of Pakistan". His charity has expanded to serve the needs of children across Pakistan in providing health and welfare services, including 18 residential homes for some 8,000 "unwanted" children.

The Edhi Foundation also provides ambulances not only for the living but also for the dead, giving decent burial to the many abandoned dead of Pakistan (Edhi, 2017). The foundation also provides "baby hatches" in which new-borns may be placed, with publicity campaigns pleading that female infants should be spared. The Edhi charity also provides health and welfare services in all areas of Pakistan, and is the worthy recipient of charitable funding in Pakistan, and from overseas.

The Edhi Foundation campaigns to prevent the murder of female infants have only been partially successful. This has been dramatically demonstrated by a powerful documentary produced by Maheen Sadiq (Sadiq, 2017; Grant, 2017). Each morning Edhi workers search the many rubbish mounds and pits in the major cities searching for bodies of infants. Almost always these are female. A few are still alive, but most are dead – some were alive when abandoned but had been eaten by rats and stray dogs; or deposited dead, usually having been smothered. Edhi began this rescue service in 2010, when 1200 infant bodies were recovered in the major cities. By 2017, Edhi reported that the number of dead infants found was increasing by about 20% each year, mainly because of the use of more workers and ambulances, which were able to retrieve more infant bodies. In 2017 Edhi workers recovered 351 bodies of female infants in Karachi, the largest city. Edhi acknowledges that they may be recovering an unknown proportion of the actual infanticides, since many bodies may be covered in garbage and cannot be found; and in rural areas bodies of murdered infants are simply buried.

The practice of female child abandonment (for whom Edhi has established a network of centres) and infanticide is certainly not diminishing. These figures on "gendercide" do not measure, of course, females who were terminated pre-birth. It is most ironic that one of the driving forces behind such murders is the still prevailing Hindu norm in Pakistan of dowry which the girl's parents must give to the groom (Wyatt, & Masood, 2010), entirely contrary to Islamic law and ethics.

11. Gaps between Religious and Secular Laws, and Everyday Moral Practice Concerning Women and Girls

Pakistan was a signatory to the UN convention on human rights, including the fair treatment of women and girls. The UN declares that Sections 16 to 30 of the universal declaration of human rights means that:

> *Honour killings are one of the most extreme forms of violence against women and hence a form of discrimination, and thus are a violation of their human rights. (YHR, 2019).*

Pakistan was also a signatory in 1996 to the principles of the UN Committee on the Elimination of Discrimination Against Women; and the convention on the rights of the child. But why is there still such a wide gap between precept and practice (Abbas & Riaz, 2012)? Answers to this question are difficult and sociologically complex. We can say that the constitution of Pakistan is still evolving, and until there is rapprochement between the warring factions of the plural society, not much progress will be made.

The chronic poverty of the nation is not only material: it is moral as well. There is clearly a moral and epistemological corruption in arguing that UN Conventions, framed by non-Muslims, cannot logically apply to an Islamic republic (Zia, 1994). The issue is whether such Conventions contradict Islamic ideals of justice and human rights: clearly they do not (Barlas, 2002; Boduel, 2017). Claiming that UN conventions can be ignored because they are un-Islamic is neither logical nor fair, and contradicts the basic principles of Islam (Mernissi, 1991).

Ali & Majeed (2018) interviewed leading scholars in Pakistan on their views on gender equality, and reveal levels of hypocrisy and ignorance in the scholars (sic) who argue for Qur'anic justification for the denial of women's rights and aspirations, seeking to confine her to a state of purdah (completely confined to the home). One 'scholar' claimed that Allah created the partner of Adam by making a woman out of Adam's rib, and she is thus an inferior being, a natural second-class citizen. This false idea does occur in Jewish and Christian versions of the creation story, but does *not* occur in The Qur'an, which offers a completely different account. Allah created Hawa ("Eve") by an act of divine will, declaring "Be!", and a piece of clay became Woman, imbued with the same soul that had created Adam. Nor was Hawa mired in original sin, as Christians assert (a sin for which all women must pay a price). Adam and his partner were created as equals, without original sin, to perform the tasks of stewardship through the naming of all things in the green earth. For an Islamic scholar to introduce Christian text and to pretend that it is Qur'anic is blasphemous indeed.

Because of patriarchal indoctrination in the education system, it is not surprising that in a study of Muslims in Northern India (Manhas & Banoo, 2013) 70% of women would prefer to have sons, and 64% actually approved of disposal of females either before or after birth. In Pakistan, most women appear to be unaware that the prevailing system of dowry is un-Islamic (Menski, 1998). This is why Zia's (2009) "faith based feminism" is so important as a political movement in Pakistan. This is "the gender jihad" of which Amina Wadud (2005) writes so convincingly, and which Durrani et al. (2017) propose as a counter to the "militarized masculinities" which dominate the distortions of Islam in favour of ideas which depart from the Qur'an and Sunnah (Ali et al., 2015). Ultimately the major changes on behalf of women's rights must begin with joint political and religious enterprises carried out by women and men (Ali et al., 2011; Zakar et al., 2013 & 2016), and must also involve curriculum reform and educational enterprise.

Pakistan has three major challenges: the improvement of children's health and safety, regardless of their gender; the improvement in the living standards of families - that is, the ending of soul-corrupting poverty; and the improvement of schools, teachers, and curricula.

12. Corruption in Pakistan

Corruption occurs when self-interest overcomes moral and religious rules, in which an individual or class of individuals seize unfair access to resources, wealth or power. The annual reports of the Human Rights Council of Pakistan from 2012 to 2018 make it clear how widespread such corruption is, a view confirmed by Leven (2011). As mentioned earlier, money which should go to schools and teachers is often diverted for other purposes, perhaps to enrich some corrupt official. How this is done, and on what scale is extremely difficult to measure, since those engaged in corruption do their best to cover their traces. Fake doctors, pharmacies and medicines is another form of cruel corruption, which worsens the health of the very poor. Stealing the lives of infant girls, or selling them into slavery is vile indeed. None of this should happen in an Islamic Republic. Allah promises that he who practises corruption will taste the reward of that corruption (Qur'an 30:41). But those who have done righteous deeds shall be righteously rewarded (Qur'an 2.188; 30:45). The Qur'anic message is simple, straightforward, easy to understand, easy to follow.

By time, indeed humankind is in loss except for those who have believed and done righteous deeds, and advised each other to truth, and advised each other to patience. (Qur'an, Surah 103)

Er (2008) comparing financial corruption in Islamic and other societies argues that Qur'an and Sunnah guidance means that it should be much easier for an Islamic society to become non-corrupt. We agree.

The corruption of Pakistan which involves the stealing of the lives of children, girls and women is so gross, so foul, that things can only improve. The police for example have great power and responsibility. Currently they use this power to execute suspects, rape women, girls and boys, and act as pimps and traffickers of children. And local judiciaries ignore or permit crimes of rape and murder imposed on women and children. Sexual corruption is practised by unnumbered men in Pakistan. Boys are brought up in the ways of corruption. The hypocrisy of this corruption is that it is profoundly at odds with the founding values of an Islamic State.

13. Conclusions

As outlined in Chapter 1, our research is framed within a critical realist methodology (Alderson, 2013; Wilkinson, 2013 & 2015a & b). This involves first, a strongly held value position by the researchers (in our case, the values of Islam concerning women and children) through which they establish the first level of a social structure in which change is advocated. This first level is that of *absence* in which a crucially important aspect of social structure is real, but missing in political policies and dialogues. In the case of Pakistan, this first level concerns the oppression of women and female children in a profoundly patriarchal and sexist culture, which purports to follow the precepts of Islam, but in reality does not.

The Hobbesian underlabouring principles by which we evaluate both evidence, and our evolving critical realist model include: the *Children First* principle of evaluating every social institution according to the degree to which it places the needs, rights and interests of children as being primary (Sawyerr & Adam-Bagley, 2017); and the *Modesty* principle, based on our ideas of what constitutes a central value in Islamic epistemology and social order (Syed, 2010). However, our full Critical Realist model for social change in Pakistan remains underdeveloped, since the challenges to the values we propose are so profound. We encountered similar difficulties in trying to construct a critical realist model of change for the English socioeconomic class system, including the oppression and disadvantage of Black and Ethnic Minority groups (Sawyerr & Bagley, 2017).

Pakistan stands at the threshold of greatness. It is an Islamic State, capable of evolving into an ethical, moral and spiritual leader amongst world nations. Islamic ideals of equality and human rights must evolve in their own fashion in Pakistan, while remaining true to Qur'an and Sunnah. Being a nuclear, highly-armed state and spending huge amounts of national budgets on warfare planning is, I suggest, un-Islamic. Peace-loving goes hand in hand with people-loving. And corruption arises from poverty; it becomes not merely the corruption of power, but the corruption of ideals and of human minds as well.

Pakistan needs the help of sister countries in her move towards the ending of mass poverty, which must include material aid that does not go towards the purchase of weaponry. Anatol Lieven (2012) in his powerfully argued *Pakistan: A Hard Country* describes a nation that is tough, strong and surviving. He concludes:

> ... *Pakistan although a deeply troubled state, is also a tough one ... Barring decisions in Washington, New Delhi – and of course Islamabad – it is likely to survive ... In the long run the greatest threat to Pakistan's existence is not insurgency, but ecological change ... Pakistani farmers are also tough and adaptable, and while some areas like the Quetta valley are likely to suffer disastrous water shortages in the near future, in the country as a whole drought will take several years to become truly catastrophic ... This allows time for human action to ameliorate the impending crisis, if the West, China and of course Pakistan itself have the will to take this action.* (Lieven, 2012, p. 477)

Women of Pakistan are strong too, and they can mould their own, Islamically inspired, feminist destiny.

CHAPTER TWELVE

GENDER EQUALITY AND PEACE-MAKING: CHALLENGES FOR THE HUMAN RIGHTS ACHIEVEMENT OF MUSLIM WOMEN, MEN AND YOUTH IN EUROPE, GAZA, BANGLADESH AND PAKISTAN

CHRISTOPHER ADAM-BAGLEY

If you raise your hand to kill me, I will not raise mine to kill you. I fear God, the Lord of all worlds, and I would rather you were burdened with my sins as well as yours and become an inhabitant of the fire: such is the evildoers' reward. Qur'an 5: 27-9.

1. Introduction: Peace-Making Solutions

We offer pacifist and peace-making solutions to all problems and issues in human civilisation, including the ways in which women and youth react to and strive against forces of ethnic an sexual discrimination, Islamophobia, external threat from an imperial power (in the case of Gaza), and the anti-women actions and attitudes of many males in Bangladesh and Pakistan. The author of this chapter has embraced Islam with delight, finding that many of the positive qualities, including a belief in the basic goodness of humans as the foundation of pacifism and peace-making which he found in Quakerism are also offered by Islam, but in a more powerful and transcendental form (Adam-Bagley, 2015a).

My argument for Islam goes like this: if you believe in God, and read the Qur'an, then you *cannot* avoid becoming a Muslim. Either The Qur'an is the final, revealed word of God to humanity; or it is a fabrication by Muhammad, who received (or invented?) The Message over a period of 23 years. Consider: Muhammad was a merchant, probably literate in the language of commerce, but not known as a scholar or poet. If he fabricated

The Qur'an he would have to be literate not only in Arabic texts, but also be a master of Hebrew texts (Torah), and New Testament Greek. He would have to be familiar with the finest traditions of Arabic poetry, and exceed the quality of these texts in reciting The Message (which in recitation, is sung rather than spoken). If Muhammad fabricated The Message, he must have been possessed of a prodigious intellect in order to construct a text which over many years emerges as an intellectually coherent document, without contradictions, and with consistent themes. The fabricator must have been a person who was able to memorise and organise over 23 years (beginning at the age of 40) the coherence of The Qur'an. And if the supposed message was fabricated, Muhammad must have pretended to have received The Message, being a master of deceit.

None of these allegations against the merchant of Mecca holds true. There is only one possible conclusion, in my opinion: *The Qur'an is the final, revealed word of Almighty God, whom we call Allah.* Further, Muhammad's life, how he lived and interpreted The Qur'anic message in simple, everyday speech addressing humanity's everyday problems, is a profound example for *all* of humanity.

I was brought up an Anglican, became a Quaker, and finally embraced Islam. Having these multiple religious identities has enabled me to compare The Qur'an with other religious texts, in trying to understand what is truth and myth, in Judaic and Christian texts and traditions. The strongest and most moral tradition in all religious texts, and the energies of religious movements (including Hinduism and Buddhism) seems to me to be that of pacificism and peace-making. Islam describes the beginning of human civilisation not in terms of "the fall" and "original sin", but of the rise of humanity through Adam and Hawa who were untainted by original sin, and who were born (as we all are) in a state of goodness, searching for spiritually guided, ethical behaviours and reunion with God, who breathed the light of the soul into every human early in our gestational life. You and I, whatever your theisms or non-theisms, each one of us is actually an Islamic soul, and to God we shall return.

The Qur'anic account of the quarrel between the two sons of Adam cited above, is unique to scripture and is also a vitally important message and example for all of us. Unlike Christianity which seems to incorporate aggressive wars into the debased form of the Christian ethic adopted by mainstream denominations, Islam has a clear and consistent view of warfare. Although Muslims may take up arms, this shall only be for defence and not for attack or imperial conquest. Killing should be avoided if possible, and prisoners treated well. All possible means of peace- and treaty-making should be explored before warfare is engaged in. But above all, pacificism is the best policy. This is exemplified on the many occasions in which Prophet Muhammad returned love and forgiveness to those who persecuted him and his companions in the early years of Islam (al 'Umari, 1995). The same ethic is exemplified in the Life of Prophet Isa (Jesus), which forms the basis of Quaker pacifism. Muslim society, friendly and accommodating to the Jewish refugees from Christian persecution (Lewis, 1984) also permits Muslims to be pacifists.[1]

2. Gaza: A Pacifist Solution

Imagine the following scenario, which could, in a better world, have occurred.

After the ending of the second world war, the nations of North and South America, Europe, and many other nations are horrified at the revelation of the Holocaust, and are ashamed at the role which Christian anti-Semitism has played in feeding the rise of National Socialism. They accept Jewish appeals that a safe homeland for the Jewish people must be created, in "the promised land" of Zion. While this demand is accepted, the major world nations agree also that the rights of the people then dwelling in Palestine should be respected, and diplomatic aid and material assistance should be given to ensure that new agricultural and building development can accommodate the Jewish refugees, without the need for the displacement of the Palestinian people. Islamic leaders, referring to the Qur'anic message (5:20-21) addressed to Jews, and to all Christians and Muslims accept that Israel is the promised homeland of Jewish people:

---

[1] Islam advises that although Prophet Daoud ("King David") uttered noble psalms, some of these "psalms" were concocted centuries afterwards for political reasons. Psalm 137 is a sad example, in which the people of Zion rejoice how they will, in acts of revenge, smash the heads of the infant Edomites against the rocks. The Kingdom of Edom is now encompassed by the southern part of Jordan, contiguous to Palestine. Some bloggers (though not thankfully, the State of Israel) equate Palestinians with the Edomites, a people who threaten Zion, and who therefore must be destroyed. See too Samuel I:17, for the manufacture of God's instruction to commit genocide against the enemies of the people of Zion. See also Deuteronomy 20:10-19 for a list of "kill everyone", "enslave others", "destroy everyone and anything" messages which purport to be from God, and are offered as advice to "the children of Israel."

And mention, O Muhammad, when Moses said to his people: 'O my people remember the favour of God upon you whom He appointed among you prophets and you possessors, and gave you that which He had not given anyone among the worlds. Oh my people, enter the Holy Land (Palestine) which God has assigned to you and do not turn back from fighting God's cause, and thus become losers. Quran 5:20-21) [2]

(After addressing Moses, and promising safe passage for the Israelites from Egypt): We caused them to inherit it, the Children of Israel. Quran 26:59

And thereafter We said to the Children of Israel: 'Dwell in the land. When the promise of the Everlasting Life comes We shall bring you all together. Qur'an 17:104

Some scholars and political commentators see this as a confirmation that Jews are accepted, equally, as a separate people: they are children of Abraham through the line of Isaac who would eventually inherit the promised land of Israel, after much wandering and travail. Muslims of course, are children of Abraham through the line of Ishmael, Abraham's eldest son. A leading proponent of Palestinian-Israeli rapprochement based on these Qur'anic texts is the American writer and scholar Ed Husain (2007, 2013, 2018).

Another vocal advocate of this view is the Italian Imam and scholar Palazzi (2001):

Anti-Jewish sentiments expressed by Islamic leaders throughout the Middle East are, in fact, not religious in nature, but, rather, political. The best proof of this is in the fact that Islamic anti-Judaism is quite recent ... the Qur'an specifies that the Land of Israel is the homeland of the Jewish people, that God Himself gave that Land to them as heritage and ordered them to live therein. It also announces that – before the end of the time – the Jewish people will come from many different countries to retake possession of that heritage of theirs. Whoever denies this actually denies the Qur'an itself. If he is not a scholar, and in good faith believes what other people say about this issue, he is an ignorant Muslim. If, on the contrary, he is informed about what the Qur'an and openly opposes it, he ceases to be a Muslim. (Palazzi, 2001)

---

[2] Translation by al-Mehri (2010). The Qur'an was not addressed to Muslims (who did not of course exist prior to The Message) but to all people of Arabia (and the wider world); polytheists, Christians, Jews and other monotheist groups such as Parsees. People only became conscious Muslims after hearing this Qur'anic revelation and instruction.

While this advocacy of the Jewish right to settle in a land which, on the founding of the Jewish state in 1948, which they then shared with Palestinians seems to have powerful Qur'anic authority, but it is not an opinion accepted by many in the Arab world. Yet the problems of Israel and Palestine seem to be mostly caused by the series of unsuccessful wars which Israel's Arab neighbours launched between 1948 and 1973. With each war being lost, more territory had to be ceded to Israel, at the expense of Palestinians, until finally Israel occupied most of Jerusalem.

There has been a "failure of empathy" with the Jews of Israel in the modern era, on the part of most countries of the Middle East. Once Israel was founded and occupied by surviving Jews from the diaspora there came great determination to survive, marked, implicitly, by the slogan: "Never again. Never again will we stand in line, heads bowed, waiting to enter the death camps. Never again." This consciousness led to great valour amongst Israelis, determined that they would engage those attempting to destroy the Jewish homeland (and all of its people), with the utmost ferocity. But this state of permanent anger, often becoming trapped by the ideologies of right wing parties (particularly those supported by emigrants from Russia), has in my reading warped the moral sensibility of many (but by means all) Israelis. I very much want Israel to survive as a nation living peacefully with the 20% of its citizens who are Arabs (Muslim and Christians), as well as with the Palestinians of the West Bank and Gaza; and negotiating a form of statehood for the Palestinian refugees in Syria, Lebanon and Jordan.

My cry to Israel is this: "Seize the moral high ground. Draw on the rich vein of Jewish ethics, and behave decently towards your minorities, and to your neighbours." [3] My pleas to Palestine, Egypt, Lebanon, Syria and Jordan are similar. Draw on the rich tradition of Muslim peace-making, recognise Israel's right to exist, and stand down your armies. Negotiate peace with more skill and determination than you negotiated the Oslo Accords. Everyone wants peace. With peace Gaza can be reconstructed, and once again grow and develop as a unique Arabic enclave.

---

[3] Alexander (2019) details many different organisations in America and Israel which are Zionist in a broad sense, both Jewish and non-Jewish, but which express disquiet and concern over current Israeli government policy and action concerning Palestinians, and the denial of full citizenship rights to the 20 percent of the population within Israel itself, who are Muslims and Christians of Arabian descent. Fundamental Jewish values declare, as does Islam, that taking one human life wrongly is to murder the whole of humankind (Kessler, 2013). See also the valuable analysis of Davidson (2019).

I am impressed by the arguments of the American Muslim academic Mehnaz Alfridi (2014) who writes about *Shoah Through Muslim Eyes*. Her argument is that Western powers, horrified at a holocaust in which their ideologies were partially complicit, washed their hands of "the Jewish problem" by creating the homeland of Israel for the unwanted Jews. The great powers then walked away, leaving their former colonies (Egypt, Jordan etc.) to sort out the mess they had made of international affairs, and their persecution of minorities. Alfridi, child of Muslim refugees from India to Pakistan offers empathic support for persecuted Jewish minorities and refugees. Rudin (2015) commented: "Alfridi musters both her considerable scholarship and her profound faith commitment to excoriate fellow Muslims for their heinous, vulgar, and religion-based attacks on Jews, Judaism, and the historical reality of the Shoah and the State of Israel."

Pacifism and peace-making in Islam, Christianity and Judaism involves compromise, loving your 'enemy', returning good for evil. Avoid boycotts. Keep talking, trying to understand the position of the other. If there are presumed sins, remember that Almighty God is the final judge, and will punish or admonish in appropriate ways. If you want to fight, fight against the destruction of our temperate climates by human-induced global warming.

If an aggressor approaches saying "I will kill you", bow your head and say: "Do what you must. But remember, if you kill me you will take away my sins, and add them to your own." But Qabil (Cain) killed Habil (Abel): Qabil's shame at the murder of his brother was great (Qur'an 5:27-31). I take this as the Qur'anic instruction to all humans to be non-violent pacifists and peace-makers.

Islam and Allah: Forgiveness and Restorative Justice

Two of the (many) strengths of Islam concern guidance on forgiveness, and on restorative justice. Each day we acknowledge in our five daily prayers in reciting *The Fatiha* (the opening book of The Qur'an) that Allah is "compassionate and merciful". Those of us who have surrendered ourselves to Allah must also try to follow this guide, being merciful and compassionate in our everyday encounters with humanity. There are numerous examples in Qur'an and Sunnah where Allah, and His Prophet are both compassionate to wrong-doers, and merciful also. What is necessary is that the wrongdoer should acknowledge their crime, express sincere regret, and offer compensation for the wrongs they have caused in the fullest way that they can. If this is a first offence, no punishment should be imposed (Pal, 2011). This seems abundantly clear from The Qur'an. But for many Muslims action takes the form of an immediate revenge, in terms of severe punishment or retribution. This, we argue, is contrary to the principles of the Qur'anic message.

All confessed "first offences" should be forgiven, and as a symbol of that regret full restoration or compensation of injured parties by the offender should be made. Then we can have a compassionate Shari'a system of the kind outlined by Brown (2017) and Esposito & DeLong-Bas (2018). Pakistan, for example could implement this model, instead of the pre-Islamic kinds of tribal law currently enforced, and wrongly given Qur'anic authority. Pakistan should *become* an Islamic nation.

3. Gaza and Forgiveness: Izzeldin Abuelaish's *I Shall Not Hate*

On December 27th, 2008 Israeli bombers, rockets, tanks and troops invaded Gaza (aided by shelling from Israeli naval vessels), for reasons which are still unclear. By January 18th, 2009 when Israelis ceased their hostilities they had killed 594 men, women and children, and severely injured about 2,600 more. About a third of those who were killed or severely injured were adolescents and children. A few Gazans tried to fight back, but with little effect. Israeli casualties were 3 dead, and 30 injured.

On January 13th, 2009 a tank parked in front of the house of Dr. Izzeldin Abuelaish, a lecturer in obstetrics. He had persuaded the tank commander that his family were not part of any armed resistance. But the tank returned three days later, and this time fired a shell into the house, without warning.

Three months before, the doctor's wife had died of leukaemia, leaving him with three teenaged daughters Bessan, Mayar and Aya and two younger sons. Staying with the girls on January 16^{th,} 2009 was their teenaged cousin Noor. Dr. Abuelaish stepped from his front door, trying to tell the troops in the tank that this was an ordinary, civilian house. He was ignored. The tank fired a round over his head, the shell penetrating the girls' bedroom. All four were killed instantly, but the boys in a different room survived, one of them with severe wounds from shrapnel.

Two years later Abuelaish (2011) wrote:

> *The catastrophe of the deaths of my daughters and niece has strengthened my thinking, deepened my belief about how to bridge the divide. I understand down to my bones that violence is futile. It is a waste of time, lives and*

resources, and has been proven only to beget more violence. It does not work, it just perpetuates a vicious cycle. There's only one way to bridge the divide, to live together, to realize the goals of two peoples: we have to find us the light to guide us to our goal ... To find the light of truth, you have to talk to, listen to, and respect each other. Instead of wasting energy on hatred, use it to open your eyes and see what's really going on ... I sometimes feel like Ayoub in the Qur'an or Job in Talmud and the Bible: the man whose faith in God was so severely tested ... I believe in coexistence, not endless cycles of revenge and retribution. And possibly the hidden truth about Gaza can only sink in when it is conveyed by someone who does not hate ... I learned from The Qur'an that the whole world is one human family. We are created from a man and a woman and made into nations and tribes that we may know one another and appreciate the diversity that enriches our lives. (pp 196-198, 228).

We can add to this account of forgiveness the memoir of Yousef Bashir (2018) *The Words of My Father*. This book is based on memories of his life in Gaza, and the wisdom and love of his father. On February 18th, 2004 15-year-old Yousef was shot in the back by an Israeli sniper. The book contains "A letter to the soldier who shot me":

... Do you ever wonder what happened to me? ... Many times I have thought about you. Were you born in Israel, or were you someone who came from Brooklyn spoiling for a fight? What did you tell the other soldiers that night, after you shot me? Did you boast? Did you cry? Were you frightened? ... It is not possible for me to forget you. The three pieces of your bullet embedded in my back, next to my spine, make me think of you every day. I wanted to hate you, but a miracle happened. No, not the miracle that I can walk again. Another miracle. One that was shown to me through my father's commitment to peace, my mother's unfathomable love, and the [Israeli] doctors and nurses who tended to me with the deepest compassion: it is the miracle of forgiveness. Without the bullet, I might never have understood forgiveness. You were created by the same God who created me. You are part of the same family as I am. I forgive you, my cousin. (pp 213-4)

4. Extrinsic and Intrinsic Attachments to Religion and Religious Ethics: The Paradox of Religious Values and their (Non)Application

Three Levels of Human Impulse and Action

The paradox and the puzzle is this. We have the values, the template, the divine authority to create a perfect society, and a perfect world order. Why then do we humans so often resort to, implement, and impose baser values, create so much violence, and even devote energies to pogroms, holocausts, ethnic cleansing, mass murder, mass rapes in warfare? In trying to answer this question I turn first of all to the work of the anthropologist Edmund Leach and his notable and much cited study *Political Systems of Highland Burma* (Leach,1974; Robinne & Sadan, 2002).

Over many years Leach immersed himself in the society of Kachin people, focussing on how rank, class, polity and religion were intertwined in how the Kachin coped with everyday life in their social system (as well as coping with threats from outside groups). Leach identified first of all "ancestor values" (including the 'creator gods') and the gradual absorption of these values into Buddhism, and the rituals which kept these ancestor or higher order values (of selflessness, sharing and peace-making) alive. In any formal gathering of tribal groups there was ritual obeisance to these higher order values. Nevertheless, Leach identified a prevailing order of "middle ground" values which the social system needs in order cope with the numerous problems of everyday living, agriculture, husbandry and trade. These might be compared to Aristotelian values, which are constructed to cope with everyday problems, trying to balance higher order values with practical ways of solving the challenges of everyday life.

Finally in Leach's study were the 'lower order values', occasionally deemed necessary to achieve a greater victory for the social system. These might involve killing not only enemies, but their wives and children also. In the wider world this "necessary" regression to the bestialities of warfare has included the bombing of Dresden and Hiroshima, the genocides of the Japanese army in China and Asia, and later genocides of minority groups (e.g. of Chinese in Indonesia in 1965-6), imposed starvation in Biafra, genocide in Rwanda, Israel's genocide of Palestinians, ISIL's rape and murder of prisoners in Syria and Iraq, American mass bombing and murder of civilians in Vietnam and Iraq. And so it goes. These atavistic acts of mass human destruction are justified (or swept from the historical record) as necessary departures from higher order morality in order to defend the order (or ordinariness) of everyday social systems.

The three levels of actions and values have their analogue in the psychodynamic account of the human mind-set. The super-ego holds the higher order values; the id contains the lusts and aggressions of the phylogenetically old brain (frequently suppressed into unconscious thinking); and the ego tries to balance these two levels in a working model of adjustment in everyday life. Sigmund Freud, the main scholar of this model of psychology observed (in correspondence with Einstein, a fellow pacifist) in 1932: "What progress we are making. In the Middle Ages they would have burned me. Now they are content with burning my books." (Einstein et al., 1933; Gay, 2006). Unfortunately Freud was wrong: if he had remained in Vienna, as a Jew he would have been first gassed, and then burnt. Freud's pacificism was based on his knowledge of the dark forces of the id, and how psychological awareness could recognise and control such impulses. Tragedy occurs when social movements convert or absorb id impulses into a set of higher order values, as happened with Fascism, National Socialism, and the grotesque distortions of Islam by Daesh, which become the impulse of collective movements.

While some psychologists see the "psychopathic personality" as being confined to a small group of individuals, we follow Moshagen et al. (2018) in seeing "the dark personality" as a lurking possibility in every human psyche, waiting for the infectious call of temptation, the deviation from "the straight path". Mary Midgley (1984) the philosopher, writing about the challenge of understanding "human wickedness" argues that: "All moral doctrine, all practical suggestions about how we ought to live, depend on some belief about what human nature is like." Reviewing the Islamic view of human evolution (Adam-Bagley, 2015a), I accepted the view that Adam and Hawa, the template models for humanity, contain the *possibility* of being tempted to commit wrongful acts. This is embodied in The Qur'anic account of shaitan's continued existence. But this is not to agree with the Christian doctrine of "Old Adam" (original sin for which an external agent has to become a blood sacrifice). One of Islam's brilliant new insights for humankind is that men and women *themselves* have the power to achieve final goodness without the need for a bizarre sacrifice (e.g. a crucifixion). In the Islamic form of humanism, it is human beings alone who gaining spiritual strength, face and overcome temptations, in pursuit of the goals of modesty, and child-centred humanism.

Intrinsic and Extrinsic Religious Commitment and Affiliation

The identification of two type of religious identity, intrinsic and extrinsic, stems from the work of the social psychologist Gordon Allport (Allport & Ross, 1967; Allport, 1973; Azis & Rehman, 1996; French et al., 2008; De Zavala et al., 2012; Donahue, 1985; McCullough & Willoughby, 2009). This dichotomy has been shown to be a valuable concept in the empirical study of values, attitudes and actions including those directed at minority or stigmatised groups (De Zavala et al., 2012). A person who has an *extrinsic* or nominal attachment to a religious label or identity does so for various self-serving reasons: conformity to the socialisation influences of culture and family; networks of social pressure and social control; and obvious benefits from being identified as an observing Christian, Jew or Muslim etc., including the public power and status of endowing religious monuments.

But the extrinsically attached person knows rather little about the essence of the religion to which they have a nominal affiliation; and if they are aware of certain rules (e.g. concerning sexual morality, conduct as a good citizen, employer or trader, tolerating the rights of others), they ignore these rules unless it is inconvenient to do so. A Christian or Jew of this type may attend weddings, funerals or baptisms because of social convention; apart from this they rarely attend church or synagogue. A Muslim will attend Friday prayers because there he will meet his friends and business associates. He has paid scant attention during the Khutbah (sermon). He rarely meets his full five times daily obligation for prayers, but will do so when others are present. He may well not fast properly during Ramadan. He does not read the Qur'an, and cannot recollect any hadiths. He is egotistical, seeking self-interest for a comfortable life. At home his wife will pray, but he rarely does.

The *intrinsically committed* Christian, Jew or Muslim accepts his or her religious affiliation with deep seriousness, and is knowledgeable about holy texts, and the guides to behaviour that they offer. This person tries to live a good and ethical life according to religious precepts. This individual attends a place of worship regularly, prays regularly, takes the rules and guidance of their religion very seriously. Subgroups within the intrinsically committed include purists of various kinds, deeply attached to some aspect of their religious heritage in particular ways (e.g. Quakers, Orthodox Jews, Pentecostals, Sufis).

There are two other important "non-theist" groups. First of all are the "ignorant agnostics" who reject or ignore religious practice and the guidance to behaviour that religion implies. They may harness a pseudo-religious identity if they have involvement with right wing movements. For this group in England the flag (e.g. the symbol of St George) is their main religious fetish. Their elaborated values are incoherent (except for insisting, for example, that ethnic and religious minorities should give up their alien identities, and conform to British values – whatever those might be). And then there are the humanists (agnostics or atheists), generally well-educated people who have adopted a clearly defined and reasoned set of values - which are not directly derived from the teachings of any particular religion – and whoengage in a co-operative social contract with fellow citizens.

I can discover no sociological study which has estimated the proportion of any national populations which fall into such groupings: but I would guess that those with intrinsic religious commitment number not more than 10% of any population. But their advocacy for tolerance and ethical behaviour could have influence beyond their actual numbers in the population. I am reminded of Quakers in Britain, containing less than 15,000 active members, but with an influence that extends well beyond their actual numbers in the population (e.g. Alton, 2018; Watson & Rowe, 2018).

Aziz & Rehman (1996) in a study of Pakistani youth aged 14 to 16, identified a group of students (less than a quarter of all research subjects) who did have some intrinsic commitment to Islam, and were keenly aware of Islam's basic teachings concerning human rights, including those concerning children and women. In an overview of studies McCullough & Willoughby (2009) show that "intrinsics" have higher educational achievements, and have better profiles on "agreeableness", "self-control" and "openness to new experience" on personality measures. They have better self-esteem, and are more able to engage in reasoned, self-control solutions when provoked:

> *The value profiles of religious people were remarkably consistent, whether the sample was Christian, Jewish or Muslim ... Adherence [to a strong religious identity] leads people to embrace principle goals, such as being respectful, helpful and positive and to eschew goals such as pleasure-seeking and hedonism, having an exciting life ... 'religious' people value positive social relationships and social harmony ... following 'sanctified goals'.* (McCullough & Willoughby, 2009, p. 85)

This profile reminds me of the Muslim students experiencing citizenship education, reported in the earlier Chapter by Nader Al-Refai and myself. In The Netherlands too, De Zavala et al. (2012) found that Muslim youth with strong intrinsic personal and religious values were those *least* likely to express any sympathy with radical terrorist groups purporting to have an Islamic identity. Similar findings have emerged from UK research (Hassan, 2018; Kaur-Ballagan et al., 2018). Such "intrinsic religiosity" can result from educational models and curricula which focus on students' strengths and personal interests, in well-funded and comprehensive educational programmes. Education *is* the answer, in Europe, Asia and the Middle East.

My thesis then is that religious people with intrinsic values concerning goodness and good conduct for themselves, in others and in the wider society; together with non-religious humanists who share many of the same general values should act (like Quakers have done) as lobby groups for social peace and social justice. These people, like the bearers of higher order religious values, are linked to the touchstone of morality which should guide all modern societies. These 'thinking citizens' are better able to resist a variety of temptations which potentially undermine moral conduct. They must work hard (and harder) in the service of their culture.

Pakistan has a core of such individuals who campaign and write on behalf of the higher values of Islam, just as Israel has a core of religious Jews who accept and work for the higher values of Judaism (Devji, 2011 & 2013). They do so in the face of hostility and even danger. If civilisation is to survive, they and their like-minded brothers and sisters across the world, of whatever religion (as well as non-religious humanists) *must* succeed.

5. Alienation and Identity, and the Descent into Terror

Where does evil (which stalks all of the societies discussed in this book) come from? As a religious person I am surprised that in the analyses of oppression, violence and exploitation of weaker people (whole ethnic groups, and whole classes of people such as women, girls and the precariat) the person of "shaitan" is so rarely mentioned. This is the creature which in the first garden refused to bow to God's new creation of Hawa and Adam, and was released by Allah to test humankind down the ages. I offer you the proposition: recognise evil, and the way that shaitan seeks to subvert human will and human justice, including those who try to follow divinely ordained or well-reasoned principles of ethical living. Evil, id or shaitan is constantly lurking in the undergrowth of the mind and the social group. Watch, and pray.

Encounter with Shaitan: A Story of Failure

Khalid Durán (2000) draws a clear distinction between Islamic values which emerged in the early years of Islam; and *islamism*, a social movement which owes more to Mussolini than to the peace-making ideals of true Islam. "Islamism" in its several manifestations (ISIL, Daesh, Boko Haram, Taliban etc) owes more to fascist ideologies than to religious ones. Durán observes:

> *Whether Islamists like the term fundamentalist or not, their understanding of religion resembles that of fundamentalists in other religions. This is not to say that Islamists are more religious or more genuinely Islamic than other Muslims . . . Islamism is a late 20th century totalitarianism. It follows in the wake of fascism and communism, picking up from those and seeking to refine their methods of domination. Few Muslims would deny that political*

commitment is part of Islamic ethics, but most disagree with the Islamist insistence that there exists a clearly defined "Islamic system," different from all other political systems. (Durán, 2000, pp 27-2).

The point is that islamism is a political movement with violent agendas, but with an "extrinsic" connection to Islam which is a useful recruiting slogan for the marginal and the disaffected, for those who have failed to absorb the proper message of Islam (Khan, 1989; Wilkinson, 2018).

Before moving to Leeds I lived in Manchester, and after becoming a Muslim I attended Didsbury Mosque in Manchester almost daily, joining in prayers, listening to Khutbahs, joining study groups on Qur'an and Sunnah. Didsbury Mosque is housed on an old Methodist church, and there are many side rooms where brothers and sisters choose to rest, pray, read and talk. In one of these rooms I met Salman Abedi, a young man who had startled me by standing up during the Sheikh's sermon, shouting at him, and then leaving, before completing prayers. I talked to Salman, and found a very distressed young man who had dropped out of school and was full of ideas which seemed to me to be at variance with The Qur'an. He swore, gesticulated, had tics, rambled on about conspiracies, and about individuals who were persecuting him.

I wrote the following article for a Quaker journal in June, 2017:

The Sad Bomber I Missed

As one of about 40 Muslim-Quakers amongst some 12,000 active, adult Quakers in Britain, I have retained a pacifist conviction, and have looked to the Qur'ran (God's final message) and the Sunnah (the life and teaching of Prophet Muhammad, based on his inspiration from the Qur'anic message) for teaching and examples which can guide pacifism. There is good teaching, and fine examples in plenty. I follow Adam's son who when faced with his murderous brother, did not fight back but accepted the murderous blows. Then his brother, aghast at his crime, asked Almighty God for forgiveness (Qur'an, 5 27-29). God tells us that "war is hateful" and should be avoided by means of treaty and peaceful negotiation. Armed conflict is permitted only in defence of one's family, never as an aggressive enterprise. The taking of innocent civilian lives is forbidden. Individuals like myself are allowed to forgo military service, in return for doing useful community work. Muhammad himself frequently turned the other cheek to aggressors, doing good to those who hated him.

I attend Didsbury Mosque in Manchester three or four times a week. When I first attended four years ago I was feeling my way, anxious to fit in, to learn the rituals of prayer and the etiquette of Muslim behaviour. I noticed a loner,

> *a sad-looking young man who often stayed in the Mosque but would not pray, and who often muttered to himself. Thinking he was, like me, a beginner in Islam I approached him, but he engaged with me in a manner that I had come to recognise (as a former psychiatric nurse, and then a clinical psychologist) as indicating a paranoid personality disorder. I asked fellow Muslims about what to do: leave him alone I was told, and I did. He soon disappeared.*
>
> *A few days ago a man detonated a bomb in Manchester, killing 22 innocent souls, mostly children and adolescents girls. The press photo of this man left me in no doubt that this was the sad young man I had seen in Didsbury Mosque two years earlier. I know now that the Mosque was concerned with respectability, not the despair of a young troublemaker. We had abandoned him. As someone who was likely a paranoid schizophrenic he was pulled into the evil affray which lurks at the edge of Islam. I failed him. We failed him. Society failed him. I pray for his soul, alongside prayers for his innocent victims, and for myself who lacked the moral courage to act decisively.*

I know now that Salman's Libyan parents had taken him back to Libya for treatment – this return to the culture of origin is one way in which Muslim parents try and cope with the needs of troubled youth, especially those who are drug users (Bakhsh, 2007). We are unsure of what happened in Libya, but it is clear now that Salman fell into the hands of islamists who in the name of their debased version of Islam, engineered and directed his terrorism. Salman's sister in an interview (Mendik, 2017) said that in his mid-teen years he had no interest in Islam or Mosque attendance, had dropped out of school, was part of a delinquent gang and a frequent cannabis smoker. Only in his late teens did he show a renewed interest in Islam, but viewed the religion through what seemed to be a psychotic lens.

In Blackburn, close to Manchester, the headteacher of a primary school with mostly Muslim pupils commented, on the second anniversary of the killings by Abedi:

> *Many pupils at Wensley Fold are Muslim and have struggled to understand Islamist extremism ... They are very proud to be Muslim and don't understand why these things happen. They come and speak to us and ask what are these people doing in the name of our religion?*

She was commenting on the prize-winning speech written by an 11-year-old in her school (Pidd, 2019). Sara Hussain imagines that she encountered Salman Abedi on his way to Manchester Arena, to commit mass murder of innocents, in the name of Islam:

I'd run for my life to try and catch up to him, to catch up to Salman Abedi, continuously I would say stop, please, talk to me. Tell me why you are doing this. What makes you think that this will justify your actions? How can this possibly be for your religion? I would explain what Islam teaches us. That he isn't doing it for me. Then I would try my hardest to show him that there's no need to do this, that this isn't an option, that there is no need to injure and harm so many innocent people. Because for what reason was he doing it? To make people hate and fear Muslims? Because Islam is about peace, not terror.

6. Alienation, Mental Illness and Support for Terrorism in Mainstream and Minority Group Members

The leading group of European researchers contributing to this field have been led by Professor Kamaldeep Bhui of the Centre for Psychiatry at London University (Bhui, 2015; Bhui & Ibrahim, 2013; Bhui et al., 2012; Bhui et al., 2014a & b; Bhui et al., 2015; Bhui et al., 2016a & b; Bhui et al., 2019; Coid et al., 2016; Dom et al., 2018; McGilloway et al., 2015; Misiak et al., 2019).This group has undertaken two kinds of research. The first is on the mental health of ethnic minority groups in countries which manifest both verbal discrimination, and overt acts of racism, discrimination and Islamophobia, judging the degree to which such discrimination and rejection may have undermined the mental health of minority groups in Britain, and in other European countries, including The Netherlands. This research does show that discriminated-against minority groups have higher levels of overt mental illness, almost certainly because of the multiple rejections and deprivation they experience.

The second strand of research by Bhui and colleagues concerns the degree to which manifesting symptoms of personality disorder and mental illness is correlated with verbal or written support of terrorism groups and activities of various kinds; and the degree to which those surviving the terrorism they have perpetrated can be identified as having longstanding mental health problems which caused them to attack vulnerable groups and communities.

Bhui et al. (2016) in a review of available studies (including their own research) identify a two stage process in the evolution of violent terrorism (by majority group members against minorities, and by minorities against majority groups). First are the pre-existing ideological groups who construct literature and websites promoting their extremist ideology (Bhui & Ibrahim, 2013). These groups work in the shadows, behind their firewalls. They include far-right, neofascist groups campaigning for "the white race";

groups acting in the name of a nationalist group (e.g. Basques in Spain; and violent groups in Northern Ireland acting for or against Catholic or Protestant interests). In this category are also groups who claim to act upon islamist principles in their advocacy of violence against established orders, groups who oppose Qur'anically supported principles such as the education of women (e.g. Taliban, Boko Haram, Al Qaida, Daesh).

These groups inspire through their web pages (and recruit through these electronic links) disaffected individuals whom psychiatrists have identified as often being depressed, alienated, poorly adjusted, loners in society. The New Zealand gunman who killed 50 Muslim worshippers attending Friday prayers in March, 2019 seems to fall into this category, as does Salman Abedi, the Manchester Arena suicide bomber. Bhui & Ibrahim (2013) elaborate their thesis with case studies of a lone individuals, recruited into terrorism by the sinister groups hiding in an electronic maze. Such individuals show:

> *Signs of chronic stress, shyness, a significant life event that acts to provide a cognitive opening, persistent isolation, and a lack of bridging social capital which may in fact be the only individual markers for vulnerability.* (p. 220)

Bhui et al (2014) further showed in a study of Muslim youth in London with cultural origins in the Indian sub-continent that most sympathy for "violent terrorism was displayed by young men who declared that religious values and texts were relatively unimportant. In contrast, those condemning terrorism had many friends both within the Muslim and non-Muslim communities. Factoring in mental health showed that those sympathetic to terrorism were often depressed loners, with suicidal feelings (Bhui et al., 2016a & b). But Bhui (2016) stresses that the large majority of minority group individuals with personality disorder, affective illness, and psychosis have *no* interest in terrorism, and no particular diagnosis stands out as having predictive value. Moreover, those individuals who do consider or act on their terrorist impulses often remain as loners, receiving their instructions (e.g. on bomb-making, and targets) through electronic communication, without ever meeting their "handlers". The findings of Bhui and his colleagues also apply to "white supremacy" terrorists, who also act as electronically-guided loners (Bhui et al., 2019).

The conclusions from this psychological work, and the educational evidence outline in earlier Chapters suggests that strong and secure family support, an intrinsic religious identity, good mental health and a firm self-concept are excellent antecedents in avoiding the temptations of extremist groups of the far right, and the neo-fascist islamist groups. If cultures treat minority groups fairly and do not "alienate" minorities in whatever fashion, then the bases of violent terrorism will be undermined.

7. Drawing the Strands Together

Muslim Women in Management and Education: Review and Conceptualisation of Word Literature, and Studies from Gaza, Palestine

This book has proposed models of equality and social justice derived from Islam, elaborated and explored by the theories of Critical Realism (Chapter 1). This is a fundamentally value-based approach based on a firm set of values justified by an intuitive and metaphysical understanding of religious teachings (the metaphysical and social-justice messages derived from Islam, Christianity, Judaism and Marxist-humanism). We explored two things: how in particular women and youth can reach for equity and justice; and what structural and ideological barriers are preventing this, in selected national case studies (from England, Netherlands, Gaza, Bangladesh and Pakistan).

We have also examined world literature in trying to establish ways in which Muslim women can survive as managers and professionals; and (in Western countries) as ethnic and religious minorities surviving discrimination in seeking employment. We have explored what barriers they face, and what kind of qualities they need to succeed in work roles outside of the family (Chapter 2). We argue that the "strong family manager" role of Muslim women is transferable to many different employment situations. A crucial first step in women's employment in Muslim Majority Cultures (MMCs) is to achieve equity with men in the sphere of education. Our case studies of Work Life Balance benefits for women professionals in the telecommunications industry of Gaza (Chapter 3) show that Islamic values of moderation and modesty, and respect for woman as family managers, can contribute to an ethical model of business practice.

The research on Gaza reported by Wesam Abubaker in Chapter 4 on how Muslim women are surviving continuous warfare and blockades presents many challenges. We gain vivid insights into the suffering and patience of women and children, and their ingenuity in using schools as analogues for new families, families which Israeli warfare had destroyed. The Islamic dignity and nonviolence of these women is a profound lesson for men, including the crass and foolish male aggression which has caused this suffering, on both sides of the fence. Their determination to follow peaceful pathways is a profoundly important example for Islamic peacemakers.

The Importance of Muslim Education

Chapter 5 offers findings from a uniquely important study of Muslim education, and the success which Muslim students in both state and religious schools may have in developing ideas and conduct as being "a good citizen". This is an important role through which young Muslims create for themselves a stable and magnanimous Islamic identity in a plural, multicultural society, that all European nations should seek to achieve. We stress this development with particular regard to two nations (UK and its four countries) and The Netherlands which we have studied intensively for the past 50 years. Comparing ethnicity, social structure and policies towards minority groups (both official, and on the part of everyday actors) we compare in the two cultures how the 'plural society' model has evolved and changed. Although there is less overt prejudice and discrimination in The Netherlands than in England, nevertheless the evolution of right-wing groups advocating Islamophobia and anti-Muslim policies is now a feature of Dutch political life (Chapter 6).

Discrimination, Islamophobia, Alienation: Islamic Dignity and the Power to Resist the Descent into Violence

In Chapter 7 we show that 'situation testing' of sending job applications (for junior level accountancy positions) demonstrates that Muslim women in England and The Netherlands are significantly less likely to be offered interviews than their "indigenous" counterparts, despite the Muslim women candidates having been born in the two European countries. This poses the question: how do Muslim women (and men, and Muslim youth of both genders) cope with the experience of discrimination, having to apply for twice as many vacancies as their "Christian" counterparts?

Is there conscious alienation in this process, and how does it influence identity, and political and social choices in adapting to society? And how does this potential alienation in employment affect individuals facing Islamophobic calls to "integrate", giving up their manifestations and loyalty concerning their Muslim heritage? Hijab-wearing women in England are particularly likely to experience public acts of discrimination, harassment, and assault. This leads us to consider the theme of *alienation* in detail.

Alienation is usually associated with the political philosophy of Marx, implying the separation of the worker from the social and material rewards of work and labour (Bhaskar, 2012). The concept had been taken up by sociologists, including the well-known paradigms of Robert Merton (1968). Merton and his followers also term the structurally enforced separation of parts of human identity as both anomie and alienation, although for theory development and empirical analysis, the latter concept of 'alienation' will suffice (Adam-Bagley, 1967; Ransford, 1968). When prejudice and discrimination (in Merton's model) block the legitimate aspirations of minority youth, various kinds of social psychological states result.

First is blaming oneself for lack of educational and occupational achievements, leading sometimes to depression, low self-esteem, rituals of working harder in lowly occupations, or dropping out of the occupational 'rat race' altogether, surviving on state benefits (perhaps by having more children). Secondly (perhaps linked to the first condition) is retreat – into rituals of religion, and sometimes into drugs, alcohol and self-medication, and in some cases the onset of frank psychiatric illness (Sadek, 2017).

Thirdly is rebellious but essentially nonviolent political activism, by those who understand the nature of their alienation. Finally are those who engage in random or self-destructive violence (e.g. that described by Bagguley & Hussain, 2016), or engage in purposive acts of self-destructive terrorism, such as the London bombers of July, 2005. The alienation model seemed to work in explaining 'deviance' a study of minority youth in The Netherlands (Adam-Bagley, 1983). However, more up-to-date work in examining the usefulness on the alienation model is needed.

The thesis, broadly stated, is that persistent, institutionalised Islamophobia in societies of the West has the potential to have harmful social and psychological consequences for young Muslims, some of whom become so psychologically marginalised, alienated and distressed that attitudes and actions supporting terrorism may result from this distress.

Following the 2019 Christchurch massacre of Muslim worshippers, 350 Muslim leaders across the world wrote:

> *Systemic Islamophobia fuels terror attacks: ... The massacre of Muslims did not just begin with bullets fired from the barrel of the racist's gun. Rather it was decades in the making: inspired by Islamophobic media reports, hundreds and thousands of column inches of hatred printed in the press, many Muslim-hating politicians and unchecked social media bigotry. Muslims have been constantly cast as suspect communities, foreigners with*

barbaric views who are a threat to our society. We are now reaping the awful outcome of systemic and institutionalised Islamophobia woven into many sections of our societies. (Letter from 350 Muslim scholars and leaders from many world countries, in *The Guardian* of London, March 18th, 2018)

The questions then concern how Muslims, women and men, and youth cope with, and counter this persistent Islamophobia in peaceful ways, drawing on the strengths and capacity for nonviolence given to us in Qur'an and Sunna? And how can Muslims avoid the temptation offered by shaitan, of retaliatory attacks on Christians, such as those which occurred in Sri Lanka in April, 2019?

In Britain, good quality, inclusive education both multicultural (as described by Modood, 2013) and religious education (e.g. the Islamic education model described in Chapter 5) can help young Muslims to exercise the dignity which the example of The Prophet has given them, of bestowing good will and good actions upon those who utter hatred. Within Islam there is the model of "the good citizen" who overcomes difficulty by studious self-control, as the work carried out with Professor Nader Al-Refai has shown.

Beloved Countries: Pakistan and Bangladesh

Our chapters on Bangladesh and Pakistan are accounts of enduring poverty which challenge the implementation and achievement of Islamic Ideals. Our beloved adopted countries, Bangladesh and Pakistan are struggling to achieve an Islamic identity which serves the high ideals of Qur'an and Sunna which every Muslim should follow. Alas, the sexual exploitation of girls and women, the practice of child marriage, the poor health of girls and women, the rape and their murder in countries in which Islam has been distorted by pre-Islamic tribal cultures in a system of patriarchal rule, is a profound tragedy. Islamic dignity, following the middle way of self-restraint and charity, is so often distorted in these countries. When people are battered by poverty, shaitan has an easy time, like a vulture pecking at the corpse of a yet-to-be born nation.

There is temptation to wickedness in the countries of East and West that we describe in this book, both for the poor and the affluent. The ambitious greed of capitalism, and the destruction of the natural environment are further temptations on which shaitan thrives.

The Critical Realist conclusion (following the work of Roy Bhaskar) is this. All human institutions, all human actions (including your own) must be critically examined through *underlabouring* dialogues, including: the degree to which these institutions and actions meet the needs, interests and rights of children, through the principle of 'children first'; the degree to which these institutions and actions meet the standards of 'Islamic modesty', the middle way of human action; and the degree to which these institutions and actions meet the goals of peace-making, accommodation, and compromise.

BIBLIOGRAPHY

Abalkhail, J. M., & Allan, B. (2015). Women's career advancement: mentoring and networking in Saudi Arabia and the UK. *Human Resource Development International*, 18(2), 153-168.

Abalkhail, J. M., & Allan, B. (2016). "Wasta" and women's careers in the Arab Gulf States. *Gender in Management: An International Journal*, 31(3), 162-180.

Abalkhail, J. M. (2017). Women and leadership: challenges and opportunities in Saudi higher education. *Career Development International*, 22(2), 165-183.

Abbas, J.A. (2005). *Islamic Perspectives of Management and Organisation.* Cheltenham, UK: Edward Elgar.

Abbas, M.Z. & Riaz, S. (2012). Legal protections provided under Pakistani law against anti-women practices: implementation gaps between theory and practice. *The Dialogue* 8(2), 173-193,

Abbas, T. (2011). Islamophobia in the United Kingdom: historical and contemporary political and media discourse in the framing of a 21st-century ant-Muslim racism. In J. Esposito and I. Kalin (Eds) *Islamophobia: The challenge of pluralism in the 21st century*, (pp 63-76.) Oxford: Oxford University Press.

Abbas, T. (Ed.). (2013). *Muslim Britain: Communities under Pressure.* London: Zed Books.

Abbas, T. & Awan, I. (2015). Limits of UK counterterrorism policy and its implications for Islamophobia and far right extremism. *International Journal for Crime, Justice and Social Democracy*, 4(3), 16-29.

Abdeen, Z., Qasrawi, R., Nabil, S., & Shaheen, M. (2008). Psychological reactions to Israeli occupation: findings from the national study of school-based screening in Palestine. *International Journal of Behavioral Development*, 32(4), 290-297.

Abdel Rahim, H. F. A., Wick, L., Halileh, S., Hassan-Bitar, S., Chekir, H., Watt, G., & Khawaja, M. (2009). Maternal and child health in the occupied Palestinian territory. *The Lancet*, *373*(9667), 967-977.

Abdelkader, E. (2017). A comparative analysis of European Islamophobia: France, UK, Germany, Netherlands and Sweden. *UCLA Journal of Islamic & Near Eastern Law, 16*, 29-59.

Abrams, D., Hogg, M. A., & Marques, J. M. (Eds.). (2005). *Social Psychology of Inclusion and Exclusion.* London: Psychology Press.

Abrams, D., Houston, D. M., Van de Vyver, J., & Vasiljevic, M. (2015). Equality hypocrisy, inconsistency, and prejudice: the unequal application of the universal human right to equality. *Peace and Conflict: Journal of Peace Psychology*, *21*(1), 28-40.

Abrams, D., Swift, H., & Houston, D. (2018). *Developing a National Barometer of Prejudice and Discrimination in Britain*. London: Equality and Human Rights Committee.

Abubaker, M. (2015). *Work Life Balance Policies and Practices: Case studies of the Palestinian Telecommunications Sector*. Bradford, UK: University of Bradford, Doctoral Dissertation.

Abubaker, M. & Adam-Bagley, C. (2016a). Work-Life Balance and the needs of female employees in the telecommunications industry in a developing country: a critical realist approach to issues in industrial and organisational psychology. *SAGE Open: Comprehensive Psychology*, 5(1), 1-12.

Abubaker, M. & Adam-Bagley, C. (2016b). Work-Life Benefits: managers' views on implementation in Jordanian telecommunication companies. *Eurasian Journal of Business and Management*, 4(1), 13-28.

Abubaker, M. & Adam-Bagley, C. (2017). Methodological issues in "correspondence testing" for employment discrimination involving ethnic minority applications: Dutch and English case studies. *Social Sciences*, 6(5) 112-120, online.

Abu-Baker, M. (2019). *Rethinking Madrasah Education in a Globalized World*. London: Routledge.

Abu Bakir, S.M. (2018). The impact of managers' emotional intelligence on employees' work life balance: a field study at Jordanian private hospitals. *European Scientific Journal*, 14(25), Online.

Abu Bakr, U. & Shukri, S. (2002). *Social Discrimination Between the Sexes*. Jordan: Supreme Council of Population.

Abu-El-Noor, N. I., Hamdan, M. A., Abu-El-Noor, M. K., Radwan, A. K. S., & Alshaer, A. A. (2017). Safety culture in neonatal intensive care units in the Gaza Strip, Palestine. *Journal of Pediatric Nursing: Nursing Care of Children and Families*, 33(1), 76-82.

Abu-El-Noor, N. I., Aljeesh, Y. I., Radwan, A. S., Abu-El-Noor, M. K., Qddura, I. A. I., Khadoura, K. J., & Alnawajha, S. K. (2016). Post-traumatic stress disorder among health care providers following the Israeli attacks against Gaza Strip in 2014: a call for immediate policy actions. *Archives of Psychiatric Nursing*, 30(2), 185-191.

Abu-El-Noor, N,I., Aljeesh, Y. I., Radwan, A. K. S., Khalil Abu-el-noor, M., Qddura, I. A. I., Khadoura, K. J., & Alnawajha, S. K. (2018). Post-traumatic stress disorder among health care providers two years following the Israeli attacks against Gaza Strip in August 2014: another call for policy intervention. *Archives of Psychiatric Nursing*, 32(2), 188-193.

Abuelaish, I. (2011). *I Shall Not Hate: A Gaza Doctor's Journey on the Road to Peace and Human Dignity.* London: Bloomsbury.

Abu Oksa Daoud, S. (2017). Negotiating space: the construction of a new spatial identity for Palestinian Muslim women in Israel. *Social Sciences*, 6(3), 72-85, Online.

Abu-Rmeileh, N. M., Hammoudeh, W., Mataria, A., Husseini, A., Khawaja, M., Shannon, H. S., ... & Giacaman, R. (2011). Health-related quality of life of Gaza Palestinians in the aftermath of the winter 2008–09 Israeli attack on the Strip. *The European Journal of Public Health*, 22(5), 732-737.

Abu-Shaban, N. (2018). Gaza shootings: an orthopaedic crisis and mass disability. *British Medical Journal*, 362, k3295.

Abu-Zaineh, M., Woode, M. E., & Giacaman, R. (2018). Youth wellbeing through the lens of the Senian capability approach: insights from the occupied Palestinian territory - a cross-sectional study. *The Lancet*, 391, S53.

Abukudair, E. (2012). The challenges facing women leaders in higher education institutions in the Kingdom of Saudi Arabia. *Saudi Journal of Higher Education*, 7(1), 87-124.

Abu-Lughod, L. (2010), The active social life of 'Muslim Women's Rights': a plea for ethnography not polemic, with cases from Egypt and Palestine. *Journal of Middle East Women's Studies*, 6(1) 1-45.

Abu-Lughod, L. (2013). *Do Muslim Women Need Saving?* Cambridge, Mass: Harvard University Press.

Abuznaid, S. (2006) Islam and management: what can be learned? *Thunderbird International Business Review*, 48 (1), 125-139.

Adam-Bagley, C. (1967). Anomie, alienation and the evaluation of social structures. *The Kansas Journal of Sociology*, 3(3), 110-123.

Adam-Bagley, C. (1970). *Social Structure and Prejudice in Five English Boroughs.* London: Institute of Race Relations.

Adam-Bagley, C. (1973). *The Dutch Plural Society: A Comparative Study of Race Relations.* London: Oxford University Press.

Adam-Bagley, C. (1976), On the sociology and social ethics of abortion. *Ethics in Science and Medicine*, 3 (1), 21-32.

Adam-Bagley, C (1983) Alienation and identity in young West Indians in Britain and The Netherlands. In C. Adam-Bagley & G. Verma (Eds.) *Multicultural Education: Education, Ethnicity and Cognitive Styles* (pp 180-193). London: Routledge Ashgate.

Adam-Bagley, C. (1997). *Children, Sex and Social Policy: Humanistic Solutions for Problems of Child Sexual Abuse.* London: Routledge Ashgate.

Adam-Bagley, C. (2008a). Crisis, rhetoric and progress in education for the inclusion of diverse ethnic groups. In G. Verma, C. Adam-Bagley and M. Jha (Eds.) *International Perspectives on Educational Diversity and Inclusion.* London: Routledge.

Adam-Bagley, C. (2008b). The educational and social inclusion of disadvantaged children in Britain. In C. Adam-Bagley & G. Verma (Eds.) *Challenges for Inclusion: Educational and Social Studies from Britain and the Indian Sub-Continent* (pp. 103-148). Leiden: Brill - Sense Education Series.

Adam-Bagley, C. (2008c). An end to apartheid? The oppression and educational inclusion of India's Dalits. In C. Adam-Bagley & G. Verma (Eds.) *Challenges for Inclusion: Educational and Social Studies from Britain and the Indian Sub-Continent* (pp. 165-182). Leiden: Brill - Sense Education Series.

Adam-Bagley, C. (2015a). *Inside Islam: A Muslim Quaker's View.* London: Quaker Universalist Group.

Adam-Bagley, C. (2015b). *The Social Psychology of the Child with Epilepsy.* London: Routledge, Classic Reprints.

Adam-Bagley, C. (2017). Book review article: Banyard's Pimp State: Sex, Money and Equality. *Dignity: Journal of Sexual Exploitation and Violence*, 2(2), 1-12, Online.

Adam-Bagley, C. (2018). Prostitution and public policy. The Nordic Model versus the Pimping of Prostitution. *Dignity: A Journal on Sexual Exploitation and Violence*, 3(1) 3-14, Online.

Adam-Bagley, C. & Abubaker, M. (2017). Muslim woman seeking work: an English case study with a Dutch comparison, of discrimination and achievement. *Social Sciences*, 6(1), 1-13.

Adam-Bagley, C., Abubaker, M. & Shahnaz, A. (2018). Woman and management: a conceptual review, with a focus on Muslim women in management roles in Western and in Muslim-majority countries. *Open Journal of Business and Management*, 6(5), 498-517.

Adam-Bagley, C., Abubaker, M., & Sawyerr, A. (2018). Personality, work-life balance, hardiness, and vocation: a typology of nurses and nursing values in a special sample of English hospital nurses. *Administrative Sciences*, 8(4), 79, 1-21.

Adam-Bagley, C. & Al-Refai, N. (2017). Religious and ethnic integration in British and Dutch cultures: historical and contemporary review of citizenship, education and prejudice. *Journal for Multicultural Education*, 11(1), 82-100.

Adam-Bagley, C., Kadri, S., Shahnaz, A., Simkhada, P. & King, K. (2017). Commercialised sexual exploitation of children, adolescents and women: health and social structure in Bangladesh. *Advances in Applied Sociology*, 7(3), 137-150.

Adam-Bagley, C. & King, K. (2003). *Child Sexual Abuse: The Search for Healing*. London: Routledge-Taylor & Francis.

Adam-Bagley, C. & King, M. (2005). Exploration of three stigma scales in 83 users of mental health services: implications for campaigns to reduce stigma. *Journal of Mental Health*, 14(4), 343-355.

Adam-Bagley, C., Madrid, S., Simkhada, P., King, K. & Young, L. (2017). Adolescent girls offered alternatives to commercial sexual exploitation: a case study from the Philippines. *Dignity: A Journal of Sexual Exploitation and Violence*, 2(8) Online 13-25.

Adam-Bagley, C., Shahnaz, A. & Simkhada, P. (2017). High rates of suicide and violence in the lives of girls and young women in Bangladesh: issues for feminist intervention. *Social Sciences*, 6(4) 140-158, Online.

Adam-Bagley, C., Sawyerr, A. & Abubaker, M. (2016). Dialectic Critical Realism: grounded values and reflexivity in social science research. *Advances in Applied Sociology*, 6(4), 400-419.

Adam-Bagley, C., Van Huizen, A. & Young, L. (1997/2018). Multi-ethnic marriage and interculturalism in Britain and The Netherlands. In D. Woodrow (Ed.) *Intercultural Education: Theories, Policies and Practice*. London: Routledge-Ashgate, Classic Reprints.

Adam-Bagley, C. & Verma, G. (1972). Changing racial attitudes: an experimental English study. *International Journal of Psychology*, 8, 55-58.

Adam-Bagley, C. and Verma, G. (1975). Inter-ethnic attitudes and behaviour in British multi-racial schools. In G. Verma & C. Adam-Bagley (Eds.) *Race and Education Across Cultures* (pp. 236-262). London: Heinemann.

Adam-Bagley, C. & Verma, G. (1979). *Racial Prejudice, the Individual and Society*. London: Routledge Ashgate.

Adam-Bagley, C. & Verma, G. (Eds.) (2008). *Challenges for Inclusion: Educational and Social Studies from Britain and the Indian Sub-Continent*. Leiden: Brill - Sense Education Series.

Adam-Bagley, C., Verma, G., Mallick, K. & Young, L. (1979) *Personality, Self-Esteem and Prejudice*. London: Routledge Ashgate.

Adichie, C. N. (2014). *We Should all be Feminists*. New York: Harper and Collins.

Adler, N. J. (1993). An international perspective on the barriers to the advancement of women managers. *Applied Psychology*, 42(4), 289-300.
Adams, J. & Owen, A. (2016). Creative pedagogies in Palestine. In J. Adams and A. Owen *Creativity and Democracy in Education: Practices and Politics of Learning*. London: Routledge.
Adida, C. L., Laitin, D. D., & Valfort, M. A. (2016). "One Muslim is enough!" Evidence from a field experiment in France. *Annals of Economics and Statistics/Annales d'Économie et de Statistique*, (121/122), 121-160.
Adjegbo, K., Kiwani, D. & Sharma, S. (2007). *Diversity and Citizenship: Curriculum Review*. London: Department for Education.
Afana, A. J., Tremblay, J., Ghannam, J., Ronsbo, H., & Veronese, G. (2018). Coping with trauma and adversity among Palestinians in the Gaza Strip: a qualitative, culture-informed analysis. *Journal of Health Psychology*, Online 1359105318785697.
Afshar, H. (2012). *Women and Fluid Identities: Strategic and Practical Pathways Selected by Women*. London: Palgrave Macmillan.
Ahmed, K. (2004). Islamization and private enterprise: can the two work together? In R. Hathaway & W. Lee (Eds.) *Islamization and the Pakistani Economy* (pp 37-44). Washington, DC: Woodrow Wilson International Center for Scholars.
Ahmed, L. (1992). *Women and Gender in Islam*. New Haven: Yale University Press.
Ahmed, M. K., van Ginneken, J., Razzaque, A., & Alam, N. (2004). Violent deaths among women of reproductive age in rural Bangladesh. *Social Science & Medicine*, 59(2), 311-319.
Ahmed, S. (2004). *The Cultural Politics of Emotion*. Edinburgh: Edinburgh University Press.
Ahmed, S. & Bould, S. (2004). "One able daughter is worth 10 illiterate sons": reframing the patriarchal family. *Journal of Marriage and Family*, 66(5), 1332-1341.
Ahmed, W. & Sardar, Z. (2012). *Muslims in Britain: Making Social and Political Space*. London: Routledge.
Akram S. & Hogan, A. (2015). On reflexivity and conduct of the self in everyday life: reflections on Bourdieu and Archer. *British Journal of Sociology*, 66, 606-625.
Al-Awadi, H. (2018). *Children Around The Prophet: How Muhammad Raised the Young Companions*. Kuwait: The American University.
Alam, S. (2018). *Perception of Self, Power and Gender Among Muslim Women: Narratives from a Rural Community in Bangladesh*. London: Palgrave-MacMillan.

Alam, N., Chowdhury, Mridha, M. & Four Others (2013). Factors associated with condom use negotiation by female sex workers in Bangladesh. *Journal for the Study of Aids*, 24, 813-821.

Alam, N., Chowdhury, M. E., Mridha, M. K., Ahmed, A., Reichenbach, L. J., Streatfield, P. K., & Azim, T. (2013). Factors associated with condom use negotiation by female sex workers in Bangladesh. *International journal of STD & AIDS*, 24(10), 813-821.

Alam, N., Chowdhury, H. R., Das, S. C., Ashraf, A., & Streatfield, P. K. (2014). Causes of death in two rural demographic surveillance sites in Bangladesh, 2004–2010: automated coding of verbal autopsies using InterVA-4. *Global Health Action*, 7(1), 25511.

Aldama, Z. (2017). For sex workers in Bangladesh, the future is as bleak as the past. *South China Morning Post International Magazine*, January 5th, 2017 Online.

Alderson, P. (2013). *Childhoods Real and Imagined: An Introduction to Critical Realism and Childhood Studies*. London: Routledge.

Alderson, P. (2015a). *The Politics of Childhoods Real and Imagined: Practical Application of Critical Realism and Childhood Studies*. London: Routledge.

Alderson, P. (2015b). Reforms to healthcare systems and policies Influences from children's rights and childhood studies. In A. Smith (Ed.) *Enhancing the Rights and Well-Being of Children: Connecting Research, Policy and Practice*, 17-32. London, UK: Palgrave.

Alderson, P. (2016). International human rights, citizenship education, and critical realism. *London Review of Education*, 14, 1-13.

Alexander, M. (2019). Time to break the silence on Palestine. *The New York Times Online*, January 19th, 2019.

Alfridi, M. (2014). *Shoah Through Muslim Eyes*. New York: White Cloud Press.

Al-Hamadi, A., Budhwar, P. and Shipton, H. (2007). Management of human resources in Oman. *International Journal of Human Resource Management*, 18 (1), 100-113.

al-Hibri, A.Y. (2002). *Islamic Law vs. Patriarchal Systems: A Woman's Perspective*. Richmond, VA: University of Richmond, Faculty of Law, for *The Commission on Women in the Profession, American Bar Association*.

Ali, A.J. (2017). Islamic view of diversity: implications for the business world. In J. Syed & A. Klarsfield (Eds) *Religious Diversity in the Workplace* (pp 100-125). Cambridge: Cambridge University Press.

Ali, F. A., Israr, S. M., Ali, B. S., & Janjua, N. Z. (2009). Association of various reproductive rights, domestic violence and marital rape with depression among Pakistani women. *BMC Psychiatry*, 9(1), 77.

Ali, F., Malik, A., Pereira, V. & Al Ariss, A. (2016). A relational understanding of work-life balance of Muslim migrant women in the West: future research agenda. *International Journal of Research on Human Management*, 28 (9), 1163-1181.

Ali, K. (2016). *Sexual Ethics and Islam: Feminist Reflections on Qur'an, Hadith and Jurisprudence* (2nd Edition), Oxford: OneWorld Books.

Ali, P. A., Naylor, P. B., Croot, E., & O'Cathain, A. (2015). Intimate partner violence in Pakistan: a systematic review. *Trauma, Violence, & Abuse*, 16(3), 299-315.

Ali, S. & Majeed, Q. (2018). Incompatibility between gender equality policies in Pakistan and Islam. *Journal of Islamic Thought and Civilization*, 8(1) Online.

Ali, T. (1983). *Can Pakistan Survive? The Death of a State*. London: Penguin Books.

Ali, T. (1992-2015). *The Islam Quintet*. London: Verso.

Ali, T. (2003). *The Clash of Fundamentalisms: Crusades, Jihads and Modernity*. London: Verso.

Ali, T. (2005). *Rough Music: Blair/Bombs/Baghdad/London/Terror*. London: Verso.

Ali, T. (2015). *A Sultan in Palermo*. London: Verso.

Ali, T. (2018). *Uprising in Pakistan*. London: Verso.

Ali, T. S., Krantz, G., Gul, R., Asad, N., Johansson, E., & Mogren, I. (2011). Gender roles and their influence on life prospects for women in urban Karachi, Pakistan: a qualitative study. *Global Health Action*, 4(1), 7448.

Ali, T. S., Árnadóttir, G., & Kulane, A. (2013). Dowry practices and their negative consequences from a female perspective in Karachi, Pakistan—a qualitative study. *Health*, 5(7D), 84.

Al Jazeera (2017). We go inside Bangladesh's biggest brothel, a town where 1,500 women work as prostitutes, some as young as 10 years old. *Al Jazeera World*, shown July 27th, 2017, and on *YouTube*, available online.

Al-Khayyat, M.H. (2003). *Woman in Islam and Her Role in Human Development*. Cairo: World Health Organisation, Eastern Mediterranean Office.

Al-Laham, N., Al-Haddad, R. & Ridwan, F. (2018). Possible haematological changes associated with acute gastroenteritis among kindergarten children in Gaza. *Annals of Medical, Health & Science Research*, 5(4), 292-298.

Allen-Green, R. (2018). A shadow over Europe: CNN Poll reveals depth of anti-semitism in Europe. Edition.CNN.Com Consulted January 27th, 2019.

Allport, G. W. (1973). *The Individual and His Religion: A Psychological Interpretation*. London: MacMillan.

Allport, G. W., & Ross, J. M. (1967). Personal religious orientation and prejudice. *Journal of Personality and Social Psychology*, 5(4), 432.

Almansour, S., & Kempner, K. (2016). The role of Arab women faculty in the public sphere. *Studies in Higher Education*, 41(5), 874-886.

Al-Mehri, A.B. (2010). *The Qur'an: With Surah Introductions and Appendices*. Birmingham, UK: Maktaba Publishers for The Qur'an Project, www.quranproject.,org

Al-Mubarak, S.-R. (2008). *The Sealed Nectar Ar-Raheequl-Makhutum – Biography of the Noble Prophet*. New York: Darussalam Books.

Al-Rasheed, M. (2013). *A Most Masculine State: Gender, Politics and Religion in Saudi Arabia*. Cambridge: Cambridge University Press.

Al-Refai, N. (2011). *An Exploration of Islamic Studies Curriculum Models in Muslim Secondary Schools in England*. Derby, UK: University of Derby, Doctoral Dissertation.

Al-Refai, N. & Adam-Bagley, C. (2012). Muslim youth and citizenship education: idealism, Islam and prospects for successful citizenship education. In F. Ahmed & M.S. Seddon (Eds) *Muslim Youth: Challenges, Opportunities and Expectations* (pp 163-182). London: Continuum Books.

Alshareef, N. (2018). *Child Trafficking from the Perspective of Islamic Law: A Case Study of Saudi Arabia*. Keele, UK: University of Keele, Doctoral Dissertation.

Alsubaie, A., & Jones, K. (2017). An overview of the current state of women's leadership in higher education in Saudi Arabia and a proposal for future research directions. *Administrative Sciences*, 7(4), 36-50.

Al-Sudairy, H. T. (2017). *Modern Woman in the Kingdom of Saudi Arabia: Rights, Challenges and Achievements*. Newcastle, UK: Cambridge Scholars Publishing.

Altaf, Z. (2011). Food security in pluralistic Pakistan. In M. Kugelman & R. Hathaway (Eds.) *Empty Bellies, Broken Dreams: Food Insecurity and the Future of Pakistan* (pp 31-45). Lahore: Vanguard Books for The Woodrow Wilson International Centre.

Altamimi, M. (2018). Could autism be associated with nutritional status in the Palestinian population? The outcomes of the Palestinian Micronutrient Survey. *Nutrition and Metabolic Insights*, 11, 1178638818773078.

Alton, M. (2018). Beliefs values and cohesion in Quaker schools. *Quaker Studies*, 22(2), 255-276.

Alvesson, M. & Billing, Y.D. (1997). *Understanding Gender and Organizations*. London: Sage.

Amin, S., Saha, J. & Ahmed, J. (2018). Skills building programs to reduce child marriage in Bangladesh: a randomized control trial. *Journal of Adolescent Health*, 63(3) 293-300.

Amin, Q. (1992). *The Liberation of Women: A Document in the History of Egyptian Feminism*. Cairo: American University in Cairo Press.

Amnesty International (2011). *Annual Report: Bangladesh 2010*. London: Amnesty International.

Alyacoubi, S., Abuowda, Y., Albarqouni, L., Böttcher, B., & Elessi, K. (2018). Inpatient management of community-acquired pneumonia at the European Gaza Hospital: a clinical audit. *The Lancet*, 391, S40.

Al 'Umari, A. D. (1995). *Madinan Society at the Time of the Prophet*. Herndon, USA: Institute of Islamic Thought.

Anderson, N. A. (2012). Psychologist's role in work-life fit is more important than ever. *APA Monitor on Psychology*, November, accessed at: www.apa.org/monitor/2012/11/ceo.aspx

Anderson, S., Allen, P., Peckham, S. & Goodwin, N. (2008). Asking the right questions: scoping studies in the commissioning of research in the organisation and delivery of health services. *Health Research and Policy Systems*, 6(1) 7, Online.

Andriessen, I. & Dagevos, J. (2008) Unknown or unmeasured? On the meaning of discrimination as a factor in unemployment among Non-Western immigrants. *People and Society* 83, (3) 279-301.

Andriessen, I., Nievers E., Faulk, L. and Dagevos. J. (2010) *Rather than Mark, Mohammed? Research into Labour Market Discrimination Against Non-Western Migrants Through Situation Tests*. The Hague, Netherlands: Social and Cultural Planning Office (Original document in Dutch).

Andriessen, I., Nievers, E., Dagevos J. & Faulk, L. (2012) Ethnic discrimination in the Dutch labor market: its relationship with job characteristics and multiple group membership. *Work and Occupations*, 39 (3) 237-269.

Andriessen, Iris, D. Van Den Ernst, M. Van Den Linden, and G. Dekker. (2015). *Foreign Origin Workers*. The Hague: Social and Cultural Planning Office, (Original document in Dutch).

Andriessen, I., Gijsberts, M. & Hujink, W. (2019). *'Fled with Little Luggage': The Living Situation of Somali Dutch People*. The Hague,

Netherlands: Social and Cultural Planning Office (Original document in Dutch).
An-Nawai (1989). *Forty Hadith* (E. Ibrahim, Translator). Lebanon: The Holy Koran Publishing House.
Ansari, N. (2016). Respectable femininity: a significant panel of glass ceiling for career women. *Gender in Management: An International Journal*, 31(8), 528-541.
Anwar, E. (2006). *Gender and Self in Islam*. London: Routledge.
Anwar, M. & Bakhsh, Q. (2003). *British Muslims and State Policies*. Bristol: Centre for Research in Ethnic Relations.
Anwar, M. & Bakhsh, Q. (2003). *British Muslims and State Policies*. Bristol: Centre for Research in Ethnic Relations.
APPG (2017). *Islamophobia Defined: Report on the Inquiry into a Working Definition of Islamophobia/Anti-Muslim Hatred*. London: House of Commons All Party Parliamentary Group on British Muslims.
Arafat, S. Y. (2018). Suicide prevention activities in Bangladesh. *Asian Journal of Psychiatry*, 36, 38, Online.
Arar, K., Masry-Harzalla, A., & Haj-Yehia, K. (2013). Higher education for Palestinian Muslim female students in Israel and Jordan: migration and identity formation. *Cambridge Journal of Education*, 43(1), 51-67.
Archer, M.A. (1995) *Realist Social Theory: The Morphogenetic Approach*. Cambridge: Cambridge University Press.
Archer, M.A. (2003) *Structure, Agency and the Internal Conversation*. Cambridge: Cambridge University Press.
Archer, M.A. (2014). *Late Modernity: Trajectories Towards Morphogenetic Society*. New York: Springer.
Archer, M.A., Collier, A. & Porpora, D.V. (2004). *Transcendence: Critical Realism and God*. London: Routledge.
Archer, T. (2009). Welcome to the Umma: the British state and its Muslim citizens since 9/11. *Cooperation and Conflict*, 44(3), 329-347.
Arens, J. (2014). *Women, Land and Power in Bangladesh*. Dhaka: The University Press.
Arif, M. (2009). *Gender and Declining Sex Ratios in North India*. Aligarh, India: Aligarh Muslim University, M.Phil thesis.
Armstrong, K. (2002). *Islam: A Short History*. London: Phoenix Press.
Armstrong, K. (2006). *Muhammad: Prophet for our Time*. London: Harper.
Arrigoni, V. (2011). *Gaza: Stay Human*. Leicester, UK: Kube Publishing.
Astell-Burt, T., Maynard, M., Lenguerrand, E. & Harding, S. (2012). Racism, ethnic density and psychological well-being through adolescence: evidence from the 'Determinants of Adolescent Social

Well-Being and Health' longitudinal study. *Ethnicity and Health*, 17, 71-87.
Attran, S. (2003). Genesis of suicide terrorism. *Science*, 99(5612), 1534-1539.
AURAT (2006 to 2018). *Annual Reports of the Aurat Foundation*. Islamabad: Aurat Publication and Information Foundation, www.af.org.pk
Awan, I. (2012). "I am a Muslim not an extremist": how the Prevent Strategy has constructed a "suspect" community. *Politics & Policy*, *40*(6), 1158-1185.
Ayaz, B. (2017). Bacha Khan: a misunderstood leader. *The Pakistan Herald*, September 17th, 2017, Online.
Aycan, Z. & Eskin, M. (2005) Relative contributions of childcare, spousal support, and organizational support in reducing work–family conflict for men and women: the case of Turkey. *Sex Roles*, 53 (7-8), 453-471.
Aycan, Z., Al-Hamadi, A., Davis, A. & Budhwar, P. (2007). Cultural orientations and preferences for HRM policies and practices: the case of Oman. *The International Journal of Human Resource Management*, 18 (1), 11-32.
Azim, T., Rahman, M., Alam, M. S., Chowdhury, I. A., Khan, R., Reza, M., ... & Rahman, A. S. M. M. (2008). Bangladesh moves from being a low-prevalence nation for HIV to one with a concentrated epidemic in injecting drug users. *International journal of STD & AIDS*, *19*(5), 327-331.
Aziz, S., & Rehman, G. (1996). Index of religiosity: the development of an indigenous measure. *Journal of the Indian Academy of Applied Psychology*, *22*, 79-85.
Bach, S. and Sisson, K. (2000) *Personnel Management: A Comprehensive Guide to Theory and Practice*. Oxford: Blackwell Business.
Badawi, J. & Beekun, R.T. (2009). *Leadership: An Islamic Perspective*. Maryland: Amana Publications.
Badawi, Z. (2003a). Foreword. *Citizenship and Muslim Perspectives - Teachers Sharing Ideas*. London: Islamic Relief.
Badawi, Z. (2003b). *Citizenship in Islam*. London: Association of Muslim Social Scientists.
Bader, V. (2005). Dutch nightmare? The end of multiculturalism? *Canadian Diversity*, 4, 9-11.
Bader, V. (2007). *Secularism or Democracy? Associated Governance of Religious Diversity*. Amsterdam: University of Amsterdam Press.
Badings, T. (2017). The price of honour: ending honour killings. *Asian Policy Forum,* May 12th, 2017. Online at www.policyforum.net

Baert, S, Cockx, B., Gheyle, N. & Vandamme, C. (2015). Is there less discrimination in occupations where recruitment is difficult? *ILR Review* 68: 467–500.

Bagguley, P. & Hussain, Y. (2016). *Riotous Citizens: Ethnic Conflict in Multicultural Britain*. London: Routledge.

Bagguley, P. & Hussain, Y. (2017). Late-modern Muslims: theorising Islamic identities amongst university students. In *Muslim Students, Education and Neoliberalism* (pp. 35-49). London: Palgrave MacMillan.

Baker, F. S. (2013). Responding to the challenges of active citizenship through the revised UK early years foundation stage curriculum. *Early Child Development and Care, 183*(8), 1115-1132.

Bakker J., Denessen, E., Pelzer, B, Veneman, M. & Lageweg, S. (2007). Attitudes towards classmates: ethnically influenced? *Pedagogiek*, 27, 201-219.

Bakhsh, Q. (2007). *Stigma: Drug Use Amongst the Muslim Community in the London Borough of Redbridge*. London: Department of Health, and the University of Central Lancashire, for the Qalb Centre, Redbridge.

Ballard, R. & Holden, B (1975) The employment of coloured graduates in Britain. *New Community*, 4, 325-336.

Bangert, M., Molyneux, D., Lindsay, L., Fitzpatrick, C. & Engels, D. (2017). The cross-cutting contribution of neglected tropical diseases to sustainable development goals. *Infectious Diseases of Poverty* 6, 73-83, Online.

Banks, J. (Ed.) (2004). *Diversity and Citizenship Education: Global Perspectives*. New York: Jossey Bass.

Banton, M. (1996) *International Action Against Racial Discrimination*. Oxford: Oxford University Press.

Banton, M. (2014). Updating Max Weber on the racial, the ethnic, and the national. *Journal of Classical Sociology*, 14(4), 325-340.

Banfield, G. (2016). *Critical Realism for Marxist Sociology of Education*. London: Routledge.

Banyard, K. (2016). *Pimp State: Sex, Money and Equality*. London: Faber and Faber.

Baqir, F. (2019). *Poverty Alleviation and Poverty Aid: Pakistan*. London: Taylor & Francis, Routledge Studies in Development and Society.

Baral, R. & Bhargava, S. (2011) HR interventions for work-life balance: evidences from organisations in India. *International Journal of Business, Management and Social Sciences*, 2 (1), 33-42.

Baral, S., Beyrer, C., Muessig, K., Poteat, T., Wirtz, A. L., Decker, M. R., ... & Kerrigan, D. (2012). Burden of HIV among female sex workers in low-income and middle-income countries: a systematic review and meta-analysis. *The Lancet Infectious Diseases*, *12*(7), 538-549.

Barbara, S. & MacQueen, G. (2004). Peace through health: key concepts, *The Lancet*, 364, 384-386.

Barber, B. K., McNeely, C., El Sarraj, Mahmoud M., Giacaman, R., Arafat, C., Barnes, W. & Abu Mallouh, M. (2016). Mental suffering in protracted political conflict: feeling broken or destroyed. *PloS One* 11, no. 5: e0156216.

Bari, S.A. (2019). Audacity of hope: stories of seven women who channelled their pain into power. *The Daily Star* (Dhaka). March 29th, 2019.

Barlas, A. (2002). *"Believing Women" in Islam: Unreading Patriarchal Interpretations of the Qur'an*. Austin, TX: University of Texas Press.

Barlas, A. (2014). An open text, and a critique of patriarchy. In M. Birkel (Ed.) *Qur'an in Conversation* (pp 48-60). Baylor TX: Baylor University Press.

Bashir, Y. (2018). *The Words of My Father: A Memoir*. London: Haus Publishing.

Basit, T. N. (2009) White British; dual heritage: British Muslim: young Britons' conceptualisation of identity and citizenship. *British Educational Research Journal*, 35(5), 723-743.

Bates, K., Leone, T., Ghandour, R., Mitwalli, S., Nasr, S., Coast, E., & Giacaman, R. (2017). Women's health in the occupied Palestinian territories: contextual influences on subjective and objective health measures. PloS One, 12(10), e0186610.

Bates, L. (2014). *Everyday Sexism*. London: Simon & Schuster.

Baxter, P., & Jack, S. (2008). Qualitative case study methodology: study design and implementation for novice researchers. *The Qualitative Report*, *13*(4), 544-559.

Baynes, C. (2019). More than 2.6M Britons are Holocaust deniers, poll finds. *The Independent Online*, January 27th, 2019.

Bazeley, P. & Jackson, K. (2013). *Qualitative Data Analysis with NVivo*. London: Sage.

BDC (2007-2017). *Monthly Statistical Bulletin, Bangladesh, July 2007 to December 2017*. Dhaka: Bangladesh Bureau of Statistics.

BDC (2015) What is work-life balance? Definition and meaning. In www.businessdirectory.com.

Bekhouche, Y., Hausmann, R., Tyson, L. D., & Zahidi, S. (2013). *The Global Gender Gap Report 2013*. Geneva: World Economic Forum.

Berry, M. & Philo, G. (2006). *Israel and Palestine: Conflicting Histories*. London: Pluto Press.

Beautrais A.L. (2006). Suicide in Asia. *Crisis*, 27(1), 55–57.
Beekun, R. (2012). Character-centred leadership: Muhammad (p) as an ethical model for CEOs. *Journal of Management Development*, 31(10), 1003-1020.
Berglund, J., & Gent, B. (2019). Qur'anic education and non-confessional RE: an intercultural perspective. *Intercultural Education*, Suppl, 20, 1-12.
Bhaskar R.A. (1978) *A Realist Theory of Science*. Hassocks, UK: Harvester Press.
Bhaskar, R.A. (1986). *Scientific Realism and Human Emancipation*. London: Verso.
Bhaskar, R.A. (2000). *From East to West: Odyssey of a Soul*. London: Routledge.
Bhaskar, R. (2002a). *From Science to Emancipation: Alienation and the Actuality of Enlightenment*. London: Routledge.
Bhaskar, R. (2002b). *Reflections on MetaReality: Transcendence, Emancipation and Everyday Life*. London: Routledge.
Bhaskar, R. (2002c). *The Philosophy of MetaReality: Creativity, Love and Freedom*. London: Routledge.
Bhaskar, R.A. (2008). *Dialectic: The Pulse of Freedom*. London: Routledge.
Bhaskar, R.A. (2010). *Reclaiming Reality: A Critical Introduction to Contemporary Philosophy*. London: Taylor & Francis.
Bhaskar, R.A. (2012). *From Science to Emancipation: Alienation and Enlightenment*. London: Routledge.
Bhaskar, R.A. (2017). *The Order of Natural Necessity: A Kind of Introduction to Critical Realism* (G. Hawke & P. Alderson, Editors). London: University College Institute of Education.
Bhaskar, R.A. & Danermark, B. (2006). Metatheory, interdisciplinary and disability research: a critical realist approach. *Scandinavian Journal of Disability Research*, 8, 278-297.
Bhaskar, R. & Hartwig, M. (2010). *The Formation of Critical Realism: A Personal Perspective*. London: Routledge.
Bhui, K. (2015). Radicalization a mental health issue, not a religious one. *New Scientist*, April 8, 30-31.
Bhui, K., & Ibrahim, Y. (2013). Marketing the "radical": symbolic communication and persuasive technologies in jihadist websites. *Transcultural Psychiatry*, 50(2), 216-234.
Bhui, K. & McKenzie, K. (2008). Rates and risk factors for suicide within a year of contact with mental health services in England and Wales. *Psychiatric Services*, 59, 414-420.

Bhui, K., Lenguerrand, E., Maynard, M., Stansfield, S. & Harding, S. (2012). Does cultural integration explain a mental health advantage for adolescents? *International Journal of Epidemiology*, 41, 791-802.

Bhui, K., Everitt, B., & Jones, E. (2014). Might depression, psychosocial adversity, and limited social assets explain vulnerability to and resistance against violent radicalisation? *PloS One*, *9*(9), e105918, Online.

Bhui, K., Warfa, N., & Jones, E. (2014). Is violent radicalisation associated with poverty, migration, poor self-reported health and common mental disorders? *PloS One*, *9*(3), e90718, Online.

Bhui, K., James, A., & Wessely, S. (2016). Mental illness and terrorism. *BMJ* September 13th, Editorial: 354:i4869.

Bhui, K., Silva, M. J., Topciu, R. A., & Jones, E. (2016). Pathways to sympathies for violent protest and terrorism. *The British Journal of Psychiatry*, *209*(6), 483-490.

Bhui, K., Otis, M., Silva, M. J., Halvorsrud, K., Freestone, M., & Jones, E. (2019). Extremism and common mental illness: cross-sectional community survey of White British and Pakistani men and women living in England. *The British Journal of Psychiatry*, Online, 1-8.

Bickmore, K., Kaderi, A. S., & Guerra-Sua, Á. (2017). Creating capacities for peacebuilding citizenship: history and social studies curricula in Bangladesh, Canada, Colombia, and México. *Journal of Peace Education*, *14*(3), 282-309.

Bindel, J. (2017). *The Pimping of Prostitution: Abolishing the Sex Work Myth*. London: Palgrave MacMillan.

Bissel, R. (2019). *The Dialectics of Liberty: Exploring the Context of Human Freedom*. New York: Lexington Books.

Blackstock O., Patel V., Felsen U., Park C., Jain S. (2017). Pre-exposure prophylaxis prescribing and retention in care among heterosexual women at a community-based comprehensive sexual health clinic. *AIDS Care*, February 11, Online.

Blanchet, T. (2001). *Lost Innocence, Stolen Childhoods*. Dhaka: The University Press.

Blanchet, T. (2005). Bangladeshi girls sold as wives in Northern India. *Indian Journal of Gender Studies* 12(3) 305-315.

Blanchet, K., El-Zein, A., Langer, A., Sato, M., Abdulrahim, S., Abouchacra, K., ... & Ansbro, É. (2018). Support for UNRWA's survival. *The Lancet*, September 18, Online.

Blanchfield, M. (2018). UNICEF: Deaths of Gaza children more than just numbers. *Toronto Star Online*, May 20, 2018.

Blommaert, L., Marcel Coenders, M. & Van Tubergen, F. (2013). Discrimination of Arabic-named applicants in The Netherlands: an internet-based field experiment examining different phases in online recruitment procedures. *Social Forces* 92, 957–982.

Boduel, C. (2017). *Pakistan: Crimes Against Female Humanity - Domestic Violence, Rape, 'Honour' Killing, Forced and Child Marriages.* Canterbury, UK: Women's Economic and Social Think Tank, Brussels School of International Studies, University of Kent.

Bogaerts, J., Ahmed, J., Akhter & Five Others (2001). Sexually transmitted infections among married women in Dhaka, Bangladesh. *Sexually Transmitted Infections*, 77, 114-119.

Boone, J. (2016a). Pakistani police admit to practice of 'encounter killings'. *Guardian Online*, September 26th, 2016.

Boone, J. (2016b). Pakistan makes 'honour killings' punishable by mandatory prison. *The Guardian Online* October 6th, 2016.

Boone, J. (2018). Pakistan's soft coup. *CAPX News*, June 6th, 2018. At https://capx.co/pakistans-soft-coup/

Booth, A. L., Leigh, A. & Varganova, E. (2012). Does ethnic discrimination vary across minority groups? Evidence from a field experiment. *Oxford Bulletin of Economics and Statistics* 74: 547–73.

Booth, R., Mohdin, A. & Levett, C. (2018). Bias in Britain. *Guardian Online*, December 2nd, 2018.

Borland, E. (2008). Class consciousness. In Parrillo, V. (Ed.) *Encyclopedia of Social Problems*, Vol. 1. London: Sage.

Böttcher, B., Abu-El-Noor, N., Aldabbour, B., Naim, F. N., & Aljeesh, Y. (2018). Maternal mortality in the Gaza strip: a look at causes and solutions. *BMC Pregnancy and Childbirth*, *18*(1), 396.

Bourdieu, P. (1989). Social space and symbolic power. *Sociological Theory*, 7, 14-25.

Bourget, C. (2019). *Islamic Schools in France: Minority Integration and Separatism in Western Society.* New York: Springer.

Bourne, J. (2015) *The Race Relations Act 1965: Blessing or a Curse?* London, UK: Institute of Race Relations.

Bovenkerk, F. (1992) *Testing Discrimination in Natural Experiments. A Manual for International Comparative Research on Discrimination on the Grounds of 'Race' and Ethnic Origin.* Geneva: International Labor Office

Bovenkerk, F., Gras, M.J.I. & Ramsoedh, D. (1995) *Discrimination Against Migrant Workers and Ethnic Minorities in Access to Employment: The Netherlands.* Geneva: International Labor Office.

Bowcott, O. (2011). Worst place in the world for a woman: violence puts Afghanistan at top of list: Congo, Pakistan, Somalia and India also in top five: rape, infanticide and poverty rife, says report. *The Guardian Online*, June 15th, 2011, Online.

Boyd, R. (2010) Scientific Realism. In E. N. Zalta (Ed.) *The Stanford Encyclopaedia of Philosophy*. Stanford, CA: Stanford University.

Boyle, H. N. (2004). *Quranic Schools: Agents of Preservation and Change*. London: Routledge-Falmer.

Bracke, S. (2013) Transformations of the secular and the 'Muslim question'. Revisiting the historical coincidence of depillarization of Islam in The Netherlands. *Journal of Muslims in Europe*, 2 (2) 208-226.

Bradley, H. and Healy, G. (2008) *Ethnicity and Gender at Work: Inequalities, Careers and Employment Relations*. London, UK: Palgrave Macmillan.

Bradley, J. (2010). *Behind the Veil of Vice: The Business and Culture of Sex in the Middle East*. New York: Palgrave-Macmillan.

Branine, M. & Pollard, D. (2010). Human resource management with Islamic management principles: a dialectic for a reverse diffusion in management. *Personnel Review*, 39 (6), 712-727.

Breen, D. (2018). *Muslim Schools, Communities and Critical Race Theory: Faith Schooling in an Islamophobic Britain?* London: Palgrave MacMillan.

Brocke, S. (2013). Transformations of the secular and the 'Muslim question'. Revisiting the historical coincidence of depillarisation and the institutionalisation of Islam in The Netherlands. *Journal of Muslims in Europe*, 2, 208-226.

Bron, J., & Thijs, A. (2011). Leaving it to the schools: citizenship, diversity and human rights education in the Netherlands. *Educational Research*, 53(2), 123-136.

Brown, J.A.C. (2015). *Misquoting Muhammad: The Challenge and Choices of Interpreting the Prophet's Legacy*. London: OneWorld Books.

Brown, J.A.C. (2017). Stoning and handcutting – understanding the Hudud and the shari'a in Islam. *Yaqueen*, January 12th, 2017, Online at http://yaqueeninstitute.org.

Brown, J.A.C. (2018). *Hadith: Muhammad's Legacy and the Medieval and Modern World*. London: Oneworld Publications.

Bryman, A. and Bell, E. (2007) *Business Research Methods*, 2nd edition. Oxford: Oxford University Press.

Brynin, M. & Guveli, A. (2012) Understanding the ethnic pay gap in Britain. *Work, Employment and Society*, 26 (4) 574-587.

Brynin, M. & Longhi, S. (2015) *The Effect of Occupation on Poverty Among Ethnic Minority Groups*. York, UK: The Joseph Rowntree Foundation.

Budhwar, P. and Mellahi, K. (Eds.) (2006). *Managing Human Resources in the Middle-East.* London: Routledge.

Bullough, A., Moore, F. & Kalafatoglu, T. (2017). Research on women in international business and management: then, now and next. *Cross-Cultural and Strategic Management*, 24(2), 211-230.

Bunzl, M. (2007). *Anti-Semitism and Islamophobia: Hatreds Old and New in Europe*. Chicago: University of Chicago Press.

Burghri, Y. (2016). Editorial: HIV/AIDS in Pakistan. *Journal of the Pakistan Medical Association*, 56(1), 1.

Burnes, B., & James, H. (1995). Culture, cognitive dissonance and the management of change. *International Journal of Operations & Production Management*, 15(8), 14-33.

Busby, E. (2018). Living in fear: one in three Muslim students attacked on compus as Islamophobic hate crime surges. *Independent Online*, March 16th, 2018.

Candela, M. & Aldams, Z. (2015). The brothels of Bangladesh. *The Diplomat*, February 23, 7-10.

Canetto, S. (2015). Suicidal behaviors among Muslim women: patterns, pathways, meanings and prevention. *Crisis*, 36(Dec), 447-458.

Carlile, A. (2013). *Permanent Exclusion from School and Institutions*. Leiden: Brill - Sense Education Series.

Carlsson, M. (2010). Experimental evidence of discrimination in the hiring of first-and second-generation immigrants. *Labour* 24(3), 263–78.

Carmichael, F. & Woods, R. (2000). Ethnic penalties in unemployment and occupational attainment: evidence for Britain. *International Review of Applied Economics* 14: 71–98.

Carter, N. M., & Silva, C. (2010). Women in management: delusions of progress. *Harvard Business Review*, 88(3), 19-21.

Catalyst (2017). *Women in Management.* New York: The Catalyst Institute.

Ceric, M. (2008) *Toward a Muslim Social Contract in Europe*. London: Association of Muslim Social Scientists.

Cesari, J. (2011). Islamophobia in the West: a comparison between Europe and the United States. In J. Esposito and I. Kalin (Eds) *Islamophobia: The Challenge of Pluralism in the 21st Century*, (pp 21-46). Oxford: Oxford University Press.

Chaillon, A., Smith, D. M., Vanpouille, C., Lisco, A., Jordan, P., Caballero, G., ... & Mehta, S. R. (2017). HIV trafficking between blood and semen during early untreated HIV infection. *Journal of Acquired Immune Deficiency Syndromes* (1999), 74(1), 95.

Chakrabortty, A. (2019). Integrate, migrants are told: but can they ever be good enough for the likes of Blair? *Guardian Online*, April 24th, 2019.
Chandra, V. (2012). Work–life balance: eastern and western perspectives. *The International Journal of Human Resource Management*, 23 (5), 1040-1056.
Channon, M.D. (2018). Son preference and family limitation in Pakistan. *International Perspectives on Sexual Reproductive Health* 43(3), 99-110.
Chao, F., Gerland, P., Cooke, A. & Alkemad, L. (2019). Sytematic assessment of the sex ratio at birth for all countries and estimation of national imbalances and regional reference levels. *PNAS (Proceedings of the National Academicy of Science, USA)*, 116(19), Online.
Charlesworth, H., & Gaita, R. (2010). Women and gender in the invasion of Gaza. In R. Gaita (Ed.) *Gaza: Morality Law and Politics*, pp 127-147. Perth: University of Western Australia Publications.
Charrad, M. M. (2011). Gender in the Middle East: Islam, state, agency. *Annual Review of Sociology*, 37, 417-437.
Charrett, C. (2019). *The European Union, Hamas and the 2006 Palestinian Elections: A Performance in Politics*. London: Routledge.
Chaudhry, A., Hajat, S., Rizkallah, N., & Abu-Rub, A. A. (2018). Risk factors for vitamin A and vitamin D deficiencies in children younger than 5 years in the occupied Palestinian territory: a cross-sectional study. *The Lancet*, 391, S3.
Chen Y-Y., Wu KC-C., Yousuf S. & Yip P.S. (2012). Suicide in Asia: opportunities and challenges. *Epidemiological Review* 34(1), 129–144.
Cherribi, A. (2011). An obsession renewed: Islamophobia in The Netherlands, Austria and Germany. In J. Esposito and I. Kalin (Eds) *Islamophobia: The Challenge of Pluralism in the 21st Century*, (pp 47-62). Oxford: Oxford University Press.
Cheung, S. Y. (2014). Ethno-religious minorities and labour market integration: generational advancement or decline? *Ethnic and Racial Studies*, 37(1), 140-160.
Chis, I.C. (2016). Problematising the critical realist positional approach to intersectionality. *Inquiries* 8(2), 1-3.
Chowdhury, F.D. (2010). Dowry, women and the law in Bangladesh. *International Journal of Law, Policy and Family*, 24, August 1, Online.
Chowdhury, F. R., Rahman, A. U., Mohammed, F. R., Chowdhury, A., Ahasan, H. A. M. N., & Bakar, M. A. (2011). Acute poisoning in southern part of Bangladesh: the case load is decreasing. *Bangladesh Medical Research Council Bulletin*, *37*(2), 61-65.

Chowdhury, F. R., Dewan, G., Verma, V. R., Knipe, D. W., Isha, I. T., Faiz, M. A., ... & Eddleston, M. (2017). Bans of WHO class I pesticides in Bangladesh—suicide prevention without hampering agricultural output. *International Journal of Epidemiology*, *47*(1), 175-184.

Clark, A. (2016). The case of Saba Qaiser and the film-maker determined to put an end to 'honour killings'. *The Guardian Online*, February 14th, 2016.

Clark J. (2015). Editorial: Bangladesh's ignored sex workers. *British Medical Journal* June 29, 350.

Clark, K. & Drinkwater, S. (2007). *Ethnic Minorities in the Labour Market: Dynamics and Diversity*. Bristol, UK: The Policy Press.

Coid, J. W., Bhui, K., MacManus, D., Kallis, C., Bebbington, P., & Ullrich, S. (2016). Extremism, religion and psychiatric morbidity in a population-based sample of young men. *The British Journal of Psychiatry*, *209*(6), 491-497.

Coleman, I. (2004). Gender disparities, economic growth and Islamization in Pakistan. In R. Hathway & W. Lee (Eds.) *Islamization and the Pakistani Economy* (pp 79-90). Washington, DC: Woodrow Wilson International Center for Scholars.

Collier, A. (1994). *An Introduction to Roy Bhaskar's Critical Realism*. London: Verso.

Collier, A. (1998). Explanation and emancipation. In M. Archer. R. Bhaskar, A. Collier, T. Lawson & A. Norrie (Eds.) *Critical Reality: Essential Readings* (pp. 444-463). London: Routledge.

Collier, A. (1999). *Being and Worth*. London: Routledge.

Collier, A. (2001). *Christianity and Marxism: A Philosophical Contribution to their Reconciliation*. London: Routledge.

Collier, A. (2002). Dialectic in Marxism and critical realism. In A. Brown, S. Fleetwood and J.M. Roberts (Eds.) *Critical Realism and Marxism* (pp. 168-186). London: Routledge.

Colucci, E. & Lester, D. (2014). *Suicide and Culture: Understanding the Context*. Cambridge, Mass: Hogrefe.

Cooney, M. (2019). *Execution by Family: A Theory of Honour Violence*. London: Routledge.

Corde, M. (2015). Dutch elections 2017: polls open amid fears of far-right surge led by Geert Wilders' PVV. *The Independent Online*, March 15th, 2015.

Corner, E. & Gill, P. (2015). A false dichotomy? Mental illness and lone-actor terrorism. *Law and Human Behavior*, *39*(1), 23.

Corraya, S. (2015). *Mapping Missing, Kidnapped and Trafficked Children and Women: Bangladeshi Perspective*. www.AsiaNews.it (*Caritas* Website)

Coyle, C. T., Shuping, M. W., Speckhard, A., & Brightup, J. E. (2015). Relationship of abortion and violence against women: violence prevention strategies and research needs. *Issues in Law & Medicine, 30*, 111-130.

Creaven, S. (2007). *Emergentist Marxism: Dialectical Philosophy and Social Theory*. London: Routledge.

Creaven, S. (2012). *Against the Spiritual Turn: Marxism, Realism, and Critical Theory*. London: Routledge.

Creaven, S. (2015). The 'Two Marxisms' revisited: humanism, structuralism and realism in Marxist social theory. *Journal of Critical Realism*, 14, 7-53.

Cresswell, J.W. (2013. *Research design: Qualitative, Quantitative, and Mixed Methods Approaches*. London: Sage Publications.

Crick, B. (2000a). *Essays on Citizenship*. London: Continuum Books.

Crick, B. (2000b). Introduction to the new curriculum. In D. Lawton, J. Cairns & R. Gardner (Eds.), *Education for Citizenship* (pp. 3–17). London: Continuum Books.

Crompton, R., Lewis, S. & Lyonette, C. (Eds.) (2007). *Women, Men, Work and Family in Europe*. London, UK: Palgrave MacMillan.

Crowe, S., Cresswell, K., Robertson, A., Huby, G., Avery, A., & Sheikh, A. (2011). The case study approach. *BMC Medical Research Methodology*, 11(1), 100. Online

Culpan, O., Marzotto, T. & Demir, N. (2007). Foreign banks: executive jobs for Turkish women? *Women in Management Review*, 22(8), 608-630.

Curwen, B., Palmer, S. & Ruddell, P. (2001). *Brief Cognitive Behavior Therapy*. London: Sage.

Daniel, W. W. (1968). *Racial Discrimination in England*. London: Penguin Books.

Das, T. K. (2000). *Social Structure and Cultural Practices in Slums: A Study of Slums in Dhaka City*. New Delhi: Northern Book Centre.

Davala, S., Jhabuala, R., Kapoor, M. & Standing, G. (2015). *Basic Income: A Transformation Policy for India*. London: Bloomsbury Academic.

Davidson L. (2019). Israel, Zionism, and the Jews. In *Essays Reflecting the Art of Political and Social Analysis. Critical Political Theory and Radical Practice* (pp. 167-207). Palgrave Macmillan.

Davis, M. K. (2013). Entrepreneurship: an Islamic perspective. *International Journal of Entrepreneurship and Small Business, 20*(1), 63-69.

De Henau, J., Meulders, D. and O'Dorchai, S. (2007) 'Parents' care and career: comparing parental leave policies across EU-15. In D. Del Boca and C. Wetzels (eds) *Social Policies, Labour Markets and Motherhood: A Comparative Analysis of European Countries* (63–106). Cambridge: Cambridge University Press.

De Zavala, C. A., Orehek, E. & Abdollahr, A. (2012). Intrinsic religiosity reduces intergroup hostility under mortality salience. *European Journal of Social Psychology*, 42, 451-461.

Dearden, L. (2017). Bangladesh child marriage – new law 'will reduce marital age to zero'. *The Independent Online*, March 8, 207.

Deitch, E. A., Barsky, A., Butz, Chan, S., Brief, A. & Bradley, J. (2003). Subtle yet significant: the existence and impact of everyday racial discrimination in the workplace. *Human Relations* 56, 1299–1324.

Den Dulk, L., Peters, P. and Poutsma, E. (2012). Variations in adoption of workplace work–family arrangements in Europe: the influence of welfare-state regime and organizational characteristics. *The International Journal of Human Resource Management*, 23 (13), 2785-2808.

Dennin, R., Lafrenz, M. & Gesk, G. (2014). HIV and other sexually transmitted infections – challenges for liberal prevention strategies. *World Journal of Aids*, 4, 258-279.

Derichs, C. & Fennert, D. (Eds.). (2014). *Women's Movements and Countermovements: The Quest for Gender Equality in Southeast Asia and the Middle East*. Newcastle: Cambridge Scholars Publishing.

DES (1999). *National Advisory Group Report on Personal, Social and Health Education*. London: Department for Education and Science Publications.

DES (2001a). *Schools Building on Success. The Green Paper.* London: Department for Education and Science Publications.

DES (2001b). *Schools Achieving Success. The White Paper.* London: Department for Education and Science Publications.

DES (2004). *Schemes of Work: Citizenship at Key Stage 3.* London: Department for Education and Science Publications.

DES (2005). *The National Curriculum for England*. London: Department for Education and Science Publications.

De Sondy, A. (2015). *The Crisis of Islamic Masculinities*. London: Bloomsbury Publishing.

Devji, F. (2008). *The Terrorist in Search of Humanity: Militant Islam and Global Politics*. New York: Columbia University Press.

Devji, F. (2011). The paradox of nonviolence. *Public Culture*, *23*(2), 269-274.

Devji, F. (2012). *The Impossible Indian: Gandhi and the Temptation of Violence*. Boston, MA: Harvard University Press.

Devji, F. (2013). *Muslim Zion: Pakistan as a Political Idea*. London: Hurst Publishers.

Devji, F. (2018). How caste underpins the blasphemy crisis in Pakistan: caste discrimination against Christians, whose ancestors were lower-caste Hindus, persists. *New York Times Online*, December 18th, 2018.

Devi, S. (2004) Health under fire. *The Lancet*, 364 (9439), 1027-1028.

Devi, S. (2018a). Funds cut for aid in the occupied Palestinian territory. *The Lancet*, 392(10151), 903.

Devi, S. (2018b). Cancer drugs run short in the Gaza Strip. *The Lancet Oncology*, 19(10), 1284, October 1.

Dex, S. and Smith, C. (2002) *The Nature and Pattern of Family-Friendly Employment Policies in Britain*. Policy Press Bristol.

Dey, I. (2003) *Qualitative Data Analysis: A User Friendly Guide for Social Scientists*. London: Routledge.

Diab, M., Peltonen, K., Qouta, S. R., Palosaari, E., & Punamäki, R. L. (2017). Can functional emotion regulation protect children's mental health from war trauma? A Palestinian study. *International Journal of Psychology*, April 19, epub.

Diab, M., Jamei, Y. A., Kagee, A., & Veronese, G. (2018). Integrating a public health and human rights approach into mental health services for Palestinians in the Gaza Strip. *The Lancet*, 391, S27.

Diab, S. Y., Isosävi, S., Qouta, S. R., Kuittinen, S., & Punamäki, R. L. (2017). The protective role of maternal posttraumatic growth and cognitive trauma processing among Palestinian mothers and infants. *Infant Behavior and Development*, June 12, epub, Online.

Diab, S. Y., Isosävi, S., Qouta, S. R., Kuittinen, S., & Punamäki, R. L. (2018). The protective role of maternal post-traumatic growth and cognitive trauma processing in Palestinian mothers and infants: a longitudinal study. *The Lancet*, 391, S39.

Diab, S. Y., Palosaari, E., & Punamäki, R. L. (2018). Society, individual, family, and school factors contributing to child mental health in war: the ecological-theory perspective. *Child Abuse & Neglect, 84*, 205-216.

Dom, G., Schouler-Ocak, M., Bhui, K., Demunter, H., Kuey, L., Raballo, A., ... & Samochowiec, J. (2018). Mass violence, radicalization and terrorism: a role for psychiatric profession? *European Psychiatry: The Journal of the Association of European Psychiatrists*, 49, 78.

Donahue, M. J. (1985). Intrinsic and extrinsic religiousness: the empirical research. *Journal for the Scientific Study of Religion, 24*(4), 418-423.

Doppen, F. H. (2010). Citizenship education and the Dutch national identity debate. *Education, Citizenship and Social Justice*, 5(2), 131-143.

Dunhill, A. (2018). Does teaching children about human rights, encourage them to practice, protect and promote the rights of others? *Education 3-13*, 46(1), 16-26.

Durán, K. (2000). Muslims and Islamists in America. *L'abbaglio dell'immigrazione (Rome: Istituto di Formazione per le Scienze Antropologiche*, 20, 27-28).

Durrani, N., Dunne, M., Fincham, K., & Crossouard, B. (2017). Pakistan: converging imaginaries in an Islamic State. In *Troubling Muslim Youth Identities* (pp. 77-125). London: Palgrave Macmillan.

Dworkin, S. & Blankenship, K. (2009). Microfinancing and HIV/AIDS prevention: assessing its promise and limitations. *Aids and Behavior*, 13, 462-469.

Dy, M. A., Martin, L., & Marlow, S. (2014). Developing a critical realist positional approach to intersectionality. *Journal of Critical Realism*, 13(5), 447-466.

Dyke, A. & James, L. (2009) *Immigrant, Muslim, Female: Triple Paralysis?* London, UK: The Quillam Foundation.

Easton, G. (2010). Critical realism in case study research. *Industrial Marketing and Management*, 39, 118-128.

Eaton, C.L.E. (2008). *The Book of Hadith: Sayings of the Prophet Muhammad from the Mishkat al-Masabib*. Bristol: The Book Foundation.

Eddleston, M., & Konradsen, F. (2007). Commentary: time for a re-assessment of the incidence of intentional and unintentional injury in India and South East Asia. *International Journal of Epidemiology*, 36(2), 208–211.

Eden, L. & Gupta, S.F. (2017). Culture and context matter: gender in international business and management. *Cross-Cultural and Strategic Management*, 24(2), 194-210.

Edhi Foundation (2017). *About Us – Edhi Welfare Organisation of Pakistan*. https://edhi.org

Edwards, P., O'Mahoney, J. & Vincent, S. (Eds.) (2014) *Studying Organisations using Critical Realism: A Practical Guide*. London: Oxford University Press.

EHRC (2009). *Ethnicity and Institutional Racism: Attitude Change Since 1999*. London: Equality and Human Rights Commission.

EHRC (2015). *Is Britain Fairer?* London: Equality and Human Rights Commission.

EHRC (2016-2018). *Annual Reports*. London: Equality and Human Rights Commission.
EHRC (2018). *Inequality in the United Kingdom*. London: Equality and Human Rights Commission.
Einstein, A., Freud, S., & Gilbert, S. (1933). *Why War?* Paris: International Institute of Intellectual Co-Operation.
Elamin, A. M., & Omair, K. (2010). Males' attitudes towards working females in Saudi Arabia. *Personnel Review*, 39(6), 746-766.
Elessi, K. (2018). The Palestinian Day of Return: from a short day of commemoration to a long day of mourning. *The Lancet*, May 18, Online.
El-Habil, M. K. (2018). Acute poisoning in the Gaza Strip: a retrospective study. *The Lancet*, 391, S29.
Elkahtib, Z. (2018). Patients' satisfaction with the non-communicable diseases services provided at UNRWA health centres in Gaza governorates: a cross-sectional study. *The Lancet*, 391, S52.
El Kishawi, R. R., Soo, K. L., Abed, Y. A., & Muda, W. A. M. W. (2017). Prevalence and associated factors influencing stunting in children aged 2–5 years in the Gaza Strip-Palestine: a cross-sectional study. *BMC Pediatrics*, 17(1), 210.
Ellis, M. (2002). *Israel and Palestine Out of the Ashes*. London: Pluto Press.
Ellsberg, M., Jansen, H. A., Heise, L., Watts, C. H., & Garcia-Moreno, C. (2008). Intimate partner violence and women's physical and mental health in the WHO multi-country study on women's health and domestic violence: an observational study. *The Lancet*, *371*(9619), 1165-1172.
Emerson, A. (2017). *Education of Pakistan's Daughters: The Intersection of Schooling, Unequal Citizenship and Violence*. Brighton, UK: University of Sussex, Doctoral Dissertation.
Emmanuel, F., Thompson, L. H., Athar, U., Salim, M., Sonia, A., Akhtar, N., & Blanchard, J. F. (2013). The organisation, operational dynamics and structure of female sex work in Pakistan. *Sexually Transmitted Infections*, *89*(Suppl 2), ii29-ii33.
Emmott, R. (2018). Palestinian U.N. aid still $200 million short after Trump cuts. *Reuter's News Agency*, www.reuters.news.com/articles/us-use-palestinians-aid/ Retrieved August 3, 2018.
ENAR (2016). *Forgotten Women: The Impact of Islamophobia on Muslim Women*. Brussels: European Network Against Racism.
Engels, F. (1845/1978). *The Condition of the Working Class in England*. London: Penguin Books.
Er, M. (2008). Corruption from an Islamic perspective. *International Journal of Islamic and Middle Eastern Finance and Management* 1(1) 31-51.

Esposito, J.L. (1998). *Islam: The Straight Path*. Oxford: Oxford University Press.

Esposito, J.L. (2003, Women in Islam. In J.L. Esposito (Ed.) *The Oxford Dictionary of Islam* (pp 339-340). Oxford: Oxford University Press.

Esposito, J. L. & DeLong-Bas, N. J. (2001). *Women in Muslim Family Law*. 2nd Edition. New York: Syracuse University Press.

Esposito, J. L. & DeLong-Bas, N. J. (2018). *Sharia: What Everyone Needs to Know*. Oxford: Oxford University Press.

Esposito, J.L. & Kalil, I. (2011). *Islamophobia: The Challenge of Pluralism in the 21st Century*. Oxford: Oxford University Press.

Essed, P. & Hoving, I. (2014). Innocence, smug ignorance, resentment: An introduction to Dutch racism. In P. Essed & I. Hoving (Eds.) *Dutch Racism*. Leiden: Brill-Rodopi.

Eva, N., Munakata, T. & Onuoha, F. (2007). Demographic correlates of constant condom use among workers in Tangail, Dhaka, Bangladesh. *Adolescence*, 42, 795-804.

Everett, H. (2018). *Faith Schools, Tolerance and Diversity: Exploring the Influence of Education on Students' Attitudes of Tolerance*. London: Palgrave MacMillan.

Ezzat, H.R. (2007). On the future of women in politics in the Arab world. In J.L. Esposito & J. Donohue (Eds.) *Islam in Transition: Muslim Perspectives* (pp 184-196). Oxford: Oxford University Press.

Ezzat, H.R. (2008). Muslim women at the cross-roads: cultural and religious rules versus religious imperatives. In H. Fadel, A. Misha'l & A. Ebrahim (Eds.) (2008). *Women's Issues: Islamic Perspective* (pp 93-100). Jordan: Federation of Islamic Medical Associations.

Farley, M., Golding, J., Matthews, E., Malamuth, N. & Jarrett, L. (2015). Comparing sex buyers with men who do not buy sex: new data on prostitution and trafficking. *Journal of Interpersonal Violence*, 11,1-25.

Farley, M. & Kelly, V. (2008). Prostitution: a critical review of the medical and social sciences literature. *Women and Criminal Justice*, 11, 29-64.

Farrar, M. (2012). Multiculturalism in the UK: a contested discourse. In M. Farrar, S. Robinson, Y. Valli & P. Wetherly (Eds.) *Islam in the West: Key Issues in Multiculturalism*. London: Palgrave MacMillan.

Fassetta, G., Imperiale, M. G., Frimberger, K., Attia, M., & Al-Masri, N. (2017). Online teacher training in a context of forced immobility: the case of Gaza, Palestine. *European Education*, 49(2-3), 133-150.

Fattah, K. N., & Kabir, Z. N. (2013). No place is safe: sexual abuse of children in rural Bangladesh. *Journal of Child Sexual Abuse*, 22(8), 901-914.

Fauveau, V. & Blanchet, T. (1989). Deaths from injuries and induced abortion among rural Bangladeshi women. *Social Science & Medicine*, *29*(9), 1121-1127.

Fazel, M., Patel, V., Thomas, S., & Tol, W. (2014). School mental health interventions in low-income and middle-income countries. *The Lancet Psychiatry*, 1, 388–398.

Fekete, L. (2008). *Integration, Islamophobia and Civil Rights in Europe*. London, UK: Institute of Race Relations.

Fekete, L. & Sivanandan, A. (2009). *A Suitable Enemy: Racism, Migration and Islamophobia in Europe*. London: Pluto Press.

Feroz, A. H. M., Islam, S. N., Reza, S., Rahman, A. M., Sen, J., Mowla, M., & Rahman, M. R. (2012). A community survey on the prevalence of suicidal attempts and deaths in a selected rural area of Bangladesh. *Journal of Medicine*, *13*(1), 3-9.

Fetzer, J. & Soper, C. (2003). The roots of public attitudes towards state accommodation of European Muslims' religious practices before and after September 11. *Journal for the Scientific Study of Religion*, 42, 247-258.

Flaschel, P. (2009). *The Macrodynamics of Capitalism: Elements for a Synthesis of Marx, Keynes and Schumpeter*. Berlin: Springer-Verlag.

Fleetwood, S. (2005) Ontology in organization and management studies: a critical realist perspective. *Organization*, 12 (2), 197-222.

Fleetwood, S. and Ackroyd, S. (2004) *Critical Realist Applications in Organisation and Management Studies*. London: Routledge.

Fleetwood, S. and Hesketh, A. (2008) Theorising under-theorisation in research on the HRM-performance link. *Personnel Review*, 37 (2), 126-144.

Forbes Magazine (2017). These women are smashing the glass ceiling in Asia – and they're all under 30. *Forbes Magazine*, December 4th, 2017, pp. 1-6.

Fortin, A. (2015). *Banishante Brothel – A Photojournal Essay*. www.alexisfortin.com/banishanta-brothel

Francke, A. (2014). *Women in Management: The Power of Role Models*. London: Chartered Management Institute.

French, D. C., Eisenberg, N., Vaughan, J., Purwono, U., & Suryanti, T. A. (2008). Religious involvement and the social competence and adjustment of Indonesian Muslim adolescents. *Developmental Psychology*, *44*(2), 597-611.

Gambles, R., Lewis, S. & Rapoport, R. (2007). *The Myth of Work-Life Balance: The Challenge of Our Time for Men, Women and Societies*. Chichester, UK: John Wiley.

Gajalakshmi, V. & Peto, R. (2007). Suicide rates in rural Tamil Nadu, South India: verbal autopsy of 39 000 deaths in 1997–98. *International Journal of Epidemiology*, *36*(1), 203-207.

Gardner, R., Cairns, K. & Lawton, D. (Eds.) (2005). *Faith Schools: Consensus or Conflict?* London: Routledge-Falmer.

Gausia K., Fisher C., Ali M. & Oosthuizen J. (2009). Antenatal depression and suicidal ideation among rural Bangladeshi women: a community-based study. *Archives of Women's Mental Health*, 12(5), 351-358.

Gay, R. (2006). *Freud: A Life for Our Time*. Boston: Little Brown.

Ghaanim al-Sadlaan, S. (1999). *The Fiqh of Marriage in the Light of the Quran and Sunnah*. Saudi Arabia: Kalmulla.Com, Online.

Ghandanfar, M.A. (2001). *Great Women of Islam*. Birmingham: Darussalam Publications.

Ghattas, H., El Asmar, K., Assi, M. J., & Obermeyer, C. M. (2017). Prevalence and predictors of double burden of malnutrition in Palestinian children younger than 5 years: analysis of data from the Multiple Indicator Cluster Surveys round four. *The Lancet*, *390*, S7.

Gholami, R. (2017). The art of self-making: identity and citizenship education in late-modernity. *British Journal of Sociology of Education*, *38*(6), 798-811.

Ghubash, R., Daradkeh, T. K., Al Naseri, K. S., Al Bloushi, N. B. A., & Al Daheri, A. M. (2000). The performance of the Center for Epidemiologic Study Depression Scale (CES-D) in an Arab female community. *International Journal of Social Psychiatry*, 46(4), 241-249.

Giacoman, R., Niveen, M., Avu-Rameiallah, A., Saab, H. & Boyce, W. (2007). Humiliation: the invisible trauma of war for Palestinian youth. *Public Health*, 121(4), 513-571.

Giacoman, R. (2018), The health of Palestinians. *The Lancet*, November 14th, Online.

Gibbs, M. (2019). Lucrative ship-scrapping sees poor Bangladeshi workers face 'abhorrent conditions with abysmal environmental protections'. *The Independent Online*, February 20, 2019.

Gieling, M., Thijs, J. & Verkuyten, M. (2010). Tolerance of practices by Muslim actors: an integrative social-development perspective. *Child Development*, 81, 1384-1399.

Gijsberts, M., & Hagendoorn, L. (2017). *Nationalism and Exclusion of Migrants: Cross-National Comparisons*. London: Routledge.

Giuliani, C., Olivari, M. G., & Alfieri, S. (2017). Being a "good" son and a "good" daughter: voices of Muslim immigrant adolescents. *Social Sciences*, *6*(4), 142, Online.

Gjelsvik, B., Heyerdahl, F., Holmes, J., Lunn, D., & Hawton, K. (2017). Looking back on self-poisoning: the relationship between depressed mood and reporting of suicidal intent in people who deliberately self-poison. *Suicide and Life-Threatening Behavior*, 47(2), 228-241.

Glass, J. and Finley, A. (2002) Coverage and effectiveness of family-responsive workplace policies. *Human Resource Management Review*, 12 (3), 313-337.

Glennon, R. (2017). The unfolding tragedy of climate change in Bangladesh. *Scientific American*, April 21st, 2017, Online.

Goffman, E. (1978). *The Presentation of Self in Everyday Life*. London: Penguin Books.

Gohir, S. (2010). The hypocrisy of child abuse in many Muslim countries. *The Guardian Online*, April 24th.

Gomes, S. (2013) Time and work/life balance of individual in society. *International Journal of Business Intelligence*, 2, 155-158.

Gone, J. P. & Alcántara, C. (2010). The ethnographically contextualized case study method. *Cultural Diversity and Ethnic Minority Psychology*, 16(2), 159-168.

Gonzales, V., Verkuyten, M., Weesie, J. & Poppe, E. (2008). Prejudice towards Muslims in The Netherlands: testing integrated threat theory. *British Journal of Social Psychology*, 47, 667-685.

Gordon, J. S., Staples, J. K., Blyta, A., & Bytyqi, M. (2004). Treatment of posttraumatic stress disorder in postwar Kosovo high school students using mind–body skills groups. *Journal of Traumatic Stress*, 17(2), 143-147.

Gordon, J. S. (2014). Mind-body skills groups for medical students: reducing stress, enhancing commitment, and promoting patient-centered care. *BMC Medical Education*, 14(1), 198-205.

Gordon, S. (2016). Women hold just a sixth of senior roles at top UK companies. *Financial Times* online, May 16th.

Gorski. P. (2013). What is Critical Realism? And why should you care? *Contemporary Sociology*, 42, 658-670.

GoP (2018). *Contraceptive Performance Report 2016-17*. Islamabad: Bureau of Statistics, Government of Pakistan, www.pbs.gov.pk

Grant, K. (2017). Discarded Daughters: the harrowing film speaking up for Pakistan's unwanted girls - review of a film by Maheen Sidiq. *INews Online*, April 7th, 2017.https://inews.co.uk

Gray, D. (2018). *Doing Research in the Real World*. London: Sage.

Gray, T. (2019). *Teaching from the Tent: Muslim Women's Leadership in Digital Religion*. St. Paul, MI: University of St. Thomas, Doctoral Dissertation.

Grech, V. & Mamo, J. (2014). Gendercide – a review of missing women. *Malta Medical Journal*, 26(1) 8-11.
Green, A. (2019). HIV epidemic in children in Pakistan. *Lancet* Vol. 393, 2288, June 8th, 2019 Online.
Greenslade, R. (2005). *New Jews: Scapegoating Muslims*. London: Institute of Public Policy Research.
Gregory, A. and Milner, S. (2009) Trade unions and work life balance: changing times in France and the UK? *British Journal of Industrial Relations*, 47 (1), 122-146.
Grierson, J. (2019). "My son was terrified": how Prevent alienates UK Muslims. *Guardian Online*, January 27, 2019.
Griffin, R. (2012). *Terrorist's Creed: Fanatical Violence and the Human Need for Meaning*. New York: Springer.
Grine, F. (2014). Empowering Muslim women through coaching and mentoring. *International Journal of Nusantara Islam*, 2(1), 54–68.
Gunnell, D., Knipe, D., Chang, S.-S. & Four Others (2017). Prevention of suicide with regulations aimed at restricting access to highly hazardous pesticides: a systematic review of the international evidence. *Lancet Global Health*, August 11, Online.
Hadi A. (2005). Risk factors of violent death in rural Bangladesh, 1990-1999. *Death Studies*, 29(6), 559–572.
Haeri, S. (2007). Resilience and post-traumatic recovery in cultural and political context: two Pakistani women's strategies for survival. *Journal of Aggression, Maltreatment & Trauma*, 14(1-2), 287-304.
Haider, Z.H. (2013). *The Ideological Struggle for Pakistan*. Stanford, CA: Hoover Press.
Haines, W. (2000). Identity and authority in citizenship education. *Muslim Educational Quarterly*, 18, 1-7.
Haj-Yahia, M. M. (2000). Wife abuse and battering in the sociocultural context of Arab society. *Family Process*, 39(2), 237-255.
Haj-Yahia, M.M. (2018). Beliefs of Palestinian women from Israel about responsibility and punishment of violent husbands. *Journal of Interpersonal Violence*, 33 (3) 442-467.
Halbfinger, D. (2019). A strange symbiosis: why Israel and Gaza keep fighting brief battles. *New York Times Online*, May 8th, 2019.
Halim K.S., Khondker L., Wahab M.A., Nargis F., Khan S.I. (2010). Various factors of attempted suicide in a selected area of Naogaon district. *Mymensingh Medical Journal* 19(2), 244-249.
Hall, S. (2000). Multicultural citizens: monocultural citizenship. In N. Perace, N. & J. Hallgarten (Eds) *Tomorrow's Citizens: Critical Debates*

in Citizenship and Education. London: Institute for Public Policy Research.

Hallaq, W. B. (2009). *Sharī'a: Theory, Practice, Transformations.* Cambridge: Cambridge University Press.

Halstead, J. M. (2018). Islamic education in the West and its challenges. In M. Woodward & R. Lukens (Eds) *Handbook of Contemporary Islam and Muslim Lives* (pp100-125). Leiden: Brill.

Hamdan, M. (2017). Burnout among workers in emergency departments in Palestinian hospitals: prevalence and associated factors. *BMC Health Services Research*, 17(1), 407, Online.

Hamid, S. (2006). Models of Muslim youth work: between reform and empowerment. *Youth and Policy*, 92, 81-89.

Hantrais, L. (2000) *Gendered Policies in Europe: Reconciling Employment and Family life.* London: Palgrave Macmillan.

Haque, R. (2015). *Voices from the Edge: Justice, Agency and the Plight of Floating Sex Workers in Dhaka, Bangladesh.* Zurich: Lit Verlag for Spectrum 111, Berlin Series on Society, Economy and Politics in Developing Countries,

Harsha, N., Ziq, L., Ghandour, R., & Giacaman, R. (2016). Well-being and associated factors among adults in the occupied Palestinian territory (oPt). *Health and Quality of Life Outcomes*, 14(1), 122.

Haseen, F., Chawdhury, F. A. H., Hossain, M. E., Huq, M., Bhuiyan, M. U., Imam, H., ... & Ahmed, J. (2012). Sexually transmitted infections and sexual behaviour among youth clients of hotel-based female sex workers in Dhaka, Bangladesh. *International journal of STD & AIDS*, 23(8), 553-559.

Hashemi, B., Ali, S., Awaad, R., Soudi, L., Housel, L., & Sosebee, S. J. (2017). Facilitating mental health screening of war-torn populations using mobile applications. *Social Psychiatry and Psychiatric Epidemiology*, 52(1), 27-33.

Hashmi, T. (2000). *Women and Islam in Bangladesh: Beyond Subjugation and Tyranny.* London: Palgrave MacMillan.

Hassan, A. & Choudhury, M.A. (2019). *Islamic Economics: Theory and Practice.* London: Routledge.

Hassan, Z. (2018). Young British Muslims are becoming more liberal – but they aren't less religious as a result. *The Independent Online*, May 5th, 2018.

Hathaway, R. M., & Lee, W. (Eds.). (2004). *Islamization and the Pakistani Economy.* Washington, DC: Woodrow Wilson International Center for Scholars.

Hawke, G. & Alderson, P. (Eds.) (2017). *Roy Bhaskar's The Order of Natural Necessity: A Kind of Introduction to Critical Realism*. London: Institute of Education, University of London.

Hawke, S., Morison, L., & Foster, S. (1999). Reproductive tract infection in low-Income areas: assessment of syndromic management in Matlab, Bangladesh. *The Lancet*, 354, 1776-1786.

Hawton, K. (2005). *Prevention and Treatment of Suicidal Behaviour: From Science to Practice*. Oxford: Oxford University Press.

Hawton, K. & O'Connor, R. (2012). *Suicide: Major Themes in Health and Welfare*. London: Routledge.

Hawton, K., Witt, K. G., Salisbury, T. L. T., Arensman, E., Gunnell, D., Hazell, P., ... & van Heeringen, K. (2016). Psychosocial interventions following self-harm in adults: a systematic review and meta-analysis. *The Lancet Psychiatry*, 3(8), 740-750.

Hayman, J. (2005) Psychometric assessment of an instrument designed to measure work life balance. *Research and Practice in Human Resource Management*, 13, 85-91.

Hayman, J. & Rasmussen, E. (2013) Gender, caring, part-time employment and work/life balance. *Employment Relations Record*, 13(1) 45-58.

Hazarika, G. (2011). Gender issues in children's nutrition security in Pakistan. In M. Kugelman & R. Hathaway (Eds.) *Empty Bellies, Broken Dreams: Food Insecurity and the Future of Pakistan* (pp 86-98). Lahore: Vanguard Books for The Woodrow Wilson International Centre.

Heater, D. (1999). *What is Citizenship?* Cambridge: Polity Press.

Heater, D. (2001). The history of citizenship in England. *The Curriculum Journal*, 12, 103-123.

Heath, A. (2018). *Social Progress in Britain*. Oxford: Oxford University Press.

Heath, A. (2019). *Ethnic Penalties in the Labour Market: Further Studies of Discrimination*. Oxford: Centre for Social Investigation.

Heath, A. & Cheung, S. (2006) *Ethnic Penalties in the Labour Market: Employers and Discrimination*. Research Report No. 341. London: Department of Work and Pensions.

Heath, A. & Li, Y. (2015a) The relationship between religion and poverty. Paper presented to SOAS-Nohoudh Muslim Integration Conference November 5th, 2015. London: SOAS, University of London.

Heath, A. & Li, Y. (2015b). Review of the relationship between religion and poverty; an analysis for the Joseph Rowntree Foundation. CSI Working paper 2015-01. Downloaded from http://csi.nuff.ox.ac.uk/

Hegewisch, A. and Gornick, J. (2011) The impact of work-family policies on women's employment: a review of research from OECD countries. *Community, Work and Family,* 14 (2), 119-138.

Heinen, B. & Mulvaney, R. (2008) Global factors influencing work-life policies and practices: description and implications for multinational companies. *World at Work Journal,* 17 (1), 34.

Held, D. & McGrew, A. (1999). *Global Transformation, Politics, Economics and Culture.* Cambridge: Polity Press.

Helgeson, S. & Johnson, J. (1990 & 2010). *The Female Vision: Women's Real Power at Work.* 1st and 2nd Editions. San Francisco: Barrett-Koehler Publishers.

Helgeson, S. (2017). *The Female Advantage: Women's Ways of Leadership.* https://sallyhelgeson.com

Helm, S. (2018). Suicide in Gaza: how the death of a talented young Palestinian writer brought to light a sharp rise in suicides. *The Guardian Online,* May 18th, 2008.

Hengartner, M. P., Islam, M. N., Haker, H., & Rössler, W. (2015). Mental health and functioning of female sex workers in Chittagong, Bangladesh. *Frontiers in Psychiatry,* 6, 176, Online.

Her Majesty's Inspectorate (HMI) (2003). *National Curriculum Citizenship: Planning and Implementation.* London: Office for Standards in Education.

Hesketh A. &, Fleetwood S (2006) Human resource management–performance research: Under-theorized and lacking explanatory power. *International Journal of Human Resource Management,* 17(12): 1977–1993.

Heszlein-Lossius, H., Al-Borno, Y., Shaqoura, S., Skaik, N., Giil, L. M., & Gilbert, M. (2018a). Severe extremity amputations in surviving Palestinian civilians caused by explosives fired from drones during the Gaza War. *The Lancet,* 391, S15.

Heszlein-Lossius, H. E., Al-Borno, Y., Shaqqoura, S., Skaik, N., Giil, L. M., & Gilbert, M. (2018b). Life after conflict-related amputation trauma: a clinical study from the Gaza Strip. *BMC International Health and Human Rights,* 18(1), 34, Online.

Hewer, C. (2001). Schools for Muslims. *Oxford Review of Education,* 27, 515-28.

Hewitt, I. (2001). Public education and Muslim voluntary organisations. *Westminster Journal of Education,* 24, 129-136.

Hilal, H. (2015). Perceptions towards female leadership in Malaysia. *Journal of Modern Education Review,* 5(1), 8-14.

Hodson, H. (2014). Gaza conflict will traumatise a generation of children. *New Scientist*, July 22, 4.
Hofstede, G. (1997). *Organizations and Cultures: Software of the Mind*. New York: McGraw Hill.
Holmes, O. & Balousha, H, (2019). Gaza generation blockade: young lives in the 'world's largest prison camp'. *The Guardian Online*, March 12th, 2019.
Holmwood, J. & O'Toole, T. (2018), *Countering Extremism in British Schools? The Truth about the Birmingham Trojan Horse Affair*. Bristol: The Policy Press.
Home Office (1999). *Stephen Lawrence Inquiry: Home Secretary's Action Plan*. London: Home Office.
Home Office (2002a). *Secure borders, safe haven integration with diversity in Britain (The White Paper)*. London: Home Office.
Home office, Community Cohesion Unit (2002b). Cited in A. Osler, A. & V. Vincent (2002). *Citizenship and the Challenge of Global Education*. Stoke, UK: Trentham Books.
Hosain, G. & Chatterjee, N. (2005). Beliefs, sexual behaviours and preventive practices with respect to HIV/AIDS among commercial sex workers. *Public Health*, 119, 371-381.
Hossain, M., Marci, K., Sidik, S., Shahar, S. & Islam, R. (2014). Knowledge and awareness about STDs among women in Bangladesh. *BMC Public Health*, 14, 774-778.
Hossain, M. G., Mahumud, R. A., & Saw, A. (2016). Prevalence of child marriage among Bangladeshi women and trend of change over time. *Journal of Biosocial Science*, 48(4), 530-538.
Hossain, S. (2010). *Urban Poverty in Bangladesh: Slum Communities, Migration and Social Integration*. London: IB Tauris Academic Studies.
Howgega, J. (2019). Most rigorous test of basic income yet. *New Scientist*, February 16th, p. 10.
HRCP (2004). *National Commission on the Status of Women: Report on Hudood Ordinance of 1979*. Lahore: Human Rights Commission of Pakistan.
HRCP (2017). *State of Human Rights in 2016*. Lahore: Human Rights Commission of Pakistan.
HRCP (2018). *State of Human Rights in 2017*. Lahore: Human Rights Commission of Pakistan.
HRCP (2019). *State of Human Rights in 2018*. Lahore: Human Rights Commission of Pakistan.
HRW (2016). *Preventing Education? Human Rights and UK Counter-Terrorism Policy in Schools*. London: Human Rights Watch UK.

HRW (2018). *'Shall I feed My Daughter or Educate Her?' Barriers to Girls Education in Pakistan.* New York: Human Rights Watch.
Huda, M.N. & Ferdous, A. (2018). The impact of HIV/AIDS education through formal curriculum and texts in Bangladesh: a study of secondary and higher secondary education students. *International Journal of Public Health,* 2(2) 94-105.
Huda T., Hayes A., El Arifeen S. & Dibley M. (2017) Social determinants of inequalities in child undernutrition in Bangladesh: a decomposition analysis. *Maternal and Child Nutrition,* March 8, Online.
Huddleston, T. & Kerr, D. (2006). *Making Sense of Citizenship: A Continuing Professional Development Handbook.* London: Hodder Murray Educational Books.
Hudy, S. (2006). Sex trafficking in South Asia. *International Journal of Gynaecology and Obstetrics,* 94, 374-381.
Huff, T. E. (2017). *The Rise of Early Modern Science.* Cambridge: Cambridge University Press.
Husain, E. (2007). *The Islamist: Why I Joined Radical Islam in Britain. What I Saw Inside and Why I Left.* London: Penguin.
Husain, E. (2013). End the Arab boycott of Israel. *New York Times Online,* March 7th, 2013.
Husain, E. (2018). *The House of Islam: A Global History.* London: Bloomsbury Publishing.
Hussain, R., Yusuf, H. R., Akhter, H. H., Rahman, M. H., & Rochat, R. W. (2000). Injury-related deaths among women aged 10–50 years in Bangladesh, 1996–97. *The Lancet,* 355(9211), 1220-1224.
Hussain, R., Yusuf, H. R., Akhter, H. H., Chowdhury, M. E., & Rochat, R.W. (2007). Causes of death among women aged 10–50 years in Bangladesh, 1996–1997. *Journal of Health, Population, and Nutrition,* 25(3), 302-311.
Hussain, Y. & Bagguley, P. (2007). *Moving on Up: South Asian Women and Higher Education.* Stoke, UK: Trentham Books.
Hussain, Y. (2017). *Writing Diaspora: South Asian Women, Culture and Ethnicity.* London: Routledge.
Hutchings, K., Metcalfe, B. D. & Cooper, B. K. (2010). Exploring Arab Middle Eastern women's perceptions of barriers to, and facilitators of, international management opportunities. *The International Journal of Human Resource Management,* 21(1), 61-83.
Ibrahim, E. & Wadoud, A. (Translators) (1989). *An-Nawawi's Forty Hadith.* Lebanon: The Holy Koran Publishing House.
Ildiagbon-Oke, M. & Oke, A. (2011) Implementing innovative flexible work practices in Nigerian local firms: Implications for management of

change in less-developed countries. *Journal of Occupational and Organizational Psychology,* 84 (3), 518-543.

IHRC (2019). *Tony Blair Institute Report a 'Narrative of Divison': A Critique.* London: Islamic Human Rights Council.

Ijaz, A. (2017a). Climate change and internal migration in Pakistan. *The Diplomat Online*, August 22nd, 2017.

Ijaz, S. (2017b). 'Honor' killings continue in Pakistan despite new law. *Human Rights Watch Dispatches* September 25th, 2017, Online.

ILO (1998). *Sex and Trafficking in South East Asia.* Geneva: International Labor Organization.

ILO (2015). *Women in Business and Management: Gathering Momentum.* Geneva: International Labor Organization.

Iqbal, Z. & Mirakhar, M. (2007). *An Introduction to Islamic Finance: Theory and Practice.* New York: John Wiley.

ISJ (2014). *Child Marriages in Pakistan.* Islamabad: Institute for Social Justice.

Islam, A. & Smith, R. (2016). Economics of prostitution in Bangladesh. In Cunningham, S., & Shah, M. (Eds.). (2016). *The Oxford Handbook of the Economics of Prostitution* (pp. 210-226). Oxford: Oxford University Press.

Islam, M. & Conigrave, K. (2008). HIV and sexual risk behaviors among recognized high-risk groups in Bangladesh: need for a comprehensive prevention program. *International Journal of Infectious Diseases*, 12, 363-370.

Islam, M. K., Haque, M. R., & Hossain, M. B. (2016). Regional variations in child marriage in Bangladesh. *Journal of Biosocial Science*, 48(5), 694-708.

Islam M. M. & Islam M. (2003). Pattern of unnatural death in a city mortuary: a 10-year retrospective study. *Legal Medicine* 5, S354–S356.

Islam, S. M., & Johnson, C. A. (2003). Correlates of smoking behavior among Muslim Arab-American adolescents. *Ethnicity & Health*, 8(4), 319-337.

Islams Women (2017). *The Fiqh of Marriage.* www.islamswomen.com, consulted August 19, 2017.

Iwuji, C. C., McGrath, N., de Oliveira, T., Porter, K., Pillay, D., Fisher, M., ... & Newell, M. L. (2015). The art of HIV elimination: past and present science. *Journal of AIDS & clinical research*, 6, Online.

Jabnoun, N. (2012). *Islam and Management: Your Ultimate Guide to Running a Business from an Islamic perspective.* Riyadh: International Islamic Publishing House.

Jaffery, R. (2018a). Pakistan's climate challenge. *The Diplomat Online*, March 21st, 2018.
Jaffery, R. (2018b). Pakistan's biodiversity is disappearing, but no one seems to notice. *The Diplomat Online*, December 1st, 2018.
Jafri, A. H. (2008). *Honour Killing: Dilemma, Ritual, Understanding*. Oxford: Oxford University Press.
Jalalzai, F. (2013). *Shattered, Cracked, or Firmly Intact? Women and the Executive Glass Ceiling Worldwide*. Oxford: Oxford University Press.
Jamal, A. (2009) *Barriers to Democracy: The Other Side of Social Capital in Palestine and the Arab world*. Princeton, NJ: Princeton University Press.
Jamaluddin, Z., Manaf, A., Sayuti, R., Rajwani, M.Z. & Noor, A.A. (2018). Sexuality and sources of information: a study of unwed teenage mothers in women's shelter in Malaysia. *International Journal of Academic Research in Business and Social Sciences* 8(11), November, Online.
James, W. (1890). Selections from *The Principles of Psychology*. In H. Thayer (Ed.) *Pragmatism: The Classic Writings* (pp. 135-179). New York: New American Library.
Jameson, R. (2016). *The Case for a Basic Income*. London: IMOS-Socrates Publications.
Jamili, D., Sidani, Y. & Safieddine, A. (2005) Constraints facing working women in Lebanon: an insider view. *Women in Management Review*, 20(8): 581-594.
Janjua, H. (2018). 'I've never been to school': child waste pickers living on Pakistan's streets. *The Guardian Online* March 25h, 2018.
Jaques, M. (2018). *Gaza Girls: Growing Up in the Gaza Strip*. New York: FotoEvidence Publishers.
Jeffrey, L. (2003). *Sex and Borders: Gender, National Identity, and Prostitution Policy in Thailand*. Vancouver: University of British Columbia Press.
Jenkins, C. & Rahman, H. (2002). Rapidly changing conditions in the brothels of Bangladesh: impact on HIV/STDs. *Aids Education and Prevention*, 14, 97-106.
Jensen, R. (2017). *End of Patriarchy: Radical Feminism for Men*. Victoria, Australia: Spinifex.
Jha, P. K., Sahu, D., Reddy, K. S., Narayan, P., & Pandey, A. (2014). Multiple sexual partners and vulnerability to HIV: a study of patterns of sexual behaviour in the slum population of India. *World Journal of AIDS*, 4(04), 373.
Joas, H. (1997). *GH Mead: A Contemporary Re-Examination of His Thought*. Boston, Mass: MIT press.

Joffres, C., Mills, E., Joffres, M., Khanna, T., Walia, H., & Grund, D. (2008). Sexual slavery without borders: trafficking for commercial sexual exploitation in India. *International Journal for Equity in Health*, *7*(1), 22-35.

Jonassen, M., Shaheen, A., Duraidi, M., Qalalwa, K. Jeune, J. & Brønnum-Hansen, H. (2018). Socio-economic status and chronic disease in the West Bank and the Gaza Strip: in and outside refugee camps. *International Journal of Public Health*, 63, 875-882.

Jones, F., Burke, R.J. & Westman, M. (Eds.) (2013) *Work-Life balance: A Psychological Perspective*. Hove, UK: Psychology Press.

Jong, A. D. (2018). Zionist hegemony, the settler colonial conquest of Palestine and the problem with conflict: a critical genealogy of the notion of binary conflict. *Settler Colonial Studies*, *8*(3), 364-383.

Jong, A.D. (2019). Gaza, Black Face and Islamophobia: intersectionality of race and gender in (counter-) discourse in the Netherlands. In K. Farquharson, K. Pillay and P. Essed (eds.) *Relating Worlds of Racism: Dehumanization, Belonging and the Normativity of Whiteness* (pp 237-257). London: Palgrave Macmillan.

Joppke, C. (2004). The retreat of multiculturalism and the liberal state: theory and practice. *British Journal of Sociology*, 55, 237-257.

Joppke, C. (2009). Limits of integration policy: Britain and her Muslims. *Journal of Ethnic and Migration Studies*, 35, 453-472.

Jordans, M. J., Kaufman, A., Brenman, N. F., Adhikari, R. P., Luitel, N. P., Tol, W. A., & Komproe, I. (2014). Suicide in South Asia: a scoping review. *BMC Psychiatry*, *14*(1), 358, Online.

Jorm, A., Ross, A. & Colucci, E. (2018). Cross-cultural generalizability of suicide first aid actions: an analysis of agreement across expert consensus studies from a range of countries and cultures. *BMC Psychiatry*, March 1;18(1):58. doi: 10.1186/s12888-018-1636-8.

Jowell, R. & Prescott-Clark, P. (1970) Racial discrimination and white collar workers in Britain. *Race and Class*, 11 (4) 398-417.

JRF (2015). *Poverty and Ethnicity: Research and Quantitative Reports by Finney, Cartney, Brynin, Nandi and Green*. York, UK: Joseph Rowntree Foundation.

Junaidi, I. (2016). Economic inequality rising in Pakistan. *Dawn Online*, July 30th, 2016.

Jung, M. (2016). *Forgotten Women: The Impact of Islamophobia on Muslim Women in The Netherlands*. Brussels: European Network Against Racism.

Kabasakal, H. & Bodur, M. (2002). Arabic cluster: a bridge between East and West. *Journal of World Business,* 37 (1), 40-54.

Kagitcibasi, C., Ataca, B. & Diri, A. (2010). Intergenerational relationships in the family: ethnic, socioeconomic, and country variations in Germany, Israel, Palestine, and Turkey. *Journal of Cross-Cultural Psychology*, 41 (5-6), 652-670.

Kalafatoglu, T. & Mendosa, X. (2017). The impact of gender and culture on networking and venture creation: an exploratory study in Turkey and the MENA region. *Cross-Cultural and Strategic Marketing*, 24(2), 332-349.

Kalin, I. (2011). Islamophobia and the limits of multiculturalism. In J. Esposito and I. Kalin (Eds) *Islamophobia: The Challenge of Pluralism in the 21st Century* (pp 3-20). Oxford: Oxford University Press.

Kamal S., Hassan C. & Salikon R. (2015). Safer sex negotiation and its association with condom use among clients of female sex workers in Bangladesh. *Asia Pacific Journal of Public Health*, 27, 410-422.

Kamali, M. (2003). *Principles of Islamic Jurisprudence*. Cambridge: Islamic Texts Society.

Kamal-ud-Din, K. (2010). *Five Pillars of Islam*. Woking: Muslim Mission & Literary Trust.

Kamenou, N., & Fearful, A. (2006). Ethnic minority women: a lost voice in HRM. *Human Resource Management Journal*, 16(2), 154–172.

Kamla, R. (2017). Religious-based resistance strategies, politics of authenticity and professional women's accounts. *Critical Perspectives in Accounting*, August, Online.

Kangaslampi, S., Punamäki, R. L., Qouta, S., Diab, M., & Peltonen, K. (2016). Psychosocial group intervention among war-affected children: an analysis of changes in posttraumatic cognitions. *Journal of Traumatic Stress*, 29(6), 546-555.

Karabell, Z. (2007). *Peace Be Upon You: Fourteen Centuries of Muslim, Christian and Jewish Conflict and Co-operation*. New York: Random House-Knopf.

Kargwell, S. (2008). Is the glass ceiling kept in place in Sudan? Gendered dilemma of the work-life balance. *Gender in Management: An International Journal*, 23(3), 209-224.

Karki, C. (2011). Suicide: leading cause of death among women in Nepal. *Kathmandu University Medical Journal* 9(3), 157-158.

Kassam, Z., Kirk-Duggan, C. A., & Ashcraft-Easton, L. (2010). *Women and Islam*. Malaysia: International Islamic University of Malaysia.

Kassam, Z. (2014). Dignity and relationality. In M. Birkel (Ed.) *Qur'an in Conversation* (pp 137-145). Baylor TX: Baylor University Press.

Katchapati, S., Singh, D., Rawal, B. & Lim, A. (2017). Sexual risk behaviours, HIV and syphilis in female sex workers in Nepal. *HIV AIDS*, 9, 9-18.

Katz, K., McDowell, M., Green, M. & Three Others (2015). Understanding the broader sexual and reproductive health needs of female sex workers in Dhaka, Bangladesh. *International Perspectives on Sexual and Reproductive Health*, 41, 182-90.

Kaur-Ballagan, K., Mortimore, R. & Gottfried, G. (2018). *A Review of Survey Research on Muslims in Britain*. London: Ipsos MORI Social Research Institute

Keating, A. & Benton, T. (2013). Creating cohesive citizens in England? Exploring the role of diversity, deprivation and democratic climate at school. *Education, Citizenship and Social Justice, 8*(2), 165-184.

Keating, A., Kerr, D., Benton, T., Mundy, E. & Lopes, J. (2010). *Citizenship Education in England 200 –2010: Young People's Practices and Prospects for the Future*. London: Department for Education, Research Report DFE-RR059.

Kemp, L. J., Madsen, S. & Davis, J. (2015). Women in business leadership: a comparative study of countries in the Arab Gulf states. *International Journal of Cross Cultural Management*, 15(2), 215-233.

Kerr, D. (2002). Citizenship education: an international comparison across sixteen countries. *International Journal of Social Education*, 17, 1–15.

Kerr, D., Lines, A., Blenkinsop, S. & Schagen, I. (2002). *England's Results from the IEA International Citizenship Education Study*. Norwich: The Queen's Printer.

Kerfoot, D. & Knights, D. (1994). Into the realm of the fearful: power, identity and the gender problematic. In H.L. Radtke and H.J. Stam (Eds.) *Power/Gender: Social Relations in Theory and Practice* (pp 67-88). London: Sage.

Kessler, E. (2013). *Jews, Christians and Muslims in Encounter*. London: SCM Press.

Kfir, I. (2014). Feminist legal theory as a way to explain the lack of progress of women's rights in Afghanistan: the need for a state strength approach. *William & Mary Journal of Women & Law*, 87(1) 5-20.

Khaderi, A. (2018). *Peacebuilding Citizenship Education in a Muslim Majority Context: Challenges and Opportunities in Bangladeshi Public Schools*. Toronto: Ontario Institute for the Study of Education, University of Toronto, Doctoral Dissertation.

Khan, A.A. (2014). Religious education and identity formation: a case study of Pakistan. *South Asian Journal of Diplomacy*, Annual Issue, 75-85, Online.

Khan, F. (2014). The Final Prophet. In M. Birkel (Ed.) *Qur'an in Conversation* (pp 148-161). Baylor TX: Baylor University Press.
Khan, M.J. & Jinnat, M.A (2019). While drug lords in jail, family members, agents oversee narco business. *Daily Star (Dhaka)*, April 25th, 2019, Online.
Khan, M. M. & Reza, H. (2000). The pattern of suicide in Pakistan. *Crisis* 21(1), 31–35.
Khan, M. M. (2005). Suicide prevention and developing countries. *Journal of the Royal Society of Medicine*, 98(10), 459-463.
Khan, M. H. (2012). *Principles of Islam*. New York & Birmingham, UK: Goodword Books and Islamic Vision Distributors.
Khan, M. (2013). Reducing harassment of female sex workers (FSWS) in low income settings: tripartite approach in Bangladesh. *Sexually Transmitted Infections*, 89,329.
Khan, S., & Ahmed, S. (2010). *Pakistani Women: Multiple Locations and Competing Narratives*. Oxford: Oxford University Press.
Khan, T. S. (2006). *Beyond Honour: A Historical Materialist Explanation of Honour Related Violence*. Oxford: Oxford University Press.
Khan, T.S. (2007). *Zina, Transnational Feminism, and The Moral Regulation of Pakistani Women*. Vancouver: University of British Columbia Press.
Khankan, S. (2018). *Women are the Future of Islam: A Memoir of Hope*. London: Penguin-Random House.
Khattab, N. & Modood, T. (2015). Both ethnic and religious: employment penalties across 14 ethno-religious groups in the United Kingdom. *Journal for the Scientific Study of Religion*, 54(3) 501-522.
Khawaja, M. (2002). The fertility of Palestinian women in Gaza, the West Bank, Jordan and Lebanon. *Population*, 58, 273-302.
King, A. & Reiss, M. (Eds.) (1993). *The Multicultural Dimension of the National Curriculum*. London: The Falmer Press.
King N. (2004). Using templates in the thematic analysis of text. In Cassell C & Symon G (Eds) *Essential Guide to Qualitative Methods in Organisational Research* (pp 256–270). London: Sage Publications.
King, K. (2016). *From Personal to Political: My Journey Through Sexual Exploitation*. Edmonton, Alberta: Sexual Exploitation Working Group.
Kisby, B. (2007). New Labour and citizenship education. *Parliamentary Affairs*, 60(1), 84-101.
Kisby, B. (2009). Social capital and citizenship lessons in England: analysing the presuppositions of Citizenship education. *Education, Citizenship and Social Justice*, 4(1),41-61.

Kisby, B. (2012). *The Labour Party and Citizenship Education: Policy Networks and the Introduction of Citizenship Lessons in Schools*. Manchester: Manchester University Press.

Kisby, B. (2017). 'Politics is ethics done in public': exploring linkages and disjunctions between citizenship education and character education in England. *Journal of Social Science Education*, 16(3), 7-20.

Kitabayashi, H., Chiang, C., Al-Shoaibi, A. A. A., Hirakawa, Y., & Aoyama, A. (2017). Association between maternal and child health and quality of antenatal care services in Palestine. *Maternal and Child Health Journal*, 21(12), 2161-2168.

Knights, D. (2015). Binaries need to shatter for bodies to matter: do disembodied masculinities undermine organizational ethics? *Organization*, 22(2), 200-216.

Knights, D. (2017). Introduction to 'Masculinities: a non/contested terrain'. Special issue of *Gender Work and Organisation*.

Koehler, B. (2011). Female entrepreneurship in early Islam. *Economic Affairs*, 31(2), 93-95.

Kolb, D. (1984). *Experiential Learning: Experience as the Source of Learning and Development*. Englewood Cliffs, NJ: Prentice Hall.

Kolda, U. & Çıraklı, M. (2019). *National Prospects and Regional Challenges for Internationalization of the Palestinian Higher Education: On the Margins of Globalization*. Hershey, PENN: IGO Global.

Kreitman, N. (1977). *Parasuicide*. Chichester, UK: Wiley.

Kremer, M. (2013). *The Netherlands: From National Identity to Plural Identifications*. Washington, DC: Migration Policy Institute.

Krug, E. G., Dahlberg, L. L., Mercy, J. A., Zwi, A. B. & Lozano, R. (2000). *World Report on Violence and Health*. Geneva: World Health Organization.

Kugelman, M. & Hathaway, R. (Eds.) *Empty Bellies, Broken Dreams: Food Insecurity and the Future of Pakistan*. Lahore: Vanguard Books for The Woodrow Wilson International Center.

Kumra, S. & Manfredi, S. (2012). *Managing Equality and Diversity: Theory and Practice*. London: Oxford University Press.

Kultab, E. (2006). The paradox of women's work. In L. Taraki (Ed.) *Living Palestine: Family Survival, Resistance and Mobility Under Occupation* (pp 231-270). New York: Syracuse University Press.

Kunert-Graf, R. (2018). Dehumanized victims: analogies and animal avatars for Palestinian suffering. *Humanities*, 7(3), 79.

Kundari, A. (2007). *The End of Tolerance: Racism in Twenty First Century Britain*. London: Pluto Press.

Kunst, J. R., Sadeghi, T., Tahir, H., Sam, D., & Thomsen, L. (2016). The vicious circle of religious prejudice: Islamophobia makes the acculturation attitudes of majority and minority members clash. *European Journal of Social Psychology*, 46(2), 249-259.

Labrique A.B., Sikder S.S., Wu L., Rashid M., Ali H., Ullah B., Shamim A.A., Mehra S., Klemm R., Banu H., West Jr. K.P. & Christian P. (2013). Beyond pregnancy - the neglected burden of mortality in young women of reproductive age in Bangladesh: a prospective cohort study. *BJOG: An International Journal of Obstetrics and Gynaecology* 120(9), 1085-1089.

Lacey, D. (2011). The role of humiliation in the Palestinian/Israeli conflict in Gaza. *Psychology and Society*, 4, 76-92.

Lakhani, A. (2005). Bride-burning: the "elephant in the room" is out of control. *Pepperdine Dispute Resolution Journal*, 5, 249-298.

Lamrabet, A. (2016). *Women in the Qur'an: An Emancipatory Reading*. Leicester, UK: Kube Publishing.

Lange-Nielsen, I. I., Kolltveit, S., Thabet, A. A. M., Dyregrov, A., Pallesen, S., Johnsen, T. B., & Laberg, J. C. (2012). Short-term effects of a writing intervention among adolescents in Gaza. *Journal of Loss and Trauma*, 17(5), 403-422.

Lancet (2017). Suicide prevention: keeping the momentum. *Lancet Global Health*, 5, e838, Online.

Lapidus, I. (2002). *A History of Islamic Societies*. Cambridge: Cambridge University Press.

Law, L. (2003). *Sex Work in Southeast Asia: The Place of Desire in a Time of Aids*. London: Routledge-Taylor & Francis.

Law, I. (2013). *Racism and Ethnicity*. London: Routledge.

Lawton, D., Cairns, J. & Gardner, R. (Eds) (2000). *Education for Citizenship*. London: Continuum Books.

Leach, E. R. (1974). *Political Systems of Highland Burma: A Study of Kachin Social Structure*. London: Athlone Press.

Lean, N. (2012). *The Islamophobia Industry: How the Right Manufactures Fear of Muslims*. London: Pluto Press.

Legge, H., Shaheen, A., Shakhshir, G., & Milojevic, A. (2018). Access to water and morbidity in children in the occupied Palestinian territory, 2000–14: a repeated cross-sectional study. *The Lancet*, 391, S8.

Lester D. & Rogers, I (2013). *Suicide: A Global Issue*. New York: Praeger; 2013.

Lester, D. (2014). *Suicide Prevention*. London: Routledge.

Levitt, H. M., Motulsky, S. L., Wertz, F. J., Morrow, S. L., & Ponterotto, J. G. (2017). Recommendations for designing and reviewing qualitative research in psychology: promoting methodological integrity. *Qualitative Psychology*, 4(1), 2-17.

Lewis, B. (1984). *The Jews of Islam*. Princeton: Princeton University Press.

Lewis, D. (2011). *Bangladesh: Politics, Economy and Civil Services*. Cambridge: Cambridge University Press.

Lewis, P. & Hamid, S. (2018). *British Muslims: New Directions in Islamic Thought, Creativity and Activism*. Edinburgh: Edinburgh University Press.

Lewis, S., Gambles, R. & Rapoport, R. (2007). The constraints of a 'work-life' balance approach: an international perspective. *International Journal of Human Resources Management*, 18(3), 360-373.

Li, Y. & Heath, A. (2008) Minority ethnic men in British labour market (1972-2005). *International Journal of Sociology and Social Policy* 28 (5), 231-244.

Lidz, V. (2009). Talcott Parsons on full citizenship for African Americans: retrospective interpretation and evaluation - thinking citizenship series. *Citizenship Studies*, 13(1), 75-83.

Lieven, A. (2012). *Pakistan: A Hard Country*. London: Penguin Books.

Lister, R. (2003). *Citizenship: Feminist Perspectives*. London: Macmillan.

Lister, R. (2011). The age of responsibility: social policy and citizenship in the early 21st century. In C. Holden, M. Kilkey and G. Ramia (Eds.) *Social Policy Review 23: Analysis and Debate in Social Policy, 2011*, (pp.63-84). Bristol: The Policy Press.

Little, J., Higgins, J. P., Ioannidis, J. P., Moher, D., Gagnon, F., Von Elm, E., ... & Scheet, P. (2009). STrengthening the REporting of Genetic Association Studies (STREGA): an extension of the STROBE statement. *Human Genetics*, 125(2), 131-151.

Lloyd, D. (2014). It is our belief that Palestine is a feminist issue. *Feminists@ Law*, 4(1), 1-19.

Lovat, T. (2012). The women's movement in modern Islam: reflections on the revival of Islam's oldest issue. In T. Lovat (Ed.) *Women in Islam: Reflections on Historical Contemporary Research* (pp. 1–9). Dordrecht: Springer.

Lovelock, J. (1979). *Gaia: A New Look at Life on Earth*. London: Oxford University Press.

Lowles, N. & Painter, A. (2011). *Fear and Hope: The New Politics of Identity*. London: The Searchlight Educational Trust.

Lunn, M. (2006). Becoming an academic woman: Islam, religious identity and career. *Asian Journal of Women's Studies*, 12(2), 33-63.

Lundblad, L.G. (2008) Islamic welfare, discourse and practice: the institutionalization of zakat in Palestine. In N. Naguib (Ed.) *Interpreting Welfare and Relief in the Middle East* (pp 195-237). Leiden: Brill.

Luopajarvi, K. (2004). International accountability for honour killings as human rights violations. *Nordisk Tidsskrift for Menneskerettigheter*, 22, 2-21.

Lydon, J. (1993) *Rotten: No Irish, No Blacks, No Dogs*. London, UK: Hodder and Stoughton.

Macintyre, D. (2017). *Gaza: Preparing for Dawn*. London: Oneworld Publications.

MacPherson, W. (1999). *The Stephen Lawrence Inquiry*. London, UK: HMSO, Cmnd 4262.

Mahadevan, J. (2017). *Cross-Cultural Management*, London: Sage.

Mahadevan, J. & Kilian-Yasin, K. (2017). Dominant discourse, orientalism and the need for reflexive HRM: skilled Muslim migrants in the German context. *The International Journal of Human Resource Management*, 28(8), 1140-1162.

Mahadevan, J. & Mayer. C.-H. (Eds.) (2017). *Muslim Minorities, Workplace Diversity and Reflexive HRM*. London: Routledge Ashgate.

Mahmood. A. (2015), Lahore: about 200 women religious scholars declare that honour killing is not allowed in Islam. *The Dawn Newspaper*, www.dawn.com/news/1185403 Consulted December 29th, 2018.

Majeed, G. (2017). Human needs theory: a significant approach to manage ethnic conflicts in Pakistan. *Journal of Political Studies*, 24(1) 17-32.

Malik, R. (2006). British or Muslim: creating a context for dialogue. *Youth and Society*, 92, 91-105.

Malik, R. (2011). The food security-governance nexus in Pakistan. In M. Kugelman & R. Hathaway (Eds.) *Empty Bellies, Broken Dreams: Food Insecurity and the Future of Pakistan* (pp 57-85). Lahore: Vanguard Books for The Woodrow Wilson International Center.

Manhas, S., & Banoo, J. (2013). A study of beliefs and perceptions related to female foeticide among Muslim community in Jammu, Jammu and Kashmir, India. *Studies on Home and Community Science*, 7(2), 125-130.

Manduca, P., Diab, S. Y., Qouta, S. R., Albarqouni, N. M., & Punamäk, R. L. (2017). A cross sectional study of the relationship between the exposure of pregnant women to military attacks in 2014 in Gaza and the load of heavy metal contaminants in the hair of mothers and newborns. *BMJ Open*, 7(7), e014035.

Manji, I. (2003). *The Trouble with Islam today: A Muslim's Call for Reform in her Faith*. London: Palgrave Macmillan.

Manji, I. (2011). *Allah, Liberty and Love: The Courage to Reconcile Faith and Freedom.* New York: Simon and Schuster.
Mann, S. (2017). Teenage couple 'electrocuted in honour killing' in Pakistan. *The Guardian Online*, September 17th, 2017.
Manzanero, A. L., Crespo, M., Barón, S., Scott, T., El-Astal, S., & Hemaid, F. (2017). Traumatic events exposure and psychological trauma in children victims of war in the Gaza Strip. *Journal of Interpersonal Violence*, Online, doi 0886260517742911.
Ma'oz, M. (2010). *Muslim Attitudes to Jews and Israel.* Brighton, UK: Sussex Academic Press.
March, A.F. (2010a) Tariq Ramadan: from a mere coexistence to an authentic contribution to Europe's Muslims. *Journal of Religion in Europe*, 3(3), 285-309.
March, A.F. (2010b). The post-legal ethics of Tariq Ramadan's persuasion and performance in *Radical Reforms: Islamic Ethics and Liberation: Middle East Law and Governance*, 2(3), 253-273.
Marett, V. (1993). Resettlement of Ugandan Asians in Leicester. *Journal of Refugee Studies*, 6(3), 248-259.
Marie, M., Hannington, B. & Jones, A (2016). Resilience of nurses who work in community mental health workplaces in Palestine. *International Journal of Mental Health Nursing*, June 13, online.
Markham, I. S. & Pirim, S. B. (2016). *An Introduction to Said Nursi: Life, Thought, and Writings.* Routledge.
Marx, K. (2013). *Capital Volumes I and II.* London: Wordsworth Classics.
Mashreky, S. R., Rahman, A., Svanström, L., Khan, T. F., & Rahman, F. (2011). Burn mortality in Bangladesh: findings of national health and injury survey. *Injury*, 42(5), 507-510.
Mashreky S.R., Rahman F. & Rahman A. (2013). Suicide kills more than 10,000 people every year in Bangladesh. *Archives of Suicide Research*, 17(42) 387–396.
Matin, K. (2014). *Income inequality in Bangladesh. Proceedings of Conference: Rethinking Political Economy of Developing Countries.* Dhaka, Online.
Martin, J., Heath, A. & Boswell, K. (2010). *Is Ethnicity or Religion More Important in Explaining Inequalities in the Labour Market?* Oxford. UK: Working Papers in Sociology 2010-2, University of Oxford.
Maulawi, S. (2012). *The Muslim as a European Citizen.* Dublin: Islamic Cultural Centre of Ireland.
McClair, T. L., Hossain, T., Sultana, N., Burnett-Zieman, B., Yam, E. A., Hossain, S., ... & Ahmed, S. (2017). Paying for sex by young men who

live on the streets in Dhaka City: compounded sexual risk in a vulnerable migrant community. *Journal of Adolescent Health*, 60(2), S29-S34.

McCullough, M. E., & Willoughby, B. L. (2009). Religion, self-regulation, and self-control: associations, explanations, and implications. *Psychological Bulletin*, *135*(1), 65-85.

McGilloway, A., Ghosh, P. & Bhui, K. (2015). A systematic review of pathways to the processes associated with radicalizaton and extremism in western societies. *International Review of Psychiatry*, 27, 39-50.

McKerman, B. (2016). Next war with Gaza will be the last because 'We will completely destroy them.' *The Independent Online*, October 24th, 2016.

McNeely, C., Barber, B. K., Spellings, C., Giacaman, R., Arafat, C., Daher, M., ... & Abu Mallouh, M. (2014). Human insecurity, chronic economic constraints and health in the occupied Palestinian territory. *Global Public Health*, 9(5), 495-515.

McPherson, P. (2018). The dysfunctional megacity: why Dhaka is bursting at the sewers. *The Guardian Online*, March 21st, 2018.

Mead, G. (1964). Mind, self and society. In A. Strauss (Ed.) *George Herbert Mead: On Social Psychology*. Chicago: University of Chicago Press.

MECA (2017). *A Child's View from Gaza: Palestinian Children's Art and the Fight Against Censorship*. Berkeley, CA: Middle East Children's Alliance.

Meer, N. (2013). Racialization and religion: race, culture and difference in the study of antisemitism and Islamophobia. *Ethnic and Racial Studies*, *36*(3), 385-398.

Meer, N. (Ed.) (2014). *Racialization and Religion: Race, Culture and Difference in the Study of Antisemitism and Islamophobia*. London: Routledge.

Meer, N. & Modood, T. (2011). How does interculturalism contrast with multiculturalism? *Journal of Intercultural Studies*, 33, 2, 175-196.

Mellahi, K., Demirbag, M. & Riddle, L. (2011). Multinationals in the Middle East: challenges and opportunities. *Journal of World Business,* 46 (4), 406-410.

Mellahi, K. and Wood, G. (2004) Human resource management in Saudi Arabia. In Budhwar, P. & Debrah, Y. (Eds) *Human Resource Management in Developing Countries* (pp 135-151). London: Routledge.

Mellahi, K., Demirbag, M. and Riddle, L. (2011). Multinationals in the Middle East: challenges and opportunities. *Journal of World Business,* 46 (4), 406-410.

Mendik, R. (2017). Salman Abedi became increasingly violent over the course of the past year. *The Telegraph Online*, May 25th, 2017.

Menski, W. (1998). *South Asians and the Dowry Problem*. Stoke-on-Trent: Trentham Books.
Mernissi, F. (1985). *The Veil and the Male Elite: A Feminist Interpretation of Women's Rights in Islam*. New York: Addison-Wesley.
Mernissi, F. (1991). *Women and Islam*. Oxford: Blackwell.
Mernissi, F. (1993). *The Forgotten Queens of Islam*. Minneapolis: University of Minnesota Press.
Mernissi, F. (2001). *Beyond the Veil: Male-Female Dynamics in Modern Muslim Society*. Indiana: Indiana University Press.
Merry, M. (2010). *Culture, Identity, and Islamic Schooling: A Philosophical Approach*. Leiden: Brill.
Merton, R.K. (1968). *Social Theory and Social Structure*. New York: Free Press.
Mesmin, D. (2017). *Bangladesh: The Prostitutes of Daulatdia*. Documentary programme (30 minutes) from *ARTE: Association relative à la télévision européenne*. Shown February 16th, 2017, consulted online December 30th, 2018.
Mesman, J., Janssen, S. & Van Rosmalen, S. (2016). Black Pete through the eyes of Dutch children. *Plos One* June 20th, 2016. http://dx.doi.org/10.1361/journal.pone.0157511.
Metcalfe, B.D. (2006). Women, management and globalization in the Middle East. *Journal of Business Ethics*, 83, (1) 85-100.
Metcalfe, B.D. (2007). Gender and human resource management in the Middle East. *International Journal of Human Resource Management*, 18(1), 54-74.
Metcalfe, B.D., Hutchings. K. & Cooper, B. (2009). Re-examining Women's International Management Opportunities and Experiences: A Middle Eastern Perspective. In Ibeh, K. & Davies, S. (Eds.) *Contemporary Challenges to International Business* (232-250). London: Palgrave-Macmillan.
Metcalfe, B. & Mimouni, F. (Eds.) (2011). *Leadership Development in the Middle East*. Cheltenham, UK: Edward Elgar Publishing.
Metcalfe, B. & Rees, C. J. (2010). Gender, globalization and organization: exploring power, relations and intersections. *Equality, Diversity and Inclusion*, 29(1): 5–22.
Metcalfe, B. D. (2011). Women, empowerment and development in Arab Gulf States: a critical appraisal of governance, culture and national human resource development (HRD) frameworks. *Human Resource Development International*, 14(2), 131-148.

Mehdi, R. (2003). Danish law and the practice of *mahr* among Muslim Pakistanis in Denmark. *International Journal of the Sociology of Law*, 31(2), 115-129.
Mehmood, M. (2017). *Understanding Prejudice: Stigma, Self-Esteem and the Dynamics of Antisemitism & Islamophobia*. London: King's College, University of London, Doctoral Thesis.
Midgley, M. (1984). *Wickedness: A Philosophical Essay*. London: Routledge.
Miller, B. (1984). Daughter neglect, women's work, and marriage: Pakistan and Bangladesh compared. *Medical Anthropology*, 8(1), 109-126.
Miller, D. (2000). *Citizenship and Nationality*. Cambridge: Polity Press.
Miller, M. (2016) Employment opportunities for Muslims in the UK. *Report of The Parliamentary Women's and Equalities Committee*. London, UK: House of Commons.
Misha, E. & Sulaiman, M. (2016). *Bangladesh Priorities: Poverty*. Copenhagen: Copenhagen Consensus Center.
Mishra, S., Thompson, L. H., Sonia, A., Khalid, N., Emmanuel, F., & Blanchard, J. F. (2013). Sexual behaviour, structural vulnerabilities and HIV prevalence among female sex workers in Pakistan. *Sexually Transmitted Infections*, 89(Suppl 2), ii34-ii42.
Misiak, B., Samochowiec, J., Bhui, K., Schouler-Ocak, M., Demunter, H., Kuey, L., ... & Dom, G. (2019). A systematic review on the relationship between mental health, radicalization and mass violence. *European Psychiatry*, 56, 51-59.
Modood, T. (2011, 7 February). Multiculturalism: not a minority problem. *Guardian Online*. Retrieved from http://www.guardian.co.uk
Modood, T. (2013). *Multiculturalism: A Civic Idea*. Cambridge: Polity Press.
Modood, T. (2017). Must Interculturalists misrepresent multiculturalism? *Comparative Migration Studies*, 5(1), 15-27.
Modood, T. (2018). *Islamophobia: A Form of Cultural Racism*. London: All-Party Parliamentary Group on British Muslims on 'Working Definition of Islamophobia' June 1st, 2018.
Modood, T., & Ahmad, F. (2007). British Muslim perspectives on multiculturalism. *Theory, Culture & Society*, 24(2), 187-213.
Modood, T. & Khattab, N. (2016). Explaining ethnic differences: can ethnic minority strategies reduce the effects of ethnic penalties? *Sociology*, 50 (2) 231-246.
Mohammad, M., Hannington, M. B. & Jones, A. (2016). Resilience of nurses who work in community mental health workplaces in Palestine. *International Journal of Mental Health Nursing*, June 13, online.

Moher D, Liberati A, Tetzlaff J, Altman DG. 2009. Preferred reporting items for systematic reviews and meta-analyses: the PRISMA statement. *Annals of Internal Medicine* 151(4):264–269

Mondal, N., Hossain, K., Islam, R. & Mian, A. (2008). Sexual behavior and sexually transmitted diseases in female sex workers in Rajshahi City, Bangladesh. *Brazilian Journal of Infectious Diseases*, 12, 400-410.

Moonis, A. (2014). *Conflict Management and Vision for a Secular Pakistan: A Comparative Study*. Oxford: Oxford University Press.

Moorse, L. (2015). Citizenship in the National Curriculum. In L. Gearon (Ed.) *Learning to Teach Citizenship in the Secondary School: A Companion to School Experience*. London: Routledge.

Morgan, D. (2010). *Essential Islam: A Comprehensive Guide to Belief and Practice*. Oxford, UK: Greenwood Publishing.

Morin, A., Fatima, H. & Qadir, T. (2018). Pakistan's slow progress to gender parity. *Lancet Global Health*, 6(2), e144, February.

Moshagen, M., Hilbig, B. E. & Zettler, I. (2018). The dark core of personality. *Psychological Review*, 125(5), 656-668.

Mosleh, M., Dalal, K., Aljeesh, Y., & Svanström, L. (2018). The burden of war-injury in the Palestinian health care sector in Gaza Strip. *BMC International Health and Human Rights*, 18(1), 28.

Moss, R. (2015). Employment Tribunal statistics released. *Personnel Today*, September 10th, online.

Morris, L. J. (1999). Citizenship and education from the perspective of religious education: a viewpoint. *Muslim Education Quarterly.* 17, 57-64.

Mufti, K. & Salman, U. (2006). *Modesty: An Overview*. www.IslamReligion.com Consulted December 1st, 2018.

Muhammad Y. & Brett P. (2019). Addressing social justice and cultural identity in Pakistani education: a qualitative content analysis of curriculum policy. In Gube, J. & Gao, F. (Eds) *Education, Ethnicity and Equity in the Multilingual Asian Context. Multilingual Education*, vol 32, 235-253. New York: Springer.

Mujahed, F., & Atan, T. (2017). Breaking the glass ceiling: dealing with the attitudes of Palestinians toward women holding leading administrative positions. *Asian Women*, 33(4) 81-107.

Mumtaz, K. & Shahad, F. (1987). *Women of Pakistan: Two Steps Forward, One Back*. London: Zed Books.

Munir, M. & Abdul-Quddus, T. (2018). Female Muslim petitioners in Pakistani family courts – cases, problems and solutions. *Al-Adwa*, 50(33), 51-56.

Munn, S.L. (2013). Unveiling the work-life system: The influence of work-life balance on meaningful work. *Advances in Developing Human Resources*, 15 (4), 401-417.

Murphy, M. & Smolarski, J. (2018). Religion and CSR: an Islamic "political" model of corporate governance. *Business and Society*, January, Online.

Murshid, N. S., & Critelli, F. M. (2017). Empowerment and intimate partner violence in Pakistan: results from a nationally representative survey. *Journal of Interpersonal Violence*, February 13th, 2017, Online.

Musofer, M.A. (2012). Pluralism in Islam. *Dawn Online*, January 20th, 2012.

Mustafa, B. (1999). Education for integration: a case study of a British Muslim high school for girls. *Journal of Muslim Minority Affairs,* 19 (1), 1-10.

Mustafa, B. (2001). Public education and Muslim voluntary organisations in Britain. *Westminster Studies in Education*, 24, 2.

Mustafa, M., Zakar, R., Zakar, M. Z., Chaudhry, A., & Nasrullah, M. (2017). Under-five child mortality and morbidity associated with consanguineous child marriage in Pakistan: retrospective analysis using Pakistan demographic and health Surveys, 1990–91, 2006–07, 2012–13. *Maternal and Child Health Journal,* 21(5), 1095-1104.

Mutalib, M. A., Hussin, S. A., Mohd, N., Sukor, K. M. N., Wan, W. M. F. A., & Razali, R. A. (2017). Islamic leadership behaviour practices among Muslim women managers. *International Journal of Academic Research in Business and Social Science*, 2017(7), Online.

Mydans, S. (2002). In Pakistan, rape victims are the 'criminals'. *New York Times Online* May 12th, 2002.

Nahar Q., El Arifeen S., Jamil K. & Streatfield P. (2015). Causes of adult female deaths in Bangladesh: findings from two National Surveys. *BMC Public Health*, Sep 18;15:911. doi: 10.1186/s12889-015-2256-6.

Nasrullah, M., Zakar, R., & Zakar, M. Z. (2014). Child marriage and its associations with controlling behaviors and spousal violence against adolescent and young women in Pakistan. *Journal of Adolescent Health*, 55(6), 804-809.

Nasrullah, M., Zakar, R., Zakar, M. Z., Abbas, S., & Safdar, R. (2015). Circumstances leading to intimate partner violence against women married as children: a qualitative study in urban slums of Lahore, Pakistan. *BMC International Health and Human Rights*, 15(1), 23, Online.

Nath, S.R. (2008). Quality of Bangladesh Rural Advancement Committee educational programmes: a review of research studies. In C. Adam-

Bagley & G. Verma (Eds.) *Challenges for Inclusion: Educational and Social Studies from Britain and the Indian Sub-Continent* (pp 183-218). Leiden: Brill - Sense Education Books.

Nath, S.R. (2017). *Competencies, Achievements of BRAC School Students: Trends, Comparisons and Prediction.* Dhaka: Bangladesh Rural Advancement Committee, Research and Evaluation Division, Research Monograph 51.

Naved, R. T., & Akhtar, N. (2008). Spousal violence against women and suicidal ideation in Bangladesh. *Women's Health Issues,* 18 (6), 442-452.

Neill, K. G. (2013). Duty, honor, rape: sexual assault against women during war. *Journal of International Women's Studies,* 2(1), 43-51

Nessa, K., Waris, S. A., Alam, A., Huq, M., Nahar, S., Chawdhury, F. A. H., ... & Das, J. (2005). Sexually transmitted infections among brothel-based sex workers in Bangladesh: high prevalence of asymptomatic infection. *Sexually Transmitted Diseases,* 32(1), 13-19.

Nessa, K., Alam, A., Chawdhury, F. A. H., Huq, M., Nahar, S., Salauddin, G., ... & Rahman, M. (2008). Field evaluation of simple rapid tests in the diagnosis of syphilis. *International Journal of STD & AIDS, 19*(5), 316-320.

Ng, E. S. W., & Sears, G. J. (2010). What do women and ethnic minorities want? Work values and labour market confidence: self-determination perspectives. *International Journal of Human Resource Management,* 25, 676–698.

Nielson, J. (1995). *Muslims in Western Europe.* Edinburgh: Edinburgh University Press.

Nielson, J. (1999). Muslims and European educational systems. In G. M. Munoz, (Ed.) (1999) *Islam, Modernism and the West: Cultural and Political Relations and the End of the Millennium.* London: Tauris.

Nielson, J. (2000). Muslims in Britain: ethnic minority, community or Ummah. In H. Coward (Ed.) *The South Asian Religious Diaspora in Britain, Canada and the United States.* New York: State University of New York Press.

Nievers, E. & Andriessen, I. (2010) *Discrimination Monitor: Non-Western Immigrants in the Labour Market in 2010.* The Hague, Netherlands: Social and Cultural Planning Office (original document in Dutch).

Noor, R., & Munna, M. S. (2015). Emerging diseases in Bangladesh: current microbiological research perspective. *Tzu Chi Medical Journal, 27*(2), 49-53.

Norrie, N. (2010). *Dialectic and Difference: Dialectical Critical Realism and the Grounds of Justice.* London: Routledge.

Nour, N. M. (2009). Child marriage: a silent health and human rights issue. *Reviews in Obstetrics and Gynecology*, 2(1), 51 Online.
NRC (2018). *6 out of 10 Children Surveyed Experiencing Traumatic Nightmares*. Oslo: Norwegian Refugee Council, www.nrc.no/news/2018/may/gaza-nightmares, Retrieved July 2, 2018.
Nuruzzaman, M. (2004) Neoliberal economic reforms, the rich and the poor in Bangladesh. *Journal of Contemporary Asia*, 34(1), 33-54.
Nwanokwu, G. (2016) *Black Shamrocks: Accommodation Available – No Blacks, No Dogs, No Irish*. Privately printed autobiography, distributed by Amazon Marketing, UK.
Nydell, M. K. (2012) *Understanding Arabs*, 5th ed. Boston MA: Intercultural Press.
Office for National Statistics (2012). *First Report of the 2011 National Census*. London: Office for National Statistics.
OFSTED (2006). *Towards Consensus? Citizenship in Secondary Schools*. London: Office for Standards in Education.
OITFET (2014). *Annual Report for 2013*. London, UK: Office of The Industrial and Fair Employment Tribunals.
Oldfield, E., Hartnell, L. & Bailey, E. (2013). *More than an Educated Guess: Assessing the Evidence on Faith Schools*. London: Theos Foundation.
Ollier-Malaterre, A. (2009). Organizational work–life initiatives: context matters: France compared to the UK and the US. *Community, Work & Family*, 12 (2), 159-178.
Ollier-Malaterre, A. Valcour, M., Den Dulk, L. & Kassek, E. (2013). Theorizing national context to develop comparative work-life research: a review and research agenda. *European Management Journal*, 31 (4), 433-447.
O'Mahoney, J., Vincent, S., & Harley, B. (2018). Realist studies of oppression, emancipation and resistance. *Organization*, 25(5), 575-584.
Omair, K. (2008). Women in management in the Arab context. *Education, Business and Society: Contemporary Middle Eastern Issues*, 1(2), 107-123.
Omair, K. (2010). Typology of career development for Arab women managers in the United Arab Emirates. *Career Development International*, 15(2), 121-143.
Omair, K. (2011). *Women's Managerial Careers in the Context of the United Arab Emirates*. Estonia: Jyväskylä University Studies in Business and Economics No. 106.
Osler, A. (1999). Citizenship, democracy and political literacy. *Multicultural Teaching*, 18, 12-29.

Osler, A. & Morrison, A. (2000). *Inspecting Schools for Race Equality: OFSTED's Strengths and Weaknesses*. Stoke-on-Trent: Trentham Books for the Commission for Racial Equality.

Osler, A. & Starkey, H. (2001). Citizenship education and national identities in France and England: Inclusive or exclusive? *Oxford Review of Education*, 27, 287–305.

Osler, A. & Vincent, V. (2002). *Citizenship and the Challenge of Global Education*. Stoke-on-Trent, UK: Trentham Books.

Ourghi, M. (2010). Tariq Ramadan: from a mere co-existence to an authentic contribution of European's Muslims. *Journal of Religion in Europe*, 3, 285-309.

Office for National Statistics (2012). *First Report of the 2011 National Census*. London: Office for National Statistics.

OFSTED: Office for Standards in Education, Children's Services and Skills, (2006). *Towards Consensus? Citizenship in Secondary Schools*. London: OFSTED.

OXFAM (2018). *Children Shed Light on Gaza's Prolonged Darkness*. Oxford: Oxford Committee for Famine Relief.

Özdil, Z. (2014). 'Racism is an American problem': Dutch exceptionalism and Its politics of denial. *Frame*, 27(2), 49-64.

Pager, D. & Shepherd, H. (2008). The sociology of discrimination: racial discrimination in employment, housing, credit, and consumer markets. *Annual Review of Sociology* 34, 181–209.

Pager, D. & Western, B. (2012). Identifying discrimination at work: the use of field experiments. *Journal of Social Issues* 68, 221–238.

Pal, A. (2011). *"Islam" Means Peace: Understanding the Muslim Principle of Nonviolence Today*. Santa Barbara, CA: Praeger.

Palazzi, A. H. (2001). The Islamists have it wrong - what the Qur'an really says. The Muslim-Jewish dialog and the question of Jerusalem. *Middle East Quarterly* 8(3) 3-12 Online.

Paludi, M. (2013). *Women and Management: Global Issues and Promising Solutions*. New York: Praeger.

Panjalingam, P. (2012). Muslim women today: challenges in achieving their potential in resources management. In H. Ibrahim and R. Islam (Eds.) *Management of Resources in Muslim Communities: Challenges and Prospects* (pp 97-112). Malaysia: HUM Press, University of Malaysia.

Pappe, I. (2016). *The Biggest Prison Camp on Earth: A History of Gaza and West Bank Occupied Territories*. London: One World Books.

Pappe, I. (2017). *Ten Myths About Israel*. London: Verso Books.

Parekh, B. (2001). Rethinking multiculturalism: cultural diversity and political theory. *Ethnicities*, 1(1), 109-115.

Parker-Jenkins, M. (1995). *Children of Islam.* Stoke, UK: Trentham Books.
Parker-Jenkins, M. (2002). Equal access to state funding: the case of Muslim schools in Britain. *Race, Ethnicity and Education*, 5, 273–89.
Parker-Jenkins, M., Hartas, D. & Irving, B. A. (2005). *In Good Faith: Schools, Religion and Public Funding.* London: Routledge Ashgate.
Parmar, B. (2014). *The Empathy Era: Business and the New Pathway to Profit.* London: Lady Geek Publications.
Parveen, S. (2007). Gender awareness of rural women in Bangladesh. *Journal of International Women's Studies*, 9(2), 253-269.
Pasamar, S. and Alegre, J. (2014) Adoption and use of work-life initiatives: looking at the influence of institutional pressures and gender. *European Management Journal*, 31(33), 1-11.
Patek, A. (2016). Blame caste for Pakistan's violent streak, not faith. *The Economic Times*, September 26th, 4.
Pathirage, C. P., Amaratunga, D., & Haigh, R. (2005). *Knowledge Management Research Within the Built Environment: Research Methodological Perspectives.* Manchester: Research Institute for the Built and Human Environment, University of Salford, Manchester.
Patrikarakos, D. (2017). *War in 140 characters: How Social Media is Reshaping Conflict in the Twenty-First century.* London: Basic Books and Hachette.
PCBS (Palestinian Central Bureau of Statistics) (1997-2014) *Labour Force Statistics*, several editions. Rammallah: Government of Palestine.
Peach, C. (2006). Muslims in the 2001 Census of England and Wales: gender and economic disadvantage. *Ethnic and Racial Studies*, 29, 629–640.
Peltonen, K., Kangaslampi, S., Qouta, S., & Punamäki, R. L. (2017). Trauma and autobiographical memory: contents and determinants of earliest memories among war-affected Palestinian children. *Memory*, 25(10), 1347-1357.
Penslar, D. J., & Kalmar, I. D. (Eds.). (2005). *Orientalism and the Jews.* Brandeis University Press.
Pepe, A., Addimando, L., Dagdouke, J., Yagi, S., & Veronese, G. (2018). Teaching in conflict contexts: dimensions of subjective wellbeing in Palestinian teachers living in Israel and the occupied Palestinian territory. *The Lancet*, 391, S6.
Peters. M., Britton, A. & Blee (Eds.) (2007). *Global Citizenship Education: Philosophy, Theory, Pedagogy.* Leiden: Brill - Sense Education Series.
Pettigrew, T. F. (2016). In pursuit of three theories: authoritarianism, relative deprivation, and intergroup contact. *Annual Review of Psychology*, 67, 1-21.

Pettigrew, T.F. (2019). The emergence of contextual social psychology. *Personality and Social Psychology Bulletin*. In press (preprint online).

Pettigrew, T. F. & Meertens, R. W. (1995). Subtle and blatant prejudice in Western Europe. *European Journal of Social Psychology*, 25(1), 57-75.

Pettigrew, T. F. & Tropp, L.R. (2008). How does intergroup contact reduce prejudice? Meta-analytic tests of three mediators. *European Journal of Social Psychology* 38: 922–34.

Phoenix, A. (2006). Intersectionality. *European Journal of Women Studies*, 13(3), 187–192.

Pidd, H. (2019). Pupil's imagined talk with Manchester Arena bomber wins award. *The Guardian Online*, May 21, 2019.

Pirzada, T. (2017). Narrating Muslim girlhood in the Pakistani cityscape of graphic narratives. *Girlhood Studies*, December, 81-104.

Pisani, E. (2008). *The Wisdom of Whores: Bureaucracy, Brothels and the Business of Aids*. London: Granta Books.

Poelman, S., Greenhaus, J. & Maestro, M. (2013). *Expanding the Boundaries of Work-Family Research: A Vision for the Future*. London: Palgrave-MacMillan.

Polderman, J. A., Farhang-Razi, V., Van Dieren, S., Kranke, P., DeVries, J. H., Hollmann, M. W., ... & Hermanides, J. (2018). Adverse side effects of dexamethasone in surgical patients. *Cochrane Database of Systematic Reviews*, August 28, (11) 8, Online.

Popper, K. (2002). *The Logic of Scientific Discovery*. London: Routledge Classics.

Porat, D. (2018). *Anti-Semitism Worldwide 2017*. Tel Aviv: Kantor Center, University of Tel Aviv.

Potter, L.B. (2001). Public health and suicide prevention. In D. Lester (Ed.) *Suicide Prevention: Resources for the Millennium*. (pp 67-82). Philadelphia, PA: Brunner-Routledge.

Poynting, S. & Mason, V. (2007). The resistible rise of Islamophobia: anti-Muslim racism in the UK and Australia before 11 September 2001. *Journal of Sociology*, 43, 61-86.

Prashad, V. (2019). Israeli bombs on Gaza. *The Guardian (Sydney) Online*, March 27th, 2019.

Presley, L. (2019). Yaba: the cheap synthetic drug convulsing a nation. *BBC News Online*, April 26th, 2019.

Pring, J. (2014) Government set to slash equality watchdog's budget ... again. *Disability News Service*, April 19th, 2014. www.disabilitynewsservice.com.

Pritchard, C. & Amanulla, S. (2007) An analysis of suicide and undetermined death in Muslim-majority countries. *Psychological Medicine, 37*(3), 421-430.

Punamäki, R. L., Isosävi, S., Qouta, S. R., Kuittinen, S., & Diab, S. Y. (2017). War trauma and maternal–fetal attachment predicting maternal mental health, infant development, and dyadic interaction in Palestinian families. *Attachment and Human Development,* 19(5), 463-486.

Purdie-Vaughns, V., & Eibach, R. (2008). Intersectional invisibility: the distinctive advantages and disadvantages of multiple subordinate-group identities. *Sex Roles,* 59(5), 337–391

Qadir, F., Khan, M. M., Medhin, G., & Prince, M. (2011). Male gender preference, female gender disadvantage as risk factors for psychological morbidity in Pakistani women of childbearing age-a life course perspective. *BMC Public Health, 11*(1), 745, Online.

Qarni, O. (2017). Panchayat in Rajanpol orders rape survivor to be stoned or sold off. *Pakistan Express Tribune Online* May 27th, 2017.

Qazi, M. (2015). Muslim women: breaking the glass ceiling of patriarchy. *Chicago Monitor,* August 28, 2015, Online.

QCA. (1998). *Education for Citizenship and the Teaching of Democracy in Schools. Final Report of the Advisory Group on Citizenship* (The Crick Report). London: Qualification and Curriculum Authority.

QCA (1999). *The National Curriculum in England: Citizenship.* London: Qualification and Curriculum Authority.

QCA (2000). *Citizenship at Key Stage 3 and 4: Initial Guidance for Schools.* London: Qualification and Curriculum Authority.

QCA (2001). *Teacher Guide KS3.* London: Qualification and Curriculum Authority.

Qeshta, H., Hawajri, A. M., & Thabet, A. M. (2019). The relationship between war trauma, PTSD, anxiety and depression among adolescents in the Gaza Strip. *Health Science Journal, 13*(1), 1-12.

Qouta, S., Punamäki, R. L., Montgomery, E., & El Sarraj, E. (2007). Predictors of psychological distress and positive resources among Palestinian adolescents: trauma, child, and mothering characteristics. *Child Abuse & Neglect,* 31(7), 699-717.

Qouta, S. R., Palosaari, E., Diab, M., & Punamäki, R. L. (2012). Intervention effectiveness among war-affected children: A cluster randomized controlled trial on improving mental health. *Journal of Traumatic Stress,* 25(3), 288-298.

Quader M., Rahman M.H., Kamal M., Ahmed A.U., Saha S.K. (2010). Post mortem outcome of organophosphorus compound poisoning cases at

Mymensingh Medical Centre. *Mymensingh Medical College Journal* 192), 170-172.

Qudus, A. (2015). Beyond the myth of puritan Bangladesh: pre- and extra-marital sexual relations among lower class urban men. *Journal of Comparative Family Studies*, 46, 456-460.

Quillan, L. (2008). A new approach to understanding racial prejudice and discrimination. *Annual Review of Sociology*, 32 (2) 299-328.

Qusar, M. S., Morshed, N. M., Kader, M. A., Azad, M. A. K., Uddin, M. A., & Shaikh, M. A. K. (2010). Psychiatric morbidity of suicide attempt patients requiring ICU intervention. *Journal of Medicine*, *11*(1), 7-19.

Rabbani, A., Khan, A., Yusuf, S. & Adams, A. (2016). Trends and determinants of inequalities in childhood stunting in Bangladesh. *International Journal of Equity and Health*, 15, 186 Online.

Rafferty, A. (2012). Ethnic penalties in graduate level over-education, unemployment and wages: evidence from Britain. *Work, Employment and Society*, 26 (6) 987-1006.

Rahim, H. F. A., Wick, L., Halileh, S., Hassan-Bitar, S., Chekir, H., Watt, G., & Khawaja, M. (2009). Maternal and child health in the occupied Palestinian territory. *The Lancet*, 373(9667), 967-977.

Rahman, A. (2001). *Consequences of Structural Adjustment Policies on the Poor*. Dhaka: 2nd National Forum of Bangladesh Structural Adjustment Participatory Review. (World Bank sponsored, documents available at: www.sappri.org/Bangladesh)

Rahman, M., Alam, A., Nessa, K., Hossain, A., Nahar, S., Datta, D., ... & Albert, M. J. (2000). Etiology of sexually transmitted infections among street-based female sex workers in Dhaka, Bangladesh. *Journal of Clinical Microbiology*, *38*(3), 1244-1246.

Rahman, M. M. (2018). The making of an Islamist public sphere in Bangladesh. *Asian Journal of Comparative Politics*, 2057891118811952.

Rahman, M.S. & Rahman, M.M. (2018). Trends in, and projections of, indicators of universal health coverage in Bangladesh, 1995-2030. *Lancet Global Health*, 6(1), 86-94 Online.

Rais, R. B. (2017). *Imagining Pakistan: Modernism, State, and the Politics of Islamic Revival*. Maryland: Lexington Books.

Raj. A. (2017). Gender empowerment index: a choice of progress or perfection. *Lancet Global Health*, 5(9), 849-850, Online.

Raj, A., Saggurti, N., Winter, M., Labonte, A., Decker, M. R., Balaiah, D., & Silverman, J. G. (2010). The effect of maternal child marriage on morbidity and mortality of children under 5 in India: cross sectional

study of a nationally representative sample. *British Medical Journal*, 340, b4258.
Ram, M., Woldensbet, K. & Jones, T. (2011). Raising the 'table stakes'? Ethnic minority business and supply chain relationships. *Work, Employment and Society*, 25 (2) 309-326.
Ramadan, T. (1999). *To Be a European Muslim*. Leicester: The Islamic Foundation.
Ramadan, T. (2004). *Western Muslims and the Future of Islam*. London: Oxford University Press.
Ramadan, T. (2007). *The Messenger: The Meanings of the Life of Muhammad*. London: Penguin Books.
Ramadan, T. (2010). *What I Believe*. Oxford University Press
Ramadan, T. (2011). Are the Dutch still Europe's least prejudiced people? Radio Interview on July 23rd, 2011 at: www.rnw.org.
Ramadan, T. (2012). *The Quest for Meaning: Developing a Philosophy of Pluralism*. London: Pelican Books.
Ransford, H. E. (1968). Isolation, powerlessness, and violence: a study of attitudes and participation in the Watts riot. *American Journal of Sociology*, 73(5), 581-591.
Rashid, S. (2006). Small power, little choice: contextualising reproductive and sexual rights in slums in Bangladesh. *Institute of Development Studies Bulletin*, 307(5), 69-76.
Rashid, T. (2018). Inside the Bangladesh brothels where Rohingya girls are suffering. *PBS: Public Broadcasting Service*, Washington. Documentary April 26th, 2018, viewed December 30th, 2018.
Rasmussen, E. (2017). Murders of teenagers show that poor communities in Karachi are becoming entrenched in conservative values. *The Guardian Online*, December 27th, 2017.
Rasmussen, S., Hawton K., Philpott-Morgan, S. & O'Connor R. (2016). Why do adolescents self-harm? *Crisis* 37(3):176-83. doi: 10.1027/0227-5910/a000369. Epub 2016 Feb 2.
Raza, M.M. (2018). Thirsty days ahead: Pakistan's looming water crisis. *The Diplomat Online* June 19th, 2018.
Redfern, C. (2018). The Bangladesh brothels where men pay child brides for sex, while police look the other way. *The Telegraph Online*, July 23rd, 2018.
Reed, M. (2001) Organization, trust and control: a realist analysis. *Organization Studies*, 22 (2), 201-228.
Reed, M. (2005) Reflections on the 'realist turn' in organization and management studies. *Journal of Management Studies*, 42 (8), 1621-1644.

Rees, S. (2018). *Peace with Justice or Collusion with Cruelty?* Victoria, Australia: Parliament of Victoria.

Renton, J., & Gidley, B. (Eds.) (2017). *Antisemitism and Islamophobia in Europe*. London: Palgrave MacMillan.

Renton, J., & Gidley, B. (2017). Introduction: the shared story of Europe's ideas of the Muslim and the Jew—a diachronic framework. In *Antisemitism and Islamophobia in Europe* (pp. 1-21). London: Palgrave Macmillan.

Reza, S.A.M., Feroz, A.H.M., Nurul Islam, S.M., Nazmul Karim, M., Golam Rabbani, M., Sha Halam, M., Mujibur Rahman, A.K.M., Ridwanur Rahman, M., Ahmed, H.U., Bhowmik, A.D., Zillur Rahman Khan, M., Sarkar, M., Alam, M.T. & Jalal Uddin, M.M. (2013). Risk factors of suicide and para-suicide in rural Bangladesh. *Journal of Medicine* (Bangladesh) 14(2), 123-129.

Rex, J. (1970) *Race Relations and Sociological Theory*. London: Weidenfeld and Nicholson.

Riach, P. A. & Rich, J. (2002) Field experiments of discrimination in the market place. *The Economic Journal*, 112 (4), 480-518.

Riaz, A. (2004). *God Willing: The Politics of Islamism in Bangladesh*. New York: Rowman and Littlefield.

Rippon, G. (2019). Do women and men have different brains? *New Scientist*, 241(3219), 28-31.

Rizzo, H., Abdel-Latif, A. & Meyer, K. (2007). The relationship between gender equality and democracy: a comparison of Arab versus non-Arab Muslim societies. *Sociology*, 41(7), 1151-1170.

Roald, A.S. (2001). *Women in Islam: The Western Experience*. London: Routledge.

Rob, U. & Mutahara, M. (2000). Pre-marital sex among urban adolescents in Bangladesh. *International Quarterly of Community Health Education*, 20, 103-111.

Robinne, F., & Sadan, M. (Eds.). (2007). *Social Dynamics in the Highlands of Southeast Asia: Reconsidering Political Systems of Highland Burma by Edmund Leach*. Leiden: Brill.

Rodriguez, J. K., Holvino, E., Fletcher, J. K., & Nkomo, S. M. (2016). The theory and praxis of intersectionality in work and organisations: where do we go from here? *Gender, Work & Organization*, 23(3), 201-222.

Rogelberg, S.G. (Ed.) (2002). *Handbook of Research in Industrial and Organisational Psychology*. Cambridge, MA: Blackwell.

Ronsmans, C. & Khlat, M. (1999). Adolescence and risk of violent death during pregnancy in Matlab, Bangladesh. *The Lancet*, *354*(9188), 1448.

Rose, J. B. & Associates (1969) *Colour and Citizenship*. Oxford: Oxford University Press.
Rossenkhan, Z., Chan, A. W., & Ahmed, P. K. (2016). Complexities of Muslim women managers' careers: an identity perspective. *Gender Studies*, 16(17), Online.
Roy, S. (2013). *Hamas and Civil Society in Gaza: Engaging the Islamist Social Sector*. Oxford and Princeton: Princeton University Press.
Rubenberg, C. (2001). *Palestinian Women*. London: Rienner.
Rubin, L., Belmaker, I., Somekh, E., Rudolf, M., & Grossman, Z. (2018). Deaths of children and women in Gaza hostilities. *Lancet*, 391(10120), 540.
Rudin, A.J. (2015). Shoah through Muslim eyes: a review. New York: ReformJudaism, www.reformjudism.org
Runciman, W. G., & Adam-Bagley, C. (1969). Status consistency, relative deprivation, and attitudes to immigrants. *Sociology*, 3(3), 359-375.
Russell, P. (2008). Hume on free will. *Stanford Encylopedia of Philosophy*. Stanford, CA: Stanford University Press.
Sabbagh, S. (Ed) (1998). *The Palestinian Women of Gaza and the West Bank*. Indiana: Indiana University Press.
Sabbir, M. (2019). Nusrat Jahan Rafi: burned to death for reporting sexual harassment. *BBC New Online*, April 10th, 2019.
Sadek, N. (2017). Islamophobia, shame, and the collapse of Muslim identities. *International Journal of Applied Psychoanalytic Studies*, 14(3), 200-221.
Sadiq, M. (2017). *Discarded Daughters: Pakistan's Unwanted Girls*. Film, 30 minutes, available at StreamTV: www.nowtv.com.
Sadruddin, M. M. (2017). Teaching human rights through global education to teachers in Pakistan. *Prospects*, 47(1-2), 73-86.
Saeed, A., Yousaf, A. & Alharbi, J. (2017). Family and state ownership, internalization and corporate board-gender diversity: evidence from China and India. *Cross-Cultural Strategic Management*, 24, 2, 251-270.
Saeed, F. (2001). *Taboo! The Hidden Culture of a Red Light Area*. Oxford: Oxford University Press.
Saeed, F. (2006). Good women, bad women: prostitution in Pakistan. In Gangoli, G. & Westmarland, N. (Eds.) *International Approaches to Prostitution: Law and policy in Europe and Asia* (pp 141-164) Bristol: The Policy Press.
Saeed, F. (2013). *Working with Sharks: A Pakistani Woman's Story of Countering Sexual Harassment in the United Nations - From Personal Grievance to Public Law*. McLean, VA: Advances Press.

Safi, M. (2017). India weighs up the return on cash handouts for the poorest. *Guardian Online*, February 6th, 2017.

Safi, M. & Rushe, H. (2018). Rama plaza, five years on: safety of workers hangs in balance in Bangladesh. *Guardian Online*, April 23rd, 2018.

Safiur-Rahman Al-Mubarakpuri (2008). *The Sealed Nectar: Biography of The Noble Prophet*. Riyadh: Darussalam Books.

Sahin, A. (2008). *Studying Islamic Education at the School of Education at the University of Birmingham*. Birmingham: School of Education, University of Birmingham.

Sahin, A. (2013). *New Directions in Islamic Education: Pedagogy and Identity Formation*. Leicester, UK: Kube Publishing Ltd.

Said, E. W. (1995). *Orientalism: Western Conceptions of the Orient*. 1978. London: Penguin Books.

Sajid, A. (2005). Islamophobia: a new word for an old fear. Paper given to *OSCE Conference on Anti-Semitism and other forms of intolerance*. Cordoba Spain, June, 2005.

Salim, N. (2004). *Sex Trade Workers in Bangladesh: An Exploratory Study in Sex Workers' Movement, and Patriarchy*. Halifax, Canada: Dalhousie University.

Sami, H. & Hallaq, E. (2018). Non-suicidal self-injury among adolescents and young adults with prolonged exposure to violence: the effect of post-traumatic stress symptoms. *Psychiatry Research*, October 9, Online.

Samuels, F., Jones, N., & Abu Hamad, B. (2017). Psychosocial support for adolescent girls in post-conflict settings: beyond a health systems approach. *Health Policy and Planning*, 32(suppl_5), v40-v51.

Sandiford, P. J. & Seymour, D. (2007) A discussion of qualitative data analysis in hospitality research with examples from an ethnography of English public houses. *International Journal of Hospitality Management*, 26 (3), 724-742.

Santos, I. S., Matijasevich, A., Tavares, B. F., da Cruz Lima, A. C., Riegel, R. E., & Lopes, B. C. (2007). Comparing validity of Edinburgh scale and SRQ20 in screening for post-partum depression. *Clinical Practice and Epidemiology in Mental Health*, 3(1), 18, Online.

Sardar, Z. (2012). *Muhammad*. London: Hodder Educational.

Sarkhar, K., Bal, B., Mukherjee, R. & Four Others (2008). Sex-trafficking, violence, negotiating skill, and HIV infection in brothel-based sex workers of eastern India, adjoining Nepal, Bhutan & Bangladesh. *Journal of Health, Population and Nutrition*, 26, 223-231.

Sarra, C. (2011). *Strong and Smart – Towards a Pedagogy for Emancipation: Education for First Peoples*. London: Routledge.

Sarwar, C. (2016). Six women kidnapped, four raped every day in Lahore. Gulamabbaskar.wordpress.com, January 3rd, 2016.
Savage, M. (2015). *Social Class in the Twenty First Century*. London: Pelican.
Savage, M. (2019). Tony Blair: migrants should be forced to integrate more to combat far right - former PM claims that 'failure' of multiculturalism has led to rise in bigotry. *The Guardian Online*, April 20th, 2019.
Sawyerr, A. & Adam-Bagley, C. (2017a). *Equality and Ethnic Identities: Studies of Self-Concept, Child Abuse and Education in a Changing English Culture*. Leiden: Brill – Sense Education Books.
Sawyerr, A., & Adam-Bagley, C. (2017b). Child sexual abuse and adolescent and adult adjustment: a review of British and world evidence, with implications for social work, and mental health and school counselling. *Advances in applied sociology*, 7(1), 1-15.
Sayer, A. (2002) *Method in Social Science* 2nd Edition. London: Routledge.
Sbardella, D. (2009). Community-based child protection in the Gaza Strip. *Humanitarian Exchange*, 44, September, Online.
Scambler, G. (2012). Resistance in unjust times: Archer, structured agency and the sociology of health inequalities. *Sociology*, 33, 275-296.
SCF & MAP (2012). *Gaza's Children Falling Behind: The Effect of the Blockade on Child Health in Gaza*. London: Save the Children Fund and Medical Aid for Palestinians;
SCF (2018). More than 250 children in Gaza shot with live ammunition as protests escalate. London: Save the Children, May 11, Online. www.savethechildrennet/.../more-250-children-gaza-shot-live-ammuniion/ Retrieved May 19, 2018.
Schäfer, S. & Holst, F. (2014). Anti-feminist discourses and Islam in Malaysia: a critical enquiry. In C. Derichs (Ed.), *Women's Movements and Countermovements: The Quest for Gender Equality in Southeast Asia and the Middle East (pp. 55-78)*. Newcastle, UK: Cambridge Scholars Publishing.
Schmitt, N. (2014). *Differences in Identity Constructions between Students of Turkish Origin and Exchange Students from Turkey in the Netherlands*. Tilburg: University of Tilburg, Doctoral Thesis.
Schwab, K., Sarrams. R., Zahidi, A., Leopold, T., Hausman, R. & D'Andrea-Tyson, L. (2017). *The Global Gender Gap Report*. Geneva: World Economic Forum.
Schuler, S., Hashemi, Riley, A. & Akhter, S. (1996). Credit programs, patriarchy and men's violence in rural Bangladesh. *Social Science and Medicine*, 43, 1729-1724.

Sev, A., Harris, N. & Sebar, B. (2012) Uncovering work-life interference among Australian Muslim men. *New Zealand Journal of Human Resources*, 12 (2) 69-80.

Sevelkoul, M., Scheepers, P., Tolsma, J. & Hagendoorn, L. (2010). Anti-Muslim attitudes in The Netherlands: tests of contradictory hypotheses derived from ethnic competition theory and inter-group contact theory. *European Sociological Review*, 8(1), 1-18.

Shaath, I., Al Haddad, L., & Eid, A. (2015). *Economic Recovery in Gaza: Supporting Livelihoods Through Women's Business Development.* Oxford, UK: OXFAM Policy and Research Studies.

Shah, A. (2014). *The Army and Democracy: Military Politics in Pakistan.* Cambridge, MA: Harvard University Press.

Shah, B., Dwyer, C., & Modood, T. (2010). Explaining educational achievement and career aspirations among young British Pakistanis: Mobilizing 'ethnic capital'? *Sociology*, 44(6), 1109-1127.

Shah, S. (2015). *Education, Leadership and Islam: Theories, Discourses and Practices from an Islamic perspective.* London: Routledge.

Shahid, A. (2013). Post-divorce maintenance for Muslim women in Pakistan and Bangladesh: a comparative perspective. *International Journal of Law, Policy and the Family*, 27(2), 197-215.

Shahjahan, M., Ara, M. & Ayaz, M. (2016). Protecting child labor in Bangladesh under domestic laws. *Open Access Library Journal*, 3(eZ543), 1-17.

Shahnaz, A., Adam-Bagley, C., Kadri, S. & Simkhada, P. (2017). Suicidal behaviour in Bangladesh: scoping literature review, and development of a public health research and prevention model. *Open Journal of Social Science*, 5(7) 254-282.

Shalhoub-Kevorkian, N. (2004). *Women, Armed Conflict and Loss: The Mental Health of Palestinian Women in the Occupied Territories.* Jerusalem: Women's Studies Center.

Shalhoub-Kevorkian, N. (2008). The gendered nature of education under siege: a Palestinian feminist perspective. *International Journal of Lifelong Education* 27(2), 179-200.

Shalhoub-Kevorkian, N., Kīfūrkiyān, N. S., & Shalhūb-Kīfūrkiyān, N. (2009). *Militarization and Violence Against Women in Conflict Zones in the Middle East: A Palestinian Case-Study.* Cambridge: Cambridge University Press.

Shalhoub-Kevorkian, N., & Shalhūb-Kīfūrkiyān, N. (2015). *Security Theology, Surveillance and the Politics of Fear.* Cambridge: Cambridge University Press.

Shamia, N. A., Thabet, A. A. M., & Vostanis, P. (2015). Exposure to war traumatic experiences, post-traumatic stress disorder and post-traumatic growth among nurses in Gaza. *Journal of Psychiatric and Mental Health Nursing*, 22(10), 749-755.

Shamim, I. (2010). *State of Trafficking in Women and Children and Their Sexual Exploitation in Bangladesh.* Dhaka, Bangladesh: Centre for Women and Children's Studies.

Shamsie, K. (2016). Why Pakistan must never forget Bacha Khan, its great unsung hero. *The Guardian Online*, January 20th, 2016.

Shannon, K., Strathdee, S. A., Goldenberg, S. M., Duff, P., Mwangi, P., Rusakova, M., ... & Boily, M. C. (2015). Global epidemiology of HIV among female sex workers: influence of structural determinants. *The Lancet*, *385*(9962), 55-71.

Shahrin, L., Leung, D. T., Matin, N., Pervez, M. M., Azim, T., Bardhan, P. K., ... & Chisti, M. J. (2014). Characteristics and predictors of death among hospitalized HIV-infected patients in a low HIV prevalence country: Bangladesh. *PloS one*, *9*(12), e113095.

Sharif, N. (2001). Poor female youth and human capital development in Bangladesh: what role for microcredit programmes? In B. Lemire and G. Campbell (Eds.) *Women and Credit: Researching the Past, Refiguring the Future* (pp 233-244). New York: Berg.

Sharmin-Salam, S., Alonge, O., Islam, M., Hoque, D., Wadhwaniya, S., Ul Baset, M., ... & El Arifeen, S. (2017). The burden of suicide in rural Bangladesh: magnitude and risk factors. *International Journal of Environmental Research and Public Health*, *14*(9), 1032-1045.

Shaw, A. (1988). *A Pakistani Community in Britain.* Oxford: Basil Blackwell.

Shehabuddin, E. (2008). *Reshaping the Holy: Democracy, Development, and Muslim Women in Bangladesh.* Washington: Columbia University Press.

Shehadeh, O. & Maaita, M. (2000). *Infanticide in Pre-Islamic Era.* Jordan: Dept of Arab Languages and Literature, Hashemite University.

Shen, J., Chanda, A., Netto, B., & Monga, M. (2009). Managing diversity through human resource management: an intersectional perspective and conceptual framework. *The International Journal of Human Resource Management*, 20 (2), 235–251.

Sheridan, L. (2006). Islamophobia pre- and post-September 11th, 2001. *Journal of Interpersonal Violence*, 21, 317-336.

Shipway, B. (2013). *A Critical Realist Perspective of Education.* London: Routledge.

Shohel, M., Ashrafuzzaman. N., Nishat, S., Ratan, D., Rasel, B., Mubarak, M. & Al-Mamun, M. (2012). Impact of education on sex workers and their children: case studies from Bangladesh. In: Sabet, D. (Ed.). *Sex Workers and Their Children in Bangladesh: Addressing Risks and Vulnerabilities.* (154-180). Dhaka: Center for Sustainable Development, University of Liberal Arts, Bangladesh.

Short, N., Turner, L. & Grant, A. (2013). *Contemporary British Autoethnography.* Leiden: Brill – Sense Education Series.

Shrivastava, A., Kimbrell, M. & Lester, D. (2012). *Suicide from a Global Perspective: Public Health Approaches.* New York: Nova Science Publishers.

Sial, M. H., Noreen, A., & Awan, R. U. (2015). Measuring multidimensional poverty and inequality in Pakistan. *The Pakistan Development Review,* 685-696.

Sian, K., Law, I., & Sayyid, S. (2013). *Racism, Governance, and Public Policy: Beyond Human Rights.* London: Routledge.

Sidani, Y. (2005). Women, work, and Islam in Arab societies. *Gender in Management,* 20 (7), 498-512.

Sidani, Y. (2017). *Muslim Women at Work.* London: Palgrave MacMillan.

Siddiqi, B. (2018). *Becoming 'Good Muslim': The Tablighi Jamaat in the UK and Bangladesh.* New York: Springer.

Siddique, H. & Hanrahan, M. (2018). Job applicants and consumers get different results depending on their perceived ethnicity. *Guardian Online,* December 3rd, 2018.

Siddique, H. (2019). Minority ethnic Britons face 'shocking job discrimination': UK research finds levels of discrimination unchanged since late 1960s. *Guardian Online,* January 17th, 2019.

Silverman, D. (2011) *Interpreting Qualitative Data: A Guide to the Principles of Qualitative Research,* 4th edition. London: Sage Publications.

Silverman, D. (2013) *Doing Qualitative Research: A Practical Handbook.* 4th ed. London: Sage Publications.

Silverman, M.M. & De Leo, D. (2016). Why is there a need for an international normative and classification system for suicide? *Crisis,* 37(2), 83-87.

Silverman, T. &Tait, M. (2016). *Dalatdia.* (Film, 11 minutes & 40 seconds) available online at www.guardian.com (accessed December 7, 2016).

Simkhada, P. and Adam-Bagley, C. (2008). Excluded and exploited: the sexual trafficking of girls and women from Nepal to India. In C. Adam-Bagley and G. Verma (Eds.) *Challenges for Social and Educational*

Inclusion: Studies from Britain and the Indian Sub-Continent (pp 219-263). Leiden: Brill - Sense Education Series.

Simkhada, P.P., Van Teijlingen, E., Winter, R.C., Fanning, C., Dhungel, A. & Marahatta, S.B. (2015). Why are so many Nepali women killing themselves? A review of key issue. *Journal of Manmohan Memorial Institute of Health Sciences* 1(4): 43-49.

Skinner, R. & McFaull. S. (2012). Suicide among children and adolescents in Canada: trends and sex differences, 1980–2008. *Canadian Medical Association Journal* 184(9): 1029–1034.

Skopek, J. & Passeretta, P. (2018). The evolution of social and ethnic inequalities in cognitive achievement from preschool to secondary schooling in the United Kingdom. In G. Passaretta and J. Skopek (Eds.) *Roots and Development of Achievement Gaps - A Longitudinal Assessment in Selected European Countries* (pp. 108-157). Dublin: Trinity College Dublin ISIOTIS Report S1.3. Available online at: www.isiotis.org

Slootman, M. & Duyvendak, J. W. (2015). Feeling Dutch: the culturalization and emotionalization of citizenship and second-generation belonging in the Netherlands. In *Fear, Anxiety, and National Identity: Immigration and Belonging in North America and Western Europe* (pp147-168). New York: Russell Sage Foundation.

Smith, R. J. (2018a). The effects of the Israeli siege on health provision in the Gaza Strip: a qualitative and theoretical analysis. *The Lancet*, 391, S37.

Smith, R. J. (2018b). Drawing urgent attention to attacks against Palestinian medical personnel. *Journal of Public Health*, August, fdy153, Online.

Sobh, R. & Silverman, T. &Tait, M. (2016). *Dalatdia*. (Film, 11 minutes & 40 seconds) available online at www.guardian.com (accessed December 7, 2016).

Sobhy S, Arroyo-Manzano D, Murugesu N, et al. (2019). Maternal and perinatal mortality and complications associated with caesarean section in low-income and middle-income countries: a systematic review and meta-analysis. *The Lancet*, March 28. DOI:10.1016/S0140-6736(18)32386-9

Sonneveld, N. (2019). Divorce reform in Egypt and Morocco: men and women navigating rights and duties. *Islamic Law and Society*, 26(1-2), 149-178.

Spangler, E. (2019). *Understanding Israel/Palestine: Race, Nation and Human Rights*. Leiden: Brill.

Spector, P., Cooper, C., Poelmans, S., Allen, T., O'Driscoll, M., Sanchez, J., Siu, O., Dewe, P., Hart, P. & Lu, L. (2004). A cross-national comparative study of work-family stressors, working hours, and well-being: China and Latin America Versus the Anglo World. *Personnel Psychology,* 57 (1), 119-142.

Spierings, N. (2015). *Women's Employment in Muslim Countries: Patterns of Diversity.* London, UK: Palgrave-MacMillan.

Stacki, S.L. & Baily, S. (Eds.) (2015). *Educating Adolescent Girls Around the Globe: Challenges and Opportunities.* London: Routledge.

Staetsky, L. D., & Boyd, J. (2016). *The Rise and Rise of Jewish Schools in the United Kingdom: Numbers, Trends and Policy Issues.* London: Institute for Jewish Policy Research.

Stahl, G. (2015). *Identity, Neoliberalism and Aspiration: Educating White Working Class Boys.* London: Routledge.

Stalker, G. (2014) Gendered perceptions of time among parents: family contexts, role demands, and variation in time-stress. *Loisir et Société/Society and Leisure,* 37 (2), 241-261.

Stallard, P. (2009). *Cognitive Behaviour Therapy with Children and Young People.* London: Routledge.

Standing, G. (2011 & 2014). *The Precariat: The New Dangerous Class* (1st and 2nd editions). London: Bloomsbury Academic.

Staples, J. K., Atti, A., Ahmed, J., & Gordon, J. S. (2011). Mind-body skills groups for posttraumatic stress disorder and depression symptoms in Palestinian children and adolescents in Gaza. *International Journal of Stress Management,* 18(3), 246.

Sternadori, M., & Prentice, C. (Eds.). (2016). *Gender and Work: Exploring Intersectionality, Resistance, and Identity.* Newcastle, UK: Cambridge Scholars Publishing.

Stone, S. L. (2003). Tolerance versus pluralism in Judaism. *Journal of Human Rights,* 2(1), 105-117.

Stoter, B. (2016). Divisive Turkey coup exposes integration problems for Dutch-Turkish community. *The New Arab,* July 22nd, pp 4-6.

Strabiac. Z. & Listhaug. O. (2008) Anti-Muslim prejudice in Europe: a multilevel analysis of survey data from 30 countries. *Social Science Research,* 37, 268-286.

Suarez, P. (2018). Child-bride marriage and female welfare. *European Journal of Law and Economics,* 45(1) 1-28.

Summerfield, D. (2012). *Global Mental health is Westernised Medicalisation of Distress.* London: School of Hygiene and Tropical Medicine.

Summerfield, D., Halpin, D., Ang, S., Balduzzi, A., Camandona, F., Tognoni, G., ... & Agnoletto, V. (2018). The maiming fields of Gaza. *British Medical Journal,* 362, k3299.

Sultan, N., Weir, D. & Karake-Shalhoub, Z. (2011). *The New Post-Oil Arab Gulf: Managing People and Wealth*. London: Saqi Books.

Sultana, H. (2015). Sex worker activism, feminist discourse and HIV in Bangladesh. *Culture, Health and Sexuality*, 17, 777-788.

Suran, L., Amin, S., Huq, L., Chowdury, K. (2004). *Does Dowry Improve Life for Brides? A Test of the Bequest Theory of Dowry in Rural Bangladesh*. New York: UN Population Research Council, Working Paper 195.

SWN & SWASA (2016). *Submission to the United Nations Committee on the Elimination of Discrimination Against Women*. Dhaka, Bangladesh: Sex Workers' Network (SWN) Bangladesh; and Sex Workers and Allies in South Asia (SWASA), Bangladesh Chapter. (Document available Online)

Syed, J. (2008). A context-specific perspective of equal employment opportunity in Islamic societies. *Asia Pacific Journal of Management*, 25(1), 135–151.

Syed, J. (2010). An historical perspective on Islamic modesty and its implications for female employment. *Equality, Diversity and Inclusion: An International Journal*, 29(2), 150-166.

Syed, J., Ali, F. & Winstanley, D. (2005). In pursuit of modesty: contextual emotional labor and the dilemma for working women in Islamic societies. *International Journal of Work, Organization and Emotion*, 1 (2), 150–167.

Syed, J. & Klarsfeld (Eds.) (2018). *Religious Diversity in the Workplace*. Cambridge: Cambridge University Press.

Syed, J., & Özbilgin, M. (2009). A relational framework for international transfer of diversity management practices. *International Journal of Human Resource Management*, 20(12), 2435–2453.

Syed, J., & Özbilgin, M. (Eds.) (2015). *Managing Diversity and Inclusion: An International Perspective*. London: Sage.

Syed, J. & Pio, E. (2016). Muslim diaspora in the West and international human relations management. *International Journal of Human Resource Management*, 10, 115-137.

Tajfel, H. (1981). *Human Groups and Social Categories: Studies in Social Psychology*. Cambridge: Cambridge University Press.

Talbi, M. (1998) Religious liberty. In C. Kurzman (Ed.) *Liberal Islam: A Sourcebook*. Oxford: Oxford University Press.

Talib, Z. & Barry, M. (2017). Women leaders in global health. *Lancet Global Health*, 5: e565–e566.

Talukder, L. (2018). How far is Bangladesh from eliminating obstetric fistula? *New Age Opinion*, May 23rd, 2018

Tanaka, C. T., Berger, W., Valença, A. M., Coutinho, E. S., Jean-Louis, G., Fontenelle, L. F., & Mendlowicz, M. V. (2017). The worldwide incidence of neonaticide: a systematic review. *Archives of Women's Mental Health*, *20*(2), 249-256.

Taraki, L. (2006). (Ed.). Living Palestine: Family survival, resistance, and mobility under occupation. New York, NY: Syracuse University Press.

Tareen, A. & Tareen, K.I. (2019). Management of psychological distress by non-specialists in conflict-affected areas. *The Lancet*, 393 (Issue 10182) 1676-1677, April 27, 2019.

Tariq, M. & Syed, J. (2017). Asian Muslim women's experiences of employment and leadership in the United Kingdom. *Sex Roles*, 68 (1), 1-13.

Tariq, M. & Syed, J. (2018). An intersectional perspective on Muslim women's issues and experiences in employment. *Gender, Work and Organisation*, 25(4), 495-513.

Tayyab, F., Kamal, N., Akbar, T., & Zakar, R. (2017). Men and women's perceptions of justifications of wife beating: evidence from Pakistan Demographic and Health Survey 2012–13. *Journal of Family Violence*, *32*(7), 721-730.

Telsur (2018). Pakistan: with peaking female infanticide, 345 newborn bodies recovered from garbage piles. *Telsur News Agency*: www.telsurenglish.net

Thabet, A. (2019). Psychological well-being of Palestinian children and adolescents: a review paper. *EC Psychiatry and Psychology* 8(3), 197-205.

Thabet, A., Tawahina, A., El Saraj & Vostanis, P. (2008). Exposure to war trauma and PTSD among parents and children in the Gaza strip. *European Child and Adolescent Psychiatry*, 17(2), 191-199.

Thabet, A. A., Ibraheem, A. N., Shivram, R., Winter, E. A., & Vostanis, P. (2009). Parenting support and PTSD in children of a war zone. *International Journal of Social Psychiatry*, 55(3), 226-237.

Thabet, A. A., Matar, S., Carpintero, A., Bankart, J., & Vostanis, P. (2011). Mental health problems among labour children in the Gaza Strip. *Child: Care, Health and Development*, 37(1), 89-95.

Thabet, A., Elhelaub, M. & Vostanis, P. (2015). Exposure to war traumatic experiences, post-traumatic growth and resilience among university students in Gaza. *American Journal of Advanced Medical Sciences*, 1(1), 1-8.

Thabet, A. & Thabet, S. (2015). Stress, trauma, psychological problems, quality of life, and resilience of Palestinian families in the Gaza Strip. *Clinical Psychiatry*, 1(2), December 6, Open Access, Online.

Thabet, A. & Thabet, S. (2016). Trauma, PTSD, anxiety and resilience in Palestinian Children in the Gaza Strip. *British Journal of Education, Society & Behavioural Science* 11(1), Online.

Thabet, A. A., Tawahina, A. A., Tischler, V., & Vostanis, P. (2015). PTSD, depression, and anxiety among Palestinian women victims of domestic violence in the Gaza Strip. *British Journal of Education, Society and Behavioural Science*, 11(2), Online.

Thabet, A. M., Thabet, S. S., & Vostanis, P. (2016). The relationship between war trauma, PTSD, depression, and anxiety among Palestinian children in the Gaza Strip. *Health Science Journal*, 10(5). Online.

Thévenon, O. (2011) Family policies in OECD countries: a comparative analysis. *Population and Development Review*, 37 (1), 57-87.

Thijs, J. & Verkuyten, M. (2013). Multiculturalism in the classroom: ethnic attitudes and classmates' beliefs. *International Journal of Intercultural Relations*, 3, 176-187.

Thomas, D. (2015). From National Liberation to Neoliberalism: 'Peace' and Aid in Palestine. www.opendemocracy.net. Consulted 6.12.17

Thomas, G. (Ed.) (2014). *Case Study Methods in Education, Volumes 1 to 4*. London: Sage.

Thomas, G. (2015). *How to Do Your Educational Case Study*. London: Sage.

Tinker, C. (2009). Rights, social cohesion and identity: arguments for and against state-funded Muslim schools in Britain. *Race, Ethnicity and Education*, 12, 539–53.

Tithi, N. (2017). Downplaying child sexual abuse. *The Daily Star* (Dhaka) October 25th, 2017, Online.

Tibbitts, F., & Katz, S. R. (2017). Dilemmas and hopes for human rights education: curriculum and learning in international contexts. *Prospects*, 47(1-2), 31-40.

Tlaiss, H. & Kauser, S. (2010) Perceived organizational barriers to women's career advancement in Lebanon. *Gender in Management: An International Journal,* 25 (6), 462-496.

Tomlinson, S. (2008). *Race and Education: Policy and Politics in Britain*. Maidenhead: Open University Press and McGraw Hill.

Tomlinson, S. (2013). *Ignorant Yobs? Low Attainers in a Global Knowledge Economy*. London: Routledge and Taylor & Francis.

Tonnessen, L. & Abbas, A. (2014). Global campaign to stop stoning of women: off target in Sudan. *CMI Field Notes*. Bergen: Chr Michelsen Institute.

Topolski, A. (2018). Good Jew, bad Jew… good Muslim, bad Muslim: "managing" Europe's others. *Ethnic and Racial Studies, 41*(12), 2179-2196.

Torry, M. (2015). *101 Reasons for a Citizen's Income*. Bristol, UK: The Policy Press.

Trew, B. (2018). Gaza's economy 'collapsing' due to Israeli blockade and massive funding cuts, World Bank warns. *Independent Online*, September 25, 2018.

Trew, B. (2019). Ticking time bomb - the water crisis which threatens chances for peace in the Middle East: climate change and crumbling infrastructure are causing water shortages in Gaza, which could soon make the enclave uninhabitable. *Independent Online*, January 21, 2019.

Tse, J. & Adam-Bagley, C. (2000/2018). *Suicide and Death Education in Chinese Adolescents: Hong Kong Studies*. London: Routledge Ashgate, Classic Reprint.

TUC (2016). *Black and Ethnic Minority Women Disadvantaged*. London: Trades Union Council Report, August, 2016.

Tyrer, D. (2013). *The Politics of Islamophobia: Race, Power and Fantasy*. London: Pluto Press.

Uddin, M. J., Sarma, H., Wahed, T., Ali, M. W., Koehlmoos, T. P., Nahar, Q., & Azim, T. (2014a). Vulnerability of Bangladeshi street-children to HIV/AIDS: a qualitative study. *BMC Public Health, 14*(1), 1151, Online.

Uddin, S. M., Hossain, M. G., Islam, M. A., Islam, M. N., Aik, S., & Kamarul, T. (2014b). High-risk behavior of HIV/AIDS among female sex workers in Bangladesh: survey in Rajshahi City. *Japanese Journal of Infectious Diseases, 67*(3), 191-196.

UNAIDS (2016). *Sex Workers: Population Size Estimates*. www.aidsinfoonline.org

UNDP (2016). *Report of the National Consultation on Law and Policies Affecting Human Rights, Discrimination and Access to HIV and Health Services by Key Populations in Pakistan*. Islamabad: United Nations Development Program, Regional Office.

UNDP (2018). *Human Development Reports*. New York: United Nations Development Program.

UNESCO (2014). *Rapid Assessment of Higher Education Institutions in Gaza*. Paris: United Nations Educational, Cultural and Scientific Organization.

UNICEF (2016). *Children at Risk in the Gaza Conflict*. New York: United Nations International Children's Emergency Fund.

United Nations (2012). *Gaza in 2020: A Liveable Place?* New York: The United Nations.
United Nations (2015). *Classification of All Economic Activities by Gender*, 3rd Edition. New York: UN Statistics Division.
UNRWA (2013). *Education in Gaza.* New York: The United Nations Refugee and Welfare Association.
UNRWA (2018). *Palestinian Refugees.* New York: The United Nations Refugee and Welfare Association.
UNRWA (2018). www.unrwa.org/what-we-do/education Retrieved 27.6.18.
UNODC (2009). *Global Report on Trafficking in Persons.* New York: United Nations Office on Drugs and Crime (available at www.unodc.org).
Unwin, J. (2011). Reading the riots. *The Guardian Online*, September 8th, 2011.
Unwin, J. (2013). *Why Fight Poverty?* London. UK: London Publishers' Foundation.
UNWOMEN (2018). *Rural Women in Pakistan: Status Report.* Geneva: UN Women: www.UNwomen.org
Urada L., Goldenberg S., Shannon K. & Strathdee, S. (2014). Sexuality and sex work. In Tolman D. (Ed.) *APA Handbook of Sexuality and Psychology, Vol 2: Contextual Approaches* (pp 37-76). Washington, DC: American Psychological Association.
Urmi, A. Z., Leung, D. T., Wilkinson, V., Miah, M. A. A., Rahman, M., & Azim, T. (2015). Profile of an HIV testing and counseling unit in Bangladesh: majority of new diagnoses among returning migrant workers and spouses. *PloS one, 10*(10), e0141483.
Urquhart, C. (2001) An encounter with grounded theory: tackling the practical and philosophical issues. In E. Trauth (Ed.) *Qualitative Research: Issues and Trends*, 104–140. Hershey, PA: Idea Group Publishing.
Vaktskjold, A., Yaghi, M., Balawi, U., Iversen, B., & Venter, W. (2016). The mortality in Gaza in July—September 2014: a retrospective chart-review study. *Conflict and Health*, 10(1), 10-15.
Valli, Y. (2012). From Madrassa to mainstream: the role of the Madrassa in shaping core Islamic values and practice amongst young British Muslims. In M. Farrar et al. (Eds.) *Islam in the West: Key Issues in Multiculturalism.* London: Palgrave MacMillan.
van Bergen, D. D., Wachter, G. G., & Feddes, A. R. (2017). Externalizing behaviours of Turkish-Dutch and Moroccan-Dutch youth: the role of

parental cultural socialization. *European Journal of Developmental Psychology*, 1-14, Online.

van den Berg, M. M., Madi, H. H., Khader, A., Hababeh, M., Zeidan, W. A., Wesley, H., ... & Seita, A. (2015). Increasing neonatal mortality among Palestine refugees in the Gaza Strip. *PloS One*, 10(8), e0135092.

Van den Berg, C., Bijleveld, C., Blommaert, L., & Ruiter, S. (2017). Veroordeeld tot (g) een baan: hoe delict-en persoonskenmerken arbeidsmarktkansen beïnvloeden. *Tijdschrift voor Criminologie*, 59(1-2), 113-135.

Vandepitte, J., Lyerla, R., Dallabetta, G., Crabbé, F., Alary, M., & Buvé, A. (2006). Estimates of the number of female sex workers in different regions of the world. *Sexually Transmitted Infections*, 82(suppl 3), iii18-iii25.

Van der Valk, J. (2015). *Dutch Islamophobia and Discrimination*. Amsterdam: Institute for Migration and Ethnic Studies, University of Amsterdam.

van Driel, B. (Ed.). (2004). *Confronting Islamophobia in Educational Practice*. Stoke, UK: Trentham Books.

Van Sandwijk, A. (2014). The rise and fall of Tariq Ramadan in The Netherlands: the interplay of Dutch politics, media and academia. *Journal of Muslims in Europe*, 3 (2), 181-208.

Värnik P. (2012). Suicide in the world. *International Journal of Environment and Research on Public Health* 9(3), 760–771.

Veenstra, G. (2013). The gendered nature of discriminatory experiences by race, class, and sexuality: a comparison of intersectionality theory and the subordinate male target hypothesis. *Sex Roles* 68: 646–59.

Velasco González, K., Verkuyten, M., Weesie, J., & Poppe, E. (2008). Prejudice towards Muslims in the Netherlands: testing integrated threat theory. *British Journal of Social Psychology*, 47(4), 667-685.

Veling, W., Selten, J. P., Susser, E., Laan, W., Mackenbach, J. P., & Hoek, H. W. (2007). Discrimination and the incidence of psychotic disorders among ethnic minorities in The Netherlands. *International Journal of Epidemiology*, 36(4), 761-768.

Vellenga, S. (2018). Anti-Semitism and Islamophobia in the Netherlands: concepts, developments, and backdrops. *Journal of Contemporary Religion*, 33(2), 175-192.

Verbeek, S., & Groenveld, S. (2012). Do 'hard' diversity policies increase ethnic minority representation? *Personnel Review*, 41(5), 647–664. doi:10.1108/00483481211249157.

Verkuyten, M. (2005). *The Social Psychology of Ethnic Identity*. New York and London: Taylor and Francis.

Verkuyten, M. & Thijs, A. (2013). Multicultural education and inter-ethnic attitudes: an intergroup perspective. *European Psychologist*, 18, 179-190.

Verma, G.K. (1989). Education for all: a landmark in pluralism. In G.K. Verma (Ed.) *Education for all: A Landmark in Pluralism*. London: The Falmer Press.

Verma, G. K., Skinner, G. & Adam-Bagley, C. (1999). *Chinese Adolescents in Britain: Identity and Aspirations*. London: Routledge Ashgate.

Verma, G. (2007). Diversity and multicultural education: cross-cutting issues and concepts. In G. Verma & C. Adam-Bagley (Eds.) *International Perspectives on Educational Diversity and Inclusion*. London: Routledge.

Veronese, G. & Pepe, A. (2017a). Positive and negative affect in children living in refugee camps: Assessing the psychometric proprieties and factorial invariance of the PANAS-C in the Gaza Strip. *Evaluation and the Health Professions*, 40(1), 3-32.

Veronese, G. & Pepe, A. (2017b). Sense of coherence as a determinant of psychological well-being across professional groups of aid workers exposed to war trauma. *Journal of Interpersonal Violence*, 32(13), 1899-1920.

Veronese, G., Pepe, A., Jaradah, A., Al Muranak, F., & Hamdouna, H. (2017a). Modelling life satisfaction and adjustment to trauma in children exposed to ongoing military violence: an exploratory study in Palestine. *Child Abuse and Neglect*, 63, 61-72.

Veronese, G., Pepe, A., Jaradah, A., Murannak, F., & Hamdouna, H. (2017b). "We must cooperate with one another against the enemy": agency and activism in school-aged children as protective factors against ongoing war trauma and political violence in the Gaza Strip. *Child Abuse & Neglect*, 70, 364-376.

Veronese, G., & Barola, G. (2018). Healing stories: An expressive-narrative intervention for strengthening resilience and survival skills in school-aged child victims of war and political violence in the Gaza Strip. *Clinical Child Psychology and Psychiatry*, 23(2), 311-332.

Veronese, G., Cavazzoni, F., & Antenucci, S. (2018). Narrating hope and resistance: A critical analysis of sources of agency among Palestinian children living under military violence. *Child: Care, Health and Development*, August 2018. https://doi.org/10.1111/cch.12608

Veronese, G., Pepe, A., Almurnak, F., Jaradah, A., & Hamdouna, H. (2018). Quality of life, primary traumatisation, and positive and negative affects in primary school students in the Gaza Strip. *The Lancet*, 391, S14.

Vijayakumar, L. (2004). Suicide prevention: the urgent need in developing countries. *World Psychiatry*, 3(3), 158-159.

von Elm E, Altman DG, Egger M, Pocock SJ, Gotzsche PC, Vandenbroucke JP, et al. (2007). Strengthening the reporting of observational studies in epidemiology (STROBE) statement: guidelines for reporting observational studies. *PLoS Medicine*, 4: e296. [pii]. doi: 10.1371/journal.pmed.0040296. pmid:17941714

Vostanis, P. (2014). *Helping Children and Young People who Experience Trauma: Children of Despair, Children of Hope*. London: Radcliffe Publishing.

Vostanis, P. (2016). *A Practical Guide to Helping Children and Young People Who Experience Trauma*. London: Speech Mark Books.

Vostanis, P., O'Reilly, M., Duncan, C., Maltby, J., & Anderson, E. (2018). Interprofessional training on resilience-building for children who experience trauma: stakeholders' views from six low-and middle-income countries. *Journal of Interprofessional Care*, 33(2), 142-142.

Wadud, A. (1999). *Qur'an and Women: Rereading the Sacred Text from a Woman's Perspective*. Oxford: Oxford University Press.

Wadud, A. (2005). *Inside the Gender Jihad: Women's Reform in Islam*. Oxford: One World Books.

Wahbalbari, A., Bahari, Z., & Mohd-Zaharim, N. (2015). The concept of scarcity and its influence on the definitions of Islamic economics: a critical perspective. *Humanomics*, *31*(2), 134-159.

Wahed, T., Alam, A., Sultana, S., Alam, N., & Somrongthong, R. (2017). Sexual and reproductive health behaviors of female sex workers in Dhaka, Bangladesh. *PloS one*, *12*(4), e0174540.

Wahlin A., Palmer K., Sternang O., Hamadani J.D., Kabir Z.N. (2015). Prevalence of depressive symptoms and suicidal thoughts among elderly persons in rural Bangladesh. *International Psychogeriatrics*, 27(12), 1999-2008.

Waller, P. & Yilmaz, I. (2011). *European Muslims, Civility and Public Life*. London: Continuum Books.

Walker, P. (2018). Divided Britain - study finds huge chasm in attitudes: far-right and anti-Islam ideas taking root in post-industrial towns. *Guardian Online*, October 17th, 2018.

Wang, P. & Walumbwa, F. (2007) Family-friendly programs, organisational commitment, and work withdrawal: the moderating role of transformational leadership. *Personnel Psychology*, 60 (2), 397-427.

Wang, P., Lawler, J., Shi, K., Walumbwa, F. & Piao, M. (2008) Family-friendly employment practices: importance and effects in India, Kenya, and China. *Advances in International Management*, 21, 235-65.

Wani, S. (2017). For too long, Pakistan schools have been a means to provide jobs, rather than education. *The Guardian Online* June 6th, 2017.
Wasserman, D., Cheng, Q & Jiang, G. (2005). Global suicide rates among young people aged 15–19. *World Psychiatry* 4(2), 114–20.
Waterston, T., & Nasser, D. (2017). Access to healthcare for children in Palestine. *BMJ Paediatrics Open*, 1(1), e000115.
Watson, A. and Rowe, D. (2018). *Experience and Faith in Education: Contemporary Essays from Quaker Perspectives*. Stoke, UK: Trentham Books.
Watt, M. (1977). *The Influence of Islam on Mediaeval Europe*. Edinburgh: University of Edinburgh Press.
WEF (2012-2019). *The Global Gender Gap Reports*. Geneva: World Economic Forum.
Weiner, M. F. (2014). The ideologically colonized metropole: Dutch racism and racist denial. *Sociology Compass*, 8(6), 731-744.
White, M. A., & Waters, L. E. (2015). A case study of 'The Good School': examples of the use of Peterson's strengths-based approach with students. *The Journal of Positive Psychology*, 10(1), 69-76.
White, S.C. (1992). *Arguing with the Crocodile: Gender and Class in Bangladesh*. London: Zed Books.
White, S.C. (2007). Children's rights and the imagination of community in Bangladesh. *Childhood*, 14(4), 505-520.
White, S. C. (2010). Domains of contestation: women's empowerment and Islam in Bangladesh. *Women's Studies International Forum* 33(4) 334-344.
White, S. C. (2015). Qualitative perspectives on the impact evaluation of girls' empowerment in Bangladesh. *Journal of Development Effectiveness*, 7(2), 127-145.
White, S.C. (2017). Patriarchal investments: marriage, dowry and the political economy of development in Bangladesh. *Journal of Contemporary Asia*, 47(2), 247-272.
Whiteley, P. (2014). Does Citizenship Education work? Evidence from a decade of citizenship education in secondary schools in England. *Parliamentary Affairs*, 67(3), 513-535.
WHO (2007). *WHO-AIMS Report on Mental Health System in Bangladesh*. Dhaka: World Health Organisation and Ministry of Health & Family Welfare.
WHO (2014). *Preventing Suicide: A Global Imperative*. Geneva: The World Health Organization.
WHO (2016). *Mental Health: Suicide Data*. Geneva: World Health Organisation.

Whyte, C. (2019). A world of pain: this unsung story of slave women in gynaecology deserves a wide audience. *New Scientist*, January 26th, p. 46.

Wilders, G. (2012). *Marked for Death: Islam's War against the West and Me*. Washington: Regnery Publishing.

Wilkinson, M.L. (2013). Introducing Islamic critical realism: a philosophy underlabouring contemporary Islam. *Journal of Critical Realism*, 12(5), 419-442.d

Wilkinson, M. L. (2015a). *A Fresh Look at Islam in a Multi-Faith World: A Philosophy for Success Through Education*. London: Routledge.

Wilkinson, M. L. (2015b). The metaphysics of a contemporary Islamic Shari'a: a meta-realist perspective. *Journal of Critical Realism*, *14*(4), 350-365.o

Wilkinson, M L. (2017). Factoring-in faith fairly: a contribution from critical realism to the authentic framing of Muslims-in-education. In *Muslim Students, Education and Neoliberalism* (pp. 67-84). Palgrave Macmillan, London.

Wilkinson, M. L. (2018). *The Genealogy of Terror: How to Distinguish between Islam, Islamism and Islamist Extremism*. London: Routledge.

Wilson, M. (1999). 'Take this child': why women abandon their infants in Bangladesh. *Journal of Comparative Family Studies*, 30(4) 682-702.

Wilson, T. (2015). *Hospitality and Translation: An Exploration of how Muslim Pupils Translate in the Context of an Anglican Primary School*. Newcastle: Cambridge Scholars Publications.

Withall, A. & Khan, M.Z. (2019). Why Pakistan is kicking out foreign charities. *Independent Online*, February 21st, 2019,

Woetzel, J. (2015). *The Power of Parity: How Advancing Women's Equality Can Add $12 Trillion to Global Growth*. eSocialScience Working Papers Id: 7570.

Wood, M., Hales, J. Purdon, S., Sejersen,T. & Hayllar. O. (2009). *A Test for Racial Discrimination in Recruitment Practice in British Cities*; Research Report No. 607. London: Department for Work and Pensions.

Woolf, N. H., & Silver, C. (2017). *Qualitative Analysis Using NVivo: The Five-Level QDA® Method*. London: Routledge.

World Bank (2012). *Gender Equality and Development*. Washington DC: The World Bank.

World Bank (2017). *Palestine's Economic Outlook*. Washington. DC: The World Bank.

World Bank (2018). *Cash-Strapped Gaza and an Economy in Collapse Put Palestinian Basic Needs at Risk*. Washington, DC: The World Bank.

Wrench, J. & Modood, T. (2000). *The Effectiveness of Employment Equality Policies in Relation to Immigrants and Ethnic Minorities in the UK*. Geneva: International Labor Office.

Wyatt, R. & Masood, N. (2010). *Broken Mirrors: The Dowry Problem in India*. New Delhi: Sage.

Yazil, C. (2017). Why is Turkey in a row with The Netherlands? *The New Statesman*, March 14th, 2017, p. 2.

YHR (2019). *Youth for Human Rights*. www.youthforhumanrights.org.

Yilmaz, G., & Schmid, M. S. (2015). Second language development in a migrant context: Turkish community in the Netherlands. *International Journal of the Sociology of Language*, 2015(236), 101-132.

Yin, R. K. (1994). *Case Study Research: Design and Methods (Applied Social Research Methods, Vol. 5)*. Beverly Hills, CA: Sage.

Yin, R. K. (2011). *Applications of Case Study Research*. London: Sage.

Yin, R. K. (2015). *Qualitative Research from Start to Finish*. New York: Guilford Publications.

Yin, R. K. (2018). *Case Study Research: Design and Methods Sixth Edition*. Beverly Hills, CA: Sage.

Yousafzai, M. (2018). *Malala: My Story of Standing up for Girl's Rights*. London: Hodder and Stoughton.

Yousafzai, M. (2019). *We are Displaced: My Journey and Stories from Refugee Girls Around the World*. London: Weidenfeld & Nicolson.

YouTube (2018). *'The Judge Kholoud Al-Faqih' – Middle East's first female judge, in Shari'a law court in Palestine*. YouTube Video, May 21, 2018.

Yusuf, H. R., Akhter, H. H., Rahman, M. H., Chowdhury, M. E. K., & Rochat, R. W. (2000). Injury-related deaths among women aged 10–50 years in Bangladesh, 1996–97. *The Lancet*, 355(9211), 1220-1224.

Zacharialis, M., Scott, S. & Barrett, M. (2010). *Exploring Critical Realism as the Theoretical Foundation of Mixed-Method Research: Evidence from the Economics of Information Science Innovations*. Cambridge: Cambridge University Judge Business School.

Zahidi, S., Geiger, T. & Crotti, R. (2019). *Global Gender Gap Report, 2018*. Geneva: World Economic Forum.

Zakar, R., Zakar, M. Z., & Kraemer, A. (2013). Men's beliefs and attitudes toward intimate partner violence against women in Pakistan. *Violence Against Women*, *19*(2), 246-268.

Zalsman, G., Hawton, K., Wasserman, D., van Heeringen, K., Arensman, E., Sarchiapone, M., ... & Purebl, G. (2016). Suicide prevention strategies revisited: 10-year systematic review. *The Lancet Psychiatry*, 3(7), 646-659.

Zareen, A. (2014). Children in brothels. *The Daily Star* (Dhaka), May 15, 2014, Online.

Zebiri, K. (2011). Orientalist themes in contemporary British Islamophobia. In J. Esposito and I. Kalin (Eds) *Islamophobia: The Challenge of Pluralism in the 21st Century* (pp 173-190). Oxford: Oxford University Press.

Zempi, I. & Imran A. (2017). Doing 'dangerous' autoethnography on Islamophobic victimization. *Ethnography* 18, 367–86.

Zia, A.S, (1994). *Sex Crime in the Islamic Context: Rape, Class and Gender in Pakistan*. Lahore: Pakistan Hoshruba Group Publishing.

Zia, A. S. (2009a). The reinvention of feminism in Pakistan. *Feminist Review*, *91*(1), 29-46.

Zia, A. S. (2009b). Faith-based politics, enlightened moderation and the Pakistani women's movement. *Journal of International Women's Studies*, *11*(1), 225-245.

Zick, A., Pettigrew, T. & Wagner, U. (2008). Ethnic prejudice and discrimination in Europe. *Journal of Social Issues*, 64, 233-251.

Zipris, I., Pliskin, R., Canetti, D., & Halperin, E. (2018). Exposure to the 2014 Gaza War and support for militancy: the role of emotion dysregulation. *Personality and Social Psychology Bulletin*, 1-13, Online 0146167218805988.

Zuzanek, J. and Manhell, R. (1998). Life-cycle squeeze, time pressure, daily stress, and leisure participation: a Canadian perspective. *Loisir et société/Society and Leisure,* 21 (2), 513-544.

SUBJECT INDEX

Alienation: Critical Realism (DCR) 19-33, 90, 109; Citizenship Education 121, 132, 155; Discrimination 177, 180; Islamophobia 313-315; Mental Illness 310-312; Negative Behaviours 209, 307; Muslim Youth, 31; Terrorism 307-312
Alderson, Priscilla & Critical Realism (DCR): 18-19, 22-33, 90, 109, 209, 293
Arab Culture & Human Resources Management: 56-73
Archer, Margaret & Critical Realism (DCR): 21-32, 57-59, 64, 90, 109, 254
Assimilation of Minorities: See Integration
AURAT Women's Foundation in Pakistan: 51
Bacha Khan, Pakistani Hero: 263-68
Bangladesh: "Absent Children" in Critical Realism (DCR) 33; Causes of Female Suicide 243-48; Child Labour & Poverty, 213-216; Child Marriage 235, 255-262; Child Murder, Maltreatment & Rape 12, 33, 216-18, 227-28, 255-262; Climate Issues 215, 234; Completed Suicide 341-45; Daughters, Valued 17; Discrimination, in UK 188-90; Dowry Issues 235-38; Gender Equality 2, 41, 51; Male Sexuality and Sexism 225-27; Patriarchy 235; Poverty & Economic Development 213-16, 228, 260-262; Poverty as Suicide Cause 235-38; Prevention of Suicide 251-54; Sexual Exploitation of Women 212-228; Shari'a Principles 12-13; Slums 238; Suicidal Behaviours 229-254; Village Brothels, 218-223; Violent Deaths in Females 238-240; Women's Education 13; Women's High Suicide Rates 229-254; Women Managers 36; Women and Political Change 254

Bangladeshis in UK: 26-27, 126, 158, 160. 188-190
Bhaskar, Roy & Critical Realism (DCR): 18-33, 57-58, 314, 316
Black feminism 43
Blockade of Gaza 61, 74-111, 312
Bourdieu, Sociology of: 9, 28-29, 282
Child Health: Child Marriage 255-262; Bangladesh 215, 228, 234, 236, 251; Gaza 78, 87; Pakistan 259, 269, 276
Childhood Sexual Exploitation: in Bangladesh 215-216, 228; of Boys, 278, 282; in Islam, 213, 216; as Male Hegemony, 228, 259; in Pakistan, 282, 286; Poverty as driver, 228; PTSD, 255-262; Trafficking, 286
Citizenship: Education in UK 26-27, 131-161; Muslim Schools 128-131; Muslim Social Contract 8, 26, 46
Corruption: 293-94 (see also *Evil*)
Critical Realism (DCR): Childhood Research 24-35; Educational Research 19, 25-27; & Islam 24-

27, 30-34, 55; Management Research 56-73; Social Change 24-31; (see also *Alderson, Priscilla*; *Archer, Margaret*; *Bhaskar, Roy*; *Wilkinson, Matthew*)
Descartes and "wonder" 31
Discrimination: Agents of 132-33; Education Against 144, 152; Effect upon Victims 156, 165, 180, 2017-10 (see also *Alienation*); Employment 158-181; History, in UK & Netherlands 163-211; Islamophobia 123-25, 156-58, 208-09; Law Versus 179-181, 186; Measurement 162-211; Muhammad endures 161; 'Muslim Penalty' 191-96; Prejudice Causes 133, 163, 183; Women 35-44, 53, 191-211
Divorce: Islamic Law & Practice 5,7, 13-17, 52, 235; Bangladesh 235, 244, 255, 262-3; Egypt 16-19; Pakistan 260-3, 272, 290
EDHI Foundation of Pakistan: 290-91
Educational Programmes: Bangladesh 212-228; England 120-161; Gaza 24-119; Netherlands 173, 175; Pakistan 263-294 (see also *Madrasahs*)
Ethnographic Research: Egypt & Palestine 44-45, 72-73; Gaza 74-119; 'Sex Work' in Bangladesh 212-228; 'Sex Work' in Pakistan 285-288; Suicidality in Bangladesh, 237-38
Egypt & Women's Equality: 14-17, 44, 49, 64, 69, 72, 298-300
Equality & Human Rights Commission, UK: 189, 192-97
Evil: 163, 293, 295, 200, 301-04, 307, 309, 311 (see also *Corruption*; & *Shaitan*)

Female Infanticide: Bangladesh 236, 260; Islam versus 5-6, 273, 288; Pakistan, 5, 12, 236, 273, 280, 289-91; Abortion of Female Foetuses 289
Feminism in Islam: 2-6, 46, 79-81 (see also *Women*)
Forgiveness in Islam: 4, 254, 263, 297, 300-02, 308 (see also *Peace-Making*)
Free Will: Critical Realism (DCR) 164; Islam 7, 105, 163; Social Action, 164, 307
Gaza: Children 74-119; Education 74-119; Israel 74-119; Warfare 56-119; Women 56-119
Genocide: 297, 303
Glass Ceiling for Women Professionals: 10, 36, 40, 50-51, 53, 56
Gulf States & Women Managers: 40, 49-54
Global Gender Gap: 40-41, 50-51
Hadith of Prophet Muhammad: 1-3, 10, 12, 46, 164, 178, 235. 252, 254, 260
Hamas & Gaza: 78, 82, 110
Hawa (Eve) & Adam: 2, 45, 120, 296, 394, 307
Hijab & Women's Equality: 8, 43, 46122-23, 127-28, 160, 166, 176, 191-92, 208, 213
'Honour' Killing: Bangladesh 12; Pakistan 12, 238, 273, 279, 281-85, 291
Human Resources Management: 36-73
Human Rights Watch (HRW): UK's Prevent 159; Children in Pakistan, 262, 274-75, 277, 281-286
HRCP - Human Rights Commission of Pakistan: 255, 258, 261-62, 269-70, 273-86
Identity: Alienation, 208, 307-14; Citizenship 121, 132, 135;

Critical Realism (DCR) 23, 26, 30, 33; Education 124-130, 137, 155-58, 160, 175; Ethnicity 121, 173, 181, 264; Islam 7-8, 26, 42, 45-46, 52, 54, 61-62, 124-28, 130, 135, 158, 173, 306; Islamophobia 118, 154, 165, 313; Multicultural 121-28, 137, 154, 160, 173. National 7, 137, 160, 173, 175, 264, 284, 315; Religion 8, 68, 122, 168, 304-06; Self-Concept 33, 165; Women, 42, 45-46, 52
Integration: Assimilation 8, 128, 159, 176; Defined 159, 174, 176; Demand for as Islamophobia 127-28, 157-59, 164, 168-69, 210-11; Education 123, 156, 158, 168; Intermarriage 208; Jews 159, 177; Muslims 159, 164-66, 177, 189; Netherlands, 17-74, 180, 187; Multicultural 160; Plural Societies 164, 170; Social Contract 164, 168
Intersection of Gender, Ethnicity & Religion: 35-6, 42-3, 191, 207
Islam and Critical Realism: See *Wilkinson, Matthew*
Islam: Economics 46; Education 121-161, 313, 315 (see also *Madrasahs*); Management 29, 44-8, 52, 55, 293; Women Scholars 1, 4, 9, 12-13 252, 266 (see also *Hadiths*; see also *Modesty;* see also *Shari'a;* see also *Sunnah;* see also *Zakat;* see also *Zina*)
Islamophobia in UK & Europe: 120-162, 166-168, 173, 177-78. 185, 190, 196-6, 208, 211, 267, 295, 311-15
Israel & Palestine: 60-61, 110, 112, 117, 165, 297-300
Jews: Anti-Semitism 165, 174, 192; Education 130-131; Holocaust (Shoah) 112, 165, 299-300; Muslim-Jewish Tolerance 8, 9, 297-99, 305-07; in Netherlands 174-75; in UK 168-69; Values of 307
Jordan & Women Managers: 41
Kidnapped Children, Bangladesh & Pakistan: 219, 237, 262, 274, 286 (see also *Trafficking*)
Leach, Edmund - Values Analysis: 302-04
Line Managers & Employment Discrimination: 56-73
Madrasahs 120-121, 158, 217-218 238, 251, 253, 271, 275
Malala (Malala Yousafzai) Pakistani Hero: 34, 110, 264-68
Malaysia & Women's Equality: 41, 50-51, 252, 266
Male Power: 48, 52, 45, 49, 228, 235, 254, 291(see also *Patriarchy*)
Manchester, UK: Prejudice & Discrimination 190, 197, 203-04; Manchester Bomber 309, 311
Marxism: Critical Realism (DCR) 18-21, 24, 27, 29-32, 90, 209; Male Class-for-Itself 237-8, 272; Humanism 312, 314
Maternal Health: 62, 81, 234, 243, 257, 259
Mental Health/Illness: Alienation 310-12; Discrimination 310-312; Terrorism Support 310-12
Minority Group Women as Managers 41-45
Modesty of Islam as Critical Realist (DCR) Principle: 6-13, 39-40, 43, 55, 122, 129,170, 176, 178, 254, 294, 302, 304, 312, 316
Morocco & Women Managers: 45
Moroccan-Dutch Minorities: 173, 183 185, 201-02
Multiculturalism: Education 136, 155, 173; Europe 54, 166;

Identity 121, 155; Islam 54, 130, 136, 313; Netherlands 164; North America, 42; Pluralism 170; UK 130, 133, 157, 160-66, 169-174; Values 169-74

Murders of Women & Children: Bangladesh 216-18; Israel 16, 105, 110, 216-18; 261, 301-03; Islam Forbids 5, 12, 105; 'Islamic' Terrorism 307-10; Pakistan 264, 267, 271, 275, 281-85, 288-93; Suicide 218, 229, 237-38, 248-49; UK Racism 133

Muslim Education: 123-161 (See also *Madrasahs*)

Muslim Majority Cultures and Women Managers: 50, 54 (see also *Global Gender Gap*)

Muslim Diaspora: 36

Muslim Schools in UK: 128-131

Muslim Women as Leaders: 45-56 (*see also Women*)

Pacifism in Islam: 265-68, 295, 300, 308 (see also *Peace-Making*)

Pakistan: "Absent" Children in Critical Realism (DCR) 33; Caste 284; Child Abuse & Exploitation 33, 281; Child Health 276-277; Child Marriage 255-262; Climate Issues 215, 269-270, 294; Corruption 292-93; Dowry 291; Education 273-76; Faith-Based Feminism, 292; Female Infanticide 236, 288-290; Gender Equality 41, 51, 238, 255, 281; 'Glass Ceiling' 10, 36, 40, 51; 'Honour' Killing 28-284; Islamic Values 2, 12-13, 51, 255, 263-64, 289, 292; Patriarchy 13, 14, 238, 271; Plural Society 256, 27-273; Poverty 268-73; Rape 281; 'Sex Work' 285-88; Sexism & Sexual Exploitation 11, 40, 25, 255-62; Shari'a Law 12-13, 231-32, 278, 280; Stoning of Women 278-289; UN Conventions 291; Women Managers 10, 36, 40, 51; Zina Law 271-72, 278-281 (See also HRCP)

Pakistanis in UK: 13, 26-27, 125-27, 143, 158, 160, 169, 180, 188-91, 198, 203, 210, 264, 314

Palestine, Women Managers: 36, 56-73

Patriarchy's Distortion of Islamic Ideals: 2, 6, 13,40, 45-54, 235, 251, 262, 290, 292, 315, 397

Peace-Making: in Gaza 98, 110-11, 295, 297, 300-01; in Plural Societies of UK, Netherlands, Bangladesh, Pakistan 126, 174, 176, 253-54, 266-67, 275, 294-97 (see also *Pacifism*)

Personality: 7, 21-22, 101, 163, 167, 304, 309-311

Poverty: Bangladesh 213-15, 228-30, 234-44, 259; Pakistan 259, 261-2. 268-9, 272-3, 276, 291-4, 313; UK Ethnic Minorities 125, 158, 191

Pluralism & Plural Societies: Bangladesh 13; Citizenship Education 135-39, 157; Gender 39; Multiculturalism 54, 135, 170; Muslims 13, 39, 164-66, 171, 176-78, 273, 313; Netherlands 164-66. 170-80; Pakistan 13, 270-73; Religion 136; Tolerance 170, 180, 313; UK 104-06, 170-80

Precariat Social Class in UK: 209, 307

Prejudice: Causes 120-181; Netherlands 179, 197; United Kingdom 20-181; Victims 38, 42 (see also *Discrimination*; see also *Islamophobia*)

Prevent (UK Programme): 127, 135, 157, 158, 168, 210-11

Prevention of Suicide in Bangladesh: 250-254
Prostitution: Boys in Pakistan 278; Drug Use 222; Girls in Bangladesh 12, 212-228; Girls in Pakistan 285-6; Girls in Philippines 251, 253, 286; Ethnographic Studies 212-228, 286-88; Madrasas 282; Rescue of 226, 286 -88; STIs/HIV 222-26; Street Children 222, 226 (see also *Rape*)
PTSD: Bangladesh 255-62; Gaza 74-119; Pakistan 255-262
PVV Dutch Far Right Party: 173
Quakers: 5, 24, 90, 130, 289. 296-97, 305-06 (see also *Pacifism*)
Qur'an: Children 43, 45, 49, 236, 288; Corruption 293; Education 120-130, 143; Exegesis 2-3, 17, 38; Female Inheritance 43; Hadiths 14, 46. 164, 235; Israel 297-300; Muhammad 263, 295-6 (see also *Hadiths, & Sunnah*); Peace-making 110, 288, 295-315; Politics 273; Sciences 131; Social Justice 34, 40, 273; Stewardship of Earth 120; Sunnah 34, 49, 110, 154-5, 251, 263; Male Hegemony versus 45, 49, 235, 254, 29; Women's Equality Issues 34, 43, 45, 47, 49, 105, 177, 235, 237, 250-1, 261, 279, 285; Women Leaders 43
Rape: Child Marriage as Rape, 255-262; Child Rape in Brothels, 216-18, 221, 226, 274-75; Dalits of India, 284; Police as Rapists in Pakistan 273-75, 287-78, 293; 'Sex Work' as Rape 286; Rape of Boys 259; Rape & Murder in Bangladesh 216-18, 221, 226; Stoning/Whipping of Rape Victims in Pakistan 279-280

Reflexivity: in Critical Realism (DCR) 24-31(see also *Archer, Margaret*)
Refugees: Bangladesh 285; Islamic Tolerance of Jews 297; Mecca 176; Netherlands 171; Pakistan 267-68, 270, 299-300; Palestine 77-78, 82, 88, 93, 99, 109; UK 171, 174
Religion: & Intrinsic Commitment to Values 303-307
Restorative Justice in Islam: 28-29, 282
Sabur – Islamic Steadfastness in Suffering: Gaza 98, 104-05, 116
Saudi Arabia & Women Managers: 40, 51, 60
'Sex Work' see *Prostitution*
Shari'a Law & Women: 10-17, 34, 48, 235,250, 260-2, 271, 276, 278-282, 301 (se also *Wilkinson, Matthew*; see also *Zina*)
Social Contract of European Muslims: 8, 121, 139, 159, 164, 169-70, 210, 135
Shaitan (Satan): 304, 307, 315-16 (see also *Evil*)
Suicidal Behaviours: In Asia & Bangladesh 229-254
Sunnah & Life of Muhammad: 1-3, 5, 9, 12, 14, 32, 34, 45, 51, 110, 235, 251, 254, 263, 282, 292-94, 302, 308
Tariq Ali, Pakistani Hero: 266-267
Teacher's Role: Bangladesh 218; Citizenship Education 120-161; Gaza 74-119; Pakistan 273 (see also *Educational Programmes*)
Terrorism: Alienation of Minorities 207-10, 314; Catholics 311; Islam 32, 34, 126; Islamophobia 123, 160, 211, 314; Israel 16; Mental Illness 209, 310-311; Netherlands 306; Prevent UK 127, 159, 210; Protestants, 311

Trafficking of Children in/from Bangladesh or Pakistan: 212, 220, 226, 236, 250-51, 262, 274, 278, 285, 293 (see also *Kidnapped Children*)
Tunisia & Women Managers: 49
Turkey & Women Managers: 39, 49-50
Turkish-Dutch Minorities: 172, 175, 181-87, 200-01, 204
UN Conventions 291
UNICEF 175
UNRWA in Palestine: 78-79, 86-111
Warfare: Gaza 74-5, 79, 82, 84, 86-108, 110, 114-15, 312; Islam 296, 308; Pakistan, 294 (see also *Peace-Making*)
Weber, Max – Cross Cultural Comparisons: 171
Wilkinson, Matthew & Critical Realism (DCR): 20-27, 32, 34, 90, 129, 161, 210, 293, 308

Women: "Absence" in Critical Realism (DCR) 44; Bangladesh 212-262; Education 42; Equality in Islam 44-45, 79-81; Family Management Model 40; Gaza 79-81; Hijab 46; Islam 1-46; Management Role Models 37; Managers 35-55; Muslim Majority Cultures 35, 50, 52; Pakistan 33, 263-294; Patriarchy versus 45, 48-9, 52; (see also *Male Power*); Suicidal Behaviours 229-254
Values in Critical Realism (DCR): 23, 312
Work-Life Balance Benefits & Women: 36, 42, 48, 53, 56-73
Zakat (Islamic Giving) Business Model: 9, 40, 47, 273
Zina Laws of Pakistan: 271-72; 278-281